Implementing Activation Policies

Sebastian Künzel

Implementing Activation Policies

An Analysis of Social and Labour Market Policy Reforms in Continental Europe with a Focus on Local Case Studies in France and Germany

PL ACADEMIC RESEARCH

Bibliographic Information published by the Deutsche Nationalbibliothek
The Deutsche Nationalbibliothek lists this publication in the Deutsche Nationalbibliografie; detailed bibliographic data is available in the internet at http://dnb.d-nb.de.
Zugl.: Oldenburg, Univ., Diss., 2012

D 715
ISBN 978-3-631-65107-0 (Print)
E-ISBN 978-3-653-04224-5 (E-Book)
DOI 10.3726/ 978-3-653-04224-5

PL Academic Research is an Imprint of Peter Lang GmbH.

Peter Lang – Frankfurt am Main · Bern · Bruxelles · New York · Oxford · Warszawa · Wien

This publication has been peer reviewed.

www.peterlang.com

Contents

List of figures

List of tables

List of abbreviations

AER	Allocation équivalent retraite (Pension equivalent allowance)
AFPA	Association pour la formation professionnelle des adultes (Agency for further training)
ALG II	Arbeitslosengeld II (Unemployment benefit II)
ALMP	Active Labour Market Policy
ANPE	Agence Nationale pour l'Emploi (National employment agency)
API	Allocation de parent isolé (Solidarity allowance for single parents)
ARE	Allocation d'aide au retour à l'emploi (Return to work allowance)
ASS	Allocation de solidarité spécifique (Specific Solidarity Allowance)
ASSEDIC	Association pour l'Emploi Dans l'Industrie et le Commerce (Local pay office for insurance benefits)
ATA	Allocation temporaire d'attente (Transition allowance)
CAF	Caisses d'Allocations Familiales (Pay offices for family assistance)
CAV	Contrat d'avenir (Subsidised employment scheme)
CCAS	Centres communaux d'action sociale (Communal Welfare Centres)
CDI	Conseil départemental d'insertion (Committee for insertion)
CDU	Christlich Demokratische Union (Christian Democratic Union)
CI-RMA	Contrats d'insertion-RMA (Subsidised employment scheme)
CLI	Commissions locales d'insertion (Local committees for insertion)
DDASS	Direction départementale des affaires sanitaires et sociales (Local social service department for health and social affairs)

DDTEFP	Direction départementale du travail, de l'emploi et de la formation professionnelle (Local department for work, employment and further education)
DRTEFP	Direction régionale du travail, de l'emploi et de la formation professionnelle (Regional department for work, employment and further education)
DIRECCTE	Direction régionale des entreprises, de la concurrence, de la consommation, du travail, de l'emploi (Regional department for enterprises, competition, consumption, work and employment)
e.g.	for example
ed.	edited
EES	European Employment Strategy
ESF	European Social Funds
et al.	et alteris (and the others)
etc.	et cetera
EU	European Union
EU2020 strategy	European Union 2020 strategy
FAJ	Fonds d'aide aux jeunes en difficulté (social allowance for young persons in difficulty)
Fig.	Figure
i.e.	id est (that means)
IAE	Le secteur de l'insertion par l'activité économique (Directorate for integration through economic activities)
ILO	International Labour Organization
MIS	Minimum Income Scheme
MoZArT	Modelvorhaben zur Verbesserung der Zusammenarbeit von Arbeitsämtern und Trägern der Sozialhilfe (Pilot project for a coordination between the public employment services and the social welfare centres)
NAPs	National Action Plans
OECD	Organisation for Economic Co-operation and Development
OMC	Open Method of Co-ordination

PARE	Plan d'aide au retour à l'emploi (Return to work plan)
PLIE	Plans locaux pour l'Insertion et l'Emploi (Local plan for insertion and employment)
RMI	Revenu minimum d'insertion (Minimum income for insertion)
RSA	Revenu de solidarité active (Active solidarity allowance)
SGB II	Sozialgesetzbuch II (German social code II)
SIAE	Secteur de l'Insertion par l'Activité Economique (Sector for Subsidised Employment)
SK	Sebastian Künzel
SMEs	Small and medium sized enterprises
SPD	Sozialdemokratische Partei Deutschlands (Social Democratic Party of Germany)
SPED	Service publique de l'emploi départemental (Local public employment service)
TIPP	Taxe intérieure de consommation sur les produits pétroliers (Tax on the consumption of petrol products)
UA	Unemployment Assistance
UB I	Unemployment Benefit I
UB II	Unemployment Benefit II
UK	United Kingdom
UNEDIC	Union nationale interprofessionnelle pour l'emploi dans l'industrie et le commerce(National social insurance)
vs.	versus

a 'fragmentation' of important welfare state institutions, we analyse not only processes of re-regulating labour markets but also the re-organisation of policies, administrations and services. Processes of re-organising institutions, policies, administrations and services are an essential part of the transformations of Bismarckian welfare states in face of the problem of inclusion of persons with non-standard employment biographies and weaker and more vulnerable groups. The opportunities and inherent problems and conflicts of such processes of re-organisation crucially involve a local dimension of the Bismarckian welfare state (Finn 2000; Künzel 2012). The local level will be consequently a focal point of our empirically informed inquiry.

The continuous increase over the last two decades in the number of persons claiming benefits from minimum income schemes or social assistance is a phenomenon that puts this institution at the centre of questions on the evolution of the Bismarckian welfare states. It triggers important issues for the Bismarckian countries: it indicates the limits of typical 'industrial risk communities' of family welfare, socially secured male-breadwinner employment and status-oriented social protection to deal with new risks (Armingeon and Bonoli 2006; Taylor-Gooby 2004). Societal and economic transformations undermine the viability of the principle Bismarckian welfare institutions (Esping-Andersen 2002; Esping-Andersen 2006; Ferrera and Hemerijck 2003). Eroding arrangements of traditional solidarity, altering ways of life, higher rates of family breakdown, rising female employment, the demographic crunch, structural changes of work and production as well as the internationalisation of the economy produce effects which weaken classical Bismarckian institutions of family welfare, socially secured male breadwinner employment and contribution-based social protection. Confronted with these new risks, the classical Bismarckian welfare state institutions increasingly fail to cover significant parts of the population. Particularly women, young, elder, migrants, low-skilled and long-term unemployed are experiencing increasing risks of minimum income receipt (Gangl 1998; Lødemel and Trickey 2001; Saraceno 2002). These groups often heavily bear the burden of the profound economic and social changes that have altered and in many cases indeed hampered the conditions for social and economic participation in Bismarckian welfare states. The new risks raise strong doubts on the capacity of the traditional Bismarckian welfare state institutions to cope with problems of minimum income receipt. The rising number of minimum income schemes defies previous patterns of social inclusion, it is connected to questions of the economic viability of the Bismarckian welfare states and it challenges the Bismarckian social protection system.

The rise in the number of beneficiaries of minimum income schemes challenges traditional patterns of inclusion of weaker and more vulnerable groups in the Bismarckian welfare states (Lødemel and Trickey 2001; Saraceno 2002). In the past, in Bismarckian countries, a guaranteed income served as primary mechanism for the social integration of weaker and more vulnerable groups. In Bismarckian welfare states, social inclusion was granted by income from socially secured male breadwinner family salaries or from rather inclusive and generous social protection systems (Esping-Andersen 1999; Ferrera et al. 2003: 350). Some studies (Møller and Hespanha 2002; Møller and van Berkel: 2002: 11) confirm the essential function of income protection for facilitating social integration. Even in the case of unemployment, they argue, a sufficient income replacement will sustain a person's integration in social networks, culture, politics, leisure-time activities, and other activities. Scrutinising the current policy agenda, reforms introduced in the European welfare states propose a new mechanism of social integration: "In the 'new welfare states, employment instead of income protection is considered to be the best remedy against social exclusion and poverty" (van Berkel and Valkenburg 2007: 8). Responding to the new social and economic risks, activation into employment appears as a new mechanism which is proposed for social integration. As income guarantees by solidarity arrangements of family welfare and generous social protection become fragile in Bismarckian welfare states, employment emerges as alternative mode for the social inclusion of weaker and more vulnerable groups. In a society where neighbourhood contacts, class affiliation or family ties are decreasing, work becomes key to enable access to important resources, social relationships and opportunities (Kenworthy 2004). Furthermore, active participation in work life not only offers income resources but simultaneously enables human and skill development which is important in an economic environment of increasingly rapid changes in skill- and production demands (Huo et al. 2008: 7; Schmid 2006). Work can also help to increase self-esteem and a person's well-being (Salais 2003). In addition, work is often attributed a disciplining and structuring effect on life (Jahoda 1982). Consequently, according to this 'new' approach to social inclusion, it is primarily activation into employment which facilitates integration into different spheres of society (income, work, different types of networks, culture, politics, sports, other leisure-time activities, etc). As income guarantees by social protection or male breadwinner family salaries prove decreasingly as a robust option for the social integration of weaker and more vulnerable groups in Bismarckian welfare states, activation into employment appears as a new option for inclusion.

Apart from the defiance of classical patterns of social integration, the rise in the number of beneficiaries of minimum income schemes raises issues of the economic viability of the Bismarckian welfare states. To cushion also weaker and more vulnerable groups against the new economic and social risks arising, the welfare state itself has to dispose of an appropriate financial basis to provide not only income replacement but also social services. However, on the revenue side, at least two developments tend to limit the possibilities of an extension of services and other welfare state tasks particularly in Bismarckian welfare states (Kenworthy 2004). Raising contributions or taxes for further tasks and services is particularly difficult to achieve for Bismarckian welfare states as employment rates only reach moderate levels (Fligstein 2001a; Schmid 2002), while significant parts of the population, as manifested by the increasing number of unemployed minimum income benefit recipients, still remain excluded from the labour market. Moderate employment rates moreover become problematic as an increasingly open economy tends to reduce alternative income options of the welfare state (Alber and Standing 2000). Although the internationalisation of the economy does not inevitably lead to a 'race to the bottom' of taxes, mobile capital reduces the state's opportunities to tax mobile resources. Given the limited room for manoeuvring on the income side, at the same time, higher demands arise on the expenditure side. Particularly in continental European welfare states, the increased failures of Bismarckian institutions for family welfare, socially secured male-breadwinner employment and status-oriented social protection to deal with new risks of an aging society, family breakdown, and structural changes of work and production cause higher demands on welfare state expenditures. The Bismarckian welfare state is thus faced with financial limits respective heightened claims for income protection and social services. In this situation, activation into employment is the primary solution to avoid raising contributions and tax rates and to simultaneously ensure the welfare state's redistributive resources for income protection and services (Kenworthy 2004). From the perspective of the Bismarckian welfare state, increased numbers of minimum income benefit recipients therefore not only reveal problems of social inclusion but are also connected to questions of its economic viability. Contesting Bismarckian welfare states typical reliance on only moderate rates of employment, besides the integrative function of work previously discussed, also the sustainability of the welfare state requires the inclusion into employment of weaker and more vulnerable groups of society who have so far been excluded from work and increasingly depend on minimum income assistance.

Apart from the social and economic challenges discussed, the rise in the number of minimum income benefit recipients in continental European welfare states defies their particular Bismarckian architecture of social protection. In the Bismarckian system, needs-based minimum income protection typically exerts a residual function in an otherwise status-based system of social protection. In contrast to minimum income programmes, which provide a general needs-based protection against the risk of exclusion, the Bismarckian model of social protection is built on specialised programmes. Programmes are specialised in so far as they insure against particular risks based on the work and contribution status of claimants. In the continental European welfare states, a risk like unemployment is therefore typically covered by generous work-status related benefits. This Bismarckian rationale of social protection is to compensate 'workers' and their families for cyclical 'industrial' risks of short-term downturns of the economy (Clasen 1999, Clasen and Clegg 2006). In this status-oriented Bismarckian social protection system, needs-based benefits fulfil a subsidiary function. Classically, needs-based benefits in continental European countries are based on residual monetary provision of poverty policy for those persons categorised as 'extreme' outsiders (Gough et al. 1997; Leibfried and Tennstedt 1985, Whiteside 2007). However, new and 'non-industrial' risks like family breakdown, structural economic change, low-paid employment, long-term unemployment or permanent exclusion increasingly require social protection systems to provide comprehensive protection also for weaker and more vulnerable groups of society (Clasen and Clegg 2006). These new and non-industrial risks test Bismarckian welfare states' 'dualistic' (Gough 2001) nature of residual minimum income benefits and generous status-based protection for workers. Nonetheless, status-oriented social protection programmes – at least for workers – appear relatively resistant against change due to their strong popularity and their vested rights' logic, which is upheld by strong corporatist institutions (Palier 2010; Palier and Thelen 2010). At the same time, status-based and work-related benefits do not present a comprehensive option for precariously employed or precarious 'non-employed' persons, not least due to an increased 'selectivity' of these specialised benefit programmes (Clegg 2007). Due to the 'dualistic' character of Bismarckian social protection systems, the greater reliance on needs-based benefits thus poses a particular defiance for continental European welfare states. Given this particular Bismarckian social protection arrangement, the focus therefore turns on so far residual needs-based minimum income programmes to deal with the new and non-industrial risks of long-term unemployment, precarious work or permanent exclusion. Activation into work of weaker and more vulnerable groups therefore evolves as an alternative to social protection by meagre to moderate minimum income benefits (Nelson 2011). In brief, employment of weaker and more vulnerable groups also presents an option to reduce the pressure from minimum income programmes in an otherwise predominantly status-based Bismarckian social protection system.

While new challenges posed for social integration, the economic sustainability, and the social protection system of Bismarckian-type continental European welfare states suggest activation into employment for weaker and more vulnerable groups, however, integration into work presents a complex issue. Activation of weaker and more vulnerable groups into employment requires taking into account diverse and simultaneous factors of exclusion in the Bismarckian welfare states. Scrutinising the causes of dependency on minimum income benefits reveals that recipients encounter different problems. While a dynamic perspective reveals that benefit receipt is by some only experienced as a short spell in their life-course, however, important groups are affected by diverse and often cumulative labour market-related and social problems of exclusion (Gangl 1998; Saraceno 2002: 12).

In the Bismarckian countries, labour market-related causes of minimum income receipt not only concern temporary problems of access to labour markets due to seasonal, frictionary or cyclical unemployment. They also relate to structural reasons of unemployment (Blanchard 2006; Blanchard and Wolfers 2000), which cause strong obstacles to employment opportunities for weaker groups of society (Ferrera and Hemerijck 2003). In Bismarckian countries, women, young, elder, migrants, low-skilled or disabled persons have been to some extent systematically excluded from employment by a labour market policy oriented towards workers (Clegg 2007; Paller and Martin 2007). The exclusive character of continental European labour market policy is due to an approach based on strongly protective labour laws, high minimum or high reservation wages and significant contributions to social security (Ferrera and Hemerijck 2003). In a rather exclusive manner, this labour market policy for workers has favoured an employment model of stable and socially well protected employment (Heidenreich 2004). Due to rigid labour market regulation and low employment growth (Clegg 2007; Ferrera and Hemerijck 2003), especially long-term unemployment has evolved as a major problem in Bismarckian welfare states. Longer spells of unemployment, particularly in a more rapidly changing environment of work and production, can lead to the deterioration of skills (Hvinden 1999; Huo et al. 2008: 7; Schmid 2006). An exclusive employment model as well as the lack or devaluation of skills produce work-related exclusionary factors which pose challenges for the work integration of minimum income benefit recipients in Bismarckian welfare states.

In addition to the employment-related risks of exclusion, the receipt of minimum income benefits is often connected to 'social' exclusionary factors. Problems of health, housing, transport, rehabilitation, child and family care are risks related to social exclusion and minimum income benefit receipt (Saraceno 2002): "Social exclusion may involve not only poverty as low income and financial resources, but also educational disadvantage, poor health and access to health services, inadequate housing, and exclusion from the labour market." (Nolan and Whelan 2010: 307). Particularly in Bismarckian countries, the partial erosion of family welfare calls into question traditional modes of dealing with issues of care, rehabilitation and other social concerns (Esping-Andersen 2002; Esping-Andersen 2006). Unresolved issues of child care, family care, rehabilitation or housing as well as psychical problems or divorce can cause dependency on minimum income benefits. For instance, unsettled issues of child or family care pose the risk of minimum income receipt for single parents (Gornick et al. 1997; Gornick and Meyers 2005). Young benefit claimants can encounter situations of crisis in the transition towards adulthood which are connected to unemployment and health deterioration (Hammarström and Janlert 2005). Health problems of unemployed can require medical consultation or psychological help (Hammarström and Janlert 2005). In addition to the problem of receiving scarce benefits, some recipients might struggle with severe financial problems of personal indebtedness. Furthermore, unemployment and notably long-term unemployment, which is a particular problem of Bismarckian countries, present causes for mutually reinforcing processes of work-related and social exclusionary factors comprising social isolation, physical and psychical annoyances (Gallie et al. 2003; McKee-Ryan et al. 2005). Blanchard (2006: 24) points to the problems of a high duration of unemployment for the take-up of work: "Such high duration was likely to lead to loss of skills, loss of morale, and thus make many of the long-term unemployed in effect unemployable." Activation into work of long-term unemployed, young persons, single parents, low skilled persons or persons with health problems thus encounters labour market-related as well as social factors of exclusion which increasingly present risks of minimum income receipt in Bismarckian countries.

At the background of labour market-related and social obstacles to employment, the Bismarckian welfare states face the issue of how employment opportunities can be facilitated for weaker and more vulnerable groups of society who increasingly need to rely on minimum income benefit receipt. Tackling this question is therefore not only a matter of re-regulating labour markets in order to provide greater employment opportunities for weaker and more vulnerable groups (Madsen 2002; Wilthagen 1998; Bekker and Wilthagen 2008). Besides a labour market policy oriented towards creating employment opportunities for broader segments of the population, activation into employment is also a matter of services to respond to the work-related and social obstacles faced by weaker and more vulnerable groups.

Taking into account work-related and social exclusionary factors of unemployment, support for the employment of weaker and more vulnerable groups requires so far predominantly passive Bismarckian welfare states to put a greater focus on services. Contrary to a strong focus on services, however, in the past, Bismarckian welfare states were characterised as 'passive' (Ferrera and Hemerijck 2003: 107–115). Bismarckian welfare states focussed on income transfers while services were primarily delivered by the family. As women aim for their proper careers, one-earner households decline and marital instability growths (Ferrera and Hemerijck 2003: 109), the family-based service arrangement in a rather 'passive' welfare state turns out problematic. Activation into employment thus requires Bismarckian welfare states to take individual exclusionary circumstances into account by an improved provision of services (Van Berkel and Valkenburg 2007: 3). The activation into employment of weaker and more vulnerable groups can be assisted by active labour market policy which comprises services for placement and training (Hvinden 1999). Apart from active labour market policy, which has increased to a moderate expenditure level in continental European countries (Bonoli 2010), social welfare services become increasingly relevant for supporting employment. In order to take into account the social exclusionary factors of weaker and more vulnerable groups, continental European countries are faced with an increasing demand for the provision of services for rehabilitation, child care, family care, housing, counselling or health care (Borghi and Van Berkel 2007). Despite the strong focus on passive benefit provision of Bismarckian-type continental European countries welfare states, attempts of the work integration of weaker groups call to respond to their service needs in the area of active labour market policies and social services.

Besides raising service supply and re-regulating labour market policy, employment support of weaker and more vulnerable groups triggers important issues of coordination (Kinder 2003), which challenge fragmented Bismarckian welfare states. Attempts to enable weaker and more vulnerable groups' work integration by assisting services demand closer co-operation between administrations traditionally concentrated on the provision of income support, placement services, providers of training programmes, and third sector organisations providing social services (Clasen and Clegg 2006). Coordination is thus a fourfold task which arises between (1) activating labour market policy and minimum income benefit programmes, (2) active labour market policy services and social welfare services, (3) between benefit provision and services and, (4) between differently funded benefit programmes.

Given the resurgent dependency of persons on needs-tested minimum income benefit programmes in Bismarckian countries, the question arises on the coupling of employment-oriented labour market policies with benefit regulation. An employment-centred welfare state implies the co-ordination between labour market policies and social protection systems in order to enhance the take-up of work of broader segments of society (Barbier 2004). However, minimum income schemes in the Bismarckian model are classically characterised as lacking a significant workfare component (Gough et al. 1997; Gough 2001). Apart from only very general stipulations for work requirements, minimum income provision in continental European countries was normally practiced either as an unconditional right to benefit receipt (Daguerre and Taylor-Gooby 2003: 629), as being subsidiary to family welfare (Gough et al. 1997; Gough 2001) or as being subsidiary to social work (Mingione et al. 2002). Furthermore, even if minimum income regulation comprised stipulations for work requirements, they were rarely applied in the pastas labour market opportunities for weaker and more vulnerable groups were limited in Bismarckian countries (Clegg and Palier 2012; Mingione et al. 2002). In light of the rising numbers of recipients of needs-based minimum income benefits in Bismarckian countries, activation can serve as an alternative to benefit receipt, if social benefits are being coupled with incentives and requirements for the take-up of work (Eichhorst et al. 2008a). By the application of work requirements and incentives, the 'activation of benefits' (Clasen and Clegg 2006) reforms social policy into an instrument suitable for increasing the 'proximity' of the unemployed to labour markets. The activation of unemployed into employment is thus a challenge for Bismarckian welfare states as it requires to couple work incentives of labour market policy with minimum income benefit programmes.

With regard to a coordinated employment support, also the coupling between social welfare services and active labour market policy services is important in order to react to weaker groups' work-related respective non-employment-related causes of minimum income benefit receipt. In Bismarckian countries, delivery of services for active labour market policy and services for counselling, health, rehabilitation or housing was usually separated between different policy fields (Champion and Bonoli 2011). Active labour market policy services normally related to a labour market policy for workers (Clegg 2007). Services were usually organised in a rather central manner primarily reacting to the general industrial risks of skill deterioration in the case of unemployment (Bonoli 2010). This 'industrial bias' towards workers in active labour market policy is explained by the prominent role of corporatist actors in the governance of active labour market policy programmes (Beyer and Höpner 2003; Streeck and Hassel 2003). In contrast, complementary to its subsidiary role to family welfare, the provision of social services in continental European countries tends to rely on more local, 'mixed' public-private systems (Mingione et al. 2002). Besides some countries, which count on a history of centralised state-run services (e.g. France, Belgium), the decentralised interventions of municipalities, regions, local welfare associations or local social workers play an important role in social service delivery in continental Europe (Bahle 2003). Fragmented between corporatist-based, skill-focused active labour market policy and local social welfare service systems, Bismarckian welfare states thus face a challenge of coordinating these services for assisting work integration of weaker groups.

With regard to requirements of a coordinated support, also the coupling between minimum income benefit provision and services is important, in order to react to work-related and social obstacles to employment of weaker groups. Taking an originally marginal, subsidiary role in Bismarckian countries, minimum income provision tends to share the same local organisational traits like social welfare services. Both the provision of social services and the delivery of minimum income schemes have common roots in local social welfare systems in continental European countries (Mingione et al. 2002; Bahle 2003). In contrast, active labour market policies were usually connected to uniform and highly centrally organised structures of status-conserving social insurance programmes (Rauch 2008). The interrelated character of unemployment insurance benefit programmes and active labour market policy matched the 'industrial bias' of policies towards workers which was enhanced by the prominent role of the social partners. Fragmented between local minimum income benefit provision and central active labour market policy programmes, Bismarckian welfare states face complicated tasks of coordinating services of minimum income benefits with social service support and active labour market policy in order to assist the work integration of weaker groups.

Coordination is, however, not only a matter of services but also relates to benefit systems. In general, social protection programmes can vary between contribution-based and tax-financed funding streams. According to the typical Bismarckian welfare state model, 'productive workers' are rewarded for their contributions by insurance-based programmes, e.g. unemployment programmes, which are typically organised by corporatist actors (Clasen 1999; Clasen and Viebrock 2006). Regarding the rather rare tax-funded social protection programmes in the Bismarckian model, to which minimum income benefits belong, budgetary responsibilities can be divided in the multi-level system of the welfare state. Governments and international organisations like the EU or the OECD have recognised the inefficiencies which can arise if differently funded programmes co-exist in an uncoordinated manner (Finn 2000). For instance, separated financial responsibilities in the multi-level system of a welfare state can lead to incentives for one programme provider to 'park' benefit recipients in other programmes (disability schemes, early retirement programmes, unemployment benefit) instead of aiming at the benefit recipients' activation into employment (Schmid 2006). Especially the Bismarckian countries are prone to this problem due to their structure which is fragmented between tax-financed, locally based minimum income schemes and centrally organised specialised contribution or work-status based programmes (Gough et al. 1997: 36). Such 'parking' in early retirement programmes, unemployment programmes or disability programmes has for a long time matched Bismarckian social policies' 'social treatment' of unemployment of weaker and more vulnerable groups (Daguerre and Taylor-Gooby 2003: 629; Eichhorst et al. 2008b), but contradicts activation attempts. As numbers of recipients of once marginal tax-financed minimum income schemes have continuously risen in continental Europe, their activation into work faces issues of a sound coordination with the different contribution-based and work-related social protection programmes. Thus, to enhance activation of weaker groups, fragmented funding structures of Bismarckian social security programmes require a better co-ordination of increasingly important tax-financed, locally based minimum income schemes with the relevant contribution-related programmes.

In the light of the requirement for coordinated and targeted policies to activate weaker and vulnerable groups of society into work, the fragmented architecture of Bismarckian welfare state institutions probes inefficient. While the fragmented nature of policies, services, administrations and provider structures matched the requirements of an industrial risk community, passive policies as well as disintegrated social and labour market policies, separated providers and disparate services turn into a problem for the promotion of opportunities of welfare and work for weaker and more vulnerable groups. The fragmentation in the organisation of important policies for the integration into life and work (income replacement, active labour market policy services, social welfare services as health care, child and family care, housing or debt counselling) can impede on taking into account the manifold causes of unemployment of weaker groups in a coherent manner. Coping with the increase of minimum income benefit recipients thus provokes questions on the (re-)organisation of policies, administrations and services between fragmented policies, levels of competences and different actors. Overall, such problems of coordination in the form of segmented and overlapping institutions, competences, funding streams, programmes and agencies that differently service minimum income benefit recipients from insured unemployed obviously reveal an important issue of current Bismarckian welfare state transformation. Consequently, the transformation towards an employment-centred Bismarckian welfare state concerns much of its organisational fabric, or, to put it more precisely, welfare state change turns into an issue of reorganising fragmented institutions. The rising numbers of beneficiaries of minimum income schemes raises the question of how Bismarckian welfare states might reorganise fragmented institutions in order to offer coordinated, service-oriented and employment-friendly policies towards weaker and more vulnerable groups of society and the labour market.

Usually, changes in policy coordination and reforms of labour market and social policy programmes, administrations and services are discussed as an issue of European regulatory processes (Visser 2009) or as a matter of national activation regimes (Barbier 2004). The Open Method of Coordination 'irritates' the functioning of Bismarckian welfare states (Heidenreich 2009) and leads to transnational learning of governance reforms (Visser 2009). Changes in Bismarckian welfare states show a 'selective appropriation' (Zeitlin 2009; Zirra 2010a; 2010b: 22) of 'good' governance comprising policy changes, administrative reforms and new service delivery models. Deviations from common European trends are explained by national patterns of implementing activation reforms (Clegg 2007): "The adoption and introduction of new forms of governance in the context of operational policy reforms are 'filtered' or shaped by (national) socio-economic, historical, cultural, institutional and political contexts." (Borghi and Van Berkel 2007: 97). As a result, reforms of labour market and social policy programmes as well as changes in administration and policy coordination are usually analysed at the national level (Clasen and Clegg 2006).

However, the exclusive focus on European and national institutions becomes increasingly problematic in understanding and analysing current welfare state reforms. Assuming that national reforms are the most important element in transforming Bismarckian welfare states may imply that important transformations at the sub national level are ignored (Clarke 2008). Such a perspective implies that characteristics of centralism and uniformity of insurance institutions still constitute the overriding principles of the organisation, administration and delivery of policies and services in Bismarckian welfare states. It closely corresponds to a welfare state that predominantly approaches unemployed by a social policy modelled on the premises of passive benefit provision and uniform rights to workers. In Bismarckian welfare states, however, to a great extent, the concrete organisation of policies to activate weaker and more vulnerable groups into employment takes place at the local level. This is due to the greater reliance of weaker and more vulnerable groups on minimum income schemes which are usually connected to decentralised elements of services, administrations or even policies in Bismarckian countries.

Moreover, reforms to render policies more 'active' and 'coordinated' (re-) introduce local discretion into social policy programmes (Finn 2000). Processes of decentralising welfare interventions, changing modes of welfare service delivery and new management techniques for controlling services are shifting issues regarding the reorganisation of employment and social welfare services to the local level. Thereby, the local level is accorded the potential to organise targeted approaches to deal with problems of income, incentives, placement, qualification, counselling, rehabilitation or care (Salais and Villeneuve 2004; Van Berkel and Borghi 2008). The idea behind this localisation of policies, administrations and services is that it is at the local level where coordinated and targeted attempts for the activation of weaker and more vulnerable groups can be organised best (Kaufmann 2009: 88–106; Kazepov 2010: 35–72). The question of coordinated and targeted approaches for the inclusion of long-term unemployed, lone parents, low skilled persons, migrants, the young, older persons, sick or disabled persons thus implies a local dimension in Bismarckian welfare regimes.

The question of the local governance of approaches towards unemployed turns the focus on the organisation of the delivery of services and policies. From a conceptual perspective, the influence of the organisation on services and policies is proven by different strands of debates on the implementation of new service delivery elements (among others Bredgaard and Larsen 2007, 2008, Jorgensen 2004 or Jewell 2007), on the different effects of decentralisation (Leibfried et al. 2005) and on the various ways to control service delivery (Hood et al. 2002). A comprehensive solution to the problem of fragmentation is sometimes equalled with the integration of policies, services and administrations into so called 'one-stop shops' (Johansson and Hvinden 2007). Indeed, the very issue of delivering services and policies is rarely discussed in a systematic manner although its elements crucially influence coordinated and targeted approaches towards unemployed.

A theoretical contribution of this book is to close this gap. Different systems of the delivery of services and policies can exist depending on the concrete local structures for policies and services, the modes of interactions for service delivery and the different control techniques of service delivery. It is thus possible to construct distinct ideal typical systems of the delivery of policies and services: the organisation of policies and services for the activation of unemployed can vary between market-oriented, bureaucratic and participatory approaches. This modelling of different organisational types of service delivery allows construing hypotheses on the reactions to rising numbers of minimum income benefit recipients in Bismarckian welfare states. Taking into account the crucial role of the local level to organise services and policies to activate weaker and more vulnerable groups into employment in Bismarckian welfare states, different local approaches of delivering services and policies might emerge. We therefore assume that the introduction of activation policies leads to transformations of Bismarckian welfare states which affect also the structures of local governance.

We will thus seek to empirically reconstruct how Bismarckian welfare states react to the challenges of fragmented policies, administrations and services. *Our general assumption is that the local level plays a crucial role in re-organising services and policies towards weaker and more vulnerable groups dependent on minimum income benefits in Bismarckian countries.* This general assumption will be tested taking the example of two selected continental European countries. In order to investigate into these questions, processes of reorganising social welfare and labour market policy programmes and services to deal with the problem of inclusion of vulnerable and weaker groups shall be reconstructed for France and Germany. Both countries present very emblematic examples of the institutionalised fragmentation of policies, administrations and services distinguishing between insiders and 'extreme' outsiders. The question of the activation of weaker and more vulnerable groups of society has both become a topic in France and in Germany thereby raising issues on the coordination of work incentives, benefits and services as for example placement, training, psychological counselling, health services, social services or childcare support. As a result of both countries belonging to the status-conserving Bismarckian welfare state model, France and Germany introduced similar social and labour market policy reforms (Clegg 2007). Reforms involved changes of the organisation of polices and services towards minimum income recipients. In France, the most important minimum income scheme was decentralised and its regulation was re-oriented towards the take-up of work (Barbier and Knuth 2011a; 2011b; Clegg and Palier 2012). In Germany, new regulation merged social assistance with unemployment assistance into one structure which is now jointly governed by local authorities and the Federal Employment Agency. National accounts of the reformed minimum income schemes portray a general move towards market-oriented activation policies in Germany (Eichhorst et al. 2008b; Jacobi and Mohr 2007) but also for France: "More recently (2003), the minimum income system was reformed in order to introduce a new welfare-to-work scheme." (Erhel and Zajdela 2004: 138). However, room for local manoeuvring in implementing approaches and the entanglement with traditionally locally bound elements make the reorganisation of minimum income programmes in both countries depend to a great extent on developments at the local level. For each country, we present local cases detailing the implementation of minimum income benefit programmes. Besides similar national regulation, we however find very dissimilar local organisations of welfare interventions and also different outcomes of activation policy.

To summarise, the local dimension of the Bismarckian activation regime is becoming more important. First, the comparative and empirically grounded work introduces the issue of rising numbers of recipients of minimum income schemes by defining the problem of fragmentation of the Bismarckian welfare state architecture in light of the transformation towards a welfare state more based on the provision of and the preparation for employment. Second, the argument focuses on a changing relationship of labour market policies, social policy and social services in Bismarckian welfare states. Third, the book takes into account Bismarckian welfare states' reform implications for an activation of weaker and more vulnerable groups by conceptualising different models of inter-organisational coordination at the local level. These arguments will be specified taking the examples of social and labour market policy reforms in France and Germany.

The structure of the book

Following the introduction, the second chapter discusses the rise in the number of beneficiaries of minimum income schemes in Bismarckian welfare states as a matter of changing patterns of inclusion and exclusion. We will conceptualise inclusion as a matter of the integration into systems of welfare production. An effective inclusion in a welfare state then depends on the particular ways how institutions as employment, the family or social security function. The rise of minimum income schemes in Bismarckian countries primarily reveals problems of recalibrating (Ferrera et al. 2000) welfare state institutions. The increasing reliance of lone mothers, older people, the young, persistently unemployed, disabled or sick persons, migrants and low skilled persons on minimum income schemes shows how the individualisation of society and the structural economic change aggravate the access to options of income, employment, qualification, care or rehabilitation in the traditional Bismarckian welfare regimes. As a result, the traditional 'division of labour' between labour market policy for 'workers' and social and family protection for weaker and more vulnerable groups becomes fragile. The increased risk of minimum income receipt for weaker and more vulnerable groups is thus a problem of the fragmented Bismarckian welfare state architecture to cope with social and economic transformations.

The third chapter discusses policy reactions to rising numbers of minimum income recipients in the Bismarckian welfare regime. European reform strategies and processes call into question the traditional Bismarckian division between labour market policy for workers and family income respectively social policy for weaker and more vulnerable groups. Due to the inertia of Bismarckian welfare state institutions, however, a better coordination of policies, programmes and services is only to some extent achieved. Reforms aiming at the institutionalisation of an activation regime rather 'selectively' (Clegg 2007) focus on weaker and more vulnerable groups. Reactions to rising numbers of minimum income schemes concentrate on attempts to institutionalise 'employment-centred welfare' as new mode of inclusion for weaker and more vulnerable groups in the Bismarckian welfare regime. While service offers are enhanced and opportunities for low-paid or in-work benefit programmes are created, issues of an effective dealing with placement, training, rehabilitation, child or family care demands of weaker and more vulnerable groups are shifted to local minimum income arrangements.

The fourth chapter discusses the question of how the local level might be able to organise activation of minimum income recipients in Bismarckian welfare states. It first analyses the local level's potential to provide individualised services to react to problems of incentives, qualification, health, counselling, child or family care of weaker and more vulnerable groups. Individualised services require a locally 'co-produced' delivery of policies and services between employment agencies, welfare centres, social associations, project executing organisations, beneficiaries' representative organisations, case-managers and benefit recipients. This question of the institutionalisation of local organisational fields for the activation of benefit recipients challenges the fragmented Bismarckian welfare state architecture at the local level. In a first hypothesis, we thus argue, that activation in Bismarckian welfare states requires a local coordination between competences from different policy levels, approaches of different actors and solutions of complementary policy fields. However, local institutional structures, local modes of interaction of service delivery and local control techniques for co-producing services and policies might differ from country to country and even in each local context. In a second hypothesis, we argue that the co-production of individualised policies and services in Bismarckian welfare states might indeed proceed differently according to distinct local approaches. We conceptualise ideal-types of a bureaucratic, a market-oriented and a participatory local organisation of services and policies.

In the fifth chapter, the methodology for a comparative empirical study of the reorganisation of minimum income schemes in Bismarckian welfare states is explained. A proper research design for the reconstruction of local reorganisation processes of social welfare and labour market policy services for beneficiaries of minimum income schemes is suggested. The employed qualitative research strategies for retrieving dense empirical data are explained. In this context, the relative strengths and weaknesses of the following research methods we used are discussed: 1.) expert-interviews with decision-makers from local employment agencies, local state agencies, territorial authorities, social welfare offices and welfare organizations; 2.) a collection of in-depth information from reviewing documents and reports; 3.) a series of detailed territorial case studies.

Turning to the empirical investigation, in the sixth chapter, policy reactions to the rising numbers of minimum income schemes are analysed for France and Germany. The typical residual character of minimum income schemes in these two welfare states is described. Analysing the position of minimum income schemes in these two welfare states, for each country, the institutionalised fragmentation of policies, programmes and services is traced. However, recent social welfare and labour market policy reforms aim at the activation of weaker and more vulnerable groups. Changes in regulation of policies and programmes simultaneously trigger questions on the organisation of minimum income schemes in both countries. It is pointed out that the activation of vulnerable and weaker groups of society, to a great extent, becomes a matter of the local level. In Germany, new labour market and social policy legislation of the so called 'Hartz' reforms led to the merging of social assistance and unemployment assistance into a general minimum income scheme for unemployed (2005). This reformed minimum income scheme is usually implemented by a new approach of joint local governance between the municipalities and the local agencies of the Federal Employment Agency. In France, the decentralisation of the general minimum income scheme (Revenu minimum d'insertion (RMI), remodelled by a new regulation for a Revenu de Solidarité Active (RSA) in 2009) to a local authority, which took place in 2004, equally raises the question of how the activation of minimum income recipients is organised at the local level. At the core of this chapter are eight case studies reconstructing the local handling of a co-production of policies and services to activate minimum income recipients in both France and Germany. The case studies analyse the institutionalisation of activating weaker and more vulnerable groups but reveal very different local paths towards re-organisation.

In the final chapter, the results and implications from the comparative study of France and Germany are put in the broader context of Bismarckian welfare state development. We draw conclusions from the empirical investigations on the causes and drivers of differently changing local governance arrangements. The mechanisms found on the local level are discussed with regard to a multi-level explanatory framework. This allows to summarise broader conclusions in view of the question in as much the local level is able to attenuate the fragmentation of Bismarckian welfare state institutions and to provide activation as a new option of inclusion for more vulnerable and weaker groups.

2. The challenge of rising numbers of minimum income recipients in Bismarckian-type continental welfare systems

The aim of this chapter is to understand the increase in the number of beneficiaries of once negligible social assistance in Bismarckian welfare states. For a long time, this last-resort minimum income protection was a residual option in insurance-based Bismarckian welfare states. Crucial economic and societal evolutions, however, in particular defy the Bismarckian welfare state model with regard to its capacity to guarantee inclusion, welfare and employment.

The development of minimum income schemes is connected to the question of how welfare states cope with fundamental social and economic transformations. Important economic changes are introduced through greater international competition and the turn towards knowledge-based patterns of production. Both developments raise productivity requirements, demand greater flexibility and orient the economy towards services (Ruggie 1982; Ferrera et al. 2000). These developments have important implications for labour markets and employment. In general, individual skill-demands are raised (Schmid 2006). As a result, employment dynamics turn out to be much more volatile and difficult for the less-skilled, weaker and more vulnerable groups of society and the labour market. This can pose problems of inclusion, welfare and employment leading to an increase in the number of beneficiaries of minimum income schemes.

Moreover, principal societal changes challenge the welfare state in important ways. Self-determination and self-fulfilment become driving choices of life and work (Beck 1983; Giddens 1991). Family formation is challenged by a greater female participation in the labour market (Esping-Andersen 2006). Increasingly instable family and solidarity situations reduce families' traditional capability of internalising welfare responsibilities. As a general trend, traditional social ties of national solidarity, class affiliation, family or neighbourhood bonds are weakening or overcome. Thus, next to the demographic crunch, urging societal issues are the changing gender roles in labour markets and households and the inclusion into society of the young, elder, migrants, sick and handicapped. Unresolved, all these developments present potential causes for an increase in the number of minimum income protection recipients.

Taken together, the flexibilisation of the economy and the individualisation of society have increased external challenges (economic development, structural and technological change) and also biographical challenges due to the discontinuities in life and work (Schmid 2002). Both developments raise serious questions on social and labour market inclusion particularly for weaker and vulnerable groups of society (Taylor-Gooby 2004). The increased risks reflect in a feminisation of the labour market, atypical employment and a growing wage polarisation and they are a potential cause for unemployment and particularly long-term unemployment. All these factors can contribute to an increase in the number of beneficiaries of minimum income schemes, thereby raising serious questions on the risk of social exclusion (Lødemel and Trickey 2001). For the welfare state, these transformations thus pose the issue of safeguarding opportunities for social and labour market inclusion in more open, market-driven and individualised societies especially of society's weaker and vulnerable groups. Such threats are common to all European welfare states, but they have differently dealt with them. As numbers of persons in need of minimum income protection have sharply risen in continental European welfare states, serious questions arise on the functioning of the established Bismarckian institutions for inclusion, employment and welfare.

At the same time, the important properties and capacities of the welfare state itself are seriously challenged by the social and economic changes. Welfare state financing, social protection expenditures and solidarity wages are increasingly under strain. Low fertility and rising longevity call into question the financial sustainability of the welfare state. In addition, welfare state expenditures nowadays compete with a nation's goal to establish attractive conditions for international investments and production (Scharpf 2000). In other words, amid the challenge to provide for solid answers for inclusion, employment and welfare, the viability of the current welfare state is at stake. Therefore, besides analysing the problems of the functioning of established Bismarckian welfare state institutions for welfare and work, it is necessary to understand how the welfare state itself changes: does the rising number of recipients of minimum income schemes in Bismarckian countries lead to a fundamental change in the established patterns of inclusion, employment and welfare or even to a general demise of its core capacities?

For explaining both the problems of inclusion and the patterns of change in Bismarckian welfare states, it is necessary to clarify the function of minimum income schemes not as an isolated phenomenon, but in the context of welfare state development. Acknowledging the transformation towards open, market-driven and individualised societies, in a first step, we define the welfare state as a matter of inclusion into systems for welfare and work. This allows, in a second step, to define the role of minimum income schemes as a subsystem of the welfare state. Using this definition permits to understand the traditionally residual and disparate role of minimum income schemes in Bismarckian welfare states. As their marginal role has been obviously questioned in face of rising numbers of beneficiaries, we discuss three concepts for understanding this phenomenon of welfare state change. The debates on retrenchment, recalibration and curtailing of social citizenship rights of the welfare state are taken as a reference to highlight different ways of how development of minimum income schemes can be interpreted. In a final step, it is analysed whether the development of minimum income schemes in Bismarckian welfare states signifies a retrenchment of the welfare state and citizenship rights or whether it refers to problems that rather pose the challenge of institutional recalibration.

2.1 The welfare system in open, market-driven and individualised societies

The current economic and social changes challenge conventional definitions of the role of the welfare state. Taking reference to the full-employment Golden Age post-war welfare state, as it existed in the 1950s and 1960s, conventional analysis stipulates the welfare state as state centred and solidarity-based entity. The welfare state is strongly regulated by a nation state and it is based on solidarity arrangements of class affiliation or family. It accounts for comprehensive benefits and the regulation of encompassing solidarity arrangements (Leisering 2003). Accordingly, welfare state efforts are defined in terms of public expenditures for programmes, benefits and welfare services (Korpi 2003). Such a welfare state, which is centred on the state and structures of association and solidarity arrangements, conveys a rather traditional concept of society. The individualisation of society and the flexibilisation of the economy, however, question this traditional concept of the welfare state (Leitner and Lessenich 2003; Obinger and Rieger 2009). Both trends raise the question on the role of the welfare state in open, market-driven and individualised societies. As societies turn towards open, market-driven and individualised modes of inclusion, the welfare state requires to be reconceptualised as consisting of systems for welfare and work (Kaufmann 1992/2009, 1999/2009; Luhmann 1981, 1984, 1987).

Welfare in an open, market-driven and individualised society is achieved by a welfare state ensuring the social right to participate in society (Luhmann 1981; Marshall 1965). The transformation towards open, market-driven and individualised societies proceeds as a process of functional differentiation (Luhmann 1984; Luhmann 1987). Functional differentiation leads to the splitting up of society into numerous social systems (as for example the economic system, the political system, the family system, the education system, the health system). As the differentiation of society proceeds, each individual has to be (at least in a basic manner) able to access the interdependent functions of the different subsystems of society. In hierarchically structured societies, groups were distinguished by very different degrees of participation in society. In modern society, however, a limited attachment or reduced access to subsystems proves very problematic. It hinders persons to benefit from complementary welfare functions (e.g. the economy, education, reproduction, health, etc.). The partial inclusion in functionally differentiated subsystems is thus a phenomenon of modern society. The abolishment of traditional bonds of the family, class affiliation or social ranks enables individual freedom but simultaneously dissolves past mechanisms of shelter, association, patronage and solidarity. Instead, modern society relates to the idea of rather equal individuals with regard to the participation in society. In open, market-driven and individualised societies, inclusion is so crucial as patriarchal private or public structures of encompassing solidarity can be decreasingly relied on. Therefore, inclusion means access to important societal functions but also dependency on them:

> "Each person has to be granted a possible access to all functional spheres. Everyone has to be capable of holding rights, to start a family, to take part in the exercise of political power or to take part in its control; everyone has to be raised in schools, to receive medical assistance in a case of emergency, and to participate in processes of economic exchange. The principle of inclusion replaces a solidarity arrangement that was based on the fact of belonging to one and only one single group." (Luhmann 1980: 30f).

In short, the transformation towards open, market-driven and individualised societies corresponds to the idea that the whole population is – at least in a basic manner – included into society's subsystems to access their different welfare functions, be it for income, education, reproduction or health. This principle of inclusion replaces rather encompassing public or private solidarity arrangements based on the family, class affiliation or social ranks. Thus, the modern welfare state is primarily an issue of inclusion into the different subsystems of society.

In open, market-driven and individualised societies, a welfare state achieves inclusion of individuals by producing synergies between state interventions and the self-regulatory subsystems of modern society, notably the economy (Kaufmann (1998: 314, 1999: 346). To promote inclusion, welfare state interventions resolve negative external effects of open, market-driven and individualised societies (Kaufmann 1996/2009). The necessity for state interventions in modern society derives from the structural indifference of different, highly specialised systems, as for instance the market economy (Kaufmann 1996/2009). Specialisation of each system enables higher performances (Luhmann 1984; Luhmann 1987). It thus permits the modern welfare state to function as a set of interdependent systems (e.g. the economic system, the political system, the family system, the education system, the health system) of welfare production (Luhmann 1981: 80).

At the same time, functional differentiation turns each system increasingly indifferent towards interrelations that do not concern its primary function. As a result, the autonomous subsystems cause negative external effects. For example, the economic system's market logic does not take into account education. Lacking education can create a negative external effect for the individual to find employment. The provision of qualified labour for the economic system would thus constitute a welfare state intervention (Kaufmann 1982/2009: 85–87). It resolves a negative external effect for an individual welfare problem by providing a collective solution (Kaufmann 1994/2009: 270). At the same time, it enables the economic system to pursuit higher performances. Therefore, the welfare state potentially has the ability to compensate for the increasing structural indifference of the economic system and the other societal systems without questioning their self-regulatory character (Kaufmann 1996: 301). Synergies between the different systems and welfare state interventions can thus lead to a higher degree of welfare production presenting the advantage of welfare states in open, individualised and market-driven societies (Kaufmann 1998: 314, 1999: 346).

In short, the welfare state is only one arena among many other functional arenas for inclusion and welfare production in modern society's welfare system. The role of welfare state interventions in open, market-driven and individualised societies is to compensate for negative external effects of the economy and other social systems in a manner which enhances the self-regulatory character of the other subsystems, notably the economic system, the political system, the family system, the education system or the health system.

To conclude, welfare production in open, market-oriented and individualised societies is based on the self-regulatory nature of subsystems of society. This confronts welfare states with the problem of inclusion. Inclusion of the whole population into crucial subsystems as the economy, the education-, health- or political system – at least in a basic manner – is a prerequisite and need of modern societies. Modern societies try to resolve this problem through a welfare state which compensates for the negative external effects of functionally differentiated social systems. This signifies a progress in comparison to hierarchically structured, patriarchal societal arrangements. As a consequence, modern welfare states 'deal with' the problems and consequences arising from increasingly autonomous social systems, notably the economy, by enhancing the subsystems' self-regulatory character with regard to their particular opportunities for inclusion. Welfare systems therefore significantly differ from a traditional welfare state based on a state-centred structure and class or family-oriented solidarity arrangements.

2.2 Minimum income schemes in the welfare system

Such a systemic perspective of the modern welfare state, which was proposed above, brings us to ask for the composition of the subsystems of the welfare state. The objective of the following discussion is to define the function of minimum income schemes in the welfare system. Minimum income schemes are embedded in particular institutional regimes of welfare states. The receipt of a 'last-resort' general minimum income benefit against social exclusion is therefore a matter of different institutional 'filters' in a welfare system (Leibfried et al. 1995; Leisering and Voges 1992: 451–453) which regulate and organise access to the production of welfare. The interdependent nature of a welfare system defines the development of minimum income programmes in three filter dimensions: the particular institutional arrangement of minimum income benefits (1), the advanced nets of social security (2), the labour market and the family as crucial institutions of a welfare regime (3), constitute a filter function that determines who will lack sufficient welfare and therefore needs to rely on the last-resort safety net (cf. Fig. 3). These internal and external institutional filters of minimum income protection can be analysed in terms of their regulatory, organisational and historical institutional development in a welfare state.

Fig. 3: The institutional filter of minimum income schemes.

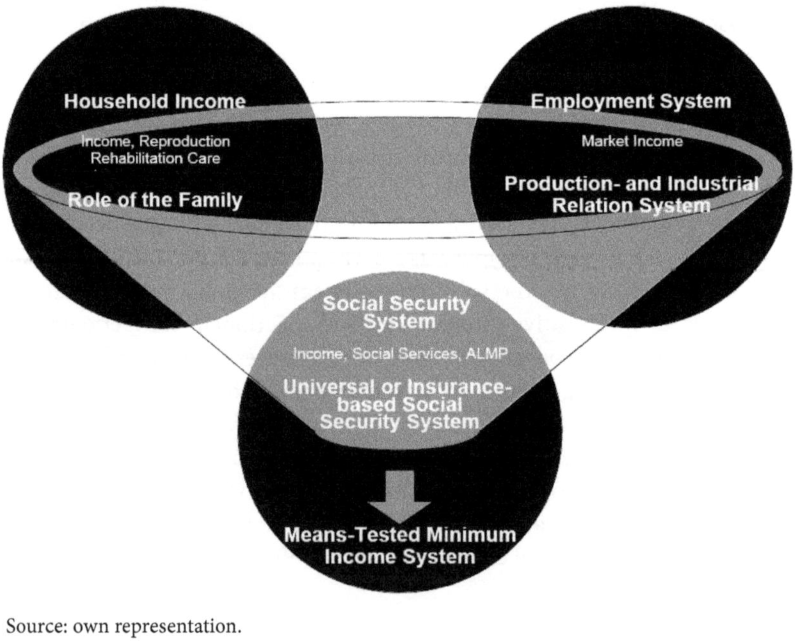

Source: own representation.

2.2.1 Institutional filter regulation of minimum income schemes

Regulation of the institutional filter of minimum income schemes refers to minimum income programmes' 'internal' access regulation as well as minimum income schemes' 'external' institutional regulation of access to the different systems of welfare production.

2.2.1.1 Internal filter regulation of minimum income schemes

If someone will receive a minimum income benefit depends in an immediate context on the institutional regulation for benefit receipt (Lødemel and Schulte 1992, Gough et al. 1997; Gough 2001). The terms of access to benefit receipt thus constitute the 'internal' filter of minimum income programmes. The internal filter of minimum income programmes, which defines eligibility to minimum income benefits, depends on regulation with regard to coverage of needs, criteria for means-testing, the degree of legal codification and work requirements (Gough et al. 1997).

Eligibility to benefits depends on the needs covered by a minimum income programme. Minimum income schemes intervene in order to prevent persons from living under an officially defined, minimum living standard (Hanesch 2001). This means that these programmes aim to provide a 'minimum' of resources to protect against poverty. However, the definition of this minimum of resources a person should be provided with is a question of societal preferences, political judgements and statistical reasoning (Behrendt 2002: 101–113; Casas 2005) related to two issues: first, coverage is a matter of the definition of the minimum income benefit level. The 'generosity' of benefits decides in an important manner on the issue who is covered by a minimum income programme (Behrendt 2002, Gough et al. 1997). Second, coverage also refers to the 'adequacy' of needs covered. Minimum income provision differs between general payments and the provision of resources 'tied' to particular needs (Gough et al. 1997: 19). Some minimum income programmes solely respond by general payments to the incident of 'poverty'. Other minimum income programmes 'tie' specific commodities or services in either cash or kind to particular needs. In these cases, minimum income programmes cover circumscribed needs by linking the provision of minimum resources to services or monetary resources for training, housing, transport or child care (Guibentif and Bouget 1997). The adequacy of services or benefits 'tied' to particular needs decides in an important manner on the question of who is covered by a minimum income programme. In brief, eligibility to a minimum income benefit programmes is a matter of societal definitions of the coverage of needs which can vary according to criteria of generosity and adequacy.

Apart from the definition of coverage, criteria for means-testing define eligibility to a minimum income benefit. For the purpose of guaranteeing a required 'minimum' of resources only, minimum income programmes rely on the principal of means-testing. According to this premise, assistance is in general subordinate to other resources of income or services of a welfare system. These other resources are meant to be exploited first. This means that the attribution of minimum income benefits is conditioned on the exact criteria of means-testing (Gough 1994). Criteria for resources susceptible to means-testing depend on two issues: first, means-testing defines eligibility according to criteria of responsibility (Gough et al. 1997: 34). On the one extreme of the responsibility scale, minimum income provision is an individual entitlement. On the other extreme, means-testing requires wider family obligations to provide resources for an individual. Second, eligibility is also a matter of the resources of income and assets which are considered as relevant for a means-test (Gough et al. 1997: 34). In this regard, criteria for means-testing can vary between the extremes of a more superficial definition and a very strict consideration of means-tested income and commodities. In brief, means-testing is a central premise of eligibility regulation to minimum income programmes which can vary regarding its strictness and responsibility obligations.

Besides coverage and means-testing, the legal degree of codification regulates eligibility of persons to a minimum income benefit (Gough et al. 1997: 34). Eligibility can be broadly codified in legal regulation which would come close to the ideal of a 'citizenship right' to minimum income benefits. On the other extreme, high discretion in legal regulation makes eligibility a very variable matter. In brief, eligibility is therefore also a matter of the legally binding character of regulation.

Finally, eligibility can depend on the strictness of work-testing requirements (Gough et al. 1997: 34). Regulation for minimum income schemes might exclude those persons not ready to work from the receipt of a minimum income benefit.

To summarise, the generosity and accuracy of needs covered, the definition of responsibility and the extent of means-testing, the degree of legal codification and the strictness of work-testing requirements define the internal filter of a last-resort safety net. By definition of the internal filter, it is decided on the immediate eligibility of persons to access benefits or services of a minimum income programme.

2.2.1.2 External filter regulation of minimum income schemes

As minimum income assistance forms only one subsystem of welfare and employment regimes (Esping-Andersen 2006; Fligstein 2001a; Gallie 2007: 1–34; Heidenreich 2004; Schmid 1997; Schmid and Gazier 2002), entry onto and exit from a minimum income programme crucially depend on how inclusion into other institutions that provide income or (social) services functions. As a result, the institutional filter of minimum income schemes is not only defined by its internal regulation, but the last-resort function of minimum income schemes also requires to ask for the possibilities of 'normal' sources of income and services (work, family and household transfers) as well as for the social protection system's alternative possibilities of benefits and services. If someone risks depending on a last-resort income programme or if someone will not be in such a need, thus also depends on how 'external' filtering institutions of minimum income benefits function (Buhr 1999: 220; Saraceno 2002).

In a welfare state, the labour market constitutes a primary external filtering institution of minimum income schemes. It serves as a central resource for creating income. Employment opportunities are determined by institutions that regulate the (potential) supply and demand of labour on the labour market (Gallie 2007: 1–34; Heidenreich 2004; Schmid 1997, Schmid and Glazier 2002). The employment model of a welfare state is in particular influenced by the production system and the industrial relations system. The production system decides upon the structure of production, as for example the opportunities of service sector employment. The industrial relation system determines the level and structure of wages as well as collective rights (Schmid 1997: 16). Both areas influence the regulation of labour markets which defines such crucial questions as regards, for example, employment opportunities for low-skilled persons. In brief, as employment provides opportunities of market income, the labour market system constitutes a primary filtering institution of minimum income schemes.

Apart from market-based income, the family is another primary filtering institution of minimum income schemes. The family respectively a partner offers important resources of income and (social) services (Esping-Andersen 1999; 2006). As regards the family or a partner, both function as an important income alternative or additional option to income from the labour market or to benefits from social security. Moreover, family welfare can fulfil important service functions for rehabilitation and care, too (Kaufmann 1994: 279). The particular functioning and role of the family in a society influences who might need to rely on minimum income programmes and who will not. Therefore, family arrangements constitute an important filtering institution of minimum income benefit receipt as it can serve as an alternative or complementary resource of welfare production.

In brief, the labour market and the family constitute a primary external filter of minimum income assistance. Regulating access to basic resources of income and (social) services, the particular functioning of the employment system and the role played by the family system regulate in a decisive manner who might need to rely on minimum income programmes and who will not.

Apart from the labour market and the family, another external filter of last-resort minimum income programmes are more elaborate and/ or 'specialised' social security programmes (Esping-Andersen 1999; Clasen and Viebrock 2006). In contrast to the broader risk of social exclusion, covered by 'general' last-resort income programmes, advanced social security programmes respond to specific risks. Advanced social security programmes specialise onto the provision of income or services for a particular risk. Unemployment, illness, incapacity, old age, family, children or survivorship are typical risks for which single programmes can exist.

Specialised social security programmes condition access on criteria as prior contributions or particular status (Atkinson 1989). In the case of access based on prior contributions, a particular risk is covered by a social insurance programme. A social insurance scheme relates allocation of income to contributions paid. Alternatively to contribution-based insurances, 'category-specific' programmes provide benefits based on the affiliation to a particular group. In contrast to general last-resort income programmes, category-specific programmes give benefits to more specific groups than only the 'socially excluded'. Single benefit programmes can exist for 'workers', 'single parents', 'disabled' or 'skilled persons'. Eventual means-testing clauses of category-specific income-related benefits do not necessarily serve to preserve a minimum income function of benefits as benefits are provided to a more specialised income group than only the 'socially excluded'. For example, a programme can relate to former employment status and contributions paid but include some broader criteria of means-testing in order to limit access by the well-off (Gough et al. 1997: 19). Programmes like the former German 'Unemployment Assistance' (*Arbeitslosenhilfe*) or the French 'Unemployment Assistance' (*allocation de solidarité spécifique*) are examples for programmes which are provided to income groups with a distinct employment status and a certain contribution-record. In other cases, apart from the exception that they define a minimum income for a specific group, category-specific programmes can also function very similar to a general means-tested last-resort income programme (Gough 1994; Gough et al. 1997: 19). As a final variant of advanced programmes of social security, instead of categorising benefit recipients, 'universal' social protection programmes relate state allocation neither to income nor to the contribution record, but to the citizen status.

In brief, alternative social security arrangements to minimum income benefits are social insurance programmes, 'categorical' income-related programmes or universal programmes for benefits and services. The crucial role of advanced schemes of social security in defining the function of last-resort assistance is underscored by the fact that they not only intervene prior to the receipt of a minimum income benefit but in some cases – for example due to administrative delay in confirming eligibility – indeed constitute a significant exit option from assistance, too (Leisering and Voges 1992). Besides the significance of family and labour market regulation, the institutional 'filter' against receipt of last resort minimum income is thus to an important extent defined by the opportunities to access onto more elaborate, insurance-based, categorical or universal programmes of social security.

To summarise, besides internal regulation of minimum income programmes, the receipt of a minimum income benefit is externally regulated by the opportunities to access income or services from the labour market, the family or specialised social security programmes. The labour market or the family constitute the two primary external filtering institutions of minimum income schemes. If these fail, higher-ranking programmes of the social protection system, which in general are more directly targeted to specific risks and social groups, can constitute a further external filter of last-resort minimum income receipt.

2.2.2 Organisational issues of specific institutional filter of minimum income schemes

Minimum income schemes are not only regulated in a particular manner but they also follow distinct organisational patterns. Reflecting specific features of an institutional filter, the organisation of crucial elements like minimum income benefits, specialised social security programmes, social services and labour market policy can differ according to their administrative linkages, their degree of centralisation and their public-private dimension.

The administrative interlinkages of elements of the institutional filter of minimum income schemes can vary. The organisation of minimum income programmes can differ from the administration of social services, advanced social security programmes and labour market policy. Originally, minimum income schemes were rooted in the organisation of social welfare services: "A key distinguishing factor is the extent to which social assistance provision has been combined with social work provision, as in the cash-care multifunctional tradition of the early Poor Laws." (Lødemel and Trickey 2001: 28). In the latter and original case, minimum income programmes were interlinked with social service administrations (Bahle 2003). In contrast, as can be exemplified at the hand of different unemployment programmes, strong interrelations have often evolved between the provision of universal or insurance-based social security and active labour market policy (Esping-Andersen 1999; Schmid 1997; Schmid and Gazier 2002).

Apart from the administrative interlinkages, the organisation of elements of the institutional filter of minimum income schemes can vary according to their degree of centralisation. Minimum income schemes have a legacy of locally based arrangements (Lødemel and Schulte 1992; Mingione et al. 2002). Besides some trends towards a more central organisation, minimum income schemes often remain more local in character (Gough et al. 1997: 35–36; Lødemel and Schulte 1992). Similarly, social services are characterised by a tradition of local arrangements (Bahle 2003: 6). While minimum income schemes and social services have often remained in important elements bound to local structures, tendencies of centralisation were much more strongly related to social insurance or more universal social security schemes in most of the European welfare states (Rauch 2008). Following industrialisation and labour movements in Europe, active labour market policy programmes often became subject to central regulation and national agencies, too. The rationale behind centralism is to guarantee for universalism and equality (Rauch 2008).

Besides the degree of centralisation, the organisation of elements of the institutional filter of minimum income schemes can vary regarding to the actors intervening. Actors intervening can be divided into belonging to the public and private sphere. Minimum income schemes as well as social service systems are often characterised by a mixed system of providers, comprising the family, the state, the for-profit or the non-profit, voluntary sector (Abrahamson 1995, 1999; Bahle 2003). In contrast, social security programmes and labour market policy have often reached a greater public dimension. However, besides the state, corporatist actors like the social partners can play a decisive role in the organisation of social security programmes and labour market policy.

The organisation of minimum income programmes, specialised social security programmes, social services and labour market policy can vary according to their administrative interlinkages, the degree of centralisation and the public private mix of providers.

2.2.3 National institutional orders of filter arrangements of minimum income schemes

Taken together in their regulatory and organisational dimensions, the internal and external filtering institutions of minimum income schemes constitute distinct institutional orders or institutional regimes (Heidenreich 2004). Institutional orders or institutional regimes are made up of key institutions, show institutional complementarities, are shaped by certain actors, their development moves to a great extent on a path-dependent track and they are usually conceptualised as national orders.

First, filtering orders of minimum income schemes are made up of the institutions described above. Being defined as institutions, the filtering elements represent relatively stable cognitive, normative and strategic patterns of interaction (Giddens 1984).

Second, the distinct filtering institutions of minimum income schemes in a welfare state tend to show complementarities. In Europe, industrialisation and labour movements often strongly advanced the broad institutionalisation of universal or insurance based social security. These 'mature' protection mechanisms reached stronger degrees of centralisation and they usually implied an involvement of the social partners in one or the other way. In these institutional orders of the 'post-war' welfare states, only a 'residual' role was left to minimum income schemes. As a result, minimum income scheme have often remained restricted to 'poverty policy' arrangements (Whiteside 2007).

Third, orders of filtering institutions are only partly influenced by current dynamics. In the institutionalisation process of the filter of minimum income schemes in a welfare state, past institutional junctions mark the development of the filtering institutions. As institutions constituting relative stabile and homogeneous orders, institutional junctions continue to shape in an important manner dynamics of filtering arrangements of minimum income schemes in welfare states (Pierson 1993: 624–628; Thelen 1999: 392–395). For instance, minimum income schemes' historical roots in poverty policy explain why minimum income schemes can be still attached to local services, social work and discretionary regulation.

Fourth, the institutional filtering arrangement of minimum income schemes is expected to be defined in the national boundaries of a welfare state. The process of institutionalisation of the filtering institutions of minimum income schemes mainly depends on national circumstances. It depends on the role of the state, the degree of communal autonomy, the relationship between the church and the state, the role of the family, the nature of the employee-employer relationship and the way private interests are publicly regulated (Alber 1995; Kaufmann 1994/2010: 282f) but also involves specific societal norms: "These safety nets are the social expression of what each European nation according to its own social consensus perceives as being the minimum floor under which poverty and social exclusion are considered as unacceptable (…)." (Casas 2005: 17).

Last but not least, despite path dependency and institutional complementarities of the internal and external filtering institutions of minimum income schemes, the institutional filter arrangements in a welfare system are not completely homogenous institutional orders. Institutional orders are not free from conflicts on the prevailing institutional design (Gallie 2007; Heidenreich 2004: 209f). A certain heterogeneity of institutions always exists that might provide room for development dynamics beyond the typical traits of minimum income schemes' 'post-war' arrangements (Streeck and Thelen 2005; Mahoney and Thelen 2010).

In brief, the internal and external institutions organising and regulating the receipt of a minimum income benefit constitute particular institutional orders of a filter for minimum income schemes in a welfare state. Based on the particular national framework defining the complementarities of internal and external filtering institutions, constellations of actors, and past institutional developments, the position of a minimum income scheme in a welfare state is defined. Historically, minimum income schemes belonged to the area of 'poverty policy' characterised by elements of social work and local arrangements. It depends on the particular institutional dynamics of a welfare state in as much minimum income schemes still take this 'residual' function of poverty policy in a welfare state.

2.2.4 Conclusion: minimum income schemes as a matter of institutional filter

To conclude, the preceding discussion allows defining the position of minimum income schemes in a welfare system. General minimum income schemes against social exclusion fulfil a particular function among the subsystems of a welfare system: they function as last-resort safety net in a welfare state. This means that an institutional filter defines who is cut off from the inclusion into important institutions of welfare production in such a way that the need arises to rely on last-resort assistance. The institutional filter of social assistance depends on the concrete function of institutions as the labour market, the social security system and the family. The precise arrangements and functions for inclusion into the subsystems of a particular welfare state are marked by path dependent developments, particular institutional constellations of actors and institutional complementarities which define the role of minimum income schemes in a welfare state. We proceed by applying this institutional regime perspective for defining the function of minimum income schemes in the Bismarckian welfare state type.

2.3 The role of minimum income schemes in the Bismarckian welfare system

Having conceptualised minimum income schemes as a function of filtering institutions, we discuss the programmes' typically residual role in the context of the Bismarckian welfare state arrangements of institutions for social security, employment and family welfare (cf. Fig. 4). The analysis for the typical Bismarckian filtering institutions of minimum income programmes refers to their regulatory as well as to their organisational dimension.

2.3.1 Bismarckian institutional filter regulation of minimum income schemes

Bismarckian regulation provides a fragmented structure between external filtering institutions of employment, family welfare and social security on the one hand and disparate means-tested minimum income programmes against the general risk of social exclusion on the other hand.

2.3.1.1 Bismarckian welfare systems' external filtering of minimum income programmes

In the Bismarckian welfare states, a socially secured employment model constitutes a principal external filter against minimum income receipt. The Bismarckian employment model is based on well protected, indefinite contracts. 'Regular' employment is full-time and turn-over is rather low. Labour markets in Bismarckian countries are characterised as exclusive regimes (Ferrera and Hemerijck 2003; Heidenreich 2004 Vogel 1999). Rigidity stems from strongly protective labour laws, high minimum or high reservation wages and significant contributions to social security. Industry remains an important factor for employment. The Bismarckian welfare state's societal preference for stable and socially secured employment leads to only moderate overall employment rates (Heidenreich 2004: 208). Usually high rates of male employment reflect the prevalence of male breadwinner careers which the Bismarckian model typically enables. In contrast, women, older people, the young or disabled people are often excluded from the labour market. The combination of a strong promotion of socially secured male breadwinner employment and low or moderate employment rates for women, older people, the young or disabled people is complementary to the functioning of the family and social protection. In the typical Bismarckian welfare architecture, weaker or more vulnerable groups, which were excluded from the labour market, therefore not necessarily had to rely on minimum income protection programmes.

In combination with socially protected but exclusive employment, components of important family welfare complement the primary external Bismarckian filter against minimum income receipt. Traditionally, the Bismarckian employment model promotes 'family' wages. It therefore corresponds to a male single earner household. In turn, the family as resource for income and social services, particularly for weaker or more vulnerable groups, plays an important role in Bismarckian welfare states (Heidenreich 2004; Ferrera and Hemerijck 2003). The Bismarckian welfare system is to an important extent based on the services of the family, or, to put it precisely, by women (Ostner 1998). Bismarckian welfare states typically rely heavily on the family for tasks related to raising children but also for rehabilitation and care. Thus, Bismarckian familialism not only accounts for reproduction but constitutes a crucial filter against minimum income dependency by providing important income resources and extended social services for weaker or more vulnerable groups of society.

Complementary to the functions of socially secured employment and the crucial role of the family for providing income resources and extended social services, predominantly passive and work status-oriented social protection programmes prepend the receipt of a last-resort minimum income. The social protection system primarily reacts to the uncertainties of – typically male – 'normal' employment careers. Descriptions of the standard Bismarckian social protection system identify highly developed social insurance institutions (Heidenreich 2004; Ferrera and Hemerijck 2003). The social protection system is dominated by a Bismarckian work-based insurance logic. This means that social security depends in a significant manner on the level of prior contributions. Social insurance schemes demand important contributions. In turn, the compensatory nature of social protection for risks as unemployment or old age has a highly status-conserving effect. In general, social protection is rather based on money transfers instead of services. Income replacement benefits tend to be generous and of long duration. Passive elements of social protection are thus strong in the Bismarckian welfare state (Esping-Andersen 1999).

The linkages between socially secured employment and social protection become strongly evident in the case of unemployment benefit programmes. As part of the specialised social protection system, unemployment is covered as a particular risk faced by workers. An unemployment policy for workers evolved in

Bismarckian welfare states (Leibfried and Tennstedt 1985). The principal idea of Bismarckian unemployment policy is to uphold and protect the status of a worker. Consequently, strategies against unemployment react to generalised, average industrial risks of workers, notably human capital deterioration and loss of income. Unemployment is covered by particular unemployment schemes oriented towards prior income (OECD 2007b). Important benefits for the insured unemployed are to a great extent unconditional in order to serve as status protection. To uphold the unemployed worker's status, important resources are allocated to programmes of further training, education schemes, early retirement schemes, or subsidized jobs (Clasen and Clegg 2003; Daguerre and Taylor-Gooby 2003: 629; Eichhorst et al. 2008b: 18; Erhel and Zajdela 2004: 129). Participation in active labour market programmes is voluntary. The rationale behind Bismarckian unemployment policy is to guarantee occupational protection for both insured unemployed and working 'insiders'.

Fig. 4: The institutional filter of minimum income schemes in the Bismarckian welfare state model.

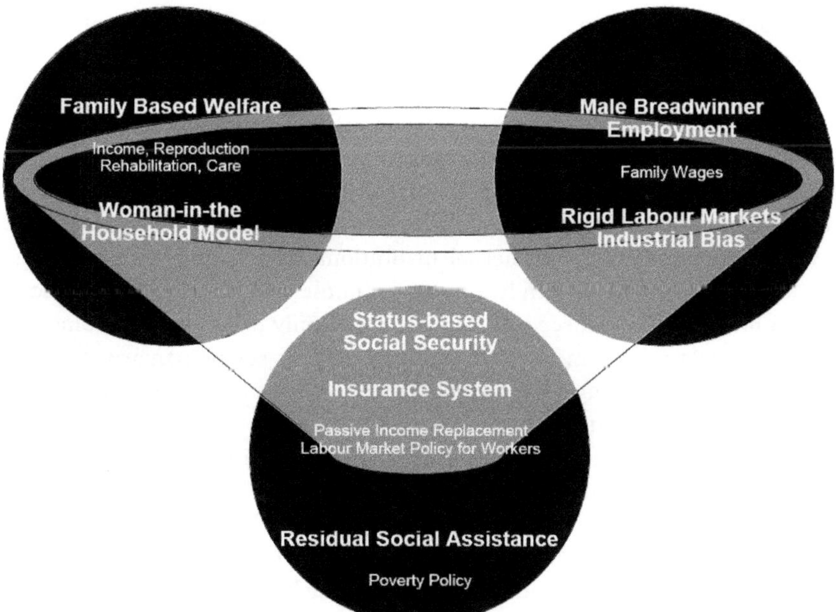

Source: own representation.

In brief, in addition to socially secured income from employment and important income and service functions of the family, the Bismarckian external filters of minimum income receipt are complemented by specialised social protection programmes like unemployment protection which dominate a worker-oriented, passive social protection system.

Summarising Bismarckian countries' external institutional filters of minimum income receipt, Bismarckian welfare states traditionally promote a particular institutional 'division of labour' between employment, the family and social security. According to the premises and hazards of an industrial risk community, the risk of minimum income receipt is externally filtered by socially secured male-breadwinner family wages, a women in the household based model of family welfare providing important social services, and status-preserving, contribution-based social programmes providing primarily monetary benefits against risks like unemployment, illness or old age.

2.3.1.2 Bismarckian welfare systems' internal filtering of minimum income programmes

In the context of the Bismarckian welfare state arrangement, the internal regulation of minimum income receipt is directed at a residual function of these disparate, tax-financed schemes (Gough et al. 1997; Gough 2001). In contrast to the broadly institutionalised functions of socially secured employment, strong family welfare and status-based social protection, minimum income programmes against social exclusion are installed as a marginal category. Regulation of the internal filter of minimum income schemes strongly refers to the income and service opportunities of the external institutional filters. Accordingly, in Bismarckian countries, minimum income programmes are principally 'subsidiary' to insurance based social security benefits and family provision of income and services. Regulation for means-testing illustrates this supplementary character of benefits. Means-testing for the eligibility to minimum income benefits tends to include wider obligations of the family to account for individual problems of inclusion. The tax-financed benefits' rather low generosity adds to the residual character of general minimum income programmes (Gough 2001: 59). Furthermore, minimum income programmes in Bismarckian Europe are only moderately formalised (Gough et al. 1997: 36f). As a result, assistance arrangements usually go along with certain discretion in granting benefits.

Minimum income programmes' linkages with labour market policy are usually rather unspecified. Receipt of a minimum income benefit is in the typical Bismarckian welfare state rather loosely coupled to work requirements. While regulation might stipulate work requirements, it does so in a rather general manner. Incentives for the take-up of work are usually not provided for in a coherent and detailed manner (Gough et al. 1997; Gough 2001) as this would undermine the model of socially secured employment (Clasen and Clegg 2006). Therefore, for a long time, 'residual' minimum income schemes did not develop an explicit component of labour market policy in Bismarckian countries.

Instead of applying stringent work requirements, residual minimum income programmes are often tied to social services. Accordingly, in Bismarckian countries, social workers have usually been assigned to recipients of social assistance (Lødemel and Trickey 2001). In general, minimum income schemes in Bismarckian countries are therefore rather related to social services than labour market policy (Lødemel and Schulte 1992; Saraceno 2002).

In short, reduced to a residual role of meagre to moderate benefits, the internal regulation of minimum income schemes accords these tax-financed programmes a strictly subsidiary function to contribution-based insurance programmes and family obligations.

2.3.1.3 The fragmented regulatory logics of Bismarckian filtering institutions

In conclusion, the archetypal Bismarckian institutional filter of minimum income assistance is based on solidarity structures of a traditional industrial risk community. It builds on a strongly socially secured, highly exclusive employment model distributing opportunities for inclusion in a very uneven manner. Policies for unemployed reflect this bias towards the industrial risk community as they are conceptualised as status protecting benefits and active labour market services for 'workers'. While being excluded from the labour market, weaker and more vulnerable groups are typically included in a separate way by socially secured family income, services of the family or contribution-based insurance. In the typical Bismarckian welfare state model, residual minimum income benefits thus follow a completely disparate logic and originally constitute a last-resort option for the 'extreme' outsiders who are not included into one of the filtering institutions of important family welfare, contribution-based benefit programmes or socially secured employment. The Bismarckian welfare state's filter of minimum income receipt is thus highly fragmented between labour market policy and contribution-based insurance for workers, socially secured family income and family welfare for weaker and more vulnerable groups as well as disparate and residual minimum income schemes for 'extreme' outsiders.

2.3.2 Organisational features of the Bismarckian filter of minimum income schemes

For the organisation of labour market policy, social insurance systems and minimum income programmes in Bismarckian welfare states, the central level and the state constitute only one point of reference among other important actors and policy levels.

2.3.2.1 Organisational features of Bismarckian external filtering institutions

The organisation of major Bismarckian welfare state institutions like the socially secured employment model, the contribution-based social protection programmes, labour market policy and status-oriented active labour market policy are in an important manner influenced by corporatist institutions and actors.

In the field of labour market policy, Bismarckian corporatism typically involves the social partners in formal bargaining processes on wages and regulations. An important complex of industrial relations and large industrial enterprises influences in significant ways the regulation of employment relations, most prominently in wage bargaining systems. The structures of the political economy contribute in an important manner to the viability of the socially secured employment model (Beyer and Höpner 2003, Streeck and Hassel 2003).

In the case of Bismarckian contribution-based social security schemes, notably in unemployment programmes, social partners usually play an important role in the set-up of these institutions (Ebbinghaus and Visser 1997). Institutions of co-management preserve a prominent role for social partners, for example, in the organisation of self-financed unemployment insurance schemes. Overall, the involvement of the social partners in the important contribution-based social security institutions, as in particular unemployment insurance, corresponds to the orientation of these schemes along the needs of an industrial risk community.

In active labour market policy and vocational training, Bismarckian corporatism involves social partners in formal and informal bargaining processes on the provision of theses services. As in social protection schemes, social partners are often involved in the provision of services for active labour market policy and vocational training (Clasen and Clegg 2006).

The competences for labour market policy, contribution-based social security programmes and active labour market policy services are in general concentrated at the national level. Bismackian welfare state's centralised logic of programmes and policies corresponds to a focus on collective rights and monetary transfers to 'workers' (Rauch 2008, Whiteside 2007). Reacting predominantly to collective risks rather than individual risks, programmes and services are organised in a more centralised and uniform manner.

As a result of the strong presence of corporatist actors in the organisation of labour market policy, social protection and active labour market policy services, an industrial bias marks these institutions. The rather centralised labour market policies, contribution-based social protection programmes and active labour market services illustrate clearly interrelated policy fields geared towards the status-protection of insured unemployed and working insiders.

2.3.2.2 Organisational features of the Bismarckian internal filtering institutions

In this original framework of corporatist, centrally organised and status conserving Bismarckian welfare state institutions, minimum income schemes constitute an 'alien' instrument (Behrendt 2002: 178). In contrast to the interlinked fields of status-oriented labour market policy, social protection and active labour market policy services, the administration of minimum income benefit programmes reveals a 'strong cleavage' (Behrendt 2002: 178).

The administration of minimum income benefit programmes is usually separated from the administration of social insurance programmes (Lødemel and Trickey 2001). Normally, the administration of these programmes is accorded to the area of 'social affairs'. It is usually not related to the administration of unemployment protection programmes or active labour market services.

Furthermore, contrary to institutions of social insurance, social assistance programmes in Bismarckian-type continental Europe are typically only to some extent centrally organised (Gough et al. 1997: 36f). Assistance arrangements usually go along with some local discretion in public delivery. In the organisation of these schemes, the local or municipal level tends to play important roles.

In the context of services to minimum income recipients, a peculiarity of the Bismarckian regimes is their 'mixed' public-private system of provision (Mingione et al. 2002: 71f). Although structures of publicly organised support are well developed, an important role in the provision of services often persists for intermediary organisations. The third sector, notably the church or other philanthropic organisations tend to be involved in the delivery of services.

As a result of this organisation of benefits and services, minimum income programmes in Bismarckian countries traditionally belong to the field of social work or treatment provision and therefore match a classical organisation of 'poverty' policy (Gough et al. 1997: 36f).

2.3.2.3 The fragmented organisation of Bismarckian filtering institutions

To summarise, the organisation of the institutional filter of minimum income schemes in Bismarckian countries reveals a cleavage between a poverty policy related field for minimum income recipients and the status-oriented fields of labour market policy, active labour market policy services and contribution-based social protection programmes for workers. While local, social and third sector actors tend to mark the poverty policy character in the former, the industrial bias of the latter is reproduced by the prominent role of the social-partners in negotiations, management and provision. As a result, carrying on the traits of classical poverty policy in form of an often locally based social work system, Bismarckian minimum income schemes, are typically strongly decoupled from a more centralised organisation of labour market policy, active labour market policy services and social insurance schemes.

2.3.3 Conclusion: Bismarckian filtering institutions of residual minimum income schemes

Summing up, the institutional division of labour of the Bismarckian welfare regime reduces last-resort minimum income programmes to a residuary function as it is meant to be purely subsidiary to socially secured employment, important family welfare or the well-developed social insurance system. Its disparate character is expressed by a regulation and organisation strongly decoupled from the characteristics of the predominant social protection institutions: minimum income schemes provide only moderate to low-level tax-based assistance benefits and traditionally belong to the field of social work. This model stipulates some local discretion in delivery and traditionally involves the third sector in delivery. Thus, residual social assistance as a form of social work is traditionally related to poverty policy for the marginalized or 'extreme' outsiders of the Bismarckian welfare state model.

Given the disparate and residual character of minimum income schemes, the Bismarckian welfare state instead accords a prevalent function for welfare production to status-based social protection, family welfare and socially secured employment. Filtering institutions of social assistance promote the idea of an industrial risk community that is built on the premises of stable male employment careers and family wages, household arrangements providing important welfare services, and passive benefits of broadly institutionalised social insurance schemes based on prior income.

Bismarckian labour market, social protection and active labour market policies typically correspond to the risks of workers. Rigid labour markets promote an exclusive employment model favouring stable male breadwinner careers and socially secured labour market income. The social insurance logic of the Bismarckian welfare state is tightly oriented along the idea of an industrial risk community. Institutions of social insurance protection are highly formalised through central regulation but typically carried in important ways by corporatist actors, as for example the social partners in the case of unemployment benefit programmes. Unemployment policy is thus conceptualised as policy towards the core workers: active labour market policy represents a mix of human capital investment and social policy. Institutions of co-management accord an important role to the social partners in the regulation of employment, social security and unemployment policy.

While being to a great extent excluded from the labour market, weaker and more vulnerable groups benefit in a separate manner from the Bismarckian welfare state model. Socially secured family income or family-based welfare services guarantee options of inclusion for the weaker and more vulnerable groups of society.

The institutional filter for minimum income programmes of the Bismarckian welfare state model is thus based on this division of labour between labour market policy for workers, family welfare for weaker and more vulnerable groups and disparate minimum income schemes for 'extreme' outsiders. However, the sustainability of this typically industrial risk related Bismarckian institutional filter of minimum income benefit receipt and its corresponding institutional division of labour is challenged. Its external filtering institutions increasingly fail to provide opportunities for inclusion in particular for weaker and more vulnerable groups as women, young, older people, low-skilled, persistently unemployed, migrants or sick. As a result, the number of persons in minimum income schemes oriented to 'need' and not previous income has drastically risen as will be discussed in the following.

2.4 Dynamics of welfare system change

The rising number of persons on minimum income schemes displays a general trend for the European welfare states, but concerns in particular Bismarckian-type continental European welfare regimes. Obviously, institutions constituting an important filter of last-resort minimum income programmes increasingly fail to provide for employment, inclusion and social protection in the Bismarckian welfare system. This problem demands for an explanatory framework. Welfare state research tries to explain the phenomena that arise due to the influence of social and economic change on the evolution of the welfare state. While researchers had concentrated on explaining the expansionary welfare state model until the 1970s, three different interpretations detail how modern welfare states react to the challenges of the transformation towards open, market-driven and individualised societies. One debate assumes a 'retrenchment' towards residual welfare, while another argument interprets recent welfare state reactions to social and economic change as a 're-commodification' of social citizenship rights. A third debate puts a different focus, as it conceptualises welfare state change as a 'recalibration' of welfare institutions in the face of new risks of open, market-driven and individualised societies. We introduce these three concepts, in order to explain the development of minimum income schemes in Bismarckian welfare states.

2.4.1 Retrenchment

A dominating interpretation views the altered social and economic conditions as causing permanent pressure on the state budget thereby defining the premises for 'new politics of the welfare state' (Pierson 2001). The argument describes a distancing of the welfare state model from a transfer-intensive welfare state that regulates rather all-encompassing solidarity structures, in particular in the form of broad social security arrangements or state employment. This debate has pointed to retrenchment as the primary trend shaping welfare state policy reactions to problems of low growth, the challenge of creating service sector employment, population ageing and the financing of existing policies. Welfare state policy takes place under the premise of 'permanent austerity'. On the long run, retrenchment is believed to manifest as the dominant principle for welfare state evolution. It raises the issue of retrenching public social expenditure or social rights. Also rising unemployment rates are identified as a sign of retrenchment from the developed welfare state as they might significantly alter distributive conditions and effect benefit spending and social rights (Korpi 2003). Consequently, with regard to minimum income schemes, this perspective highlights changes made to the social security net. Benefit cuts and more rigid criteria to access universal or social insurance systems make a growing number of people refer to social assistance benefits (Hanesch 2001: 168).

From the perspective of the retrenchment debate, a rebalancing of social security from higher-ranking social security programmes towards minimum income protection fits into interpretations of a welfare state regress. In this light, the rising significance of minimum income schemes in the Bismarckian welfare states then indicates broader processes of retrenchment increasing the likeliness of a residual welfare state model (Pierson 1995: 20–27).

2.4.2 Re-commodification

Another explanation interprets current trends as re-commodification of the welfare state. This argument describes a detachment of the welfare state model from a welfare state whose core function was– at least theoretically – based on guaranteeing an income independent from the market (Esping-Andersen 1996). From this perspective, ideal typically, social citizenship in a welfare state was based on unconditional, collective rights (Marshall 1965). Accordingly, a worker would not have to submit to any wage conditioned by business. However, changing socio economic power relationships make the welfare state become subject to a re-commodification (Serrano Pascual 2007a).

Consequently, from this angle, the increase in the number of beneficiaries from minimum income schemes is analysed as a curtailing of social citizenship rights. The debate highlights in as much social security's level and conditions of benefit receipt provide an encompassing and independent resource of welfare. Claims on minimum income protection are usually means-tested against income (from the market). In some countries, social benefits are too weak to promote beneficiaries above the poverty line. Moreover, strict procedures of means-testing and other forms of administrative control can provoke higher non take-up rates. Both factors can limit an efficient material provision of social benefits in order to alleviate poverty (Behrendt 2002). Consequently, similar to the retrenchment argument, the debate on re-commodification tends to interpret the rise of beneficiaries of minimum income schemes as turn towards a restricted welfare state.

2.4.3 Recalibration

A more recent debate explains the evolution of the welfare state in terms of recalibration (Ferrera et al. 2000; Ferrera and Hemerijck 2003). This argument refers to the idea of a 'new' welfare state (Esping-Andersen 2002) for employment, inclusion and social protection. It responds to the recognition of new problems and risks caused by open, market-driven and individualised societies (Armingeon and Bonoli 2006; Taylor-Gooby 2004). New risks arise from structural economic change, changing life forms, a change of demographics, the feminisation of the labour market, or higher frequencies of family break-down (Schmid 2002). Risks translate into unemployment and particularly long-term unemployment, atypical employment or a growing wage polarisation. Such new risks tend to concern weaker and more vulnerable groups of society: the young, women, older people, lone-parents, the sick, migrants, low-skilled or persistently unemployed. In this context, it is increasingly perceived to be necessary to remodel the welfare state in such a way that opportunities for inclusion are safeguarded for the growing number of persons with non-standard employment biographies. By doing so, recalibration means that reforms are above all about the question of restructuring welfare states in a more efficient and effective way in view of new risks.

With regard to minimum income schemes, the debate on recalibration highlights changes in the institutions of the welfare state. From this perspective, a rise in the number of beneficiaries of last-resort income schemes signals institutional problems to deal with de industrialisation, long-term unemployment, atypical employment, low-paid employment or lone-parenthood (Lødemel and Trickey 2001: 28). It translates into the question on opportunities for a more effective welfare state with regard to the inclusion of groups vulnerable towards new risks, as these groups can constitute significant shares of beneficiaries of social assistance. Consequently, from the perspective of the recalibration debate, rising numbers of beneficiaries of last-resort social assistance point at filtering institutions of social assistance that fail to provide options for welfare and inclusion for weaker and vulnerable groups of society.

Summing up, the debate on welfare state change suggests three different reactions to the challenges of the transformation towards open, market-driven and individualised societies. As one trend, increasing the likelihood of a residual welfare state, a policy of retrenchment sets in aimed at cuts in public social expenditure or social rights. As another development, increasing the possibility of a market-oriented welfare state, a trend of re-commodification of social citizenship evolves, submitting welfare state rights onto market requirements. As a third trend, increasing the potential of a more effective welfare state for weaker and more vulnerable groups of society, a policy of recalibration reacts to new risks by attempting to provide fresh approaches for inclusion.

From these three different policy trends, we can derive three broader explanations for understanding the rise of beneficiaries of minimum income schemes. In face of the economic and social transformations, the retrenchment debate assumes greater restrictions of the *state* to provide welfare. As a result, the rise of beneficiaries of social assistance is explained mainly as a problem of retrenchment of 'advanced' social security arrangements. In a different vein, the re-commodification argument assumes a more important role of the market for welfare production. As a result, the rise of beneficiaries of social assistance is explained by restrictions of the *market* to provide for welfare opportunities.

Offering another interpretation of welfare state evolution in open, market-driven and individualised societies, the debate on recalibration views the rise of beneficiaries of minimum income schemes as a problem of traditional welfare state institutions, like the *family*, to react to new risks. From this perspective, the welfare state is increasingly lacking efficient and effective institutions to provide broader inclusion and welfare options for weaker and more vulnerable groups of the labour market and society.

Applying these three interpretations, we try to assess each positions explanatory potential for rising claims on 'residual' assistance in Bismarckian welfare states.

2.5 Development dynamics of minimum income schemes in Bismarckian-type continental welfare systems

Scrutinizing the impact of economic and social changes on central Bismarckian institutions, like socially secured employment, status-based social security and the important family welfare system, reveals dynamics that, in particular, polarise in the development of minimum income schemes. Developments show that the Bismarckian model's external filtering institutions for minimum income schemes increasingly fail to provide options of welfare production in particular for weaker and more vulnerable groups including women, young, older people, low-skilled, persistently unemployed, migrants or sick persons.

2.5.1 The erosion of the Bismarckian employment model's external filter function

Among the primary institutions covering against minimum income receipt, employment has decreasingly constituted a robust external filter in Bismarckian welfare states. The Bismarckian employment model of stable, male bread-winner careers has been strongly affected by structural economic change. Declining 'Fordist' employment options heavily impacted on the highly industrialised Bismarckian countries (Ferrera and Hemerijck 2003). The reduction of industrial labour was furthermore accelerated by 'labour-shedding' inclinations caused by high contributory rates to generous social protection and highly protective labour laws (Clegg 2007). As a result of the sharp rationalisation of industrial labour, opportunities for socially secured employment were particularly curbed for low-skilled industrial workers. Given the exclusive character of Bismarckian labour markets, new risks of unemployment and particularly long-term unemployment therefore derived for low-skilled persons from the structural changes of the economy.

At the same time, the creation of new jobs was hampered by strong obstacles to service sector employment growth. Ferrera and Hemerijck (2003: 108) analyse this problem as 'continental syndrome': elevated contributory financing and the generosity of insurance-based income replacement benefits led to a high productivity threshold. As a result, high wages prevented a market solution for employment creation. In particular, job opportunities in the personal and social service sector remained restricted (Iversen and Wren 1998). On the other hand, soaring commitments to social security institutions put such a pressure on the public budget that made public sector service employment growth difficult. These developments prohibited new employment options for laid off industrial workers furthering trends of unemployment and persistent unemployment.

However, the ever more exclusive Bismarckian employment model also inhibited labour market access for those persons who could not rely anymore on advanced social protection programmes due to trends of partial retrenchment (cf. discussion below). Furthermore, exclusive labour market regulations turned out increasingly problematic as family structures changed. Due to higher rates of divorce and family break-up, the family decreasingly proved being a robust welfare option for women, older persons, young persons or sick persons (cf. discussion below). For these groups, the labour market as alternative option for welfare production remained limited due to its weak employment dynamics. This trend furthered risks of unemployment and persistent unemployment. Additionally, stronger aspirations of higher-skilled women to realise proper employment careers not only contributed to changing family structures but also exerted new pressure on weaker (male) groups that had been included by socially secured employment in the past. Due to the exclusive labour market character, this trend further heightened unemployment risks for low-skilled persons. As a result, the exclusive employment model decreasingly proved as a robust welfare option for low-skilled but also revealed problems to offer opportunities for weaker and more vulnerable groups who could not rely anymore on family welfare or advanced social security programmes (Esping-Andersen 2002; Ferrera and Hemerijck 2003)

Consequently, against new risks of unemployment created by changes in the economy, the family and individual role types, the Bismarckian employment model proves difficult to still function as a comprehensive welfare option. The partly erosion of the socially secured employment model concerned particularly low-skilled workers. However, exclusive structures of labour markets also turned into a problem for young people, women, older persons, low-skilled people, sick or disabled people as other welfare options as the family or the advanced social protection programmes became less reliable. This problem of welfare production on the labour market is increasingly recognised as a 'dualisation' between 'insiders' and 'outsiders' (Ferrera and Hemerijck 2003; Heidenreich 2004; OECD 2007b; Palier and Thelen 2010): 'insiders' hold well protected jobs while a growing part of the population are extreme 'outsiders' of the labour market. As other options of welfare become limited, extreme 'outsiders' risk unemployment or long-term unemployment. As employment dynamics were weak in the past, increasing unemployment and, in particular, long-term unemployment impacted on the development of minimum income schemes.

In short, as changes in the structure of the economy, the family and the individual role models produce new risks of unemployment and long-term unemployment, the highly socially secured Bismarckian employment model proves increasingly difficult to function as institutional filter against minimum income receipt. The partly erosion of the socially secured employment model, weak employment dynamics and exclusive labour markets have limited employment as a welfare option for weaker groups of the labour market, more vulnerable groups of society, low-skilled and long-term unemployed.

2.5.2 The erosion of the Bismarckian family model's external filter function

In parallel to the problems, which the traditional employment model increasingly encounters, the strong reliance on family welfare causes growing difficulties for Bismarckian welfare arrangements. New social and economic transformations have created increasing burdens on comprehensive family welfare. The realisation of women employment careers, increasing educational levels of women, rising female employment rates and professional aspirations of women, increasing marital instability and erosion processes of sustainable one-earner households pose obstacles for family welfare (Ferrera and Hemerijck 2003: 109).

In parallel, the strong emphasis of Bismarckian welfare institutions on 'passive' income transfers instead of services could not ease the increasing problems to produce family welfare. As a result of the erosion of the family model as well as the passive Bismarckian welfare state character, the stress on the family as welfare provider becomes problematic. For example, important care demands on the family, and women in particular, stage a trade-off between careers and children which leads to low fertility (Billari and Kohler 2004; Rindfuss et al. 2003). Particularly for lone parents, this situation bears the risk of poverty. These trends hint at the increasing welfare problems caused by the strains put on the Bismarckian familialistic welfare system. The familialistic welfare system more and more emerges as a 'sub optimal strategy' against the protection of risks (Esping-Andersen 1999). Its strong reliance on the family to fulfil employment, reproductive and rehabilitative functions turns out to pose increasing difficulties.

In more individualised, open and market-oriented societies, the strong reliance on family welfare proves difficult for women and lone-parents. However, the problems of traditional Bismarckian family welfare equally raise welfare questions with regard to those groups that, in the past, benefited from rehabilitation services and income options offered by the family (young people, sick people, older people, weaker groups of the labour market in general and persistently unemployed). As a result, Bismarckian last-resort minimum income schemes directly experience the problems of the family-based welfare arrangement as assistance was here usually conceptualised as highly subsidiary to family welfare.

Consequently, greater risks of family breakdown, the increasing significance of women employment careers and erosion processes of the reliable one-earner household model impede on the function of family welfare to serve as comprehensive institutional filter against minimum income receipt. The obstacles put on the family as income option, reproduction function and rehabilitation opportunity weigh so heavily for weaker and vulnerable groups as alternative welfare options like social services or employment have remained restricted in Bismarckian welfare states or had been privileging workers, as in the case of unemployment benefit programmes.

2.5.3 The erosion of the status-based Bismarckian social protection's external filter function

Obstacles to welfare production on the labour market and in the family have been accompanied by changes in the social security system.

For a long time, strong rationalisation pressure on employment in Bismarckian-type continental European countries was complemented by the possibility to exit the labour market onto specialised, often status conserving social security programmes. Bismarckian countries reacted to problems of inclusion of weaker groups of the labour market, low-skilled and long-term unemployed by an expansion of their social policy for 'workers': "(…) governments, especially in continental Europe, also increased the generosity of social benefits, notably for those who were particularly hard-hit by the economic crisis (redundant industrial workers, lone parents, poor elderly, long-term unemployed, etc.)." (Palier and Martin 2007: 547). As a result, in the past, Bismarckian unemployment policy addressed problems of inclusion and labour market integration of weaker groups of the labour market, low-skilled unemployed, persistently unemployed, sick people, the handicapped or older people by generous higher-ranking social protection programmes. This 'social treatment' of unemployment (Daguerre and Taylor-Gooby 2003: 629) led to a continuous expansion of specialised schemes for unemployment, (early) retirement, disability or sickness (Ebbinghaus 2001). In parallel, contributions to social insurance increased. While employment and the family increasingly failed as primary external filtering institutions against minimum income receipt, for a certain period of time, expansive 'higher-ranking' programmes of social security stepped in as filtering institution. Generous social protection thereby partly covered problems of family welfare and employment to deal with new risks such as long-term unemployment, lone parenthood or skill devaluation.

However, large scale expansion of the advanced social security net came to a halt in the end of the 1990s.While retrenchment did not take place globally in continental European welfare states, changes made to the social security system in these Bismarckian countries proceed as 'qualified cost-containment' (Clegg 2007: 605). For important higher-ranking social protection schemes, access was partially limited. As a general trend in continental Europe, the Bismarckian principle of 'contributiveness' was reinforced (Clegg 2007). By reducing redistributive elements of the social insurance system, it (re-)turned towards a stricter actuarial logic. This means, the link between the amount of contribution and the volume of benefits was tightened. Benefit eligibility to higher-ranking programmes of social security thus became much more restrictive regarding prior income. Alternatively, benefit entitlements were cut in a selective way. Retrenchment was thus 'selective' in that sense as it reduced earlier opportunities for unemployed persons with non-standard employment biographies, single parents, redundant low-skilled workers, sick persons, handicapped people or long-term unemployed to rely on specialised programmes of social security.

In this context, reforms in the area of unemployment benefit are particularly striking (Clegg 2007: 605–607): considering the overall development of unemployment benefits for the period from 1985 to 2003, expenditures in important Bismarckian countries remained stable or even increased to some extent. Some benefits for the older unemployed or those with the longest contribution records were still expanded (Palier and Martin 2007: 547–549). However, selective expansion of unemployment benefit was accompanied by contractions in other parts. Criteria of access, levels and duration of unemployment benefits were more closely linked to employment history, prior contributions and seniority.

As a consequence, the unemployment insurance system became much more selective. In turn, coverage of risks by this important higher-ranking scheme of social security became much less exhaustive.

Selective retrenchment in unemployment schemes and other specialised social security programmes increased a 'dualistic' character (Gough 2001) of the Bismarckian social security system. While persons with standard employment biographies remain widely covered by higher-ranking programmes of protection, as a result of partial cost-containment, specialised programmes of social security decreasingly cover unemployed persons with non-standard employment biographies, persistently unemployed, redundant low-skill workers, or other vulnerable groups of society. Parallel to the obstacles of employment and family welfare, specialised social security programmes thus neither function anymore as a comprehensive filtering option against minimum income receipt: "Unemployment insurance systems have, in short, often distanced themselves from the management of 'bad' risks." (Clegg 2007: 605). As a result of selective retrenchment of the specialised social protection programmes, formerly marginal means-tested minimum income benefits gained more significance (Palier and Martin 2007: 550). Weaker groups of the labour market and more vulnerable groups of society increasingly need to rely on general minimum income schemes instead. 'Dualisation' is therefore not only a matter of the labour market but it is also reflected within the social security system.

Resuming the changes in the social security system, selective retrenchment of unemployment programmes and other specialised social security schemes have shifted increased benefit claims from the higher ranking social security programmes towards residual minimum income assistance. Without family welfare nor employment as reliable options for welfare production, particularly weaker and more vulnerable groups of society, who are depending on social security, increasingly have to rely on meagre to moderate level, residuary Bismarckian minimum income schemes.

2.5.4 The rise of minimum income claimants: a crisis of classical Bismarckian filter institutions

Issues on the sustainability of the Bismarckian welfare state in light of the social and economic changes are illustrated by rising numbers of beneficiaries of minimum income schemes. The current debate on welfare state change offers three interpretations to discuss these trends: the debate on retrenchment points out restrictions of the state to provide welfare, the re-commodification argument highlights a greater relevance of the market for welfare production, and the debate on recalibration points out the general need to remodel the Bismarckian welfare state institutions in face of new risks for the inclusion of weaker and more vulnerable groups.

To some extent, changes of Bismarckian social security present a process of retrenchment. Attempts of cost containment in the social security system took place in a selective manner. While the expansion of higher ranking programmes of social security had first served as an option to cover welfare problems caused by the decline of industrial labour and the erosion of traditional family solidarity structures, Bismarckian social security has become less encompassing. Cost-containment of generous and often status-protecting higher-ranking social security programmes has proceeded in such a way that large challenges of welfare production are shifted onto originally residual minimum income benefits.

The debate on re-commodification underscores the greater relevance of the market for welfare production. Structural changes of the economy, the family and the individual role models put strains on the Bismarckian welfare model of exclusive, socially secured male breadwinner employment careers. Low or moderate employment rates of Bismarckian countries increasingly turn into a problem of inclusion of weaker and more vulnerable groups as traditional solidarity structures of socially secured, family-wage based employment, comprehensive family welfare or encompassing social protection are withering away. While the Bismarckian employment model decreasingly fulfils functions of a comprehensive provision of welfare, the exclusive structures of the labour market simultaneously inhibit new market-based options for welfare production. Both trends limit the function of the labour market to externally filter against dependency on minimum income programmes.

Reflecting on the consequences of social and economic transformations for the Bismarckian welfare state, the debates on recalibration and re-commodification draw a similar conclusion. In a rather 'pessimistic' outlook, retrenchment and re-commodification arguments interpret the consequences of welfare state change as a sign of a general demise of the welfare state. However, to present the problem of rising numbers of beneficiaries of minimum income schemes from such a perspective only, would present a very narrow analysis. It appears to be too fast of an assumption to accord the changes in the Bismarckian social security system to a general demise of the welfare state.

Notwithstanding the thesis of 'selective retrenchment', most of the problems, which the Bismarckian welfare state is exposed to, however, are to a great extent due the particular Bismarckian architecture of important welfare institutions. In light of the social and economic changes, it is not the welfare state in general but the traditional institutional set-up of the Bismarckian employment and welfare regime which is in crisis. Indeed, the rise of the numbers of beneficiaries in Bismarckian welfare states rather illustrates the problems to provide reliable and broad opportunities for inclusion, that a welfare state still modelled around an 'industrial risk community' encounters in light of the transformation towards an increasingly open, market driven and individualised society. As traditional Bismarckian modes of inclusion by the family become fragile, an important filtering institution for weaker and more vulnerable groups in the Bismarckian welfare state fails. Alternative Bismarckian welfare options are not prepared to cope with the new risks of the weaker and more vulnerable groups as they cover the needs of an industrial risk community. The socially secured and exclusive employment model as well as the predominantly passive social security system do not offer robust options for weaker groups which are therefore highly susceptible to the new risks of long-term unemployment, devaluation of skills or family break-up and erosion processes of family solidarity. In the case of the Bismarckian countries, the recalibration problem therefore describes very unequal opportunities for women, older people, the young, disabled or sick people, migrants, low-skilled or persistently unemployed to participate and combine the benefits of crucial welfare functions – notably employment, education, social security, care and rehabilitation. A dualisation between insiders and extreme outsiders has therefore evolved as a new challenge for the Bismarckian welfare state: core workers have well protected jobs and regularly qualify for social insurance benefits. At the same time, unemployment or long-term unemployment concern an increasing part of the population that is now being qualified as extreme outsiders of the classical Bismarckian institutions of socially secured employment, family welfare and status-based social protection. Dualism thus signals new challenges of employment, inclusion and social protection of weaker and more vulnerable groups of society. From the perspective of the recalibration debate, the Bismarckian division of labour between institutions to provide for income, education, care and rehabilitation is now turning into a problem of fragmentation as it does no longer fit together to produce solid answers for inclusion, employment and welfare for weaker and more vulnerable groups of society.

Qualified cost-containment and the problems of recalibration thus explain how the classical Bismarckian 'filtering' institutions are failing in light of the new risks: they highlight how the Bismarckian welfare arrangement of socially secured employment, family-based services and contribution-oriented and passive social security experiences increasing obstacles of welfare production in face of the new risks arising. To put it in a nutshell, as the male bread-winner model erodes, family welfare is under strain, coverage of generous income replacement benefits decreases and effective and efficient social services remain scarce, the institutional filter of the 'residual' Bismarckian assistance model does not function anymore in a reliable manner. As a result, the number of minimum income benefit recipients has risen provoking anew the question of inclusion, social protection and employment of low-skilled, weaker groups of the labour market and persistently unemployed arises.

Consequently, the decreasing reliance on traditional structures of solidarity arrangements, contribution-intensive institutions of social protection, and strong regulation of welfare production does not necessarily signify a demise of the welfare state. Instead, it rather raises the question on the drivers, pitfalls and directions which the institutionalisation of new opportunities for inclusion and options of welfare production might take in the realm of employment, education, care, rehabilitation and social security. We assume that the development of Bismarckian welfare states in particular raises questions on how fragmented institutions of employment, education, care, rehabilitation and social security are reformed to offer more efficient and effective welfare options of inclusion to beneficiaries of minimum income schemes. Therefore, the increasing number of beneficiaries of minimum income schemes does only to some extent a more limited welfare state. It raises in particular questions of how the Bismarckian welfare system might recalibrate to deal with the inclusion of low-skilled, weaker groups of the labour market and persistently unemployed.

2.6 Conclusion: recalibration demands of Bismarckian institutions in face of rising numbers of minimum income beneficiaries

In this chapter, we discussed the phenomenon of rising numbers of beneficiaries of minimum income schemes in the Bismarckian welfare state model. The transformation of economy and society turns the focus onto the question of inclusion, employment and social protection for weaker and more vulnerable groups of society who have often become dependent of minimum income schemes in Bismarckian welfare states.

A sociological definition of the role of the welfare state in open, market-driven and individualised societies pointed out the welfare state as a system of welfare production. While traditional welfare arrangements were based on the premises of vested solidarity arrangements (as the family or an industrial community) and the state as guarantor of welfare production and regulation, welfare production in more open, market-driven and individualised societies necessitates broad inclusion into different, autonomous subsystems. In this context, welfare states are about the promotion of universal access to a set of subsystems for welfare production, as for example the labour market, education, care or rehabilitation.

According to the particular arrangement of different subsystems for welfare production, distinct filtering orders of minimum income receipt can be distinguished. In a system of welfare production, minimum income schemes take a particular function. Minimum income schemes are accorded the function of last-resort safety net. By regulation of the generosity and accuracy in defining needs, definition of responsibility and the extent of means-testing, the degree of legal codification and the strictness of work-testing requirements, minimum income programmes internally filter between who is eligible and who not. At the same time, the development of minimum income schemes is tightly interrelated with and depends on the functioning of crucial institutions of welfare and employment regimes. The opportunities of labour market inclusion, the functions of family welfare, the conditions to access insurance-based, universal or categorical programmes of social protection and the range of services of social, active labour market and education policy externally filter minimum income benefit receipt. Barriers to employment, education, care and rehabilitation or social security then reflect back on the development of minimum income schemes.

The rise of the numbers of beneficiaries in Bismarckian welfare states illustrates how in light of the economic and societal transformations a traditional welfare arrangement increasingly fails to provide and combine opportunities for employment, education, social protection, care and rehabilitation in particular for women, older people, the young, disabled or sick people, migrants, low-skilled or persistently unemployed. Institutions of the Bismarckian welfare and employment regime are typically structured along the premises of an industrial risk community. Here, minimum income programmes are strongly subsidiary to social security and family welfare. In the Bismarckian welfare state model, 'workers' are subject to labour market policies which serve to uphold an exclusive and socially secured employment model. A risk as unemployment is centrally regulated and managed by corporatist arrangements for particular unemployment schemes oriented to previous income. Accordingly, an 'industrial bias' of Bismarckian social and unemployment policy promotes the status protection of core workers by contribution or category related and in many aspects passive social security programmes and an active labour market policy upholding the human capital of 'workers'. In this Bismarckian welfare state model, weaker and more vulnerable groups are normally covered by family-wage based household income or family services for care and rehabilitation. A residual function is therefore attributed to general minimum income benefit programmes against exclusion. Based on a disparate logic, the tax-based programmes traditionally belong to the field of poverty policy, provide meagre to moderate benefits only, and they are geared towards the 'extreme outsiders' or 'undeserving' poor. As such it is typically marked as a field of social work, which is intertwined with social services, characterised by important local discretion and counts on actors from the third sector intervening.

However, the analysis of this chapter has shown that disparate and residual minimum income programmes against social exclusion lose their marginal character in Bismarckian welfare states. Bismarckian filtering institutions of minimum income schemes have changed in important aspects. To better grasp these changes of welfare institutions, we discussed in as much rising numbers of beneficiaries of minimum income schemes relate to a retrenchment of the welfare state, obstacles to a market-oriented welfare state, and to what extent it relates to unresolved new risks of inclusion of weaker and more vulnerable groups of society. The erosion of the familialistic welfare system, which had provided broad opportunities for income, care and rehabilitation for weaker and more vulnerable groups, exposes these groups to new risks of unemployment and long-term unemployment. In parallel, selective restrictions of formerly more expansive higher-ranking social security programmes in Bismarckian welfare regimes refer welfare claims of unemployed persons with non-standard employment biographies, redundant industrial workers, single parents, handicapped or sick persons, unemployed low-income groups, or long-term unemployed onto general minimum income programmes. At the same time, employment opportunities remain limited due to a high-productivity threshold, reduced employment options in the shrinking industrial sector and the small sector of personal and public services. The rise of minimum income beneficiaries is thus connected to the particular problems of Bismarckian external filtering institutions for employment, social security, training, education, rehabilitation and care to recalibrate towards new risks caused by economic and societal changes: the widely passive, contribution-based and increasingly selective character of the higher-ranking social security system as well as a labour market policy for 'workers' tend to exclude weaker and more vulnerable groups of society. A dualisation process between core-workers and new, extreme outsiders of the labour market like the young, women, the elderly, migrants, low-skilled, disabled or sick persons and long-term unemployed points out increasing problems of inclusion. All these developments put an ever increasing burden on residual and disparate minimum income schemes in Bismarckian welfare states. As a consequence, the problems Bismarckian institutions face to deal with the transformation of society and economy polarise in a drastic rise in the number of persons in minimum income schemes which are oriented to 'general need' and not previous income or special risks.

Bismarckian welfare states thus encounter the problem of recalibration in order to provide alternative options to minimum income receipt for weaker and more vulnerable groups of society. In particular with regard to weaker and more vulnerable groups, Bismarckian welfare states are confronted with the problem to promote and combine access to employment, social protection, education, rehabilitation, care and child services. This problem of fragmentation of important welfare institutions is reflected by the exclusion from labour markets but it is also mirrored in the structures and approaches to deal with unemployment. Minimum income protection is tightly connected to poverty policy. As such it is intertwined with meagre to moderate level benefits and social welfare services. It is marked by some local discretion and involves third sector organisations intervening. In contrast, workers are covered by generous insurance institutions and active labour market policy services oriented towards upholding human capital. Accordingly, labour market policy, active labour market policy and insurance programmes are highly institutionalised through central regulation and marked by the influence of corporatist institutions.

The development of minimum income schemes in Bismarckian welfare states thus turns the fragmented nature and organisation of important elements of filtering institutions of minimum income schemes into a problem. It raises the question on the drivers, obstacles and directions which processes of recalibrating and re-organising institutions of employment, education, care and social security are taking towards the inclusion of weaker groups of society as low-skilled, persistently unemployed, sick persons or lone mothers.

The next chapter therefore concentrates on the question if and how social, welfare and labour market policy in Bismarckian welfare states attempt to deal with the increasing claims on residual minimum income programmes.

3. Activation reforms in Bismarckian-type continental welfare systems

The aim of this chapter is to understand changing patterns of social and labour market policy reactions in view of the increasing claims on residual minimum income programmes in Bismarckian countries. As explained in the previous chapter, minimum income schemes in Bismarckian countries were originally connected to classical poverty policy and social work. New approaches for welfare and employment are put forward by the European Commission's strategies for sustainable social protection systems as well as inclusion and labour market participation of society's weaker and vulnerable groups who have increasingly become dependent on minimum income schemes in Bismarckian welfare states. The EU2020 strategy and the Lisbon agenda as well as the European Employment Strategy (EES) and the Open Method of Co-ordination (OMC) in the field of Social Inclusion and Social Protection (Heidenreich 2009; Zirra 2010a) have also evolved in continental welfare states as references for reforming distressed mechanisms of inclusion, social protection and employment.

As a reaction to welfare state transformations, these European strategies propose employment as key to welfare state reform (European Council 2000). Inspired by European strategies for Employment and Social Inclusion (Visser 2009), activation into employment becomes a central feature of welfare state remodelling. The activation concept suggests integration into the labour market as best remedy against risks of exclusion and poverty (van Berkel and Valkenburg 2007: 8). Notably for weaker and more vulnerable groups, which were in Bismarckian welfare states usually excluded from employment, the European strategies propose integration into employment as new mechanism for inclusion. Furthermore, activation is being considered key to a financeable welfare state, in particular with regard to the sustainability of social protection systems.

For increasing employment, particularly for the weaker and vulnerable groups in society, the European policy approaches aim at reducing institutional and individual barriers against participation in the labour market. For increasing welfare and employment opportunities for low skilled, women, younger and older people, migrants, sick or long-term unemployed, concepts as the EU 2020 strategy intent to support new patterns of inclusion that can facilitate transitions between the labour market, social services and social protection (EU COM

(2009) 647 final). For this purpose, flexicurity strategies are proposed which aim to combine flexible labour markets, employment-friendly and reliable social protection systems as well as employment-oriented services (Madsen 2002). Flexicurity strategies are thus a central tool to achieve labour market activation as a reform strategy for the welfare state.

Consequently, the flexicurity concept, which is a qualitative reference for a welfare state based on the activation into work, implies the idea of a 'coordinated' approach for fostering equal opportunities on the labour market. To promote labour market access of long-term unemployed and otherwise disadvantaged groups, European strategies for inclusion point out the necessity to reach beyond mere labour market incentives. According to these strategies, increasing weaker and more vulnerable groups' individual responsibility for a labour market-based welfare production (Serrano Pascual 2007a) simultaneously requires addressing the complex problems of persistently unemployed and weaker groups of the labour market (e.g. low qualifications, social protection, housing, transport, indebtedness, health, alcoholism, addiction, child and family care). Besides reliable and employment-friendly social protection, a focus is therefore put on the provision of client-centred counselling and placement as well as different social services tailored to individual needs (van Berkel and Valkenburg 2007). Consequently, advancing equal opportunities for disadvantaged groups (e.g. low skilled, women, younger and older people, migrants, sick or long-term unemployed) involves issues of a coordination of labour market regulation, social protection and services in a manner, which enhances the take-up of employment. As a result, the issue of coordinated approaches questions prevalent institutional and organisational infrastructures regulating the labour market, social protection, social, health and educational services which is in particular a problem of the fragmented Bismarckian welfare regime.

As a recent trend in Bismarckian welfare states, in particular minimum income recipients have become subject to new policy approaches towards unemployed (Clegg 2007; Lødemel and Trickey 2001). These new policy programmes, which are especially aimed at weaker groups of society, partly resemble European flexicurity strategies for activation into the labour market. The concrete institutionalisation of reforms, however, can be only understood when taking into account the dynamics of Bismarckian welfare state institutions originally modelled around the needs of an industrial risk community (Zirra 2010a). We argue that recalibration in Bismarckian welfare states and the opportunities for coordinated policies need to be analysed at the background of the particular dynamics and problems of Bismarckian filtering institutions of minimum income programmes: theorising on the path Bismarckian social and labour market policy reforms are about to take requires to take into account the obstacles to family welfare, moderate employment rates, restricted access to higher-ranking social security programmes, worker biased labour market policy, limited intervention of services, and residual minimum income assistance.

For this purpose, first, at a more general level, we outline the new European agenda for unemployment policy which is based on the premises of activation into employment by applying flexicurity strategies. At the core of the agenda is the idea of an employment-centred welfare state in order to decrease structural unemployment and increase the inclusion of weaker groups into the labour market. For understanding this widespread paradigm for national social and labour market policy reforms, it is important to consider diffusion mechanisms of policy concepts among European welfare states, notably through the role of the European Commission, the OECD or the ILO. However, for understanding the institutionalisation of social and labour market policy reforms and the opportunities for coordinated approaches in continental European countries, the particular dynamics of Bismarckian institutions have to be taken into account. The principle argument of the chapter is that the particular constellation of Bismarckian institutions frames reforms in such a way that 'activation' is institutionalised as a new and specific Bismarckian institutional filter for minimum income schemes. The new institutional filter targeted at the labour market inclusion of weaker and more vulnerable groups, who are often in the receipt of minimum income benefits, can be described as 'employment-centred welfare'. It introduces significant employment-friendly reforms of labour market policy, social security and social services in a 'selective' (Clegg 2007) manner: the primary premise of the activating Bismarckian system is to institutionalise a new institutional filter in order to decrease the pressure on formerly marginal minimum income programmes.

3.1 Activation into employment as a new concept for welfare systems

New concepts for policies towards unemployed mainly put forward at the international level differ from status-oriented unemployment policies for 'workers', social policy as 'social treatment' against unemployment or classical poverty policy which were approaches practised in Bismarckian countries. According to the idea of an employment-centred welfare state, unemployment policy needs to be reconceptualised. Unemployment policies in an employment-centred welfare state aim at the inclusion of all potential groups, including weaker and more vulnerable groups, into the labour market. In contrast to the classical welfare state approach of income protection by social policy, the activation approach defines the inclusion into employment as new mechanism against social exclusion and poverty (van Berkel and Valkenburg 2007: 8). By doing so, activation policy in particular raises the issue of the inclusion of weaker groups of the labour market and persistently unemployed.

Over the last two decades, the OECD (*The OECD Jobs Study, 1994)* and the European Union have proposed reform paths and enhanced the spreading of new policy concepts among nation-states (Armingeon 2007). The rigidities of product markets, labour markets and labour protection laws are analysed as impeding on countries' ability to adapt to change, causing an increase in structural unemployment. This supply-side analysis has heightened attention on labour markets' 'inclusiveness', notably towards weaker groups of the labour market (that often include women, young, migrants, sick, disabled and the elderly), low-skilled unemployed, and persistently unemployed:

> "(...) unemployment is essentially the result of an excess supply of low-skill labour, and low-skilled workers may find it difficult to earn more from work than what their benefits are worth. The result is the development of a new role of ALMPs, which emphasises stronger work incentives and employment assistance." (Bonoli 2010: 20).

In this context, obstacles to labour market dynamics and the flipside effects of social protection systems are discussed. The reform concepts propose a different idea of social protection: employment instead of 'dependency' on monetary benefits is suggested as best remedy against poverty and exclusion. In contrast to the classical Bismarckian approaches of inclusion into the family or a 'social treatment' of unemployment by social policy or poverty policy, the employment-centred welfare state's concept against exclusion relies on employment policy instead.

By recalibrating unemployment policy towards activation into work, a multitude of problems shall be solved which Bismarckian countries but also other welfare states are facing in light of the current societal and economic transformations. Foremost, the reform concepts shall enhance equal opportunities for inclusion (on the labour market). At the same time, the new unemployment policy approach shall ensure the viability of the social security systems, and contribute to the consolidation of the states' budget (Bonoli 2010; van Berkel and Valkenburg 2007).

In short, the attempt to activate all unemployed including weaker groups of the labour market, low-skilled unemployed and persistently unemployed contrasts fundamentally with past Bismarckian policies towards unemployed and approaches of the inclusion of weaker and vulnerable groups. By propagating to target disadvantaged groups, who have often become dependent on minimum income programmes in Bismarckian welfare states, policies for inclusion into the labour market offer an alternative to Bismarckian approaches of classical 'poverty' policy, 'social treatment' by social policies or family inclusion. As explained in the following, flexicurity' strategies for better employment assistance, employment-friendly social protection and new labour market options are a strategy to achieve activation into work.

3.2 Flexicurity as reference point for employment-centred welfare systems

The European Union's employment strategy is inspired by the idea of 'flexicurity' as basic architecture for how to sustain a welfare state based on activation into employment (EU COM 2007). Flexicurity strategies for an employment-centred welfare state suggest to establish a 'nexus' between security arrangements and the flexibility of labour markets (Wilthagen 1998; Bekker and Wilthagen 2008) which comprises flexible labour markets, reliable and employment oriented social protection as well as employment assistance. The reform concepts put forward are particularly meant to increase opportunities – including low-paid employment – for weaker groups of the labour market. Entry jobs and less precarious employment situations shall hereby arise for the low-skilled, long-term unemployed, women, migrants, young or the elderly who are often faced with new risks and difficult employment prospects (Wilthagen and Tros 2004) and therefore, in Bismarckian welfare states, increasingly risk to rely on minimum income schemes.

In practise, the drive for a welfare state based on the activation into employment encounters the problem that flexibility of labour markets and security for unemployed and employees are often strived for in an isolated and hence, antagonistic matter. For reaching one objective, often the other is neglected. The consequences of policy choices are either detrimental to employment creation or mean bad news for social protection in terms of income (replacement), work standards, human capital development or self-realisation. While stressing the employment opportunities created by flexible labour markets and low-paid employment, the flexicurity debate simultaneously recognises the detrimental effects that flexible labour markets can have in terms of social protection:

> "On the one hand employment is (being) created that would not be created otherwise – thus offering opportunities for specific groups in the labour markets, such as women and ethnic minorities -, whereas on the other hand flexible employment is accompanied

by negative social effects (very weak and dependant position of the workers involved)." (Wilthagen 1998: 12).

In order to sustain social protection particularly for weaker and more vulnerable groups, the flexicurity concept proposes to reinterpret the trade-offs between flexible, low-paid employment and security in a manner that can bring about mutual benefits of activation both in terms of security and employment (Clasen and Viebrock 2009). In this context, the concept of transitory labour markets (Schmid 2002) highlights the need for an interdependent understanding of labour markets and adjacent institutions. The idea is to encourage and facilitate individual action by the right institutions for sound labour market transitions (Schmid 2002). The concept proposes to reshape institutions in such a way that individual transitions between employment and other productive activities (e.g. education, training, care, rehabilitation or reproduction) are facilitated.

In order to achieve such sound transitions on labour markets, the institutional interplay between labour markets, social benefit systems and services becomes key (Madsen 2002). Such an integrated concept for reforming the structure of labour markets thus promotes flexible labour markets on the one hand (EU COM 2007). On the other hand, it also comprises measures to improve both employment prospects and social protection (Wilthagen and Tros 2004, Wilthagen 2007). This is done by, first, a generous social benefit system (unemployment or social benefits), and, second, by simultaneous policies and services which set work incentives, but also assist and equip unemployed people with the necessary skills, opportunities and assets needed. From the concept of flexicurity strategies, it thus not only derives the proposal for flexible labour markets, but also for the reform of social policies and services in order to promote the take-up of employment.

To conclude, flexicurity strategies present an architecture for how to achieve both employment and welfare. To establish a welfare state based on the activation into employment, the Flexicurity concept, which is promoted by the European Employment Strategy, suggests an agenda of flexible labour markets, generous and employment-friendly social protection, and active unemployment policy and services. A successful interplay of these different components might create employment opportunities – including low-paid employment – in particular for weaker groups of the labour market, low-skilled unemployed and persistently unemployed. Flexicurity strategies might therefore frame attempts to remodel the distressed Bismarckian welfare state. A shift towards an employment-based mode of welfare production might offer new opportunities for welfare production for those groups that risk dependency on minimum income programmes.

3.3 Areas of an employment-centred welfare system

Given the flexicurity strategies' focus on an interrelated concept of employment and social protection, central elements of an activating welfare state can be detailed. In order to promote access to the labour market also for low-skilled, persistently unemployed and other weaker groups, the flexicurity strategy implies an activation agenda which comprises (1) flexible labour markets, (2) work incentives of social benefits, (3) a 'homogenisation' of benefit systems and (4) the introduction of enabling services. The activation paradigm thus demands employment-friendly reforms of the welfare state in different fields including training, social security, labour market, care and rehabilitation policy (Barbier 2004, Barbier and Ludwig-Mayerhofer 2004).

3.3.1 Flexible labour markets for the activation into employment

First, in order to allow for activation into employment, flexible labour markets are one component which European flexicurity strategies propose. Flexicurity strategies suggest a comprehensive and universal flexibilisation of labour market regulation – also for the 'normal employment relations' of core-workers which define the Bismarckian employment model. Flexible labour markets comprise possibilities for part-time jobs and temporary work arrangements. They also include the possibility of low-paid employment.

Part-time jobs, temporary work and low-paid jobs are meant to create greater employment opportunities for weaker groups of the labour market, low skilled unemployed and persistently unemployed. In an increasingly open, flexible and service-oriented economy, employment prospects for low-skilled or persistently unemployed are offered by those parts of the service economy which suffer from a 'cost-disease' (Baumol 1967): high-productivity thresholds induced by 'solidarity' wages or strict labour market regulation turn out being problematic for the creation of these jobs (Iversen and Wren 1998; Scharpf 2000). The acceptance of an equality-jobs trade-off is therefore increasingly an option to make up for the low productivity of many service oriented jobs (Iversen and Wren 1998; Kenworthy 2004). Employment situations shall hereby arise for the low-skilled, long-term unemployed, women, migrants, young or the elderly who are often faced with new risks of exclusion and difficult employment prospects (Wilthagen and Tros 2004) and therefore, in Bismarckian welfare states, increasingly risk to rely on minimum income schemes.

In brief, flexibilisation strategies challenge worker-biased Bismarckian labour market policy as they suggest the comprehensive flexibilisation of labour markets in order to improve labour market access and upward mobility opportunities for weaker and more vulnerable groups, who often rely on minimum income benefits in Bismarckian welfare states.

3.3.2 Workfare elements for the activation from benefits into work

Second, to realise the activation from benefits into work, 'workfare' elements are a complementary component to flexible labour markets. In the context of activation programmes, 'workfare' elements put forward various instruments to push unemployed to integrate into the labour market or to participate in certain activities. Contrasting Bismarckian welfare state practices of the 'social treatment' of unemployment and status conservation of insured workers, workfare elements promote the idea of 'conditionality' of benefits and services. The rationale of 'conditionality' is to counteract disincentive problems posed by flexible labour markets or low-income employment, which might especially exist for weaker groups of the labour market (Clasen and Clegg 2006). To respond to this problem, workfare components of activation strategies make use of various elements connected to the receipt of benefits or income. Thereby, mandatory and disciplining elements take a prominent role. Workfare elements might introduce a restrictive definition of the duration and level of benefits. Also, the acceptability of job-offers can be defined in a rather broad sense. Or the participation in services and active labour market policy programmes can be demanded. As an alternative, beneficiaries might have to work for benefits in public schemes (Lødemel and Trickey 2001). In addition, individual activity to actively search and prepare for employment can be required, for example, on the basis of integration contracts between the beneficiary and a public agency. A sanctioning-regime might apply in the case of non compliance (Eichhorst et al. 2008a). At the same time, work incentives not only include mandatory and disciplining effects, but can comprise regulations of the tax and benefit system (e.g. 'tax credits' and 'in-work' benefits) to 'make work pay'.

In brief, workfare strategies challenge the Bismarckian social treatment of social policy as they suggest the application of workfare elements to activate also weaker and more vulnerable groups who increasingly have to rely on minimum income programmes.

3.3.3 Integrated social protection systems for unemployed

Third, to cushion against risks of flexible and changing labour markets and non-standard employment biographies, activation policy reform concepts propose a 'homogenisation' of the social protection systems for unemployed (Clasen and

Clegg 2006: 533). The activation concept implies a recalibration of the criteria for eligibility and entitlement to social protection during unemployment. Two-tier systems of unemployment support (higher-ranking insurance or category-specific programmes on the one side, and last-resort general minimum income programmes on the other side), which for example divided unemployed in continental welfare states between 'deserving' unemployed workers, 'deserving poor' and 'extreme outsiders', are increasingly perceived as problematic. Unemployment schemes that reward entitlements to persons according to status and skill differentials, notably status conserving arrangements as characterising the Bismarckian model, are regarded as unapt to deal with the conditions of flexible and changing labour markets and non-standard employment biographies. In particular for low-skilled and weaker groups of the labour market status-based insurance tends to fail to provide protection and incentives needed for inclusion into open, market-oriented and individualised societies. A more generalised access to a basic support during unemployment is instead regarded as a mechanism that can also account for those weaker and more vulnerable groups experiencing particular and increased risks by the turn towards more open, market-oriented and individualised societies. As a result an integration or 'homogenisation' of unemployment support systems is suggested. This stated, adjustment might take place between the extremes of 'upgrading' towards the top tier so far protecting the 'workers' or downward alignment towards schemes protecting the 'undeserving' poor.

In short, a greater 'homogenisation' or integration of social protection for unemployed to also provide protection and incentives for the inclusion of weaker groups into open, market-oriented and individualised societies, be it in form of an 'upgrading' or 'downgrading' of social protection, would represent a crucial break with the dualistic Bismarckian unemployment system which is biased towards the needs of an industrial risk community.

3.3.4 Services as enabling elements of activation

Fourth, in addition to flexible labour markets, workfare and integrated social security, an 'active' welfare state refers to services that shall enable the activation of unemployed in various ways. The argument of 'capacity-building' or 'capability' approaches explains well the idea to take into account societal, structural impediments of persistently unemployed, weaker and more vulnerable groups of society for the take-up of work (Bonvin and Farvaque 2007; Salais 2003): "The welfare state is expected to enable all citizens to participate actively and to take responsibility for themselves by providing a framework of infrastructure and services that offsets unequal opportunity structures." (Dingeldey 2007: 825) Therefore, welfare state interventions do not only gain importance for enforcing individual ownership to engage in job-search or related activities, but also with regard to assist in dealing with risks or problems mainly deriving from non-standard employment biographies. For Bismarckian welfare states this implies the challenge to intervene in such a way that those out of work due to diverse and often simultaneous reasons –parenthood, disability, health, indebtedness, alcoholism, addiction, housing, transport, long-term unemployment or lack of skills – will be (again) equipped with a perspective for work or work-related activities.

In this context, active labour market policy acknowledges a range of measures as job-placement, training and further education to offset barriers related to immediate labour market integration (Hvinden 1999). However, in particular in Bismarckian welfare regimes, this interpretation of unemployment policy was tightly bound to a concept for guaranteeing the status of 'workers'. In the framework of an active and dynamic welfare state, approaches link up not only training policies to benefits but various adjacent policy fields. Particularly, in light of the objective to create broad and equal labour market access conditions not only for 'workers' but also for low-skilled, persistently unemployed, lone mothers, disabled or sick persons, other policy fields gain prominence. The turn towards employment-friendly policies especially sheds light on the functioning of social services. Social services as for example housing, family care, child care, health services (including drug and alcohol counselling), social counselling, psychological counselling or debt counselling are increasingly identified as crucial components in the context of employment-friendly policies (Dingeldey 2007; Eichhorst et al. 2008a). As a consequence, in the active and dynamic welfare state, social services for rehabilitation or care are turned towards the goal of labour market integration (Hvinden 1999; Van Berkel and Møller 2002). For example, social work or family policies are increasingly guided by the idea to improve individual capacities for facilitating labour market participation.

In short, challenging Bismarckian welfare state's passive character and its worker-biased active labour market policy, the implementation of employment-friendly services is suggested as a strategy to enable the activation into work of persons with work-related and particularly non-work related, social problems who are increasingly dependent on minimum income schemes in continental Europe.

3.3.5 Summarising the components of an employment-centred welfare state

To summarise, according to the concept of an employment-centred welfare state, effective unemployment policies are a necessary complement to flexible labour markets: the goal is to activate all groups of unemployed, thereby raising the issue of labour market inclusion of weaker groups of the labour market, low-skilled unemployed and persistently unemployed – also in order to reduce the pressure on minimum income systems. In particular for these groups, participation in the labour market is proclaimed as an alternative to benefit receipt, for example, from minimum income assistance which is in particular a problem in Bismarckian welfare states. In order to assist and enable work integration of long-term unemployed, vulnerable groups and those persons with risks of non-standard employment biographies unemployment policies are required to react to the risks and problems of open, individualised and market-oriented societies. For this purpose, the activation agenda suggests the flexibilisation of labour markets, sustainable social protection systems through the standardisation of benefits, the conditioning of benefits on participation in different social and labour market policy services, and the implementation of employment-friendly services reacting to social and work-related problems of unemployed. By propagating the goal of facilitating labour market integration for all groups of society, activation policies thus call for a crucial recalibration and recombination of different welfare state policies, which notably calls into question Bismarckian welfare states' fragmented unemployment policies of classical poverty policy for the 'extreme' outsiders, status-conserving social policy for the 'deserving' poor and worker-oriented active labour market policies.

In face of fragmented institutions in Bismarckian welfare states, the turn towards an employment-centred welfare state is here to a great extent about the recalibration and reorganisation of classical poverty policy, social policy for workers, labour market policy and services in order to provide approaches for the inclusion of weaker groups of the labour market and persistently unemployed.

Having defined both the flexibilisation of labour markets and integrated benefits, the application of incentives, and a range of services for activation into work, as components of an employment-centred welfare state, the question arises of how such a concept, which is promoted by the European Union and other international institutions like the OECD or the ILO, might be institutionalised in Bismarckian welfare states. It poses the questions of the consequences of its application in the Bismarckian welfare states which are particularly confronted with the problem of rising numbers of benefit recipients of once marginal minimum income schemes.

3.4 Between European diffusion of 'good' governance and national activation regimes

For a long time, strong rigidities of the continental European welfare regime led to the assessment of 'frozen' Bismarckian welfare state institutions (Esping-Andersen 1996). In the meanwhile, overcoming institutional inertia, changes in the institutions for welfare and work are also observed for Bismarckian countries. In the debate on the implementation of activation policy reforms in Bismarckian welfare states, processes of European 'diffusion of good governance' and the institutionalisation of national activation regimes are discussed. The general premises of both trends are laid out in the following.

Particularly in the European context, the European Employment Strategy (EU COM 2010) and the European policy for social inclusion (EU COM 2008a; EU COM 2008b) have strongly propagated the idea of an employment-centred welfare state (Pochet and Zeitlin 2005; Heidenreich and Zeitlin 2009; Graziano and Vink; Zirra 2010a; Preunkert 2009). Faced with the need to strengthen a 'social Europe' in light of progressing market integration, while simultaneously being confronted with the diversity of European welfare and employment regimes, the Open Method of Coordination (OMC) was introduced as a new European regulatory approach. First applied in connection with the European Employment Strategy (*EES; Treaty of Amsterdam 1997*), the Lisbon Process and the Lisbon Agenda (European Council 2000) led to the broader application of the OMC in policy fields as social cohesion and inclusion. The basic idea of the OMC is to develop co-ordinated European strategies through a soft approach, while the EU member States remain responsible for defining social and labour market policy. A process of periodically renewed guidelines, national action plans (NAPs), joint reports, country surveillance and 'peer review' (and – eventually – recommendations in the field of employment) shall enable mutual learning between governments and national bureaucracies. For employment, the member states agreed on the 'Lisbon' targets to raise general employment rates at 70%, to increase women participation on labour markets at a minimum of 60% and to promote the inclusion in the workforce of workers aged 55–64 at 50% (Fischer and Tholoniat 2006). Such a 'soft-law' approach encounters limits as it cannot directly enforce social and labour market policy through 'hard-law' and sanctions therefore leaving a great extent of policy definition at the national level (Scharpf 2002). However, as a 'one-size fits all approach' might not suite the different national welfare and employment regimes in Europe, the approach of experimental, learning based policy has its virtues: 'diffusion through learning' of successful practices via the OMC Mutual Learning Programme has fundamentally changed the mind-maps of European decision-makers (Visser 2009). It resulted into a paradigmatic change in the European member states in the conception of employment policies away from 'managing' unemployment towards activation into labour markets.

Heidenreich (2009) explains the often cited 'delivery gap' from European strategies to concrete national policy and organisational reforms: the OMC has been proven capable to 'irritate' national regimes but it cannot steer them intentionally in a planned direction. The influence of the OMC depends on how European ideas, resources and procedural arrangements can be of use for interaction, bargaining and compromise between national actors in specific national policy arenas. Apart from European diffusion processes, this observation points out the crucial explanatory role of existing national welfare state institutions in order to understand reform paths towards the activation principle. Variations from common European trends are explained by national patterns of activation reforms (Barbier 2004 and Serrano Pascual 2007b): "The adoption and introduction of new forms of governance in the context of operational policy reforms are 'filtered' or shaped by (national) socio-economic, historical, cultural, institutional and political contexts." (Borghi and van Berkel 2007: 97). According to this debate, activation regimes are thus defined as a result of the particular national coordination of labour market regulations, social services and social security programmes and policies at the national level (Clasen and Clegg 2003; Clasen and Clegg 2006). As a result, activation reforms of labour market and social policy programmes are usually analysed at the national level (Clasen and Clegg 2006).

Given the disposition of welfare regime reform pressure and administrative capacity as well as the high misfit between European programs and national institutions(Börzel and Risse 2000), incremental changes and a strong impact of the OMC can be expected in Bismarckian-type continental European countries (Heidenreich 2009; Heidenreich and Bischoff 2008). Taking into account the previous discussion, beyond European diffusion of 'good' governance, different national institutional factors and the national coordination of policies and programmes are key for explaining the institutionalisation of particular activation regimes. Therefore, to understand change in Bismarckian welfare states in reaction to rising numbers of beneficiaries of minimum income programmes, we not only have to account for the European premises for an active and dynamic welfare state (as explained above) but we also have to take into account the particular institutional set-up of the Bismarckian welfare state. Theorising on how the reactions to rising numbers of minimum income assistance recipients changes Bismarckian welfare state institutions, demands to discuss reforms of social and labour market policies at the background of the distressed Bismarckian institutional filter for minimum income programmes which was made up of socially secured employment, important family welfare, and a social and labour market policy geared towards status protection of workers. As illustrated in the following, the attempt to institutional a new institutional filter guides reforms in continental European countries.

3.5 Employment-centred welfare as new filter for minimum income schemes in Bismarckian-type continental welfare systems

The European diffusion of the activation paradigm in Bismarckian welfare states defies exclusive labour market structures, the dualistic benefit system, and its status-conserving and passive welfare state character. Challenges of unemployment policy reform therefore not only concern the internal regulation of residual Bismarckian minimum income programmes. They also raise issues of recalibrating the welfare functions of employment, social security, rehabilitation and care in general. Labour market and social policy changes thus relate to the question of how the institutional filter of minimum income programmes, which is defined by the structure of assistance programmes and their institutional context for welfare and work, might be reformed. In other words, the defiance of increasing numbers of beneficiaries of minimum income schemes poses the question of how the difficulties of traditional family welfare and moderate employment rates are reacted to by Bismarckian welfare state policy. We argue that the reforms introduced in Bismarckian countries are presenting attempts to institutionalise activation as a new institutional filter of minimum income programmes.

In reference to European strategies for an employment-centred welfare state, Bismarckian countries adopt changes in labour market regulations, implement reforms of the dualistic benefit system, put a greater focus on incentives and pay attention to services. Acknowledging the important changes in the external and internal filtering institutions of minimum income schemes, these reform strategies are, however, introduced in a 'selective' manner (Clegg 2007: 607; Zirra 2010a, 2010b) as important parts of Bismarckian welfare state institutions for 'workers' remain stable. The particular way continental European countries implement central premises of activation reforms as a new institutional filter of minimum income schemes shall be thus discussed in the area of reforms of the labour market, the benefit system, the work incentives of benefits and the issue of service provision.

reform against the will of the social partners (Clegg 2007; Palier and Martin 2007). Moreover, the insurance system remains popular, not least due to the important claims of a large part of the population, which arise from its contributory nature. As a result, governments refrain from undertaking fundamental changes of the whole social security system (Palier 2010: 365).

Despite this inertia, however, divisions in-between the systems have partly been recalibrated in continental Europe. With regard to the higher-ranking systems of social security, a trend with only some exceptions (for example measures to improve social insurance coverage of part-time workers in the Netherlands, cf. Hemerijck and Marx 2010) has set in: a remodelling of the higher-ranking social security programmes towards a more exclusive social insurance character has taken place (Palier 2010; Palier and Thelen 2010). This has been the result of measures which led to the reinforcement of contribution-based programmes towards a more acute logic of social insurance (Clegg 2007; Palier and Martin 2007). In some cases, it was also achieved by the dissolution of category-specific and status-conserving programmes which had belonged to the higher-ranking system of social security but which were not based on direct contributions (Clegg and Palier 2012; Hinrichs 2010). As a result, atypical risks are decreasingly covered by social insurance programmes (Clegg 2007) or category-specific and status-conserving programmes.

From the bottom of the system, the division of the two tier system is to some extent realigned by a consolidation of the means-tested general minimum income programmes as a protection mechanism for vulnerable groups, long-term unemployed, persons with unsteady employment (Palier 2010) and even low income earners (Clegg and Palier 2012; Barbier and Knuth 2011a). As a general trend (cf. chapter 2.4), the selective recalibration of social insurance programmes towards a more acute insurance logic caused an increase in the numbers of beneficiaries of minimum income schemes (Palier and Martin 2007; Hemerijck and Marx 2010). Furthermore, in the cases of a dissolution of higher-ranking, category-specific or status-conserving social security programmes (for example for 'long-term unemployed workers' or 'lone mothers'), the former programmes were usually merged into the generalised minimum income programmes (Clegg and Palier 2012; Hinrichs 2010). Such 'mergers' also added to an increase in the numbers of beneficiaries of generalised minimum income schemes as well. These realignments between the 'higher-ranking' Bismarckian system and the generalised minimum income programmes, however, usually triggered only a limited 'upgrading' of generalised minimum income programmes (Clasen and Clegg 2006). Bismarckian generalised minimum income benefits' main traits, namely their residual and subsidiary nature at low to moderate benefit level, remained mostly unchanged.

Due to the inertia of Bismarckian institutions blocking a comprehensive integration of the social security system, processes of European diffusion of 'good governance' are implemented in a selective manner in Bismarckian countries. Generous social insurance programmes reinforce their exclusive character for 'workers' with a steady contribution records. At the same time, general minimum income programmes tend to emerge as principle social protection for workless weaker and more vulnerable groups, long-term unemployed and unemployed persons with unstable employment biographies and even low-income earners. In view of a limited upgrading, generalised minimum income programmes mostly keep their residual and subsidiary character of benefits. The reforms thus trigger realignment of the two-tier benefit system as they strengthen a more exclusive contribution-based character of higher-ranking system while they increase the significance of generalised minimum income programmes for social protection.

3.5.3 Work incentives and requirements in continental European welfare states

The selective remodelling of the two-tier benefit system is accompanied by a similar application of European strategies for a greater focus on increasing benefits' incentives and requirements for the take-up of work. The stronger reinforcement of requirements and incentives for the take-up of work, which constitutes a further pillar of institutionalising employment-centred welfare, proceeds in a selective manner. This selective application of workfare elements is also related to the resistant character of corporatist Bismarckian welfare state institutions (Clegg 2007; Palier and Martin 2007).

In continental European countries, the increased focus on work incentives is primarily directed at generalised minimum income programmes (Clegg 2007). Although in a rather unspecified manner, regulations for the take-up of work had often been formally provided for as part of the traditionally disciplining and subsidiary Bismarckian minimum income assistance arrangements. In addition, regulation of work and activity requirements of minimum income benefits has increasingly been detailed. Workfare elements to increase incentives for the take-up of work are now often explicitly stipulated in the regulation of generalised minimum income programmes (Clegg and Palier 2012; Barbier and Knuth 2011a). However, such elements of workfare receive greater relevance when labour markets become more 'inclusive' (Clegg and Palier 2012). The trend towards more flexible labour markets for weaker and more vulnerable groups of

including low-paid, part-time or temporary work. This new institutional filter is directed at a remodelling of both internal and external institutional regulation of minimum income benefit receipt (cf. Tab. 1).

Tab. 1: Continental European filtering institutions of minimum income schemes

National Orders of Filtering Institutions		Classical Bismarckian Filter	Activating Bismarckian Filter
MIS Internal Filter	Coverage of Needs	Residual	Extension on working-poor but still low to moderate generosity
	Definition of Responsibility	Family or Social Work	Active Citizen
	Degree of Legal Codification	Moderate	Moderate
	Extent of Means-testing	Subsidiary to Family Welfare or Social Insurance	Subsidiary to Work Income, Family Welfare or Social Insurance
	Activity requirements	Social treatment	Workfare
MIS External Filter	Employment System	Socially Secured Male-breadwinner Employment	Partial Flexibilisation
	Household System	Family-based Welfare for Income, Reproduction Rehabilitation and Care	Restricted Family Welfare
	Higher-ranking Social Security Programmes	Status-based, generous Social Security,	Employment-friendly Social Insurance for Strong Contributors
	Services	Passive Welfare State and active Labour Market Policy for Workers	Focus of Active Labour Market Policy and Social Welfare Services on Weaker Groups
	Dominant Mode of Inclusion/Exclusion	Between workers and non-working groups	Between insiders and outsiders of the labour market

Source: own representation.

The new institutional filter remodels internal regulation of minimum income programmes. The trend towards low to medium benefit level, generalised minimum income programmes in the social security system is consolidated. In parallel, specific regulation for minimum income benefits puts a stronger focus onto work incentives. Work requirements, which often built up on traditionally subsidiary minimum income benefit regulation, make eligibility to generalised minimum income programmes increasingly conditional on the willingness to work. Moreover, employment is enhanced as an alternative to benefit receipt by the introduction of earnings supplements or tax exemptions which explicitly try to make low-paid jobs more attractive. In sum, incentives for the take-up of work and the focus on activity requirements are remodelling internal minimum income regulation: in particular low-paid employment is institutionalised as alternative welfare option for weaker groups of the labour market.

At the same time, activation as a new institutional filter of minimum income programmes also affects its external filtering institutions, which had been characterised by Bismarckian traits of exclusive labour markets and passive benefits. Labour market policy increases employment opportunities by a greater flexibilisation of formerly exclusive labour market regulation. Thereby, employment arises as a new option for welfare production for groups which had been usually excluded from the labour market in the classical Bismarckian world. Particularly for low-skilled, weaker groups of society or long-term unemployed, employment opportunities are offered by low-paid, part-time or temporary jobs. For the higher-ranking programmes of social security, the contribution-based logic of social insurance is reinforced. Work-incentives are introduced in a very limited and more indirect manner for higher-ranking social security programmes. Furthermore, a greater focus is put onto services in order to enable activation into employment also for persons with demands for care, rehabilitation or training. To some extent, activation policy concepts, have thus affected Bismarckian 'worlds' of employment, social security and services: minimum income benefits external institutions change to the extent that they better filter against minimum income receipt.

Given this very circumscribed extent of change of Bismarckian institutions compared to the concepts for an activating welfare state, which are diffused by the European Union, the implementation of labour market and social policy reforms proceeds in a selective manner in continental Europe. In order to achieve employment as a new way of social protection, European and international strategies propose the coupling of both security and labour market flexibility. The new institutional filter of minimum income schemes implemented in continental European countries, however, introduces a new dualism. Rather exclusive segments of the labour market are still strongly protected by labour market regulation. Simultaneously, persons with a steady contribution-record qualify for generous and largely non-conditional, status-protecting unemployment insurance programmes. In contrast, offering significantly weaker monetary protection, still residual general minimum income programmes are consolidated as the fallback option for weaker and more vulnerable groups, long-term unemployed and persons with low or unsteady contribution records. Particularly for minimum income benefit recipients, work incentives and requirement are provided for, in order to make benefit recipients grasp the new employment opportunities. However, employment for weaker and more vulnerable groups, long-term unemployed or low-skilled persons tends to be concentrated in low paid, part-time or temporary work arrangements. These groups thus constitute a significant and also rather exclusive segment of labour market outsiders.

Explanations for the resistance of continental European institutions and the institutionalisation of a specific Bismarckian activation filter against minimum income schemes point to the 'Bismarckian character' of institutions. An important representation of corporatist actors in the Bismarckian institutions for welfare and work, strong personal claims of important parts of the population on benefits due to their contributory character and persisting cognitive patterns are among the reasons which make it difficult to change social insurance regulation, labour market regulation or spending patterns more radically.

3.6 Conclusion: activation as a new institutional filter of minimum income receipt

Summing up this chapter, Bismarckian welfare states react to the rising numbers of beneficiaries of minimum income schemes by a remodelling of social and labour market policy. The activation agenda promulgated by the European Union and other international organisations entails reforms to safeguard social and labour market inclusion for weaker and more vulnerable groups within open, market-oriented and individualised societies. The idea of greater employment dynamics through flexible labour markets is matched in flexicurity concepts with employment-friendly arrangements for reliable social protection and different services. For protecting, assisting and enabling inclusion into flexible labour markets, the activation agenda therefore also comprises propositions for sustainable social protection systems through the homogenisation of the benefit system, work incentives and different social and labour market policy services. Such reform concepts in particular confer to continental European welfare states where problems to provide reliable arrangements for employment, care, or rehabilitation for persistently unemployed, weaker groups of the labour market and low-skilled unemployed cumulated in an increase of the numbers of beneficiaries of minimum income schemes.

The debate on the European diffusion processes of activation policy reforms points out general changes in the mindsets of national decision-makers that increasingly lead to a different understanding of unemployment policy away from 'managing unemployment' towards the more comprehensive idea of an employment-centred welfare state. Concentrating on developments in the Bismarckian welfare state model, the analysis of national institutions reveals 'selective' welfare state policy changes only, due to problems of coordination and re-organisation of central institutions at the national level. Core institutions of the traditional Bismarckian risk community, as the strong corporatist role of the social partners and the contribution related claims on social insurance, are identified as factors which block a more comprehensive remodelling of the regulation of labour markets or the integration of the two-tier, dualistic social security system. Instead, reforms of selective cost-containment in the social security system reinforced the logic of social insurance institutions privileging labour market insiders. At the same time, although proceeding at the 'margin' of the benefit system (Clegg 2006, Palier 2010), the distancing of persons with non-standard employment biographies from social insurance onto minimum income programmes raises fundamental questions of institutional recalibration: the rising numbers of minimum income recipients in Bismarckian welfare states was analysed not as a problem of minimum income programmes only but it was connected to the increasing obstacles for traditional Bismarckian institutions to produce opportunities for income, rehabilitation or child or family care particularly for weaker and more vulnerable groups, low-skilled and long-term unemployed. For those groups, family-based welfare, a highly regulated labour market and worker-oriented social protection systems increasingly fail as institutional filter against assistance receipt.

The reform trajectories taken by continental European countries suggest that these welfare states tend to react to social and labour market problems of long-term unemployed, weaker groups of the labour market and low-skilled unemployed by establishing a particular regime for the activation into employment. As a consequence of the reforms introduced to the social security system and as a result of societal, family and economic changes, persons with non-standard biographies and vulnerable people are often found on minimum income schemes. 'Employment-centred welfare' was identified to intervene as a new institutional filter in the Bismarckian welfare regime. It introduces flexible labour markets, notably low paid employment, and puts a stress on work incentives and services. Hereby, Bismarckian countries aim at the labour market inclusion of weaker groups of the labour market, low-skilled unemployed and persistently unemployed. To put it in a nutshell, employment-centred welfare in Bismarckian welfare states evolves as a new institutional filter to reduce the burden of still residuary minimum income schemes.

Consequently, the focus of the Bismarckian activation regime provokes question of the labour market integration of long-term unemployed, low-skilled unemployed and weaker groups and more vulnerable groups of society. The institutionalisation of employment-centred welfare in Bismarckian countries also raises the question of how services for placement, counselling, qualification, training, rehabilitation or child and family care might be effectively coordinated in order to move welfare recipients into work. As will be argued in the following, the implementation of an activation strategy of long-term unemployed, low-skilled unemployed and otherwise disadvantaged groups is to a great extent a matter of local level processes.

4. Re-organising minimum income schemes: the local dimension of Bismarckian activation regimes

This chapter theorises on the question of how Bismarckian regimes for the activation of long-term unemployed and weaker and vulnerable groups of society might be organised at the local level. To understand the remodelling of Bismarckian welfare states towards an employment-centred institutional filter of minimum income schemes, we argue that it is necessary to go beyond analysing processes of European diffusion of 'good' governance and national regimes of activation. The predominant focus of the Bismarckian activation regime on weaker and more vulnerable groups as well as long-term unemployed, who are now being usually referred to minimum income schemes, invigorates a local dimension of the continental European welfare regime. For the implementation of activating services, labour market- and social policies in Bismarckian-type continental Europe, the local level plays a crucial role.

The recalibration of tasks for the promotion of employment, inclusion and social protection for weaker and more vulnerable groups of society onto minimum income programmes fits into dynamics of a decentralisation of the Bismarckian welfare system. It tends to reinforce or revive the development of decentralised welfare state institutions: this is due to the fact that important parts of minimum income assistance are in continental European welfare regimes bound to the local level (cf. chapter 2.2.2). Social services as well as minimum income benefit schemes are traditionally based on locally bound structures in many European welfare states (Bahle 2003) and the local level is therefore principally implied in the question of the activation of minimum income claimants.

In addition to the important share of local authority in Bismarckian minimum income arrangements, the strong focus in Bismarckian countries on the work integration of long-term unemployed and vulnerable groups makes local processes key in the implementation of the activation regime. The local level's significance in the activation of groups difficult to place by the application of work incentives, social welfare services and active labour market policy derives from the particular organisational requirements of such attempts (Finn 2000; Künzel 2012). To achieve the activation of long-term unemployed and weaker groups of society, a logic of local 'co-production'of tailor-made policies and services of placement, training, rehabilitation, child or family care is required

(Pestoff 2009). For the 'production' of these different policies and services, it requires the interventions of different providers, the exploitation of competences from different policy fields and the coordination of tasks from different policy levels. For this co-production of tailor-made interventions, the local level is the relevant place as it is here where the different providers intervene, competences are applied and tasks are executed (Kazepov 2010).

A local co-production of tailor-made services and policies therefore raises the question of remodelling and combining different competences, tasks and providers towards the common activation of minimum income benefit recipients in continental European welfare states. So far, the organisation of crucial policies and services mirrored the fragmented Bismarckian institutional filter of minimum income schemes as it also accorded to minimum income arrangements a disparate role in the organisation of policies and services (cf. chapter 2.2.2). According to this organisation, local elements of minimum income schemes' arrangements have traditionally been connected to the provision of classical poverty policies, a social treatment of beneficiaries or social work. In contrast, active labour market policies followed logics of rather generalised and centralised public services in Bismarckian welfare states as they were usually strongly related to the centralised unemployment insurance programmes. Co-produced interventions for the activation of benefit recipients into employment thus present attempts at the local level to call into question the so far disintegrated character of policies, services and providers. In a first argument of this chapter, we will therefore argue that the evolution of employment-centred welfare in Bismarckian welfare states proceeds as an institutionalisation of distinct local organisational fields (Scott 2001) which combine the interventions from different policy fields, crucial policy levels and various providers according to a common logic of co-producing services and polices for the activation of persons difficult to place (Niklasson 2007; Heidenreich and Künzel 2010).

This increased reliance on locally bound structures and the attempts to institutionalise a co-produced delivery of policies and services not only raise the local level's relevance in the welfare state but also increase the probability of different local responses. Reforms to render public policies more 'co-produced' (re-) introduce local discretion into the implementation of policies and services towards minimum income benefit recipients (Finn 2000). Processes of decentralising welfare interventions, changing modes of welfare service delivery and new management techniques for controlling services are shifting issues regarding the reorganisation of employment and social welfare services to the local level. At the local level, however, policies and services to activate unemployed are being embedded in different local structures, local interactions to co-produce policies and services can vary and different techniques exist to locally control the implementation of services. As the institutionalisation of policies and services can proceed differently at the local level, divergent ways might arise how to co-produce services for the targeted activation of benefit recipients into work. Presenting a second hypothesis of this chapter, we therefore assume that the introduction of activation policies causes transformations of Bismarckian-type continental European welfare states which evolve differently depending on distinct structures of local governance. To be able to grasp such variance, three possible ideal types of the local co-production of activation policies are theorised. The local organisation of the activation of benefit recipients might be governed by a bureaucratic approach, by a market-oriented model or by participatory attempts.

4.1 The local level's role in institutionalising employment-centred welfare

In Bismarckian-type continental European welfare states, locally bound structures experience an increasing boost of relevance with regard to responsibilities for the activation of long-term unemployed as well as weaker and more vulnerable groups. This is due to the involvement of local authority, the importance of the delivery of services and the co-produced character of these policies.

4.1.1 The traditional role of local authorities in continental European welfare systems

In continental European countries, social services and minimum income assistance arrangements have typically been connected to a local dimension (Mingione et al. 2002; Saraceno 2002). The local level has been usually involved in the provision of minimum income benefits and the delivery of social welfare services (rehabilitation, care, social work). In contrast to the social insurance institutions, these welfare state institutions have always been more discretionary in nature and usually remained more locally bound in Bismarckian-type continental Europe. Although this traditional role of the local level in minimum income provision and social services varied in its extent from country to country in the past, recent reforms have led to a reinvigoration or 'revival' of the local level in general.

Above all, the significant shifting of welfare claims from Bismarckian insurance institutions and family welfare onto minimum income schemes in some way automatically boosts local elements as these have been traditionally more pronounced in minimum income structures than in insurance institutions. In addition, in many continental European countries we witness a trend towards an increased devolution of responsibilities for social tasks onto the local level, thereby reviving the relevance of the local level in minimum income arrangements or social services (Borghi and Van Berkel 2007; Clegg and Palier 2012). Explicit measures of decentralisation have in some cases added to the revival of local elements of social services and minimum income programmes, furthering the process of 'vertical subsidiarisation' (Kazepov 2008) of welfare state policies in Bismarckian countries.

In short, for the handling of opportunities of welfare and work for the unemployed in continental European welfare states, decentralised policies and actors (once again) play an ever increasing role as Bismarckian welfare state policies are more heavily relying on minimum income benefit protection and attempts to focus on social services which are both traditionally 'local' areas of welfare state policy.

4.1.2 Activation as a matter of the local delivery of services and policies

Given the relevance of local authority for minimum income benefit provision and social services, the question arises on the particular capacities of the local level for an activation of persistently unemployed and weaker groups of the labour market.

In order to activate weaker and more vulnerable groups of the unemployed into the labour market, which is the priority of activation strategies in Bismarckian countries, the focus turns on effective welfare state services. Besides the national provisions for increased opportunities for low-paid, part-time or temporary employment, an increasing focus is shifted on services and possibilities to set work incentives in Bismarckian countries (cf. chapter 3). The activation of long-term unemployed and vulnerable groups of society, who increasingly have to rely on minimum income programmes in Bismarckian countries, poses issues of different and sometimes simultaneous demands of labour market placement, training, social counselling, care or rehabilitation. The "enlargement of the target groups of activation, including sick people, the handicapped, older people, highly vulnerable groups, single parents" (van Berkel and Borghi 2007: 278) therefore requires "that services should be adjusted to individual circumstances in order to increase their effectiveness" (van Berkel and Valkenburg 2007: 3). As a result, a cornerstone of the activation strategy is the intervention of personalised, tailor-made services to react to the challenges of work integration of long-term unemployed as well as weaker and more vulnerable groups of society. Activation strategies for these groups thus imply the application of tailor-made services to set labour market incentives, place, train or counsel unemployed.

However, service-based welfare interventions to activate unemployed difficult to place are very different from the predominant social policy interventions of the typically passive Bismarckian welfare state model which mainly aimed to improve social rights and monetary resources of beneficiaries. A service-orientation of approaches, as postulated important by the activation concept, confers to pedagogical forms of welfare interventions (Kaufmann 2009: 103–106). Pedagogical forms of welfare interventions aim to increase a person's competences through improving her or his ability for social interaction (education, health, knowledge, abilities, etc.) and to increase her or his readiness to act (normative orientation, motivation and willingness to perform): "The aim of welfare state policy in this context is typically a direct increase of a persons' ability to act through educational, counselling, rehabilitative or informative efforts." (Kaufmann 2009: 106; translation SK). As they strongly rely on services, activation strategies are thus different from centralised or generalised acts of income provision, social rights formulation or investments in infrastructure. Instead, activation approaches primarily rely on services for counselling, placement, education, instruction or rehabilitation, application of benefit incentives or sanctions in order to enable, orient and spur unemployed towards inclusion into employment. Consequently, activation policy can be interpreted as "an attempt to put 'one-size-fits-all' approaches in the provision of social services in the past, and to promote tailor-made or personalised services – concepts that are usually treated as synonyms of individualised services." (van Berkel and Valkenburg 2007: 3).

The difficulties of centralised or generalised social policies to realise individualised activation strategies are due to the interactive character of service-based strategies which makes implementation highly contingent upon the local context (Kaufmann 2009: 88–106). A transformation from the universal and generalised social treatment of unemployment towards a service-based logic of work incentives, active labour market policies and social service thus shifts tasks onto the local level. A great extent of the outcome of approaches to enable, orient and incite unemployed towards inclusion into employment depends on the interactions between the local service delivering organisations and the individual citizens (van Berkel and Valkenburg 2007). To enable a service-based orientation of policies, discretion for context-based and flexible interventions is important (Kaufmann 2009: 88–106). This requirement of local room for manoeuvring corresponds to the typically discretionary Bismarckian local arrangements of minimum income programmes and social services (cf. previous chapter) as well as the revived role of the local level due to decentralisation tendencies.

Salais and Villeneuve (2004) describe opportunities for context-based and flexible welfare interventions as 'situated public action'. The concept of situated action refers to a modified governance concept of the welfare state which is identified as a premise for tailor-made welfare interventions. It contrasts modes of centralised and standardised social policy interventions which tended to underlie logics of a social treatment of unemployment in Bismarckian welfare states. Situated public action means instead, that design, implementation and evaluation of social policy proceed in a more interrelated and process-like manner. A social policy process which separates steps of action in a hierarchical manner is viewed as problematic to reach the goals of individualised, service-oriented welfare interventions. To a great extent, the realisation of situated, service-based interventions therefore takes place on the immediate, interactive level of service implementation which is very remote from the central level of legislation (Kaufmann 2009/1982: 103–106). As a result, situated governance for activating unemployed difficult to place is accorded to forms and elements of localised interventions. Principally, the premises for situated services for the activation of long-term unemployed, weaker groups of society thus correspond to the tendency in Bismarckian welfare regimes to shift tasks onto the locus of local service agencies and organisations (Finn 2000).

To conclude, the national uniformity of benefits and regulation in Bismarckian welfare states is partially challenged by the strong focus on strategies for the activation of long-term unemployed and other weaker groups of the unemployed. The application of services and incentives to activate long-term unemployed and other weaker groups into low-paid, part-time or temporary employment is strongly contingent on the local context. The interrelated and interactive character of these interventions, which aim to improve a person's individual capacities, behaviour and motivation, makes their implementation depend on local service delivery processes. Correspondingly, the greater reliance on locally bound structures of minimum income schemes increases possibilities of interactive and situated local service delivery in Bismarckian welfare states. It thus offers opportunities for implementing service-based welfare interventions to activate persistently unemployed and weaker groups of society. The recalibration of tasks of social protection of persistently unemployed and weaker groups of society onto locally bound structures of minimum income schemes and the relevance of services for the activation of unemployed difficult to place thus requires to take into account a local dimension of the Bismarckian welfare state and activation regime.

4.1.3 The co-production of services: a matter of institutionalising local organisational fields

The Bismarckian activation agenda for persistently unemployed, weaker and more vulnerable groups of society raises the question on the parameters and processes which define the local institutionalisation of individualised services and policies for recipients of minimum income benefits in Bismarckian welfare states. The issue of local service delivery for the activation of weaker groups of the unemployed is in the following conceptualised as a matter of the local co-production of different policy fields, various policy level's tasks and between different providers of services: it requires the institutionalisation of distinct local organisational fields and challenges the boundaries of the fragmented Bismarckian welfare state architecture.

Raising the issue of individualised welfare interventions for the activation of unemployed implies important questions of the organisation of local service delivery in Bismarckian welfare states. To implement individualised and situated welfare policies and services at the local level, the activation concept formulates the idea of organising a local co-production to activate weaker and more vulnerable groups of society (Pestoff and Brandsen 2009). The idea is to make participate national and local authorities, public and private organisations, employment and social services, social workers and placement officers, beneficiaries and case-managers in a process of service delivery. The question of a co-production of individualised services suggests conceptualising the local level as organisational field. An organisational field is defined as the collective and interrelated influences which structure the relations between actors and their environment for a particular organisational arrangement (Scott 2001: 83, 136), in this case the delivery of services to activate recipients of minimum income schemes: "By organizational field, we mean those organizations that, in the aggregate, constitute a recognized area of institutional life: key suppliers, resource and product consumers, regulatory agencies, and other organizations that produce similar services or products." (DiMaggio and Powell 1983: 148).

The concrete local organisational fields which might evolve in the realm of minimum income schemes are distinct service delivery systems for the activation of benefit recipients: "By service delivery system I include such issues as who are the clients to be served, the services to be provided, the manner in which the services will be provided, and, (…), the patterns of client-staff regulations." (Hasenfeld 1992b: 39). Actors in this particular organisational field of the delivery of services towards minimum income recipients are defined as human service organisations. Human service organisations as for example public employment services, welfare offices, placement and counselling services, rehabilitation or education services are involved in the activation of benefit recipients:

> "(…) the core activities of the organization are structured to process, sustain, or change people who come under its jurisdiction. It is this transformation process to which people are subjected that defines them as the raw material of the organization, and it is precisely what differentiates human service organizations from other bureaucracies." (Hasenfeld 1992a: 4).

As human service organisations aim to achieve a co-production of services, public services' welfare and employment offices, placement and counselling services, rehabilitation or education services are strongly embedded and interrelated with their environment (Hasenfeld 1992b: 36). The organisational field human service organisations interact in for the activation of benefit recipients thus constitutes a local service delivery system. As a result, the organisation of the co-production of activation policies in Bismarckian countries is a problem of institutionalising local organisational fields. In the present analysis, we are thus interested in the structures and interactions which define the institutionalisation of local organisational fields in the Bismarckian welfare states.

By recalibrating responsibilities for persistently unemployed, weaker and more vulnerable groups of society to a great extent towards in important aspects locally organised minimum income schemes, challenges of coordination to organise a co-production for the activation of assistance recipients are conferred to the local handling of minimum income schemes. The co-production of individualised activation of persistently unemployed, weaker and more vulnerable groups of society raises the issue of construing distinct local service delivery systems for minimum income schemes. This process of a local co-production to realise the activation of beneficiaries of minimum income schemes is framed by central features of Bismarckian welfare state institutions. The particular problems of coordination derive from the functional separation of institutions for welfare and work which is strongly pronounced in the Bismarckian welfare system. Analytically, the local field for organising the activation of recipients of minimum income schemes is set by the Bismarckian welfare state's problems of coordination between the local and national level, between different policy fields and between private, not for profit and public actors. In other words, the Bismarckian welfare system projects three different challenges onto the local level which set the context for a local co-production of services (Niklasson 2007):

- the demand for a closer cooperation between formerly separated policy fields and organisations (for example between placement and training services,

income substitution, services of counselling and social work, family and health policies);
- the requirement of a closer co-operation between national, regional and local actors;
- and the necessity of a closer co-operation and collaboration between public, not-for profit and private organisations (Green and Orton 2009; Lindsay et al. 2008: 717).

Co-produced, tailor-made welfare interventions for recipients of minimum income schemes in Bismarckian welfare states thus pose a threefold organisational problem of coordination: challenges of coordination arise between the local and national level, between different policy fields and between private, not for profit and public actors. It is primarily at the local level where these problems of coordination are dealt with in order to organise situated public action for recipients of minimum income schemes. By summarising the main patterns of the Bismarckian welfare system according to these three analytical dimensions, it becomes clear how the problem of fragmented competences in the Bismarckian welfare state is a challenge for the reorganisation of minimum income schemes at the local level.

4.1.3.1 Co-producing policies and services of different fields

A first inter-organisational challenge of the co-production of tailor-made services for minimum income recipients is the local inter-organisation of different policy fields and the coordination of their logics for the activation process. When analysed for a local organisational field, benefit schemes, labour market policy, active labour market policy services and social welfare services will not necessarily correspond in a coordinated manner to the activation logic (Genova 2008). Distinct approaches as 'social welfare policy' or 'active labour market policy' might define rather separated fields of policies and services (Champion and Bonoli 2011) which require coordination at the local level for the activation of recipients of minimum income schemes.

Particularly in Bismarckian welfare states, benefit schemes, labour market policy, active labour market policy services and social services are typically defined as separate policies and services (cf. chapter 2.2.2). In the Bismarckian countries, actors, services and policies are structured very differently according to the policy field they belong to: forming a policy field of 'social welfare policy', minimum income programmes are traditionally related to services of social work or treatment provision, but they are rather weakly connected to labour market policy and services of active labour market policy (Gough 2001; Saraceno 2002). Rather separated from the field of 'social welfare policy', labour market policy, active labour market policy, and contribution-based (or –related) unemployment benefits have a legacy of being connected to a field of 'labour market policy' which was, in the past, oriented towards status protection.

Challenging this fragmentation, activation policies introduced in Bismarckian countries are now proposing a new policy field which requires local coordination between labour market policy's work incentives, minimum income benefits, social welfare services (counselling, rehabilitation and social work) and active labour market policy services (placement and training) for the work integration of beneficiaries of minimum income schemes. In this context, locally based minimum income assistance institutions are required to apply instruments of labour market policy and active labour market policy which, in the past, belonged to the separate field of status-based 'labour market policy'. The local inter-organisation of minimum income benefits, active labour market policy and labour market policy according to a logic of activation into work is a crucial corner-stone to enhance employment as a welfare option of still residuary minimum income schemes.

Besides the inter-organisation between formerly different policy fields of 'social welfare' and 'labour market policy', usually locally based minimum income assistance institutions also encounter the problem to remodel the logic of the 'social welfare policy field' in a manner enhancing work-integration of minimum income beneficiaries. Minimum income programmes in continental European countries were typically organised along structures of social work services (Gough 2001; Mingione et al. 2002; Saraceno 2002). For the co-production of services to activate persistently unemployed or weaker groups of the labour market, the issue arises to connect social welfare services more effectively to income support and labour market policy. As the family's typical institutional functions of care and rehabilitation increasingly fail to intervene subsidiary to minimum income assistance in Bismarckian welfare states, the challenge arises to bound social welfare services for rehabilitation or child care in a more comprehensive and efficient manner to benefit provision and the take-up of employment. Thereby the challenge arises to connect social welfare services to minimum income provision in order to serve the new goal of labour market integration of weaker groups and persistently unemployed.

In brief, the institutionalisation of an organisational field for the local co-production of services to activate persistently unemployed, weaker groups of the labour market or low-skilled unemployed is a matter of the coordination and interaction of different policy fields. Particularly for the Bismarckian countries, the local handling of activation policies for recipients of minimum income schemes encounters the challenge of adjusting and reorganising different approaches, services and policies for labour market integration.

4.1.3.2 Co-producing services and policies from different policy levels

As a second inter-organisational issue, the co-production of tailor-made social welfare services, active labour market policy, and instruments of labour market policy for the activation of minimum income recipients requires contributions from different policy levels in the local policy process (Hooghe and Marks 2001). The question of the institutionalisation of local organisational fields for the activation of long-term unemployed as well as weaker and more vulnerable groups of society is therefore structured in important ways by a central-regional-local dimension.

The co-production of activation policies for beneficiaries of minimum income schemes depends on a closer co-operation between national, regional and local actors (Green and Orton 2009). In Bismarckian welfare states, different policy levels are usually implicated in the delivery of labour market policy, active labour market policy, minimum income benefits and social welfare policies. Important responsibilities for minimum income provision and social service delivery are in Bismarckian welfare states often based at the local level. At the local level, public and third sector actors fulfil important tasks in providing benefits or social welfare services as for example counselling, housing or health services (Mingione et al. 2002). The local implication in social minimum income benefits and social services has often long-standing historical roots (Whiteside 2007). In other cases, recent trends of decentralisation have often revived local arrangements for services and benefits in Bismarckian welfare states (Kazepov 2010). But beyond mere social benefits and social work, which are tasks strongly based at the local level, the co-production of activation services requires drawing on competencies of active labour market policy and labour market policy. In Bismarckian countries, labour market policy is usually conceived by the central level and it is subject to a strong influence of the social partners. Thus, local tasks for benefits and local skills in the field of social work, on the one hand, and national competences for labour market policies and active labour market policy, on the other hand, frequently remain separated in the Bismarckian multi-level system of the welfare state. In order to locally co-produce the activation of weaker and more vulnerable groups as well as persistently unemployed, it arises the local task to draw on the different levels' competences for social welfare services, benefit provision, active labour market policy and labour market policy.

In short, the institutionalisation of an organisational field for the local co-production of services to activate persistently unemployed, weaker groups of the labour market or low-skilled unemployed thus proceeds as a matter of the coordination of services delivered by the national, the regional and the local level. Particularly in the Bismarckian countries, the local handling of activation policies for recipients of minimum income schemes encounters the challenge to draw on competences for income replacement, labour market policy, active labour market policy and social work, which are often separated between the local and central level.

4.1.3.3 Co-producing services between public, private and third sector providers

A third inter-organisational problem of the co-production of various services and policies for the activation of beneficiaries of minimum income schemes is the integration of public, private and third sector service providers in the local policy process. The state, the for-profit sector and the non-profit sector can intervene in different ways and to a different extent in the provision of benefits, active labour market policy services and social services.

Co-produced activation policies for beneficiaries of minimum income schemes imply a closer co-operation and collaboration between public, not-for profit and private organisations in the local policy process (Osborne and McLaughlin 2004; Pestoff et al. 2006). In the Bismarckian welfare state the involvement of private actors has always played a certain role in the provision of welfare. Despite a highly elaborated public dimension, unemployment benefit arrangements, labour market policy and active labour market policy are in the continental European countries typically influenced by corporatist institutions of the social partners (Ebbinghaus and Hassel 2000). In the area of social services or minimum income benefits, various providers, comprising the municipalities or other local bodies as well as third sector organisations, typically intervene (Bode 2006). A coherent involvement of these third sector organisations in a co-production of services is necessary for responding to the various needs of persistently unemployed and weaker and more vulnerable groups of society (Lindsay and McQuaid 2008). Stipulated by activation policies' attempts to combine labour market policy, social welfare services, active labour market policy and benefit provision, a broad integration of public, private and third sector service providers in the local policy process is crucial.

In brief, the institutionalisation of an organisational field for the local co-production of services to activate persistently unemployed and weaker groups of society proceeds as a matter of the local coordination of different service providers. In Bismarckian welfare states, the local handling of activation policies for recipients of minimum income schemes proceeds as an issue of the local interplay of public providers and for-profit or non-profit private actors in the local service delivery.

4.1.3.4 Three local challenges of activating minimum income recipients

To conclude, the institutionalisation of services and policies for the activation of persistently unemployed and disadvantaged groups in continental Europe encounters three crucial problems of coordination at the local level. In the past, the Bismarckian welfare states' policies and services in the fields of social welfare, benefits, active labour market policy and labour market policy were strongly separated, collaboration of public, non-profit and for profit actors between these fields was not assured, and tasks were divided between the local and central level. Consequently, local attempts to co-produce individualised and situated interventions for the activation of long-term unemployed and weaker groups of society challenge the particular architecture of the Bismarckian welfare state. Therefore, the institutionalisation of work incentives, training, rehabilitation or care according to the individual situation of minimum income recipients, demands the development of local organisational fields which co-produce benefits and services across the fragmented policy fields, between the divergent actors and from the different policy levels.

4.1.4 First hypothesis: local organisational fields as requirement to implement the Bismarckian activation regime

While processes of European diffusion and national regulation introduce a new focus on work incentives, social services and active labour market policy in Bismarckian welfare states, the activation of long-term unemployed and vulnerable groups dependent on minimum income schemes opens up a local dimension of the Bismarckian activation regime.

The Bismarckian activation regime attempts to rely on work incentives, social services and labour market policies to reduce the pressure on minimum income schemes. Taking into account these areas stressed for the activation of minimum income benefit recipients, at least two tasks are to an important extent under local authority in continental Europe. Usually, social welfare services imply an important part of local responsibility. Furthermore, and central to the question of activation of minimum income benefit recipients, authority for the delivery of minimum income benefits tends to be based to a crucial extent at the local level. Both trends either derive from historical circumstances of social benefit and welfare service provision or they are (re-)introduced by fresh tendencies of decentralisation.

This relevance of the local level in Bismarckian welfare states for recipients of minimum income benefits, furthermore, confers to a key requirement of the activation of persistently unemployed and weaker groups of society: the Bismarckian welfare states' attempt to activate long-term unemployed and weaker groups of society implies the need for a local co-production of individualised welfare interventions. Generalised or centrally applied policies and services, which conferred to the classical Bismarckian welfare state logic of passive benefit provision, are problematic for achieving the activation into work of long-term unemployed, weaker groups and vulnerable groups. Responding to weaker and more vulnerable groups' individual situation, the local level has the potential to coordinate the application of work incentives, social services and active labour market policy, in a tailor-made manner. By the institutionalisation of distinct local organisational fields, local authorities or local public service providers can make different policies and services and their various providers take part in a co-production of individualised and coordinated policies and services. The local handling of minimum income benefit arrangements in Bismarckian welfare states thus opens up opportunities for the activation of recipients of minimum income schemes through a local co-production between national and local authorities, public and private organisations, employment and social services, social workers and placement officers, beneficiaries and case-managers.

The institutionalisation of such distinct local organisational fields for the co-produced provision of welfare and work opportunities challenges fragmented, separated and uniform policies and services in the Bismarckian welfare state. Due to the decentralisation of policies and services as well as the requirement for a local co-production of tailor-made activation by different providers, policies and services, it is to a great extent at the local level where the threefold division of important policies and services in Bismarckian welfare states is called into question: the local coordination of policies and services therefore defies fragmentation and separation between different policy levels, providers and policy fields. The possibilities of institutionalising employment-centred welfare as a new filter of minimum income schemes in Bismarckian countries thus to a great extent depend on the local handling of services and policies to activate weaker and more vulnerable groups of beneficiaries. Consequently, the realisation of attempts to reduce pressure on minimum income schemes by the activation of benefit recipients depends in a crucial manner on the effective local delivery of work incentives, social welfare services and active labour market policy.

We can therefore formulate a first hypothesis with regard to the institutionalisation of employment-centred welfare for minimum income benefit recipients in Bismarckian-type continental European welfare states: *decentralised competencies and possibilities of co-production enable the local level to challenge the fragmented Bismarckian welfare state architecture by the institutionalisation of organisational fields coordinating resources for activation between the local and central level, between fields of labour market and social welfare policy and between public authorities, third sector organisations, private providers and social partners.*

4.2 Different local governance patterns of employment-centred welfare

The decentralised (re-)structuring of organisational fields towards a local co-production of policies and services proceeds according to certain governance patterns of approaches for the activation of benefit recipients (Künzel 2012). Local organisational fields are about the co-production of individualised and tailor-made work incentives and services for benefit recipients. Decentralisation and activation reforms imply important local room for manoeuvring for the institutionalisation of governance arrangements for the activation of minimum income recipients in Bismarckian welfare states. As a result of the greater local room for manoeuvring, locally different governance approaches might develop in Bismarckian countries for the activation of persistently unemployed, weaker groups and low-skilled persons:

> "The new institutional context allows unprecedented opportunities for a region to opt out of certain existing domestic regulatory regimes, to stay out of newly established ones, (…): in other words, regions can increasingly constitute themselves as distinctive localities, bounding or debounding themselves according to their own region-building strategies." (Ferrera 2005: 179).

Theoretically, we thus have to account for the evolvement of different local governance patterns in the activation of unemployed. This raises potential for discussion about different activation approaches.

To explain different activation approaches, in a first step, it is highlighted that the local co-production of an activation of beneficiaries of minimum income schemes underlies specific assumptions on individual behaviour. The changing conception of the individual from a social citizen towards an 'active' recipient in the process of co-production of active inclusion is discussed. It is underscored that assumptions on individual behaviour of 'active' recipients partaking in the co-production of welfare and employment opportunities can differ. We highlight different premises of the conception of the individual which underlie market-oriented, bureaucratic, and participatory strategies to activate recipients of minimum income schemes. But the decentralised co-production also implies that intervening services set an important organisational context for activation (4.4.2). In a second step, the implications of the institutionalisation of service delivery systems for the activation of benefit recipients are discussed. We theorise how distinct organisational conditions of the local provision of welfare condition different strategies of activation (market-oriented, bureaucratic or participatory). Thus, local fields for the (re-)organisation of minimum income schemes in Bismarckian welfare regimes might vary between at least three different ideal typical paths of local governance of activating services.

4.2.1 Concepts of individual behaviour underlying the co-production of activation

Activation policies mark a conceptual shift away from providing social citizens with collective rights and uniform citizenship towards the idea of active recipients partaking in a contract-based co-production of individualised welfare interventions.

The idea of social citizenship corresponds to social programmes that guarantee income protection (Marshall 1965). From this perspective, adequate benefits suffice to enable social citizens to make use of their capacities to act. Inclusion is supported via collective rights but remains open to definition by the individual. In an ideal typical manner, this 'social citizenship' approach has matched Bismarckian social policy conceptions of a social treatment of unemployment.

The introduction of activation policy is marking a deviation from this idea of uniform social citizenship as it depends on individualised strategies. Activation policy fosters the idea of an individualised concept of unemployment policy. Thereby, the activation concept reinterprets the relationship between the state and its citizens. It signifies a shift from the idea of uniform social citizenship and collective rights towards greater individual responsibility (Serrano Pascual 2007a). The idea of unconditional social citizenship and collective rights, which was ideal typical for the traditional Bismarckian welfare state model, is at least partially replaced by the principle of contract (Serrano Pascual 2007a). In an ideal sense – and today often in a practice – the beneficiary and the state agree on a contract that defines reciprocal responsibilities (Pestoff et al. 2006). Without the beneficiary taking an active role in this process of welfare 'co-production', the intended benefits and services will not be delivered (Pestoff 2009).

Notwithstanding this general focus on the responsibility of the individual, the activation concept comprises competing approaches to deal with precarious life situations as unemployment and social exclusion. Their differences mainly derive from concurring assumptions on individual behaviour in the co-production of tailor-made services. This is evidenced by situating active inclusion among different concepts to deal with the inclusion of recipients of minimum income schemes. We distinguish three approaches of activation: individuals can be conceived as clients, beneficiaries and autonomous citizens (Van Berkel and Møller 2002: 51–56).

Individuals as clients of market-oriented activation approaches

As a first variant of activation policy, a *market-oriented concept* explains precarious life situations as a consequence of a lack of individual incentives to generate income. From this angle, the receipt of benefits is a sign of an individual problem leading to dependency. Following the rational argument "generosity (...) makes it irrational for individuals to reject benefits in favour of work." (Lødemel and Trickey 2001: 18). Thus, a market-oriented strategy interprets activation primarily as a matter of enforcing the right incentives for labour market inclusion. Individuals play the role of *clients* contracting work-first services that expect their quick integration into any kind of work. Active labour market policies or social welfare services are conceptualised for the short-run while financial work-incentives are strongly applied, often in a disciplining manner, to enforce labour market inclusion.

Individuals as beneficiaries of bureaucratic activation approaches

As a second type of activation policy, a *bureaucratic* concept views the individual as being limited in many aspects, notably living conditions, care, qualifications or health. Individuals are, however, regarded as potentially unwilling to seize opportunities for inclusion. For the good of the people but also for the benefit of society in general, service organisations therefore need to provide for ways to eventually enforce measures upon citizens. Individuals are treated as *beneficiaries* of a set of integrated services defined by the enabling state. Beneficiaries are bound to benefit from placement, counselling, social welfare services and active labour market policies (Eichhorst et al. 2008a: 5). This concept of 'enforced emancipation' is reminiscent of practices from the early poor laws and the workhouse tradition (Whiteside 2007). Enabling contract-based services match a "policy of producing individuals and identities" (Serrano Pascual 2007a: 12) for labour market inclusion (Rose 1999).

Individuals as autonomous citizens of participatory activation approaches
A third approach to activation policy shares structural explanations for precarious life situations but proposes a participatory concept for the activation of unemployed into work. Individuals are viewed as *autonomous citizens* willing to seize participation opportunities. According to this perspective, individuals are not only accorded needs for financial resources and a set of services, but they require encouragement to choose between options for employment and services (Sen 1985; 1993; Sen 1999: 88): "Without the substantive freedom and capability to do something, a person cannot be responsible for doing it." (Sen 1999: 284). Co-produced placement, counselling and training services can provide for choice by promoting a citizen's capability for voice (Bonvin and Orton 2009): "In welfare approaches, this suggests a shift away from freedom from want toward freedom to act. (...) the purpose of welfare intervention is to provide people with the necessary capability that allows them to act freely (...)." (Salais 2003: 322). Participatory services rely on the individuals' commitment to use their capabilities to choose active participation in society.

Different programmatic strategies of co-producing activation
To conclude, individualised strategies underlie different programmatic priorities of activating benefit recipients. Different from a concept of uniform social citizenship and collective rights for income protection, which underlay the typical Bismarckian social treatment of unemployment, three programmatic approaches of an individualised co-production of activation policies can be distinguished. A market-oriented activation concept focuses welfare interventions on enforcing work-incentives for welfare clients to generate income on the labour market. In contrast, in the bureaucratic version, an enabling state defines beneficiaries' needs for integrated services to surmount structural deprivation for labour market integration. Alternatively, a participatory approach promotes autonomous citizens' capabilities to choose among different individual options given by placement, training and counselling activities.

These market-oriented, bureaucratic and participatory variants of co-producing individualised activation approaches require different forms of organising welfare state interventions in order to include persistently unemployed, weaker groups of the labour market or low-skilled into employment or social services.

4.2.2 The organisation of co-produced policies and services for minimum income recipients

Parallel to the programmatic aspects of the implementation of activation policies and services, the organisational context is crucial for applying individualised approaches. The local co-production of policies and services to activate recipients of minimum income benefits raises the question on the practices and processes that structure an organisation of individualised services. This connects activation reforms to questions on how the provision and delivery of individualised services, policies and benefits is organised at the local level. As the institutionalisation of employment-centred welfare in Bismarckian welfare states calls for a greater focus on individualised services and work incentives, the techniques and processes that regulate the interactions between bureaucracies, agencies, welfare associations, case-managers and unemployed are crucial. The co-produced character of activation strategies heightens the relevance of the particular organisational arrangements which structure the interactions between these different actors for the delivery of individualised policies and services. Questions arise on the local institutional conditions for the delivery of individualised policies and services, the local modes of interaction for service provision and the organisational techniques that are applied to 'steer' interactions in the direction that employment friendly reform programmes wish to take (Van Berkel and Borghi 2008). Possible local organisational models to offer tailor-made services can be therefore explained in view of these three dimensions: individualised welfare interventions are determined by the local institutional conditions for policies and services (Finn 2000), the institutionalisation of local modes of interaction for welfare intervention (Garrow and Hasenfeld 2010: 33–57) and the local implementation of techniques for controlling service delivery (Clarke et al. 2000b; Hood et al. 2002).

Due to the important local room for manoeuvring in Bismarckian countries' handling of minimum income schemes, differences in the local conditions for policies and services become relevant, and the local modes of interaction as well as the local control techniques can vary. As a result, the localisation of policies and services, an institutionalisation of local modes of interaction for welfare intervention, and the local implementation of techniques for controlling service delivery can develop according to different patterns of the inter-organisation. Different organisational approaches of the implementation of individualised policies and services for recipients of minimum income schemes might evolve at the local level which can be distinguished in an ideal typical manner by a market-based, a bureaucratic and a network-based organisation (Williamson

1979). Thus, complementary to the individual dimension of activation policy programmes, particular organisational structures promote particular types of individualised approaches which might vary between market-oriented service delivery, bureaucratic interventions or participatory service models.

4.2.2.1 Local institutional conditions for co-produced policies and services

The decentralisation of competences for welfare interventions to the local level is an important prerequisite for providing a broader range of situated policies and services – independently of the specific form of the activation approach (either market-oriented, bureaucratic or participatory) (Lindsay et al. 2008). This localisation reduces the capacity of national legislation to define universal, collective rights. Increasingly, the range of policies and the concrete services, which are implemented, are decided upon at the local level. However, the ability of public authorities, third sector organisations, placement and welfare offices to locally provide individual, tailor-made or even participatory solutions varies strongly. The delivery of policies and services is increasingly determined and provided by local communities specified either by market-orientation, bureaucracy or partnership.

Local institutional conditions for a market-oriented approach

As a first variant, market-oriented activation policies are linked to conditions of decentralisation leading to structural and financial retrenchment of the welfare system (Pierson 1995; Rauch 2008). In the market-oriented model, local institutions are weak and fragmented. The capacities of public administrations, community organisations or welfare associations are not strongly developed and relationships between them are only weakly institutionalised. The weakness of local institutions and actors is related to limited human, technical, financial or legal resources. For example, local legal or financial capacities are weak as they are subject to greater constraints than at the national level. In addition, decentralisation further aggravates the situation of weak local providers, authorities and community-based groups as it shifts costs and complex problems onto the local level. In the market-oriented model, actors intervening in the local delivery of services and policies therefore try to evade engagement in resource consuming or too complex strategies for welfare interventions. Consequently, local actors will tend to concentrate on resource-minimising strategies for the activation of recipients dependent on minimum income protection (Pal and Weaver 2003). Local accounts of activation reforms in Poland (Sztandar-Sztanderska 2009) and Italy (Monteleone and Mozzana 2009) suggest that weak institutional settings and weak local actors delivering important services and policies contribute to a cost-minimising, market-oriented strategy.

In short, weak and fragmented local institutions describe a local setting permeated by cost and resource minimising strategies.

Local institutional conditions for a bureaucratic approach

According to the bureaucratic concept of co-producing policies and services, national, regional and local efforts in a territory are integrated by strong public agencies (Niklasson 2007: 188). The local institutional fabric for the take-up of decentralised policies and services is marked by strongly entangled bureaucratic structures: while institutional resources for the co-production of policies and services are available at the local level, the issue is monopolised by public agencies. Public administrations pull the strings by holding onto the crucial competences to integrate efforts in a region (Niklasson 2007: 188). Well established in a territory, public agencies and bureaucracies command important financial, legal and human resources of which they make actively use. Usually, established single organisations stand out in the territory as they monopolise crucial functions (Pfeffer and Salancik 1978). Stability of this institutional arrangement is maintained by insulating important functions in organisations rather independent from their environment. Influences from the local institutional environment by other local service providers on the main public organisations are weakly developed. In local structures based on bureaucratic entanglement, local institutions for a broader legitimisation of policies and services are not strongly elaborated. Legitimacy for policies is derived from processes of political representation and legislation (Peterson and Rom 1990). Accordingly, the local institutional role and capacity of civil society groups, welfare associations or other project executing organisations is rather weak and peripheral.

Thus, while bureaucratic approaches of co-producing services and policies are based on strong and locally entangled public agencies, local institutional ties to citizens and associations are weakly developed in this institutional setting.

Local institutional conditions for a participatory approach

In an institutional setting characterised by local partnerships, issues are not only taken up at the local level but various local actors are in a comprehensive manner involved in conceptualising welfare interventions. Local institutions of partnership are based on active local communities (Lindsay et al. 2008: 717–721). Capacities in local organisations and communities are strongly developed (Lindsay and McQuaid 2008: 354f; Lindsay et al. 2008: 717–719). In the case of institutionalised partnerships, local configurations bring up strong citizen groups, important social service providers and established local administrations eager to seize opportunities arising from decentralisation (Francis 1998: 143–147). The transfer of authority to decentralised levels thus places policy processes where a network of support for social issues is strong and actors are inclined to use discretionary room as 'laboratory for social experimentation' (Leibfried et al. 2005).

Local partnership structures are characterised by broadly institutionalised arrangements for participation opportunities. In a local partnership setting, institutions for legitimating policy choice are highly established at the local level. Co-produced services and policies are conceptualised and organised by strongly institutionalised local project groups, networks and similar open co-ordination approaches between subordinate actors: "They provide a forum that can allow groups to combine their resources to develop complementary projects that provide multidimensional responses to complex individual and collective problems." (Finn 2000: 54). With regard to services and policies, institutionalised partnerships have the advantage of being close to the affected citizens (Niklasson 2007: 145). For example, in the UK, authority was devolved in the form of 'working neighbourhood', 'pathfinder' or 'pathway to work' projects. In the pilot projects, flexibility was provided in planning processes to define mutual tasks and to secure local agreement. Strong communities indeed fostered activation approaches for persistently unemployed or vulnerable groups of society through local 'partners' (Green and Orton 2009; Lindsay et al. 2008).

In brief, local partnerships rely on strong relationships between various local 'partners' and strong community capacity in order to implement local authority and institutional flexibility for activation approaches.

Varying local institutional conditions for co-produced policies and services

To conclude, co-produced public action shifts welfare interventions from the relatively homogeneous definition provided by national legislation towards local milieus, structures and initiatives. Local institutional conditions support different approaches towards the activation of persistently unemployed or vulnerable groups. In the case of a market-oriented concept, weak and isolated local actors opt for cost-minimising strategies. Bureaucratic localisation of activation policies is based on an important but exclusive structure of decentralised public agencies that integrate issues of activation. In the case of a participatory concept, strong local communities use devolved authority for locally bound partnerships to encourage an activation approach.

4.2.2.2 Local modes of interaction for the delivery of co-produced policies and services

Decentralised, co-produced forms of public action imply a shift from the hierarchical provision of standardised services towards more inclusive types of local service organisation. This increases the significance of interactions within a region. However, interaction between public authorities, placement and welfare offices, placement officers and management, case-managers and persons in receipt of benefits may proceed according to different logics (Garrow and Hasenfeld 2010: 33–57). Local coordination processes for service delivery can be distinguished according to competition, bureaucratic regulation or participation.

Competition-based modes of local interaction

Local interactions organised in the form of competition for 'cheaper' services support a market-oriented logic of activation (Bredgaard and Larsen 2007). Contracts and economic incentives then form the basis of relationships in a given region. Actors responsible for managerial, executive and operational tasks act at arm's length as they are competing for 'input' in the process of delivering social and labour market policy services (Lindsay et al. 2008: 716).

The market-oriented mode of local interactions applies different elements of competitive regulation for organisations and persons involved in service delivery. A crucial element of a market-oriented local organisation is the marketisation of services. According to this principle, services are subject to 'contracting-out' procedures. So called 'quasi-markets' are established for services by introducing a competition during which external service providers, not-for profit or for profit organisations, submit an offer to bid for the delivery. According to the idea of outcome payment, reimbursement on the service delivered is usually only guaranteed upon the successful realisation of the offer: "The principle idea is to create a free market for employment services in which (primarily private) service providers bid in open competition by public tendering. This is expected to produce 'better and cheaper' employment services (..)." (Bredgaard and Larsen 2007: 289). According to a similar market-oriented logic, welfare offices and management typically function according to 'merit pay'.

The market-oriented mode of interaction gives providers in the public sector, for-profit and non-profit organisations the opportunity to intervene in a transparent and open bidding process for service offers. Thereby, opportunities arise for the intervention of new actors in approaches towards persistently unemployed or weaker groups of society (Lindsay et al. 2008: 716–717). At the same time, the terms of regulation of a transparent contracting-out regime produce several restrictions for interactions. The marketisation of services excludes interactions on equal terms between the service providing and the service-demanding actor (Lindsay and McQuaid 2008: 361; Lindsay and McQuaid 2008: 361), which makes it difficult for both to find common responses to complex issues. In a similar vein, the market-model leads to disincentives between the actors in a region to build up specific and stronger relationships (Williamson 1981). Furthermore, in order to enable the marketisation of services, services need to be to some extent centrally regulated (Osborne and Gaebler 1992) thereby adding to the problem of cooperation. Market-oriented interactions for a co-production of services thus privilege competition over broader agreements on complex social issues between actors (Bredgaard and Larsen 2007; Green and Orton 2009).

Local studies from the UK in particular show how the introduction of competitive tendering among service providers transformed the local delivery of services into a market-oriented concept of activation (Green and Orton 2009; Lindsay et al. 2008): a very strict and standardised contractual model for which the public employment service largely controlled the design and content for, focused the coordination between local actors, private and third sector providers towards a market-oriented mode of activating unemployed.

In brief, in market-oriented processes of the delivery of policies and services to active persistently unemployed and vulnerable groups, efficiency arguments outrival broader agreements on complex issues.

Competence-based modes of local interaction

In contrast to arm's length relations, bureaucratic welfare interventions for the activation of unemployed are based on an expert system (Kaufmann 2009: 258f). Bureaucratic modes of service delivery are typically organised by a competence-based style of interaction. The needs and interests of the beneficiaries are believed to be represented by experts' knowledge and judgements. Rationality is considered important in the local co-production of services and policies (Hasenfeld 1992a: 26). Accordingly, local coordination for the co-production of services is viewed as an issue for the professionals involved in the necessary technical details (Kaufmann 2009: 258f). The issue of coordinating services and policies remains at the hands of expert decisions. Forms of co-production are therefore highly technical and based on consultation. A formalised, juridical style of social regulation dominates. Judgements demand a background of distinctive knowledge or profession. Such forms of competence-based coordination are highly technical and complex. They are often shaped by micro politics, and thus fail to develop a greater participatory dimension (Derlien 2000). More spontaneous, immediate forms of interaction in the delivery of services are not enabled by the model. Regulatory activity tends to lead to a high density of rules, complex arrangements and the co-production of services in a more or less pre-defined way (Niklasson 2007: 188).

In brief, an expert-system defines a bureaucratic local mode of service delivery for the activation of beneficiaries of minimum income schemes.

Arguing as mode of local interaction

A participatory mode of organisation involves autonomous stakeholders who participate in arguing processes regarding the co-production of welfare interventions. In the participatory model for co-producing the local delivery of services and policies, interactions are thus based on a deliberative mode. Local action relies on processes taking into account and exchanging different arguments, world-views and knowledge bases. Diversities and differences are acknowledged by making them subject to 'reason-giving'. In these local arguing processes, diverging arguments are tested with regard to their consistency and claims of validity. The idea is to persuade others of the right service by the 'power of the better argument' (Elster 1991; Elster 1998). Arguing processes involve autonomous stakeholders in the local co-production of welfare interventions. The number of stakeholders intervening is not limited. Options for 'voice' and 'exit' exist to express disaccord as stakeholders are autonomous.

Local interactions in a participatory model for service delivery count both on formal as well as informal arguing processes (Isett et al. 2011). Mutual agreements and common declarations are the regular outcomes of a participatory mode of interaction while official contracts are only used sparsely for formalising interactions (Provan and Milward 1995). For example, according to a participatory mode of interaction, arguing processes between the service- demander, the provider organisations, case-managers, advocacy groups and possibly beneficiaries define action-plans and service provisions. However, although participatory modes of interaction rely on the idea to benefit from the continuous exchange of arguments between diverse stakeholders there is no guarantee that all voices and perspectives are necessarily represented. Informal networks particularly risk causing exclusion. In contrast, formal networks provide greater opportunities for institutionalising criteria to ensure broad inclusion of stakeholders (Monge and Contractor 2003).

A participatory mode of local service delivery therefore achieves definition of minimum income recipients' needs by deliberative processes. Through this deliberative style of interaction, norms and values are found for interaction (Salais 2008). For example in the city of Vienna, arguing processes entailing participation of different and autonomous stakeholders led to an activation approach offering broad support and choice to autonomous citizens (Atzmüller 2009).

Arguing processes as a local mode of interaction between different stakeholders lead to the common definition of action plans and service provision. Consequently, arguing processes co-produce a participatory concept of activation.

Different forms of interaction for the delivery of co-produced policies and services

To conclude, a shift from hierarchical provision towards co-produced services and policies for the activation of persistently unemployed and vulnerable groups of society demands greater local coordination for service delivery. However, different logics shape local interactions. In the case of a market-oriented activation concept, the delivery of services is organised in the form of competition between rational actors. For a bureaucratic activation concept, experts in a competence-based system regulate the delivery of services. In the participatory model, agreement on service delivery is a matter of local arguing processes between numerous autonomous stakeholders.

4.2.2.3 Local control techniques for the delivery of co-produced policies and services

Decentralised, co-produced public action requires ways to locally control differentiated activities between public authorities, third sector organisations, management, case-managers and benefit recipients. Local mechanisms of control thereby partly replace or complement guarantees of collective social citizenship rights by national legislature or law courts. However, techniques employed to locally control service delivery can vary considerably (Hood et al. 2002). We distinguish between market-oriented, bureaucratic and participatory local attempts to control welfare interventions for activation.

Market-oriented control techniques for the delivery of policies and services

Market-oriented control is organised by benchmarking in the form of publishing rating systems or league tables of standards (Hood et al. 2002: 192). Steering techniques concentrate on strategic control at distance of actors being overseen. Operational control is weak, as this would imply a closer engagement and implication of the local controller in the process of service delivery. As a result, relations between planning bodies and actors charged with direct delivery, as for example between management and services or case-managers and clients, are rather separated and controlled by benchmarking. Therefore, outcome oriented indicators dominate. Indicators concentrate on quantifiable, immediate and often short-term results. Opportunities to evaluate long-term procedures and more complex interventions of services and policies are limited (Lindsay and McQuaid 2008). Benchmarking as mechanism of control therefore has an inherent tendency to facilitate the implementation of a market-oriented concept of activation policy (Bredgaard and Larsen 2007).

Local accounts of activation reforms in the UK (Green and Orton 2009; Lindsay et al. 2008), Italy (Monteleone and Mozzana 2009) and Poland (Sztandar-Sztanderska 2009) illustrate how the introduction of simple job-entry statistics for controlling purposes shifts the focus of services onto job placement efforts for clients with lesser obstacles. Studies on the British Jobcentre Plus, that serves recipients of minimum income schemes, show how simplistic job-entry statistics spread a market-oriented, 'work-first ethos' among staff and project executing organisations (Lindsay and McQuaid 2008). Given the outcome-oriented, distanced control character, possibilities to evaluate long-term procedures and more complex interventions are restricted (Lindsay and McQuaid 2008).

Thus, the local implementation of benchmarking for controlling co-production processes of policies and services supports a market-oriented type of activation.

Bureaucratic control techniques for the delivery of policies and services

In the case of a bureaucratic concept of co-produced policies and services, not only strategic but also operational control is high. Control techniques concentrate on the inner coherence and integrated character of services. The idea of bureaucratic control techniques is to control the application of welfare interventions according to generalised standards (Hughes 1998). To make policies and services confer to legislative prescriptions, programme regulations and government authority, bureaucratic supervision highly formalises the internal division of tasks, the definitions of role positions, and the distribution of authority in the process of service delivery (Hasenfeld 1992a, 1992b, 2010). Bureaucratic control of the delivery of services and policies thus proceeds in a more remote and formal style. The application of impersonal rules for the assignments to positions, the formal distribution of authority, and the formulation of detailed rights and duties of each position serve to guarantee standards of welfare interventions. General standards, formal rules, detailed reporting and indicators are applied by local actors to guarantee accountability and efficiency in the delivery of policies and services (Du Gay 2000).

Hasenfeld (1992: 25) gives evidence for a typical case of bureaucratic control by implementers:

> "Having defined a specific set of goals – placing welfare recipients in educational and training programs in order to make them employable – they [the implementers] then developed a careful flowchart of how recipients should be processed through the system, specifying the precise decision rules workers were to follow. They wrote an elaborate manual of procedures that detailed the role of the case-managers, and what standard operating procedures they had to follow. A very elaborate management information system was developed to keep track of the clients and of every decision made by the workers, assuring accountability. Clear lines of authority were enunciated. Viewed as a whole, the design seemed to be logically driven by the aim of the program."

Due to the formal and dense style of bureaucratic control, room for discretion in devising and delivering welfare services is rather limited, for example between case-managers and beneficiaries. Instead, the behaviour of staff is fully determined by their formal goal prescriptions (Hasenfeld 2010: 34). Discretion in service delivery, for example between case-managers and beneficiaries, is traded for consistency and accountability (Du Gay 2000). Typically, goals are highly explicit in the bureaucratic model of supervision.

Overall, a more formalised but dense style of supervision with regulators being at distance from the actors involved in the delivery of policies and services confers to the bureaucratic concept of welfare interventions.

Participatory control techniques for the delivery of policies and services

Supposing a participatory concept for activation, control is based on trust, reputation and the reciprocal dependency of actors. In the participatory model of local co-production of service provision, trust ensures and increases the effectiveness of goal delivery (Isett et al. 2011: 164).

The participatory mode of control enables different ways individuals are controlled through the influence of a group. In the one case, local, personal and informal relations play an important role for controlling the delivery of services and policies (Langan 2000). In this context, control is based on the reputation of actors (Hood et al. 2002: 14–16). Behaviour intent on pursuing reputation among peers is widespread and leads to conformity. An informal rating of trustworthiness might take place. In the other case of group control, control is based on the reciprocal dependency of actors. Reciprocal dependency between actors in a local organisational field derives from mutual decision-making and resource-sharing. In the case of reputation-based as well as mutual control, respect for overall goals is strengthened by the continuous character of common action. A common 'history' of reciprocal activities and the build up of reputation foster trust among actors in a territory (Powell 1990).

In order to achieve control based on reputation and reciprocal dependency, effective structures for group processes are crucial. In this context, committees and other institutionalised forms of communication exert an important function (Hood et al. 2002: 16). Committees can restrain individual action by group decision-making. In addition, committees create a climate of expectations and mutual obligations. Consequently, in the model of participatory control of the local delivery of policies and services, relational distance between the controller and the controlled is rather low (Hood et al. 2002). Interactions are often direct and immediate. This enables continuous changes and modifications to the content of services if this is required in the process of delivery. At the same time, trust-based control leaves flexibility in the course of delivery of policies and services. It leaves room for those realising a service to adapt to specific circumstances (Bredgaard and Larsen 2007). Effective trust-based control therefore allows for steering complex goals of welfare interventions.

Overall, trust and mutuality as techniques of controlling the co-production of policies and services confer to a participatory concept of activation policy.

Different control techniques for the delivery of co-produced policies and services
To conclude, unlike the oversight of collective rights by members of national parliament or law courts, decentralised, co-produced forms of the delivery of policies and services suggest various local ways to control services. In the case of market-oriented co-production, actors are controlled at a distance by outcome-oriented local benchmarking. In contrast, standards and detailed rules are locally applied to guarantee the coherence of policies and services for a bureaucratic concept. Local group processes and mutuality control a participatory concept for co-producing policies and services for the activation of unemployed.

4.2.3 Second hypothesis: activation approaches increase variance in local service delivery

In conclusion, decentralised, co-produced attempts of work activation of the persistently unemployed and weaker and vulnerable groups of society mark crucial shifts in the way welfare interventions proceed in Bismarckian-type continental European welfare states. The institutionalisation of employment centred welfare suggests a shift away from a fragmented configuration of labour market policies, benefits, social welfare services and active labour market policies towards a local co-production of tailor-made and coordinated welfare interventions. The recalibration of responsibilities for long-term unemployed, unemployed low-skilled persons, and needy vulnerable groups onto much locally bound minimum income programmes as well as the requirement of co-produced work incentives, benefits, social welfare services, placement and training services for the activation of these groups increase legitimacy and relevance of a local dimension of the Bismarckian activation regime. Given this local room for manoeuvring in Bismarckian welfare states, the local structuring of distinct organisational fields for the activation of recipients of minimum income schemes might proceed differently.

First of all, in programmatic terms, different assumptions can exist on the local level for how to deal with unemployment of long-term unemployed and weaker and more vulnerable groups. Programmes for the activation of unemployed into work are based on different assumptions on individual behaviour. Market-oriented thinking views unemployed as clients of short-term service interventions which stress the application of strong work incentives in order to enhance direct labour market access. Bureaucratic approaches view the individual as rather inactive beneficiary who requires strong prescription of different policies and services in order to be activated into work. Participatory variants of activation regard the individual as autonomous citizen who requires enhancement of his or her abilities to make choices among a set of different social welfare services, training and employment options.

While different assumptions on individual behaviour underlie activation programmes, the variance in local activation strategies is above all an issue of the local organisation of co-produced services and policies (cf. Tab. 2). Local organisational differences can exist in the co-production of services and policies between local authorities, national agencies, social associations, public employment services, private service providers, organised civil society, case-managers and recipients. Besides the programmatic aspects, the structuring of organisational fields for a local co-production of welfare and employment opportunities for weaker groups of the unemployed proceeds in three dimensions: It decentralises resources and rights to existing local institutional structures, it implies local interactions between actors for the co-produced delivery of policies and services and it is conditioned by the way control techniques for goal-attainment of co-produced policies and services are implemented locally.

Tab. 2: Ideal types of the local organisation of welfare interventions

	Universal Logic of Social Citizenship	**Market-Based Logic of Active Inclusion**	**Bureaucratic Logic of Active Inclusion**	**Participatory Logic of Active Inclusion**
Concept of the Individual	Social Citizen	Client	Beneficiary	Autonomous Citizen
Mode of Interaction	Hierarchy	Competition-Based	Competence-Based	Arguing
Local Conditions	Central Definition by Legislation	Local Fragmentation	Bureaucratic Entanglement	Local Partnerships
Techniques of Control	Parliaments and Law-Courts	Benchmarking	Standards, Rules and Indicators	Trust and Reciprocity

Source: own representation.

Correlating to the different individual activation premises, the local organisation of the different services and policies for the activation of unemployed can ideal typically either match a market-oriented logic, a bureaucratic logic or a participatory logic. These ideal types derive from assuming a coherent pattering of different types of welfare intervention over the three crucial explanatory dimensions for the organisation of local service delivery systems: the local structures for decentralised policies and services, the local modes of interaction for service delivery and the local implementation of control techniques.

We thus assume that the greater reliance on more decentralised minimum income programme arrangements and its related services as well as the introduction of activation policy produces variance in the way distinct local organisational fields are evolving for the institutionalisation of Bismarckian activation regimes. *In a sequential and thus, second hypothesis, we assume that the implementation of Bismarckian activation regimes varies at the local level according to the existing local structures for the take-up of decentralised policies and services, the local interactions for service delivery and the local implementation of control techniques of service delivery. This local variance will manifest around three ideal types of the activation of recipients of minimum income schemes. The local governance of service delivery of minimum income schemes either structures towards a market-oriented, a bureaucratic or a participatory organisation of services and benefits of minimum income schemes.*

4.3 Conclusion: two hypotheses on a local dimension of activation

In this chapter, we argued that activation reforms in continental European countries boost a local dimension of the welfare state. The increasing legitimacy and relevance of a local governance of social protection and activation of unemployed in Bismarckian countries mainly derives from two developments. A first development implying a more important role of the local level in Bismarckian welfare states is the greater reliance on minimum income schemes to protect unemployed and the greater significance accorded to services. The shifting of tasks of social protection against unemployment onto minimum income schemes and the increased significance accorded to services reinvigorates or revives local elements of the Bismarckian welfare states. This is due to the fact that in the continental European welfare states, the local level was typically involved in tasks of social welfare services, social work and minimum income benefit provision. Such 'social' tasks are in an important manner and to different degrees historically and traditionally intertwined with the delivery of minimum income schemes in Bismarckian countries. Moreover this trend towards a greater relevance of the local level for 'social' tasks is often reinforced by explicit transfers of competences to the local level.

A second development, which increases the relevance of the local level, is the Bismarckian welfare state's activation focus on long-term unemployed, low skilled and weaker and more vulnerable groups of society. The activation of long-term unemployed as well as weaker and more vulnerable groups, who are targeted by Bismarckian welfare state policies, proceeds to a great extent as a local co-production of the various providers, policies and services involved. Reactions to the different social and labour market issues inhibiting the work integration of long-term unemployed and vulnerable groups require the intervention of different providers, policies and services. This co-produced implementation of work-incentives, social welfare services and active labour market policies is a matter of the local level. It is at the local level, where public agencies, which are responsible for minimum income benefit recipients, attempt to combine services and activities of different policy fields, policy levels and actors.

The activation of long-term unemployed and weaker and more vulnerable groups of society thus proceeds as a matter of the institutionalisation of distinct local organisational fields. A local organisational field for co-produced policies and services to activate recipients of minimum income schemes results of the rules and resources which are reproduced by the interventions and interrelations between local authorities, national agencies, social associations, public employment services, private service providers, organised civil society, case-managers and recipients. Such a local organisational field develops services and policies to activate persistently unemployed, weaker groups of the labour market and low-skilled unemployed who are often in receipt of minimum income benefits and who are at the focus of Bismarckian activation policies. The local co-production thus aims at the organisational realisation of the new Bismarckian employment-centred institutional filter for minimum income recipients: the fragmented Bismarckian organisation is responded to by attempts of a local inter-organisation of formerly separated policy fields, providers and policy level competences in order to activate minimum income recipients by social welfare services labour market policies, social protection and active labour market policy.

We thus put up a first hypothesis: *Due to the recalibration of social protection onto decentralised structures and the possibilities of a local co-production, distinct local organisational fields to activate persistently unemployed, more vulnerable groups of society and low-skilled unemployed challenge the fragmented Bismarckian welfare state architecture at the local level.*

In a second step, we argued that a co-production of services and polices for the activation of minimum income recipients can locally vary. Our argument stems from the assumption that different activation strategies are influenced by distinct types of local organisation.

Different activation programmes are normally distinguished according to the diverging assumptions on individual behaviour which underlie them. Assumptions on individual behaviour are of particular relevance as activation strategies aim to make the individual 'actively' contribute to the co-production of welfare and work opportunities. Contract-based active inclusion, however, can rely on very different assumptions of individual behaviour: In a market-oriented approach, individual clients are assumed to primarily lack incentives to seize opportunities for the inclusion into work or welfare service. In a bureaucratic model of activation, individual beneficiaries are perceived as lacking self-determination to overcome various social and labour market barriers to placement. Finally, in a participatory model, autonomous individuals require support of various services in order to have an opportunity to choose.

However, activation approaches not only differ with regard to conceptions on how to deal with unemployed, but are also a matter of the distinct local organisation of policies and services. The co-production of welfare and employment opportunities for long-term unemployed and weaker groups of society relates to questions of the configuration and capacity of local institutions for the take-up of services, it raises issues of how actors interact at the local level for organising the delivery of services and polices, and it confers to issues of how actors control the goals of welfare interventions. In a second hypothesis we consequently assume: *Given the room for local manoeuvring in continental European welfare states, we expect local conditions for the usage of decentralised resources, local interactions for service delivery and the local implementation of control techniques of services determine whether the local governance of Bismarckian activation regimes evolves around ideal types of either a market-oriented logic, a bureaucratic concept of active inclusion or a participatory approach for autonomous citizens.*

Distinct institutional settings and structures of the local organisational field can thus lead to different types of governing activation policy reforms. Reactions of Bismarckian welfare states to rising numbers of benefit recipients of minimum income schemes crucially involve the local level. Attempts in the Bismarckian welfare states for including persistently unemployed, weaker groups of the labour market or low-skilled unemployed in work increase the relevance of the local level. Decentralisation and the idea of a co-production of policies offer new resources, rights as well as concepts and legitimacy at the local level. The local room of manoeuvring thereby introduced in the Bismarckian welfare states provokes problems of rule interpretation and enforcement which open up space for the local level to implement welfare state interventions in different ways. This might lead to the definition of distinct local fields of service delivery. The viability of the assumptions of distinct local regulatory regimes and the conception of certain ideal types might therefore grasp a crucial change in the provision of welfare and work in Bismarckian welfare states: these questions decide upon the way welfare and work is provided in Bismarckian welfare states. This work will therefore foremost concentrate on exploring the assumption and phenomenon of local regulatory arrangements in Bismarckian welfare states. While focusing on the structural explanations for activation policies, this does, of course, not mean that concrete processes and procedures of change are not important. Local reforms towards activation policy proceed as processes which are determined by different intentional and unintentional influences and effects caused by the opportunities for incremental change of institutions (Crouch and Farrell 2004; Streeck and Thelen 2005) and the manoeuvres of skilled actors (Mahoney and Thelen 2010). While foremost focussing on the structural explanations for activation policy, we will try to explore further explanations for change processes in an inductive way resulting from the following empirical inquiry.

5. A methodology for comparative empirical studies on the reorganisation of minimum income schemes

This work raises the question on the reaction of Bismarckian-type continental European welfare states to rising numbers of beneficiaries of minimum income schemes. The attempt to institutionalise an activation regime for persistently unemployed and vulnerable groups was identified as a general response to this problem. However, we argue that the institutionalisation of such an activation regime can only to some extent be explained by processes of European diffusion of 'good governance' and national institutional coordination. A recalibration of tasks of social protection of unemployed onto much locally bound minimum income schemes, and the requirements of a local co-production of tailor-made services to activate persistently unemployed, unemployed persons with health problems, and other disadvantaged groups excluded from the labour market makes the local level play an important role in the Bismarckian activation regime.

We transformed this observation of an essential role of the local level in the continental European welfare states' policy answers to rising numbers of recipients of minimum income schemes into two hypotheses. First, the institutionalisation of distinct local organisational fields to activate recipients of minimum income schemes challenges the fragmented Bismarckian welfare state architecture. The institutionalisation of such local organisational fields rises up to the challenges of the Bismarckian welfare states' problems to coordinate between separated policy levels, policy fields and actors. Second, the way recipients of minimum income schemes are activated at the local level is influenced by the local organisation. Namely, it can strongly vary according to the local institutional structures, the local interactions for service delivery and the local implementation of control techniques for service delivery.

Contrasting conventional types of standardised benefit provision, which underlay logics of social treatment of unemployment in Bismarckian regimes, we propose three ideal types of local governance in order to determine market-oriented, bureaucratic or participatory activation approaches. The proposed ideal types serve to account for possible distinctions of local procedures in a systematic manner:

> "(…) the construction of a strict logic of instrumental action serves sociology, (…) to understand real social action as a deviation from those processes which would take

place if action was not distracted due to irrationalities of all kinds (affectional action, inaccuracy) from purely rational behaviour. (…) for this purpose sociology needs to construe 'pure' ('ideal') types of those types, which internally show a strict logic of up most consistency, although they will as little appear in reality in this absolute ideally strict form as a physical reaction would take place which is programmed on the premises of an absolutely vacant room." (Weber 1972: 2 and 10; translation SK).

A probe into both hypotheses on the essential role of the local level for the institutionalisation of the Bismarckian activation regime makes empirical inquiries at the local level a sine qua non of the research design. Thus, to explore our assumptions and the mechanisms behind, a focus of this work is put on local case studies in selected continental European countries. At the same time, the Bismarckian welfare state architecture has been pointed out as crucial context for understanding the issues and challenges, which frame practices at the local level in these countries. We can therefore not solely concentrate on the developments at the local level, but we also need to contextualise our local findings by analysing the particular architecture of these Bismarckian countries. The resulting methodological challenge is to combine tasks of thorough and in-depth case studies with a comparative design allowing for some generalisation of developments among continental European welfare states. We selected France and Germany among the continental European countries and conducted four in-depth local case studies on the implementation of activation reforms in the area of minimum income schemes in each of the two countries. We will explain this choice made, by, first, elaborating on the nature and challenges of a qualitative approach to conduct 'local' case studies. Secondly, taking into account these challenges, we put forward our strategy for a comparative qualitative research design which combines in-depth study with possibilities for generalisation. And, finally, we elaborate on the single methodological instruments which are applied for putting this research design to practice, notably by the use of expert interviews and the drafting of detailed case study reports.

5.1 Exploring the local level's role: elements of a case study approach

The practices to device and implement programmes and services for beneficiaries of minimum income schemes at the local level in France and Germany constitute the 'case' this work aims to analyse. To study the mechanisms of local governance of the 'general' minimum income scheme, in each country, four local territories were selected. This procedure thus matches a case study based explanation strategy which is aimed at a comprehensive exploration of a phenomenon:

"To reconstruct a case means to collect all the information that is needed for understanding it." (Gläser and Laudel 2006: 34; SK). A case study is a preferred method to analyse contemporary events that are 'uncontrollable' (in contrast to experiments) (Yin 2007: 15). The purpose of "a case study is best defined as an in-depth study of a single unit (a relatively bounded phenomenon) where the scholar's aim is to elucidate features of a larger class of similar problems." (Gerring 2004: 341).

5.1.1 The strengths of a case study approach: explaining and exploring

Case studies mainly serve explanatory purposes (Gerring 2004; Yin 2007). Case studies thus serve a different purpose than quantitative analysis, which above all concentrates on the calculation of the probability of a causal effect. Being based on a single unit or on small numbers of units, case studies cannot inform on the probability of a causal effect. However, stating a causal argument is not only a matter of estimating causal effects. The construction of a causal argument is also an issue of the exact causal mechanism at work. For the purpose of explaining a case's exact causal mechanisms at work, the research strategy has to be explanatory. Case studies exactly serve this purpose of 'process-tracing'. They unravel and analyse operational links: "Case studies, if well constructed, allow one to peer into the box of causality to the intermediate causes lying between some cause and its purported effect. Ideally, they allow one to 'see' X and Y interact (…)" (Gerring 2004: 348). A case study is therefore able to inform on the existence of a causal relationship of two correlating variables X and Y. It identifies causal mechanisms by providing general knowledge with empirical insights on the way two variables interrelate. By in-depth analysis, case studies thus serve our attempt to gather precise information on causal mechanisms in the process of the local implementation of Bismarckian activation regimes.

A second main characteristic of a case study research strategy is its exploratory nature (Gerring 2004; Yin 2007). Case studies are less useful in proving or disproving a well-established theoretical argument. If a subject is relatively unknown, however, or a new hypothesis is put up, as in the present argument on the relevance of the local implementation processes of the Bismarckian activation regime, an exploratory design is necessary. Different from a strategy of trying to confirm or disconfirm, a case study approach does not necessitate very detailed and specified knowledge on the independent variable. It rather serves to investigate more detailed and specific relationships and mechanism in the course of analysis: "It is the very fuzziness of case studies that grant them a strong advantage in research at exploratory stages, for the single-unit study allows one to test a multitude of hypotheses in a rough-and-ready way." (Gerring 2004: 350). Case studies are therefore 'pilot-studies', 'theory-building' exercise or 'plausibility probes'. As we predominantly find cross-national research on Bismarckian activation regimes (cf. chapter 3.4), local studies on the cases of implementation can produce new insights. Thus, the qualitative case studies' strength of exploring matches our attempt to study local cases in order to analyse the implementation of Bismarckian activation regimes.

In short, the case studies' explanatory and exploratory potential confer to our aim of probing into the crucial local procedures for implementing a Bismarckian activation regime.

5.1.2 Defining the case, unit, levels and timeframe of analysis

Applying a case study design to practice requires definition of the exact case analysed, of the levels and units of analysis focussed on as well as the concrete period of time studied.

The immediate focus of this work thus lays on the case of the implementation of minimum income schemes at the local level in France and Germany. By having defined as case relevant for our interest the general minimum income schemes, we are explicitly renouncing on studying the group or category specific minimum income schemes in France and in Germany. In France, the general minimum income scheme against social exclusion is the 'Revenu de Solidarité Active (RSA), which replaced the former Revenu Minimum d'Insertion (RMI), while in Germany, 'Arbeitslosengeld II' (ALG II; unemployment benefit II) is the general minimum income scheme.

Different levels of analysis are involved in our attempt to analyse the local implementation of activation regimes in Bismarckian welfare states. To clarify the position of the local units for case study in our analysis, it is useful to explain all the levels of analysis relevant for our research design (Gerring 2004: 342): in our case, all continental European welfare states (France, Germany, Italy, Austria, Switzerland and the Benelux countries) make up the 'population' of the analysis. A 'population' consists of a 'sample' distinguishing between unstudied and studied cases. In the present analysis, France and Germany are sampled as cases for study. This sample consists of a certain number of 'units'. A local case of the implementation of Bismarckian activation regimes is situated in a 'unit' of study. A single unit is defined as a spatially bounded phenomenon. In our case, the 'unit' for case study is represented by the local entity whose political and administrative structures are most directly charged with the delivery of services to minimum income recipients. For the purpose of our analysis, the relevant local units are the departments ('Départements') in France and the municipalities ('Kommunen') in Germany. Both local units hold crucial elements of authority for the organisation and planning of delivery of the minimum income schemes RSA and ALG II.

A unit is either observed at a single point in time or it represents a development over a defined period of time. As we want to analyse policy reactions and changes in Bismarckian countries' approaches to increasing numbers of beneficiaries of minimum income schemes, we need to identify reforms that might be of relevance. We identify a significant involvement of the local level in the institutionalisation of Bismarckian activation regimes in particular with regard to the following events: In France, the organisation of the RMI was fully decentralised following reforms during the years 2003–2004. In Germany, in 2005, the ALG II was implemented as a new minimum income scheme entailing important responsibilities for the municipalities. Field research was undertaken in Germany in 2008, and in France in 2009. Therefore, our case studies cover the most important phase of institutionalisation of these central activation reforms in Germany (2005–2008) and France (2004–2009).

A case to be explained is then the local implementation of the activation regime in a local unit. Relevant dimensions of these cases are the events marking the decentralisation of social protection for unemployed, the application of activation reforms, the local usage of decentralisation, the local interactions for service delivery, and the local implementation of control techniques of services. These dimensions are re-constructed in the detailed case studies.

Summing up, the case of the Bismarckian activation regime that we want to study is the institutionalisation of the governance of the RMI/RSA in four local departmental units in France since its crucial decentralisation reforms in 2003–2004 and the governance of the ALG II in four municipal entities in Germany since a key governance reform implemented in 2005. This raises the question on the generalisation of our results with regard to the question of the institutionalisation of Bismarckian activation regimes.

5.2 Proposing a design for the local study of Bismarckian activation regimes

Case studies are meant to expand theories or to 'generalise' an analytical observation (in contrast to statistical generalisation) (Yin 2007: 15) but they face a number of ambiguities and issues to do so (Gerring 2004). Above all, we want to analyse the viability of the argument that activation in Bismarckian countries much depends on developments that take place at the local level. While our demand for an in-depth study corresponds to the ultimate advantages of the case study (Gerring 2004: 348), however, securing a wider scope of a case study-based argument demands particular attention. One of the greatest challenges of a case study design is its representativeness. A well-founded study of our argument is only possible for a small number of units. Therefore, the chosen case study strategy encounters the ambiguous task to inform about the particularity of the single units but also to deliver general knowledge. Ambiguity arises from the case study's inherent character to "study a single unit with intent to shed light upon other units (…)." (Gerring 2004: 344). This raises the issue how we connect the mechanisms found in the local units to other units not studied in-depth, other levels not studied in-depth and other points in time not studied in-depth. The ambiguity of the case study approach requires a solid generalisation strategy for our local findings.

Case studies therefore confront the problem to cope with the distinction between 'two empirical worlds' (Gerring 2004: 344f). By studying cases of the local implementation of activation regimes in continental European countries, we refer in a narrow sense to the empirical world of eight local units. On these units, being central to our analysis of the implementation of the activation regime in a Bismarckian country, we are producing in-depth knowledge. But at the same time, by referring to the local implementation of activation regimes in continental European countries in general, we try to suggest that the mechanisms found in our eight case studies have larger relevance for a quite huge population of adjacent units, that they are connected to different levels and that they interrelate with other points in time. This distinction between 'central' and 'peripheral' empirical worlds is a gradual one introduced by the balance between the case study, being at centre, and the weight given to the peripheral units, levels and points in time of the analysis. Our aim is to 'contextualise' and 'embed' the results of the cases studied within their 'periphery', which refers to past and current practices of the local implementation in general, of the wider implementation of activation regimes in France and Germany, and of the general development of Bismarckian activation regimes in continental Europe. We want to connect our case studies to these 'other' empirical worlds which are, from our perspective, considered as 'peripheral'. However, in contrast to the eight in-depth case studies, these peripheral empirical worlds can only be surveyed in amore superficial manner. Thus, by connecting central and peripheral analysis and by interrelating in-depth insights with general results, our case studies describe a typical 'double function' of the case study design (Gerring 2004: 345). To enable this 'double function' of in-depth study and generalisation, we will (1) cover the various units, levels and points in time of the analysis with different data collection techniques, we apply (2) a comparative, multiple case research design, and we (3) use theory.

5.2.1 Application of various data collection techniques

First, to correspond to the double-function of the case study design, for every level of analysis, different data collection techniques are used (Yin 2007: 46–64). While the case-studies of this work rely on multiple evidence in-depth studies comprising expert interviews and documents, broader developments are described in a more superficial manner. The circumstances of the local implementation of the minimum income schemes in a unit are contextualised by taking into account secondary literature or documents on general past practices of the implementation of the minimum income scheme and with regard to practices in other parallel units. The particular architecture of the implementation of minimum income schemes in France and Germany with regard to the crucial policy fields, levels and actors involved are described by referring to secondary literature. The implementation of the Bismarckian activation regime in general is analysed at the national regime level by the study of secondary literature.

In brief, to enable the double-function of in-depth study and generalisation for our case study approach, we use various data collection techniques to cover the local cases as well as its surrounding local, national and Bismarckian regime context.

5.2.2 Selection of local cases in two 'critical' Bismarckian countries in continental Europe

Second, for our research, we select a multiple cases design in order to strengthen the double-function of the case study (Yin 2007). A comparative research study combines single unit-analysis with an across-unit analysis in a formal manner. The eight local units of case study in France and Germany allow for a 'comparative' study not only in a single country but in two Bismarckian countries. As we not only attempt to study one case, but a series of eight, we distance ourselves from the classical form of a single case study. Apart from the fact of being very demanding in resources and time, however, comparative case studies promise greater analytical benefits. This multiple cases design can take advantage of insights of across-unit analysis of a group of eight cases. Due to this 'replication' design, the robustness of its findings is increased. Furthermore, a careful selection of local units adds to the representativeness of the case series. Selection of local units for comparative studies can follow according to 1) the selection of cases to predict similar results or/and 2) the selection of cases to predict contrasting results but for anticipatable reasons. The eight local cases chosen as units for study were selected according to a most-similar-most-different design (Przeworski and Teune 1970). In the present analysis, criteria for selection of the local units were 'weak' and 'strong' territorial entities. 'Weak' and 'strong' subgroups were distinguished according to criteria of socio-economic development. The idea was to account for some possible local characteristics that might be crucial for the development of the cases and that could be identified beforehand. Hereby, we might account for a further explanatory variable: the local usage of decentralisation might also depend on the socio-economic conditions of a territory. For each country, we selected two local units for the weak as well as two for the strong subgroup. This selection strategy matches requirements of a reliable multiple case study: for comparison, each of the subgroups should at least count two individual cases (Yin 2007: 54). In addition, all local units were selected among urban agglomerations. Long-term unemployment and social exclusion are phenomena very present in urban agglomerations (Häußermann et al. 2008). We therefore assumed actors in these local agglomerations to be sensible to this topic. This comparative, most-similar-most-different multiple local case study design thus serves to increase opportunities for generalisation both from a country specific but also from a cross-country perspective on the local mechanisms relevant for the implementation of a Bismarckian activation regime in France and Germany.

Apart from the selection of most-similar-most-different local cases, France and Germany were chosen as two 'crucial' continental European countries in order to sharpen our argument on the relevance of a local dimension of the Bismarckian activation regime. Selection of two countries of the same welfare state type confers to a 'most similar systems' design (Przeworski and Teune, 1970). For the purpose of comparative study, sampling systems as similar as possible reduces the number of factors accounting for differences: both countries represent 'archetypes' of the status-conserving and industrial risk-community based Bismarckian welfare states. In both countries, a fragmentation of important providers, policies and services fits in many aspects the typical Bismarckian arrangements for social protection and labour market policy (Clegg and Clasen 2006). Furthermore, in the last decade, France and Germany have both introduced important institutional reforms towards an activation of unemployed (Hinrichs 2010; Palier 2010). Apart from belonging to the status-conserving Bismarckian welfare state model, France and Germany, however, show some 'crucial' differences which might provide larger explanatory relevance for the local practices of implementing activation reforms (Gerring 2004: 348). First, Germany and France differ in their state architecture. France is typically characterised by a strong central state (Levy 1999). The relevance of a 'central' state might impose important consequences for local developments, although this generalisation is partly challenged in the field of social- and employment policy (as we will later see). In contrast Germany is a federal state (Schmid et al. 2004). This is relevant for the field of social- and employment policy but this generalisation will also be subject to specification in the following chapters. Secondly, while both countries' general minimum income programmes reflect the Bismarckian subsidiarity principle, they set different priorities. Germany's general minimum income scheme has a legacy of being strongly subsidiary to the family or to work (Behrendt 2002). France, in contrast, has developed a very strong tradition of 'politique d'insertion' (social inclusion policy) (Morel 2004), which accords to the minimum income scheme a backup function to social work and treatment.

In sum, the selection of eight local cases according to a most-similar-most-different approach in two 'critical' Bismarckian countries in continental Europe sets important parameters of a comparative study aimed at synthesising the local mechanisms found in a broader perspective.

5.2.3 The theoretical framework: a guide for the exploratory analysis of local mechanisms

Third, generalisation of the argument of the relevance of the local level for the implementation of the Bismarckian activation regime is increased by guidance of a theoretical framework. In particular on the basis of theory guided arguments more general mechanisms can be pointed out. Theory is a sine qua non of case studies. It helps to specify and orient the inquiry. Moreover, it allows for the kind of 'analytical generalisation' case studies aim at (Yin 2007: 35–40):

> "An important step in all of these replication procedures is the development of a rich, theoretical framework. The framework needs to state the conditions under which a particular phenomenon is likely to be found as well as the conditions when it is not likely to be found. The theoretical framework later becomes the vehicle for generalizing (…). (…) if some of the empirical cases do not work as predicted, modification must be made to the theory." (Yin 2007: 54).

By defining the institutionalisation of local organisational fields as premise for an implementation of the Bismarckian activation regime and by spelling out the conditions for the implementation of possibly varying types of local governance of activation reform, a clear theoretical framework guides the exploratory empirical analysis on the mechanisms of local governance.

To conclude, local practices in eight cases of the implementation of activation regimes in Bismarckian countries are put in a broader perspective by a threefold strategy: first, the general implications of the local findings are increased by additional secondary literature analysis which covers important levels of analysis and different points in time surrounding the local cases. Second, a most-similar-most-different design of eight local units in France and Germany, that represent two crucial Bismarckian welfare states, shall allow for a broader comparison of explanatory factors of the local practices. Third, theoretical assumptions of local organisational fields and different types of local governance guide the analysis on the conditions for the local implementation of activation reforms. Having explained both the essence of local case studies as well as our general design chosen, we close this chapter by explaining the key techniques used for the concrete local inquiry.

5.3 Methods and techniques applied for the local case study series

The case study method possesses the advantage to incorporate a full variety of evidence: documents, artefacts, interviews, and observations can be used as resources to re-construct information on a case (Yin 2007: 15). In general, reliability and validity is increased by referring to multiple sources of evidence (Yin 2007: 98–126). Good case studies will therefore use as many sources as possible (Yin 2007: 115). Principal methods and techniques applied for the eight local case studies were semi-structured expert interviews, qualitative content analysis and case study reports.

5.3.1 Semi-structured expert interviews

For studying cases of the local governance of activation reforms in selected local entities in France and Germany, interviews of the involved actors as well as relevant documents were used as resources. Central insights of our empirical inquiry rely on 80 expert interviews. Experts are defined as persons who possess an outstanding knowledge on a case. Consequently, expert interviews serve as a method to exploit this knowledge (Gläser and Laudel 2006: 10). Interview partners were selected experts occupying central positions in the key organisations involved in local planning and delivery processes of crucial services and policies for recipients of minimum income schemes. After a broad search process via the internet and first contact phone calls, all selected interview partners were contacted by mail and via telephone. Apart from one expert, all experts envisaged for interviews agreed to a conversation. The author of this book normally conducted an interview of one and a half to two hours' duration with only one expert. Interviews took always place in the facilities of the interviewed experts' organisations and were conducted in the language of the country investigated in. Interviews in Germany were conducted between March and July 2008. Interviews in France took place during March till July 2009.

A major concern of the case study interviews and their results was to preserve anonymity of the persons involved. Anonymity is usually not a desirable option as it eliminates some important background information and makes composition of the cases more difficult. Anonymity though serves to protect identities in case of a controversial topic or if research outcomes could (negatively) affect the persons involved. Full anonymity is therefore necessary if the three following options are not possible (Yin 2007: 181f): can the anonymity of individuals alone be sufficient while leaving the case itself identifiable? Is it possible to name the individuals but to avoid attributing any particular point of view or comment to the individual while allowing the case to be identifiable? Is it possible to report only a cross-case analysis instead of single-case reports? As the introduction of labour market and social policy reforms was in both France and Germany a highly controversial topic and the persons interviewed were regularly embedded in a strict organisational hierarchy, full anonymity was an essential and professional condition for retrieving in-depth information from the expert discussions (Gläser and Laudel 2006). Consequently, all three options of limited anonymity were not feasible for the present research. Anonymity therefore has to be guaranteed for the local units studied as well as the actors interviewed.

On the basis of anonymity guarantees, interviews were led as 'guided conversations' on the relevant issues (Yin 2007: 106; Witzel 2000). The non-standardised interviews were conducted along the premises of an interview guideline. Interview guideline based interviews comprise topics to be discussed in the interview and a list of questions (Gläser and Laudel 2006: 39–40). The topics of the field manual aimed to include central questions of the research in a manner that would be practicable for questioning during an expert interview. The interviews were conducted as semi-structured interviews (Mayring 2005). This means that the phrasing and order of the questions varied from one interview to another. The advantage of semi-structured interviews is to give the expert room for narration while nonetheless focussing the discussion on relevant issues. Thereby, a dense and interrelated informational basis on a case was retrieved. The interviews were recorded with a digital recording device. For documentary reasons of the research process and for further analysis, all interviews were transliterated[2].

2 Transliteration followed a coherent set of rules. The following basic rules applied for transliteration: Interviews were completely and word by word transliterated in their

In short, central insight of the empirical inquire rely on the results of overall 80 semi-structured expert interviews in four local entities in France and four local entities in Germany. These interviews were conducted with local experts involved in the implementation of activation reforms.

5.3.2 Qualitative content analysis and case study reports

Analysis and interpretation of the empirical raw data, which comprised both the full interview transcripts[3] and the collected documents, proceeded according to central methodological steps of qualitative content analysis (Mayring 2005; Witzel 1996). This procedure served the goal of a structured and comparable integration of the empirical raw data in single, detailed case study reports on each local entity studied (Yin 2007). At the centre of this method is the process of 'explication' of the collected raw material (Mayring 2005). As a basis for analysis, an analytical grid is constructed according to preliminary theoretical ideas. 'Explication' means to scan a text, which in our case consisted of the full interview transcripts, with regard to information that can be accorded to categories of the analytical grid. Via the process of extraction, information is taken from the text analysed. Thereby, the theory-based system of categories of an analytical grid is a rather flexible instrument. This means, it can be altered throughout the process of extraction, notably by creating and remodelling categories, if relevant information is discovered that had not been anticipated. In line with this method of 'explication', the eight case study reports for France and Germany were structured according to cross-case, transversal issues under which information were subsumed. The aim of this procedure was to construct an informational basis different form the original text of the transcript. The informational basis was on the one hand guided by the preliminary theoretical ideas but on the other hand it was influenced by the collected information from the empirical material, too (Gläser and Laudel 2006: 191–211). In the end, it comprised the relevant information needed for answering the research question. Qualitative content analysis and structured and detailed case study reports increase reliability and comparison of the research (Yin 2007: 81).

---

original version, standard orthography of the language of origin was used and no literal rewording was applied. Non-verbal expressions were only transliterated if they were of relevance for a statement. Interruptions of an interview were marked in the transcript and incomprehensive sections were marked as "(…)".

3 Upon request, access to full interview transcripts can be made available by the author.

In the present work, based on theoretical arguments hypotheses were formulated with regard to the empirical analysis. Validation, falsification or modification of the hypotheses will proceed according to the empirical analysis illustrated in the following chapters. The presentation of the empirical material for this work will proceed as condensed presentation of the eight written case study reports. To embed the detailed case studies in their particular welfare state context, the case studies are preceded by a general discussion of the evolution of the generalised minimum income schemes in the French and German welfare state. This introduction is followed by stylised presentations of each single written case study report. Each case study responds to the reconstruction of the relevant local dimensions of this research: the local usage of decentralisation, the local interactions for service delivery, and the local implementation of control techniques of services. For a better coherence, we dedicate separate sections to the French and the German presentations. At the end of each country section, country results are discussed in cross-case analyses (Yin 2007: 170–175). The conclusion of this book then serves the purpose of synthesising the results of the local studies in France and Germany by pointing out to an explanatory model of the mechanisms of the local institutionalisation of Bismarckian activation regimes.

In brief, qualitative content analysis, case study reports and the construction of theoretical hypotheses serve to assess in a systematic way the empirical information retrieved from the interview transcripts and the documents studied.

To summarise, a main technique for data collection on the local implementation of services and programmes to activate recipients of minimum income schemes were semi-structured interviews with 80 experts involved in the local governance. The collected raw material for each local unit studied was analysed according to qualitative content analysis and it was transformed into detailed case studies. This method permitted a structuring of the empirical raw material in single detailed case study reports in a comparative manner according to an analytical grid. Eight detailed case studies resulted from this procedure each describing a local case of the implementation of the minimum income scheme in France and Germany. Embedded in the context of French and German social and labour market policy development, in order to investigate the assumptions made in the theoretical part and to deepen our understanding of relevant procedures, the detailed case studies are presented in the following empirical part.

5.4 Conclusion: combining local study and welfare state analyses

The aim of this chapter was to make explicit the methodological approach for analysing the local implementation of a Bismarckian activation regime. The challenge was to find an approach combining our argument of the relevance of local practices to activate recipients of minimum income schemes with the general development of Bismarckian activation regimes (cf. Tab. 3). A comparative, qualitative case study design was identified as an instrument to account both for the possibility of in-depth case study of the local governance of minimum income schemes as well as to offer opportunities for generalisation. In the present work, we are studying the local case of the implementation of the minimum income scheme 'RMI'/'RSA' in four French local authorities and the local practices of the implementation of the minimum income scheme 'ALG II' in four municipalities in Germany.

Tab. 3. Research design

<table>
<tr><td rowspan="10">T
H
E
O
R
Y</td><td>METHO-
DOLOGY</td><td colspan="10">EMPIRICAL RESEARCH</td><td rowspan="10">T
H
E
O
R
Y
-
B
U
I
L
D
I
N
G</td></tr>
<tr><td>Most Similar Welfare Systems</td><td colspan="8">Two Bismarckian Countries</td><td rowspan="4">Secondary Literature, Documents</td><td rowspan="7">P
E
R
I
P
H
E
R
Y
C
E
N
T
R
A
L</td></tr>
<tr><td rowspan="3">Crucial Cases</td><td colspan="4">France</td><td colspan="4">Germany</td></tr>
<tr><td colspan="4">Central State</td><td colspan="4">Federal State</td></tr>
<tr><td colspan="4">MIS as Backup of Social Inclusion Policy</td><td colspan="4">MIS Subsidiary to Family and Work</td></tr>
<tr><td>Most-similar local systems</td><td colspan="8">Urban Agglomerations</td><td rowspan="3">Interviews, Case-study Reports, Documents Secondary Literature</td></tr>
<tr><td rowspan="2">Most-similar-most-different Local Systems</td><td>F-A</td><td>F-B</td><td>F-C</td><td>F-D</td><td>G-A</td><td>G-B</td><td>G-C</td><td>G-D</td></tr>
<tr><td>strong</td><td>weak</td><td>strong</td><td>weak</td><td>weak</td><td>strong</td><td>strong</td><td>weak</td></tr>
<tr><td colspan="11">PROBING ALONG TWO HYPOTHESES</td></tr>
<tr><td colspan="11">EXPLORING ALONG TWO HYPOTHESES</td></tr>
</table>

Source: own representation.

Aiming at a 'double-function' of in-depth study and generalisation we use multiple sources of empirical data comprising expert interviews, case study reports, documentary analysis and study of secondary literature. Dense information on the local units studied was gathered by techniques of documentary analysis and 80 interviews with experts from key organisations involved in the local governance of the minimum income scheme. Based on techniques of qualitative content analysis, the empirical raw material for each local unit studied was transformed in detailed case study reports. Proceeding according to a common analytical grid, eight detailed reports structured in a comparative manner for analysis were written. For comparative purposes 'weak' and 'strong' local units for study were selected according to a most-similar-most-different design.

Simultaneously, generalisation of the local mechanisms is aimed for at a more general level by the following steps. To account for the 'national' architecture surrounding the local governance of minimum income schemes, France and Germany were selected as 'critical' cases among the continental European welfare states. Both countries are 'critical' cases as – apart from their commonality of belonging to the Bismarckian model – they can be distinguished in important matters: with regard to issues of the local governance of the minimum income scheme, further explanatory value might arise from the fact that France is a centralised country with a pronounced tradition of a 'social inclusion policy' for minimum income recipients while Germany is a federal country with a minimum income scheme more strongly based on regulation for family and work responsibilities. We will thus not only account for the local developments but, based on secondary analysis, we will also discuss these contextual conditions. Combining both results from the in-depth local case studies and the contextual welfare state conditions will allow retrieving interrelated mechanism, drawing comparisons and generalisation of the empirical inquiry.

Furthermore, generalisation is enhanced by our preliminary theoretical assumptions. We assumed that the local governance of services and policies to activate recipients of minimum income schemes will depend on certain conditions. First of all, it requires the institutionalisation of local organisational fields with different actors, policy fields and levels intervening for a local co-production of services to recipients. Secondly, we formulated the assumption of varying local practices to realise the implementation of activating programmes and services. Conditions for a market-oriented, a bureaucratic and also a participatory pattern of activation were construed. Along the lines of these two hypotheses, the empirical analysis thus serves to test and further explore our argument of the relevance of the local level for the implementation of activation regimes in Bismarckian countries.

The following empirical part is therefore introduced by a description of the national and territorial labour market and social policy situation which contextualises the local governance of minimum income schemes in France and Germany. It is followed by the presentation of eight detailed case studies on the local governance of the minimum income schemes in France and Germany each represented in one separate section. The empirical part concludes with country-specific comparisons of the local procedures of the case studied. A broader comparison of the results for France and Germany as two Bismarckian welfare states will be discussed in the last chapter.

6. The traditional role of minimum income schemes in France and Germany

In both France and Germany, the delivery of benefits and services towards unemployed and persons at risk of exclusion is traditionally framed by strong differences in the distribution of competences among levels of government, in the role of public providers and private actors, and the specific characteristics of policies and social protection programmes. Taken together, these three categories define the particular and established context a local co-production for the recipients of minimum income schemes is confronted with in these Bismarckian welfare states (cf. chapter 4.2.2). In the following, we identify this context of the inter-organisation of benefit schemes, active labour market policy services and social services in France and Germany *before* crucial social and labour market reforms took place.

6.1 A circumscribed field: unemployment policy in France and Germany

The traditional organisation of benefits, policies and services for the unemployed in France and Germany corresponds to a typical Bismarckian labour market policy for workers (Clasen and Clegg 2006; Clasen and Clegg 2003; Daguerre and Taylor-Gooby 2003). In both countries, the organisation of policies and services has been strongly influenced by Bismarckian corporatist institutions.

6.1.1 Corporatist institutions in social and labour market policy in France and Germany

In France, the social partners take an extremely important position in the management of the contribution-financed public unemployment insurance (Clasen and Clegg 2006: 536–538). The French unemployment insurance, UNEDIC ('Union nationale interprofessionnelle pour l'emploi dans l'industrie et le commerce'), has been a private institution, entirely financed out of contributions by workers and employers since 1984. This has so far legitimised the social partners to de facto act alone on important decisions as for example changes to unemployment benefits and contributions. The state would then validate such collective agreements for the generalisation across all firms, but be kept out from further 'political interference'. This is why the French central state, at the same time, has always held tightly to other competencies in unemployment policy, for example over placement, which was organised by a separated National Employment Agency ('Agence Nationale pour l'Emploi', ANPE) (Clasen and Clegg 2006: 536–538).

In Germany, the state has traditionally exerted a much larger influence on the unemployment insurance system than in France. Like in France, unemployment insurance has been funded by employers and employees, too. But eventually arising annual deficits have usually been covered out of revenues from general taxation (Clasen and Clegg 2006: 538–539). In Germany, it is primarily the Bismarckian corporatism in the political economy, which produces a bias towards industrial social and labour market policy (Clasen and Clegg 2006: 538–539). Germany's unemployment insurance has been tightly coupled to the collective wage bargaining system. Insured unemployed are by rule protected against being forced to accept a job-offer below the wage reached in collective bargaining (Eichhorst et al. 2008b). This regulation has served as an important prerogative for the functioning of the industrial relations system.

In conclusion, labour market and unemployment policy in both France and Germany is influenced by a strong industrial bias. In France, the autonomous role of social partners in predominantly self-financed unemployment insurance schemes influences crucial aspects of unemployment policy. In Germany, the regulation of unemployment protection and policy is influenced by devolved governance structures or structures of the political economy of wage bargaining in Germany.

6.1.2 Services and programmes for 'normal' unemployed in France and Germany

In France and Germany, the industrial bias in labour market and social policy was expressed by the fact that important benefits for the unemployed were to a great extent unconditional in order to guarantee occupational protection for both insured unemployed and working insiders. As a result, also services of active labour market policy were de facto offered on a voluntary basis. Active labour market policy had a legacy of functioning as a social treatment (Daguerre and Taylor-Gooby 2003: 629; Eichhorst et al. 2008b: 18; Clegg 2007) of unemployment: programmes and services for active labour market policy were typically tailored to uphold the status of the core labour force. In line with this social treatment approach, in France and Germany, important resources were in the past allocated to programmes of further training, early retirement schemes, education schemes or subsidized jobs (Bonoli 2010; Clasen and Clegg 2003; Daguerre and Taylor-Gooby 2003: 629; Eichhorst et al. 2008b: 18; Erhel and Zajdela 2004: 129).

In Germany, services of active labour market policy and status-oriented unemployment benefits were always delivered by a single Federal Employment Agency. In the past, the organisation's rationale, management and staff strongly identified with voluntary service offers to core-workers (Ludwig-Mayerhofer 2005: 110). While unemployment benefit regulation for the insured unemployed stipulated some 'demanding' and 'enabling' elements, they were rarely applied by the public employment service (Eichhorst et al. 2008b). For a long time, services of the Federal Employment Agency were in practice offered on a voluntary basis only to those insured unemployed who were actually inclined to take part in the active labour market policy programmes (Ludwig-Mayerhofer 2005).

In France, the non-conditionality of unemployment benefits and active labour market policy was mirrored by an organisational separation of the private social insurance institutions (UNEDIC) and its local pay offices (Association pour l'Emploi Dans l'Industrie et le Commerce, ASSEDIC) from separate central state-run agencies for placement (ANPE) and training (AFPA, 'Association pour la formation professionnelle des adultes'). In contrast to Germany, this led to greater, although unsystematic attempts of the state-run services to dedicate its programmes also towards those unemployed excluded from social insurance, as for example recipients of minimum income benefits (Daguerre and Taylor-Gooby 2003: 631).

In short, services and benefit programmes towards unemployed in both Germany and France have been typically based on the principles of a social treatment of unemployment which is not only expressed by regulation but also by the rationale of important organisations.

6.1.3 Conclusion: status-oriented unemployment policy fields in France and Germany

To conclude, in both France and Germany, an interrelated structure of unemployment benefits as well as programmes and services of active labour market policy typically defined a distinct field of unemployment and labour market policy geared towards the status protection of unemployed. Competences for labour market policy were concentrated at the national level and social partners played an important role in the governance of this policy field. In Germany, the logic of a social treatment of unemployment was implemented by the Federal Employment Agency. This agency served unemployed receiving status-based benefits and it offered de facto 'voluntary' services. In France, the logic of a social treatment of unemployment was implemented by different national bodies: The private insurance institution (UNEDIC) and its pay offices (ASSEDIC) delivered benefits to the insured. The training agency (AFPA) and the placement agency (ANPE) delivered programmes to both insured and non-insured unemployed.

6.2 A field apart: minimum income schemes in France and Germany

In France and Germany, means-tested minimum income benefits shared the typical traits of residual, subsidiary and isolated continental European social assistance regimes (Saraceno 2002; Mignione et al. 2002; cf. chapter 2.3.2.2). The organisation of minimum income schemes was in both countries strongly divided from the administration of other social security benefits and differed from the organisation of 'normal' unemployment policy. Nonetheless, distinct social welfare systems still showed some important differences between France and Germany.

6.2.1 The traditional role of the general minimum income scheme in France

In France, regulation of the means-tested general minimum income scheme (RMI), which was introduced in 1988, was rooted in a broader concept of social exclusion. A tradition of 'politique d'insertion' based the French regulation of minimum income assistance on a rationale that did not establish a direct link between lack of income and unemployment (Morel 2004). While regulation encompassed formal activity requirements, it referred to work only in a more indirect manner (Clasen and Clegg 2003: 376). Instead, minimum income assistance regulation was strongly rooted in the idea of social 'insertion' (Erhel and Zajdela 2004; Enjolras et al. 2001). In the realm of 'insertion', social rehabilitation played a significant role in the regulation of the French minimum income assistance regime: "(…) here lack of income is considered a symptom of problems requiring solutions other than just obtaining a job. In these systems availability for work is integrated, and sometimes substituted, with other requirements concerning health, education or housing." (Mignione et al. 2002: 21). In France, the social treatment of unemployment was thus paralleled by a 'social work' dimension for minimum income recipients (Clegg and Palier 2012). Social insertion was the guiding principle for the general minimum income programme (RMI) (Daguerre and Taylor-Gooby 2003: 629).

In line with this social insertion logic, the implementation of minimum income assistance has strongly reflected the policy field's rationale of social work. The introduction of the general minimum income scheme (RMI) in 1988 indeed 'universalised' the prior system of largely discretionary, local 'social help' in France (Clegg and Palier 2012). Although social assistance benefit was universalised through national regulation and the delivery by state-run field services, the French minimum income scheme continued being strongly embedded in a local culture of social work. At the local level, the system confirmed the strongly institutionalised role for the intervention of social workers (Mingione et al. 2002: 58). Social workers typically accounted for the benefit delivery by the central state-run field services and they also accounted for the social counselling offers, which were organised by a local authority (départements).

While the state and its central state-run field services dominated the provision of the general minimum income scheme and the local authority was responsible for the social services attached to it, the third sector's role remained rather limited in the French social welfare system (Fraisse 2009; Mingione et al. 2002: 58). The originally weak third sector involvement in the social work services, which were run parallel to the general minimum income scheme, has been explained by the historically marginalized role of the church in France (Bahle 2003). In France, the church did not set up important welfare organisations. The French Revolution and the separation between the church and the state in 1905, limited the Catholic Church's scope of activity in social welfare to a 'private' matter towards its believers. Instead, social services in France were always marked by a stronger public role. A third sector for social service delivery has nonetheless evolved in France, but it is described as not well organised in representative bodies and influenced by very different ideologies (Bode 2006; Fraisse 2009).

Summarising the disparate position of the means-tested general minimum income scheme in France, its organisation can be described as a 'centrally-regulated local system of welfare' (Mingione et al. 2002: 58). Decoupled from labour market policy and social insurance institutions, the introduction of a general means-tested minimum income programme in 1988 institutionalised by central regulation the principle of social 'reinsertion' for persons at risk of social exclusion. This idea of rehabilitation, social work and social treatment of assistance benefit recipients has been mirrored by a form of delivery that embedded minimum income benefits in the social welfare system. The original system of delivery of the general minimum income scheme (RMI) was organised by a delivery of benefits through central state run social field services and asocial treatment by social workers of local services.

6.2.2 The traditional role of the general minimum income scheme in Germany

Similar to the situation in France, also in Germany regulation of the general minimum income scheme against social exclusion, which was introduced by law in 1962, strongly differed from the occupation-related logic of the dominant social security institutions. However, social assistance in Germany was rather loosely footed on the idea of being an instrument of social rehabilitation. Instead, it was much more strongly defined as being subsidiary to family solidarity and 'self-help'. By demanding the support of the wider family in case of individual neediness, family solidarity was strongly stipulated in the German minimum income legislation (Behrendt 2002: 181). Furthermore, in contrast to the French 'politique d'insertion', the German minimum income assistance system established a direct link between lack of income and the fact of being unemployed (Buhr 1999: 224–227; Saraceno 2002: 21). The principle of 'self-help' formulated the idea that social assistance should not function as a permanent alternative to income independent from the labour market (Behrendt 2002: 179; Buhr 1999: 224–227; Saraceno 2002: 21).

While the introduction of national regulation for minimum income assistance was aimed at reducing differences in the level and administrative practices of benefits against social exclusion, in contrast to France, however, the delivery of the minimum income benefit and its attached policies and services remained more strongly rooted at the local level. Despite the introduction of a general minimum income programme, the federal state's role in the organisation of the benefit provision and its attached policies and services was limited to setting legal frameworks (Behrendt 2002; Mingione et al. 2002: 63). Minimum income benefits therefore remained embedded in the structure of a much decentralised German social welfare system that has traditionally accorded municipalities as well as regions an important role. Following up on their traditional role for 'social aid', the communes (*Kommunen*) and also the regions respectively states (*Länder*) remained to a large degree in charge for minimum income assistance (Behrendt 2002: 179) as well as for important social services (e.g. child care, psychological care, housing).

Compared to France, a further particularity of this German local social welfare system is the strongly institutionalised role of the third sector both in services and in local policies (Zimmer et al. 2009). Historical cooperation between the third sector organisations and local authorities for 'social aid' to the undeserving poor or extreme outsiders has evolved into a powerful 'welfare corporatism' in public social service delivery and policies towards persons at risk of exclusion.

The prominent role of the third sector is explained by historical religious heterogeneity (Bahle 2003). In the course of time, the Protestant and Catholic Church had developed dense networks of welfare services. In the Weimar Republic these services became part of the public system. Today, the concept of subsidiarity guarantees these organisations a prominent legal status in many areas of social service delivery (Bahle 2003; Bode 2006; Zimmer et al. 2009). Accordingly, third sector organisations have been strongly implicated in public social service provision in areas such as healthcare, psychological care, housing, leisure activities or school education. While the third sector remained subordinate to public intervention, its organisations have retained an important complementary role and receive substantial public funding (Mingione et al. 2002: 63). Thereby, the third sector has gained such a large autonomy which makes it carry traits of an independent 'semi-public institution': "(…) in Germany local communities are dealing with a highly organised and internally closely cooperating non-profit sector that is able to establish an oligopolistic, often even monopolist, system of local service provision." (Bahle 2003: 13). Thus, traditionally, the third sector has been strongly involved in the local policies and services which are run in parallel to the minimum income scheme.

In a development, which was largely decoupled from the activities of the Federal Employment Agency (Czommer et al. 2005: 14–17; Schmid et al. 2004), since the 1990s, the German local authorities and the third sector organisations began to initiate approaches for work integration for minimum income recipients (Voges et al. 2001). As increased numbers of benefit recipients increasingly presented a problem for the locally financed minimum income assistance budget, job placement developed as an own area of social work in many communes (Kantel 2008: 99). "In the meantime it can be said that at the municipal level (…) a substantial level of contacts, networks, knowledge and experience has been accumulated, particularly in the area of labour market integration of groups that tend to be excluded from the labour market." (Schmid et al. 2004: 177). These initiatives remained, however, bounded to the system of a social treatment of unemployment (Hanesch 2001: 183–185; Kemmerling and Bruttel 2005; Schmid 2006; Voges et al. 2001). Mostly publicly subsidized work-schemes often promoted a different goal than the integration into the rigid regular labour market. Figuring prominently among these initiatives was the municipal practice to temporarily subsidise employment in order to (re-)establish social assistance seekers' eligibility to status-oriented unemployment benefits financed by the Federal Employment Agency and the state (Buhr 1999: 224–227; Gangl 1998: 216, 226; Kantel 2008: 99).

Summing up, the disparate position of minimum income schemes in Germany is described as a 'network-based local system of welfare' (Mignione et al. 2002: 63). The idea of self-help by referring to family solidarity or taking up employment guided the German social assistance regime. In parallel to its subsidiary and means-tested logic, also the minimum income programme's system of delivery reflected traditional traits of a social welfare system. National regulation only set a framework to guarantee some uniformity for benefits while benefit provision and its attached services and policies were organised by municipalities, the states and an important third sector. Despite its premises for 'self-help', the implementation of the minimum income scheme remained nonetheless connected to the prevalent logic of a social treatment of unemployment and minimum income receipt. Temporarily subsidised public employment initiatives by the local authorities often served the goal to (re-)establish assistance recipients' claims on status-oriented unemployment benefits.

6.3 Conclusion: a Bismarckian legacy of fragmented providers, services and policies

To conclude, the institutionalisation of local organisational fields to co-produce targeted activation services for minimum income benefit recipients in France and Germany confronts challenges of typically fragmented institutions of labour market policy and social protection.

Typical characteristics of rigid Bismarckian labour markets mirror in the regulation and organisation of benefits and services to unemployed in France and Germany. Means-tested, minimum income assistance in France and Germany reveals a 'strong cleavage' (Behrendt 2002: 178) with regard to status-oriented arrangements for unemployed. Rather closed and highly centrally organised structures define labour market policies, social insurance programmes and active labour market services towards 'workers'. In the governance of labour market and unemployment policy, social partners play an important role. Accordingly, active labour market policy programmes rely on training, subsidised employment or further education for the status-protection of core workers. In Germany, this institutional complementarity was manifested by the Federal Employment Agency's activities of voluntary and status-conserving offers of active labour market policy alongside the delivery of status-based benefits. In France, the deliberate nature of active labour market policy was enhanced by an organisational separation between the exclusively corporate insurance institution and a state-led placement agency.

Typical for the Bismarckian countries, in France and Germany, the administration of means-tested minimum income benefits was in the past strongly decoupled from the providers, programmes and policies for the 'normal' unemployed. In both countries, the minimum income benefit scheme exemplified the traits of a residual and subsidiary continental European minimum income assistance regime. In France and Germany, minimum income benefits were embedded in distinct social welfare systems. These social welfare systems though structured in some aspects differently in Germany and France. In Germany, the subsidiarity principle in assistance regulation stipulated stronger demands of family solidarity or 'self-help'. Furthermore, in the German federal state, the provision of benefits and its attached policies and services, was primarily a matter of the local authorities and third sector organisations. Benefits remained in practice decoupled from services, e.g. from social services delivered by 'quasi-public' but autonomous not for-profit welfare organisations. In France, social assistance was regulated by the principle of 'social insertion' making benefit receipt an instrument of social work and rehabilitation. Social field services for benefit provision were organised by central government while delivery of the generalised minimum income programme was locally embedded in a social work system dominated by the interventions of social workers.

Turning from the illustration of this traditionally disparate role of minimum income schemes from 'normal unemployment policy', attempts to institutionalise employment-centred welfare for minimum income recipients are in the following analysed for France and Germany.

7. The institutionalisation of employment-centred welfare in Germany

In the following parts, it is analysed how recent labour market and social policy reforms are introduced in Germany in order to react to increased numbers of recipients of minimum income benefits (cf. Fig. 1). We investigate into the introduction of activation policies and attempts of re-organising the traditional approaches towards unemployed and persons at the risk of social exclusion.

7.1 Labour market- and social policy reforms in Germany

Reacting to a longer trend of rising minimum income benefit recipients, new government priorities for employment policy have been introduced in Germany (Jacobi and Mohr 2007: 227). Especially a series of reforms during the years 2002 till 2005, which are referred to as 'Hartz' reforms, introduced radical changes to German labour market and social policy. According to Eichhorst et al. (2008a) and Jacobi and Mohr (2008) these reforms aim to react to the problem of unemployment by giving priority to work-first strategies:

> "(...) the aim of this reform was to lower unemployment but also to ease the burden of taxation and non-wage labour costs by reducing benefit dependency. The major lever to achieve this goal was the shortening of individual unemployment spells through accelerated job placement and more coherent activation of the beneficiaries (...)." (Eichhorst et al. 2008a: 23).

Challenging the traditional approaches of a social treatment of unemployment, these reforms comprise a series of different reform programmes which are identified as a shift towards activating labour market and social policies (Dingeldey 2007; Ludwig-Mayerhofer 2005). Impacting on the internal and external filter of minimum income schemes, changes concern the benefit system, the labour market, work incentives and services.

7.1.1 A reformed entitlement structure of the benefit system

Significant changes in the entitlement structures of protection against unemployment have taken place in the course of the Hartz reforms (Eichhorst et al. 2008a; Barbier and Knuth 2011b). Principles of status- and job protection by unemployment benefits were radically circumscribed. A shorter but still generous contribution-financed unemployment insurance scheme remains in place only for the short-term unemployed (Unemployment Benefit I, UB I). Apart from some exceptions[4], the maximum duration of this insurance-based unemployment benefit was reduced to one year. Being subject to strict eligibility criteria, this status-based benefit is reserved for those unemployed who have acquired a steady contribution record to the insurance scheme. Apart from the changes of the unemployment insurance programme, however, the most significant reform programme (Hartz IV) suggested the pooling of social assistance and former unemployment assistance. This newly created benefit scheme (Unemployment Benefit II, UB II) introduced a tax-funded, means-tested and flat-rate minimum income benefit at the level of prior social assistance as support for the long-term unemployed. Benefit recipients of former income-related protection for long-term unemployed (Unemployment Assistance, UA) and of former means-tested social assistance became eligible to the new minimum income scheme. Most of the assistance seekers who had been relying on the former scheme of means-tested social assistance became recipients of the new minimum income scheme. This was due to a new and very broad definition of the 'ability to work' introduced by the reform. It excludes only those persons from the new minimum income scheme who are judged not being able to work at least three hours a day, who have reached the age of retirement, and who do not have a work permit as they are asylum seekers. For each of these three groups separated category specific programmes persist which are social assistance schemes with a rather limited scope of recipients. The majority but not all benefit recipients of the new minimum income scheme are long-term unemployed. Freshly unemployed persons, who had an unsteady employment record, a low-income or no employment at all usually have to rely on the new minimum income scheme as well. This is due to the stricter eligibility criteria of contribution-based unemployment benefit I, which was tightened as part of the reform.

While unemployment insurance (Unemployment Benefit I) remains in place for those with strong contribution records, Unemployment Benefit II thus presents a new generalised minimum income scheme for the weaker groups of the labour market, long-term unemployed, and otherwise disadvantaged groups of society. In this new system, only a very restricted role is left to category specific programmes, namely for older persons, those not capable to work and asylum seekers.

---

4 Privileges of longer periods of benefit receipt were reintroduced for older unemployed in the aftermath of the reform.

7.1.2 A new organisation of services and work incentives

In particular the new generalised minimum income scheme (UB II) for those at the general risk of exclusion has been at the focus of activation reforms. Compared to these changes, unemployment insurance (UB I) was not decisively remodelled, and the three small category specific social assistance programmes for asylum seekers, old persons and those not fit for work even remain disconnected from a new work orientation.

Regulation of the new minimum income scheme is guided by the idea of 'demanding' and 'enabling' elements for the benefit recipients' activation into work. The legal regulations (German Social Code II and Social Code III) bring together abroad range of workfare and service elements for the activation of benefit recipients (Dingeldey 2007; Eichhorst et al. 2008b; Ludwig-Mayerhofer 2005). Carrying on a principle of former social assistance regulation, the main idea of the new minimum income scheme is that beneficiaries shall solve neediness through 'self-help' either by employment or wider family responsibilities (Knuth 2009). Conditionality is therefore an important criterion of benefit payments. Numerous elements stress the benefit recipients' individual activity requirements. Overall, regulation aims to promote the (re-) integration into the labour market. For this purpose, acceptability requirements for suitable work are defined in a very broad manner. In contrast to recipients of the status conserving insurance scheme against unemployment (UB I), benefit recipients of the minimum income scheme (UB II) are required to accept jobs paid below the rate of collective wage agreements or the wages normally paid in a region. Also the signature of integration contracts is mandatory for benefit claimants. A sanction regime exists for the non-compliance of benefit recipients. Sanctions comprise the temporary deduction of benefit payments or, in case of repeated violations, a three step suppression of benefit payment. Young unemployed (under 25) can be sanctioned by complete benefit withdrawal already upon a first breach of rules. A sanctioned person having temporarily lost his or her complete rights to cash benefits can ask for in-kind benefits instead. Sanctions are provided for in cases of breaching duties of declaration, denial to accept job-offers, decline to participate in active labour market policy programmes, refusal to sign integration contracts or deviation from agreed on contracted activities (Eichhorst et al. 2008b).

In principle, minimum income benefit recipients have access to basically the same set of active labour market policy programmes (German Social Code III) as offered to the short-term unemployed. To enable minimum income benefit recipients to take-up work, a set of supporting activities is proposed (Dingeldey 2007; Eichhorst et al. 2008b; Ludwig-Mayerhofer 2005). Active labour market policy instruments comprise training schemes, programmes of further education, start-up grants and mobility grants. Further activities that can be offered to those persons who do not immediately find a job are low paid workfare community jobs ('Arbeitsgelegenheiten mit Mehraufwandsentschädigung'). Low paid workfare community jobs can also serve to test the benefit claimants' willingness to work. A workfare community job usually lasts three to six months. A benefit recipient shall work no longer than eight month in a workfare community job. In addition, another instrument of publicly subsidised employment retains the possibility of granting a regular income being subject to social contributions (Arbeitsgelegenheiten in der Entgeltvariante). Apart from this set of active labour market policy instruments, as a peculiarity of the new organisation, also social welfare services shall be made available to assist benefit recipients. These services comprise coverage of 'reasonable' costs for housing. They can also include further social measures as for instance debt counselling, child-care, drug counselling or psychological assistance. Finally, the regulation orders that benefit recipients' access to jobs or the social welfare and active labour market policy programmes, shall be facilitated and imposed by both active (personal) placement and case management.

While a similar set of services is offered to both insured and means-tested unemployed, work requirements are much stronger for the means-tested unemployed than for the insured. Regulation of the new means-tested minimum income scheme stipulates a strong coupling of benefits with work incentives and services.

7.1.3 Increased flexibilisation of the German labour market

In parallel to work requirements and a focus on services, the German labour market has become less rigid. Greater flexibility was introduced in labour market regulation albeit in a 'selective' manner (Clegg 2007). This is evidenced by an important increase of forms of atypical employment. Instruments for greater labour market flexibility as 'making-work pay' schemes (Mini- and Midi Jobs) or temporary employment tend to focus exclusively on lower-income segments or are explicitly applied for weaker groups of the labour market (Eichhorst et al. 2008b). Furthermore, low earners support by complementary payments of the general minimum income scheme (UB II) indeed presents an instrument of "hidden subsidies for low-paid jobs of 11 billion Euros annually." (Barbier and Knuth 2011a: 6).

Thus, similar to the reforms of the entitlement structure, the introduction of greater labour market flexibility centres on opportunities for the activation into employment of long-term unemployed and weaker groups of society who are dependent or at risk of dependency of the new minimum income scheme.

7.1.4 The selective focus of a Bismarckian activation regime in Germany

Despite the far-reaching changes in labour markets, social policy and active labour market policy in Germany, the rather 'selective' (Clegg 2007) focus on the activation of weaker and more vulnerable groups illustrates the difficulties of a typically Bismarckian country to reform its distinguished structures of status-based social and labour market policy in a broader manner (cf. chapter 6.1). A full harmonisation and integration of the different benefit systems and services for all unemployed could not be realised due to opposition of actors in the national bargaining process which led to the reforms. While the general ideas of the German labour market reforms are regarded as an outcome of European learning processes, the governance structures were a result of difficult negotiations in the corporatist and multilevel system of the German welfare state (Fleckenstein 2008). Questions of efficient governance of labour market and social policies coincided with the traditional distribution of authority in the multi-level system of the German welfare state, institutionalised interests, and the strong division between tax-financed and contribution-based logics in the financing of the social security system (Czommer et al. 2005). The negotiated governance structures illustrate the persisting influence of the structures of the distinct policy fields of status-based unemployment policy and social welfare policy. Fragmentation therefore persists between benefit regulation, administrative structures and services of the insurance-based (UB I) and a means-tested system (UB II) against the risk of unemployment (Knuth 2009).

In contrast to reforms in France (cf. chapter 8.1), however, by the merging of tax-financed former status-based long-term unemployment assistance and tax-financed social assistance, the changes achieved a more far-reaching national framework for the integration of benefits, social welfare and unemployment policy into one organisational field for the activation of weaker and more vulnerable groups.

7.1.5 Conclusion: activation as new filter against minimum income receipt in Germany

Summing up, the German labour market and social policy reforms fit into typical Bismarckian attempts to institutionalise a new, employment-centred filter as alternative to minimum income benefit receipt for weaker and more vulnerable groups (cf. chapter 3.5). While the German labour market and social policy reforms did not principally call into question the fragmented benefit system for unemployed typical for a Bismarckian welfare state, the changes have fundamentally remodelled the benefit system. As a full integration or greater harmonisation of benefits and services for all unemployed was blocked, it persists a status-protecting unemployment scheme (UB I) insuring core-workers which has however been limited in extent. At the same time, the Hartz reforms have led to the creation of a new generalised minimum income scheme, which pools social assistance and previously status-based unemployment assistance. As a result of the reforms, the social protection claims of long-term unemployed and other groups at the risk of exclusion are now referred to this general minimum income scheme. At the same time, the reforms put a focus on an increased application of placement, active labour market policy, social welfare services and work incentives particularly for the recipients of the minimum income benefit. Furthermore, the reforms of social security and services were paralleled by a flexibilisation of the labour market. This flexibilisation is limited as it foremost aims at increasing work opportunities for permanently unemployed and weaker groups of the labour market in subsidised and contribution-reduced work schemes or temporary work. Reformed elements of labour market policy, social services and work incentives thus primarily aim at the activation of long-term unemployed, weaker groups of the labour market and vulnerable groups of society who are now to a great extent receiving this new general minimum income scheme against social exclusion. Consequently, employment is suggested as a new way to deal with the increased numbers of means-tested minimum income claimants.

However, a large number of the benefit recipients of the new minimum income scheme are regarded to face strong barriers with regard to the activation into the labour market (Kantel 2008). As a result, among the long-term unemployed benefit recipients, many persons are considered as facing different and often multiple problems with regard to the take-up of work. This raises the question of how services and benefits might achieve a targeted and individualised activation of persistently unemployed.

7.2 The re-organisation of service delivery for minimum income recipients in Germany

The re-organisation of the minimum income benefit provision and its attached services aims at a closer interplay of benefits with active labour market policy instruments (incentives, placement, training, advanced education, job creation measures) and social welfare (housing benefits, psycho-social counselling, drug-counselling services, debt counselling and other social work activities) in order to account for work-related as well as social problems of the activation of needy persons (Czommer et al. 2005: 14–17). Triggered by the labour market reforms, the traditional German local system of welfare, based on social assistance provision and attached services and policies by municipalities and a semi-autonomous third sector, is subject to change. It is challenged by the idea of a 'Jobcenter' which pools delivery of the new minimum income assistance benefit programme, municipal social services and placement activities of the Federal Employment Agency.

The issue of achieving coordinated services of social welfare and labour market policy is to a great extent left to the actors implementing the new minimum income scheme at the local level, notably the local employment agencies and the municipalities. The national framework for the organisation of the Jobcenter principally continues to respect former competences of the local and federal level and only outlines broader responsibilities of each actor at the local level. The institutionalisation of an organisational field for a targeted and individualised activation of recipients of the minimum income scheme thus depends to a great deal on the extent to which the Jobcenter, the municipalities, the local agencies of the Federal Employment Agency, and the third sector are capable to co-produce policies and services. The basic organisational traits of the Jobcenter are explained in the following.

7.2.1 An integrated framework for different benefits and services

The framework for the delivery of the minimum income benefits and its attached services through the Jobcenters is marked by a principal division of labour between the local employment agencies and the municipalities. This structure leads to some peculiarities of the organisation and preserves a prominent role for the two authorities responsible for the Jobcenter. According to legal regulation, the municipalities are responsible for the following benefits and services of the Jobcenters (BMAS 2007; Kantel 2008):

- housing (costs for 'reasonable' accommodation) and heating,
- social welfare services as childcare, youth welfare, social assistance, drug-counselling, debt counselling and psychosocial care, to the extent that these services are necessary for the integration into employment,
- new clothing and furniture for housing,
- financing school trips.

The Employment Agencies are responsible for all other benefits and services for minimum income claimants (BMAS 2007; Kantel 2008):

- placement services and programmes of active labour market policy,
- securing means of subsistence (unemployment benefits, social allowance, additional, temporary surcharge after payment of short-term unemployment benefit),
- payment of contributions to statutory health, nursing care and pension schemes.

7.2.2 The distribution of financing responsibilities for the Jobcenter

Principally, each authority is responsible for financing its proper tasks in the realm of the Jobcenter. By bearing expenditures for the means of subsistence, placement services and active labour market policy programmes, the federal government accounts for the largest share of funding for the minimum income benefit and its attached services. The municipalities are responsible for the expenditures for housing benefit recipients and the accompanying social welfare measures. The federal government reimburses approximately one third of municipal expenses for housing benefits. Municipalities account for approximately 12% of the administrative charges, which include Jobcenter staff. Federal funding bears the costs for the remaining share. While the federal government thus finances the greatest share, it also benefits first from possible reductions of financing obligations. In the case of labour market integration of a person, it is first the federal government, which is relieved from its unemployment benefit payment obligations. Only if a person accesses enough resources from the labour market to also sustain its housing costs, the municipalities are relieved from their financing duties (BMAS 2007; Kantel 2008).

7.2.3 The organisation of services reacting to work-related and social exclusionary risks

Apart from the crucial implications of the federal level in financing, it also sets an important national framework for the delivery of services, which, however, leaves local discretion on important issues.

Important aspects of placement and active labour market policy programmes are defined at the national level. The federal parliament designs and defines the existing labour market policy instruments, which may be applied by the Jobcenters. For the provision of training schemes and programmes for further education, the Federal Employment Agency demands centralised procedures of public-tendering on quasi-markets. Price, concept and past record of the bidding project executing organisations are the central criteria for tendering, which is organised by centralised regional tendering bodies of the Federal Employment Agency.

In contrast, the way of organising procurement of all types of subsidised work, including the widespread workfare community jobs, is a local matter. Moreover, active labour market policy programmes financed from federal funds explicitly exclude components of social work like psychological counselling or debt-counselling. This is due to the fact that those 'social' exclusionary factors of benefit recipients have to be accounted for by social welfare services of the municipal partner. Therefore, labour market policy's measures, which are defined in the German social code III, are supposed to be inter-organised with instruments – such as debt counselling, drug counselling, child care, psychological and social care. The organisation of these services and the coordination with active labour market policy programmes is not detailed in the social code. Consequently, it is also an issue of local practices. Furthermore, the local level is asked to compile a specific local labour market programme which defines the mix of active labour market policies deemed locally appropriate (BMAS 2007; Czommer et al. 2005; Kantel 2008).

In short, while instruments and procurement of labour market policy instruments are to an important extent defined at the national level, programmatic priorities, procurement of the important workfare community jobs and the inter-organisation with social welfare services are left to the local level.

7.2.4 Instruments for controlling local activities

Apart from services, an important national framework is also set for controlling activities, which, however, leaves local discretion on important issues. For the Jobcenters, management objectives, indicators on minimum standards or the assessment of clients into different categories form a set of important steering mechanisms.

Centralised control by objectives is aimed at ensuring a mutual obligations' approach of contract-based services for placement but also leaves some discretion at the local level. For this purpose, the Federal Employment Agency aims to steer the merged organisations for minimum income recipients through a nationwide process of management by objectives. In this process the Federal level annually suggests initial figures. Local actors can reply to these by their proper propositions. The final decision rests with the Federal Agency. Federal steering is based on the following five nationwide indicators which have been in place since 2005:

- Expenses for benefit payments (not counting costs for placement services),
- the number of integrations of unemployed (into the labour market, education, publicly funded employment),
- the number of integrations of unemployed under the age of 25,

- the average duration from the initial request for benefit payments to the day of decision,
- cost per integration.

For assessing the federal objectives a software run by the Federal Employment Agency collects data. Controlling on management objectives takes regularly place and is guaranteed by the local Federal Employment Agencies and their regional authorities. The system of management by objectives is generally regarded as important for action of the Jobcenters (Kantel 2008).

In contrast to this national framework for labour market indicators, reporting on the effects of social welfare services is neither foreseen in the technical arrangements of the Jobcenter nor much developed among communally financed but traditionally 'autonomous' third sector organisations. Local actors can however complement the five national indicators with additional local management objectives which they might deem necessary.

Besides the management objectives, the Jobcenters accepted to obey certain minimum standards on indicators which are reported to the Federal Employment Agency. These minimum standards define expectations with regard to the frequency of contacts with clients, the share of clients with whom integration contracts have been agreed on, or the progress in the assessment of clients into differentiated groups. In 2006, the Federal Employment Agency called on the Jobcenter to group clients into one of five categories differentiating with regard to chances to find an employment. It remains however up to the local level how to contextualise or use these indicators in the course of their actions. Consequently, the Federal Employment Agency introduces general objectives and indicators for steering the Jobcenter while leaving it up to the local level to detail the general premises.

In short, given these broader national prerequisites for controlling activities for work integration, actors at the local level can additionally complement local management objectives, for example by goals for social welfare issues.

7.2.5 Staff of the Jobcenter

For delivering services, the Jobcenter has been staffed with personnel sent by the municipality and the Federal Employment Agency. In general, former social workers of the social welfare centres are a potential source of staff for the municipality while the federal government can provide placement officers of the Federal Employment Agency. Due to the usually limited responsibility for personnel and professional supervision transferred to the Jobcenter, the employees of the Jobcenter remain subject to the personnel and participation rights of their authorities of origin. Consequently, for the different bodies of staff, different personnel and operational legal arrangements might exist in a Jobcenter which can lead to different salaries and working arrangements (Kantel 2008).

In short, both placement officers and social workers are provided for assisting benefit recipients with their work integration.

7.2.6 Decision-making bodies of the Jobcenter

The existing local room for manoeuvring provided for by national regulation for policies, services and controlling raises questions on the local structures for decision-making.

The Jobcenter is principally governed by a joint management and a common supervisory board. The two decision-making bodies shall represent both the municipality and the local employment agency. A joint management of the Jobcenter is generally formed by a municipal civil servant and a civil servant from the Federal Employment Agency. One of them acts as a chief executive officer. As a rule, the municipality shall be granted the option to choose first whether it desires to send the chief representative onto the management board.

The order of authority on the management board may change annually. The Jobcenter and its management, however, are usually accorded only limited budgetary control and responsibility for staff themselves (Kantel 2008). To an important extent, these responsibilities remain in the hands of the municipality and the local employment agencies.

As a second official decision-making body, the supervisory board of the Jobcenter reunites the municipality and the local employment agency. The municipality and the local employment agency usually preserve their authority to take final decisions on the budget, staff and the annual programming of employment measures in the sessions of the supervisory board. Generally, regulation suggests that the local employment agency concentrates on supervising benchmarks and the correct legal implementation of payments and services. The municipality shall be offered the ultimate decision power on the local activities, notably by taking the chairmanship on the local supervisory board to the Jobcenter. The organisational capacities of the Jobcenter therefore depend much on its supervising authorities.

In addition to the supervisory board, an advisory board exercises consultative tasks in relation to the activities of the Jobcenter. According to the German social code SGB II, the Jobcenter shall take into account advice on its activities from representative bodies as for instance charity organisations, trade unions, employers' associations, the chambers of commerce and other professional associations. The advisory function replaces traditional 'co-management' by the trade unions and employer's which had been a typical Bismarckian feature of the field of labour market policy in Germany. Formerly, the social partners were accorded an important stake in local decisions-making, for example on which active labour market programmes to implement. The institutionalisation of an advisory board might also change the influential role of the third sector which had been a central actor in the local social welfare system prior to reform.

In short, a supervisory board, an advisory board and the management drive decision-making processes of the Jobcenter, whereby important formal authority is preserved for the supervisory authorities which are the municipality and the local employment agencies.

7.2.7 Conclusion: an integrated framework for the local activation of benefit recipients

To conclude, the aim to activate recipients of minimum income schemes is based on a complex local governance structure that principally requires local coordination between previously separated fields of benefits, active labour market policy and social welfare services. Municipalities and their social welfare services merge their competences with local agencies of the Federal Employment Agency to deliver benefits and services to recipients of minimum income schemes. A local co-production to activate in particular long-term unemployed and other vulnerable groups depends on how the Jobcenter, the local agencies of the Federal Employment Agency, the municipalities and other actors work together to combine competences of counselling and placement, active labour market policy programmes, social welfare services, housing and unemployment benefits. It is up to the local level to decide on the specific mix of activities of the Jobcenter, to decide how counselling staff of social workers and placement officers will be made up and organised, if social welfare services as drug counselling or child care will be offered in the frame of the activities of the Jobcenter, what role civil society, the third sector and social partners might play in the devising of activities, and how subsidised employment programmes are organised. Therefore, activation of the long-term unemployed crucially depends on the way, the Jobcenters, the municipalities, the local Federal Employment Agency, third sector organisations and other representative bodies interact at the local level. This raises the question of how there-combining of previously separated tasks might create local organisational fields of coordinated and targeted activities to activate recipients of minimum income schemes.

7.3 The local implementation of activation reforms in Germany

At the example of four local case studies (local authorities G-A, G-B, G-C and G-D), the question is traced how requirements of local coordination are dealt with between the field of social welfare and active labour market policy, between the competences of the national and local level and between different providers. We investigate how process of re-organisation might lead to the institutionalisation of local organisational fields for a targeted and individualised co-production to activate long-term unemployed and weaker groups of the labour market.

7.3.1 Local governance of welfare interventions in local authority G-A

Welfare interventions in region G-A are confronted by problems of a weak socio-economic development. The level of unemployment has been persistently elevated and the rate of minimum income benefit recipients is high. The city, which is situated in the former part of West Germany, had witnessed a decline of its strong industrial basis. After heavy restructuring, it has entered a period of recovery during the last decade by focussing economic development on new technological priorities. Despite the slight economic recovery, the city's recent financial record has been characterised by high debt. As a result, over the last decade, a primary local policy objective has been to limit new indebtedness.

At the time of research (2008), the city is governed by a leftwing coalition government formed by the Green Party ('Bündnis 90/Die Grünen') and the Social Democrats ('SPD'). The mayor is a social democrat.

7.3.1.1 Local institutional conditions for the take-up of services and policies

The local government generally supports taking social concerns into broader account but widely leaves the handling of matters related to the Jobcenter to its civil servants. The local administration is an established actor with a wide influence over local activities. In the administration, principal responsibility for executing municipal authority over the Jobcenter is given to a proper labour market policy directorate. At the same time, single social directorates in the administration, notably for health and social affairs, remain responsible for the municipal housing benefits and the social welfare services of the Jobcenter. The local administration runs important social welfare services itself and tightly pulls the strings of those municipal social welfare services delivered by third sector organisations. Overall, the labour market policy directorate of the local administration is accorded the role to coordinate the municipal activities and exert authority over the Jobcenter.

The municipal administration actively makes use of its competences over the Jobcenter. A civil servant from the municipal directorate of labour market policy views the Jobcenter as an opportunity to set distinct regional priorities within the federal guidelines for labour market policy (G-A-6: 16):

> „The construct of the Jobcenter principally has the advantage that it is not determined by federal programmes that completely define what to do in the region, but which offer the opportunity to set regional priorities, and this is exactly, what we can achieve in governing the Jobcenter (…). I believe this is a good thing." (G-A-6).

Between the leading civil servants of the municipality and those of the local employment agency long-standing relations exist. Both authorities' civil servants stress a tradition of working together which dates back well before the founding of the Jobcenter. This facilitates collaboration on matters of the Jobcenter as a high civil servant of the municipal directorate for labour market policy highlights:

> "(…), I believe this is a very collaborative process, which leads to the decisions of the supervisory board. So, yes, I know of other municipalities and Jobcenter, and I really think that we in region G-A, perhaps because it is so small and everyone has been involved for many years, we work together in a very positive manner." (G-A-6).

In region G-A, the organisation of the Jobcenter can thus build up on established bureaucratic working relationships between a municipal labour market unit and the local employment agency, which are even strengthened as the municipal government de facto confers to its municipal labour market unit the municipal supervisory role.

7.3.1.2 Local modes of interaction for the delivery of services

In region G-A, the supervisory board of the Jobcenter, which reunites the leading civil servants from the local authority and the local employment agency every three to six months, serves as a body for formally agreeing upon matters of the Jobcenter. In practice, however, the civil servants of the municipality and the local employment agency actively and informally intervene in the daily operations of the Jobcenter. Civil servants from the municipality and the local employment agency indeed highlight the importance of closed and regular dealings with each other. The most urgent and important issues which require consideration, are dealt with directly between the heads of the municipal labour market policy directorate, the director of the local employment agency and the management of the Jobcenter. The advantages of a closed circle of actors are stressed by a leading civil servant of the municipal labour market policy directorate:

> "Yes, we have informal meetings, so that there is some space for an open exchange of opinion, so that everyone can directly raise its voice if something bothers him. The intention behind is that problems remain on a practical level, (...)." (G-A-6).

Other actors in the city, as for example the case-managers of the Jobcenter, the social partners or the many local welfare service organisations active in the region, are not much involved in devising the principal activities of the Jobcenter. The third sector and the social partners are only being involved if they can strongly mobilise on a particular issues. However, strong mobilisation through representative associations is described difficult. The landscape of welfare organisations in region G-A is characterised as dense but very diverse. Different ideologies and competition are common phenomena among welfare organisations which inhibit a stronger organisation of common interests. According to statements of the leading local representatives of the third sector, the unions as well as the business sector, who are all on the advisory board to the Jobcenter, their influence on activities of the Jobcenter is small. Thus, relying on long-standing administrative relations, the local Employment Agency and the local administration rather exclusively negotiate 'what is good for the beneficiaries' of the Jobcenter.

The management of the Jobcenter, the local employment agency and the municipality agree on an overall strategy to help people by placing them on the labour market. The actors principally aim to activate all recipients including those deemed having only a low likelihood of finding work. To do so, they claim that the activities of the Jobcenter have to differ from an approach for short-term unemployed. The director of the local employment agency explains why a local strategy of the Jobcenter is crucial:

> "On the contrary, our task is to offer and develop measures with low exigencies for this group of clients in order to bring them closer to the labour market. These are measures that are not aimed at immediate integration, but at developing their employability. The problems our clients have and carry around with them are partly very manifold. Therefore, we have first of all the task to reduce such a bundle of problems somehow before we can talk about qualifying someone for the labour market." (G-A-7).

In short, a closed planning circle exclusively made up of the civil servants from the municipality and the local employment agency defines the Jobcenter's goal to achieve activation of long-term unemployed and otherwise disadvantaged groups by integrated services which shall combine benefit delivery with the provision of both social counselling and placement, rehabilitation as well as labour market programmes.

Devising and organising the local employment programme and its services

The local 'employment programme' is described as an outcome of negotiations and discrete planning which takes place between the management of the Jobcenter and the civil servants from the local employment agency and the municipality. The Jobcenter may propose ideas but as the local authority and the local employment agency did not transfer crucial responsibilities for the budget onto the management of the Jobcenter, it is them who take the crucial decisions. A work group made up of local civil servants principally prepares the Jobcenter's employment programme. It is chaired by the municipal directorate for labour market policy. The deputy manager of the Jobcenter observes that the municipality uses its coordinating role to advocate local interests.

In the negotiations on the employment programme, different priorities are voiced by the city and the agency. The municipality deems it important to put a stress on public employment schemes as it deems those instruments as beneficial for both long-term unemployed and the local economy. Therefore, it especially aims at the expansion of public employment schemes subject to social insurance contribution and it seeks continuity in the local project executing organisations offering the public employment schemes. In addition, the civil servants from the local authority consider it necessary for the Jobcenter to offer also social welfare services in order to tackle possible multiple obstacles to the labour market integration of long-term unemployed. By contrast, the local employment agency stresses its duty to act as an authority on behalf of federal requirements. As a local agency of the federal level, its civil servants deem it necessary to limit the extent of publicly funded employment measures and to promote training programmes instead.

The services and instruments finally offered by the Jobcenter G-A correspond to a 'negotiated' consensus. According to the annual local employment programme, besides a moderate share of training programmes, the Jobcenter in region G-A usually makes predominantly use of workfare community jobs. Their share of local means spent of total active labour market measures is continuously above 40%. Alongside workfare community jobs and training, social welfare services as debt counselling or health services are also offered in the framework of the Jobcenter.

Procurement of the active labour market instruments to external project executing organisations thereby corresponds to a traditional division of labour between the Federal Employment Agency and the municipality. As stipulated by national regulation, training and further training programmes are subject to competitive tendering processes of a centralised authority of the Federal

Employment Agency. In contrast, authority over procurement of the programmes of publicly funded employment was to a large extent transferred to the municipal authority. The Jobcenter had to give away this competence to the municipality due to great municipal political pressure. The municipality was eager to hold onto this task in order to determine how the local third sector organisations implement the publicly subsidised jobs. Third sector organisations are paid a standard tariff for the execution of the workfare community jobs, which is independent from the intensity in clients' support needed. Similar to practices under the former social assistance regime, the municipality thus exerts a strong influence on publicly subsidised work but it focuses on workfare community jobs instead of generous public employment opportunities which were widely applied in the prior regime.

In contrast to the delivery of labour market instruments, integration of social services in the realm of the Jobcenter required more far reaching local changes. At the time of the creation of the Jobcenter, access of assistance-seeking persons to the municipal welfare services (e.g. drug counselling, debt counselling, psychosocial counselling, child care) had been subject to very discrete and disintegrated practices. Responsibility for services was fragmented between different social directorates of the city administration. Resembling the traditional German local welfare system, each service offer was subject to longstanding cooperation processes between the social administration of the city and the local welfare organisations. Funding was mostly granted without any explicit conditions attached to it. Stepping up as coordinator for the municipal activities, the municipal labour market policy department regarded it as crucial to attach social services to the Jobcenter herby making them available for the case-managers. To integrate social services in the system, an organisation plan was drawn up by the local civil servants. It principally conditions funding granted to welfare organisations on compliance to guidelines, prescribes a reporting system and lays out detailed instructions to social workers and the project executing organisations. The Jobcenter was given a key role in this system as it is made responsible to fill a predetermined number of places, which are reserved for minimum income benefit recipients in the social welfare services. Principally, in region G-A the case-managers of the Jobcenter are now deciding if a minimum income recipients' is given access to social services like debt counselling or psychosocial counselling. The Jobcenter uses this situation to include the utilisation of social welfare services as activity conditions in integration contracts agreed on with benefit recipients. This is a major change in practice as, prior to the reform, persons in need of a social counselling had been able to directly contact a social welfare organisation.

In short, exact procedures of an integrated implementation of active labour market and social services are prescribed to case-managers and third sector organisations on the basis of very technical and competence-based negotiations between the civil servants of the municipal labour market department and the local employment agency.

Definition and organisation of placement and counselling

A social dimension is not only provided in the employment programme but also in instructions to staff. The municipal labour market administration, the local employment agency and the Jobcenter management agreed to conceptualise case management in region G-A as an approach every social worker and placement officer of the Jobcenter should master. This means that field service staff involved in counselling benefit recipients is instructed to react to both social and work-related problems of a benefit recipient.

For placement and case management, both the Federal Employment Agency and the municipality transferred staff to the Jobcenter. The Jobcenter disposes of a total staff of approximately 700 employees. The Federal Employment Agency asked its placement officers to take up jobs at the Jobcenter. In parallel, the local authority in region G-A transferred significant numbers of social workers from its social welfare offices to work at the Jobcenter. However, as nationwide estimates fell short of the large number of households applying for minimum income benefits, the Jobcenter in region G-A needed approximately 100 to 150 additional employees. As the local authority and the local employment agency in region G-A did keep competences for hiring personnel, the Jobcenter has not been able to hire staff itself. Given the situation that the local welfare offices have already transferred a large part of their social workers to the Jobcenter, the local authority fills vacancies by municipal staff with different professional background, especially from municipal field services in which staff was redundant. The federal partner authority stocked up personnel of the Jobcenter in a similar way. Staff has been provided from a rescue company, pooling laid off staff of former state owned companies. In addition, new personnel, often highly qualified but not skilled in social work or job placement, is hired, often for temporary employment only.

Despite some training efforts, competences of staff to autonomously interact with benefit recipients and to recognise social and work-related problems are described as limited. Representatives from the trade unions and the social welfare organisations as well as the manager of the Jobcenter observe a widely lacking 'sense' for case management. Representatives from the trade unions and the social welfare organisations criticise particularly that staff in the Jobcenter often lacks mutual awareness of both social and work-related issues. According to the manager of the Jobcenter, a fundamental problem for the application of a case management approach to activate benefit recipients are shortages in skills of a major part of personal, be it from social work, placement or other fields:

> "Most employees that came into the new organisation, were rather rustic, simple officers from the employment agencies or welfare office and don't have this comprehensive case management background, not yet. They must actually master in a more comprehensive manner this case management approach that each employee working in the area of activation should know, (...). Even if politicians love to speak of case management, only a quarter of my employees in the area of activation are real case-managers and perhaps a sixth are well-trained case-managers who really understand something of case management." (G-A-4).

In consequence, decision-makers in the Jobcenter in region G-A describe similar behavioural patterns of their staff in daily work: many employees would stick very closely to legal texts and rules, often deficits would exist in knowing all the existing regulations. In counselling, a tendency would exist to offer measures that can be easily administered such as short-term training schemes or communal workfare jobs. Employees would not dare to develop their proper room for manoeuvring, refrain from measures that are more difficult to administer or described in less detail in the legal texts. Due to the qualification problems observed, the Jobcenter but also the supervising authorities believe that it is important to have clear and detailed regulations that prescribe to staff what to do. The director of the local employment agency expresses this view:

> "So sometimes an employee says, and I also hear this from higher levels of hierarchy, clearer instructions, that do not leave so much room, would possibly be more workable." (G-A-7).

In short, although both placement officers and social workers are working for the Jobcenter to provide advice to minimum income benefit recipients, their social work and placement competences are described as too limited in order to autonomously interact with benefit recipients.

7.3.1.3 Local control techniques

Given the problems of staff to autonomously master relations with benefit recipients and to practice case management, a tight system of control is established in region G-A to ensure the application of both programmes of social rehabilitation and labour market policy by the Jobcenter.

National benchmarking on the integration of recipients demands the Jobcenter, its management and staff as well the third sector organisations to place beneficiaries into employment, education or subsidised employment. This system of management by objectives is accepted by virtually all actors in region G-A as a guide to services oriented towards the goal of labour market integration of benefit recipients. The management of the Jobcenter identifies 'expenses for benefit payments' as most important benchmark goal. Also, it explains to accord great importance to the 'number of integrations of unemployed into employment, education or publicly funded employment'. While the local employment agency advocates the fulfilment of the national benchmarking objectives, the municipal authority warns that the system of management objectives can exert a certain pressure on management, staff and project executing organisations to take action in the direction of short-term and cost effective measures. A leading civil servant of the municipal directorate for labour market policy views this effect as potential problem:

> "The idea is, of course, to get quickly rid of the people with short-term measures. It must be fast, and it shall cost nothing. That is sometimes difficult to implement." (G-A-6).

The municipal administration has therefore advocated the introduction of additional local indicators in order to 'balance' national benchmarking. Following up on the initiative of the municipal administration, also the local employment agency agreed to take advantage of the discretion of the national framework for benchmarking. Further local indicators and reports were introduced which require project executing organisations to give a broader account of their efforts towards activating assistance recipients.

The local administration and the local Employment Agency for example set 'employability' as a local management objective for the Jobcenter to report on. Jobcenter G-A implemented the Federal Employment Agency's request in 2006 to group benefit recipients into one of five categories differentiating benefit recipients with regard to chances to find an employment. The local authority's administration and the local employment agency use the categorisation to control the Jobcenter, its case-managers and the benefit recipients' with regard to efforts and progress on the benefit recipients' 'employability'. The local concept developed for this purpose tries to measure the influence of the provision of social welfare services and other labour market programmes on the 'employability' of benefit recipients. Progress towards 'employability' shall be measured with regard to benefit recipients advancing onto a group of benefit recipients regarded closer to the labour market. 'Employability' as an indicator shall measure the explicit local goal to also reach those groups of benefit recipients that are regarded to have the least chances of reintegration.

Besides indicators on 'employability' to ensure recognition of social concerns, a detailed guide for reporting was drawn up by the civil servants. According to this guide, the associations counselling a benefit recipient, for example on a debt problem, will have to report back to the Jobcenter on the benefit recipients' rehabilitation progress. This is not done by direct exchanges or roundtables between the staff of the Jobcenter and the social workers of the welfare association but by formal reporting. Legal problems of privacy with regard to exchanging reports on personal issues as debt or alcoholism are resolved by asking the benefit recipient to transfer the reports him- or herself. In consequence, due to the fact that most of the clients only find access to social services through the Jobcenter, formal and systematic reporting by social associations to the Jobcenter is enabled. The supervisory authorities and the management of the Jobcenter endorse this change as it allows to not only include the utilisation of a social welfare service in integration contracts with benefit recipients but to effectively control the project executing organisations' efforts as well as the benefit recipients' behaviour, too. By contrast, actors from the third sector complain about the registration of debt problems or alcoholism in reintegration contracts being potentially subject to sanctions. The project executing organisations nonetheless comply with this regulation as their funding depends on it.

The local authority and the employment agency thus aim to ensure activation of benefit recipients into work, social rehabilitation programmes or active labour market policy programmes by closely supervising placement and counselling activities of staff and third sector organisations. Detailed reporting requirements and local benchmarks added by the local actors to the national benchmarking combine into a comprehensive local system of control supposed to not only account for integration into the labour market, workfare jobs or further education but also for supervising the use of social welfare services and the gradual development of benefit recipients towards an improved employability.

7.3.1.4 Towards a bureaucratic activation logic in region G-A

In region G-A, civil servants steer the activities of the Jobcenter by dense and tight regulation. To a wide extent, local politicians leave tasks of joining up local social welfare services and national placement services to their civil servants. Thereby, a rather closed circle of civil servants is privileged. While the municipal labour market policy department actively advocates municipal 'social' concerns, the local employment agency upholds Federal Employment Agency's interests of an efficient and placement oriented organisation. Resulting from this situation, the organisation and activities of the Jobcenter are to a great extent a matter of technical negotiations between these two actors. They define and instruct what is 'good' to achieve an activation of the benefit recipients. The third sector, the social partners, benefit recipients or case-managers tend to be rather excluded from the crucial planning processes of the Jobcenter activities.

In region G-A, long-standing bureaucratic relationships are boosted by the new constellation of the Jobcenter. As the local government readily gives supervisory authority over the Jobcenter to its municipal labour market department, long-standing relationships between this unit and the local employment agency gain outstanding relevance. The experienced civil servants of the municipal labour market department use their new municipal coordinating role to actively promote municipal social and labour market interests in established and often informal bargaining processes with the local employment agency. In the meanwhile, the local social partners and third sector organisations are referred to the official advisory committee, which has no significant legal influence.

In the area of activation measures, civil servants of the local employment agency and the local authority's administration rely on their competences to negotiate an employment programme defining beneficiaries' social and work-related needs. Coupled to the provision of benefits, benefit recipients in region G-A are offered both active labour market policy as well as programmes for social rehabilitation. In addition to training and workfare community jobs, social rehabilitation as drug counselling, psychological and social counselling are important measures the Job-Centre makes regularly use of. The imprints of social welfare policy on the strategy of the Jobcenter can be traced back to the influence of an active local labour market department.

The deficits of field service staff in skills and experiences to autonomously master a case-management approach are paralleled by a broad set of detailed steering mechanisms. This tight system of control has the tendency to strongly condition action of the Jobcenter in region G-A. The Federal framework for benchmarks guides services towards a logic of activating benefit recipients. Besides the obligatory national benchmarks on integration into the labour market, further education or subsidised employment, the system is enlarged by controlling 'employability' and the use of social welfare services. Upon initiative of the municipal labour market department, it was reached a consensus with the local employment agency to add these elements to the reporting system. As a result, the system of evaluation takes into account gradual developments of clients and the use of social welfare services. Overall, the supervisory provisions on labour market measures and social indicators locally control activities of the Jobcenter in a very strict way leaving hardly any discretion for interactions between case managing staff of the Jobcenter, third sector organisations, and benefit recipients. At the same time, this tight system of control and regulation is an important guide to staff as skill deficits and problems of staff policy make it difficult to institute a case management approach which would give more autonomy to the interactions between benefit recipients, staff and project executing organisations.

To conclude, the organisation of the minimum income scheme in region G-A comes close to a bureaucratic logic of activation. Instead of giving authority to the market or adopting broader participatory procedures, an established local coalition of civil servants from the local administration and the local employment agency works out a system for integrating national placement services with local social services. Implementation of a confined set of ALMP and social services by the Jobcenter, case-managers and third sector organisations is closely monitored by detailed local standards and reporting

7.3.2 Local governance of welfare interventions in local authority G-B

Efforts to activate long-term unemployed and weaker groups of the labour market in region G-B take place in a dynamic socio-economic context. Region G-B, situated in former West Germany, belongs to the strongest economic regions in Germany. Unemployment is at a level below German average and numbers of minimum income recipients are moderate. The city's economy has strongly grown over the last years thanks to a boost in skill demanding and production-related services, its international trade orientation, and a comparatively moderate but modernised industrial basis. At the time of research in 2008, the city is led by a conservative government (CDU) which has been in power since the beginning of the decade. The mayor is a conservative. The local government puts a priority on economic development. Savings and privatisation permitted the local government to advance at a time large public investments in economic infrastructure and to move forward the consolidation of the highly indebted city. In line with this economic policy, the city government backs a budgetary conscious social and labour market policy which is focussed on programmes for the activation of the unemployed into the labour market.

7.3.2.1 Local institutional conditions for the take-up of services and policies

The city government supports activation of the unemployed into the labour market but leaves tasks related to the Jobcenter mainly to its municipal administration.

The official authority representing the city in the context of the Jobcenter is the municipal directorate for economic policy. The city administration's directorate for economic policy counts on a proper labour market policy department. Simultaneously, the municipal directorate for social affairs and family also plays an important role for the Jobcenter, as it is in charge of the municipal tasks for housing and welfare services. In the municipal directorate for social affairs, competences for housing and the different rehabilitation services are distributed over different, specialised departments.

The local employment agency and the municipal directorates for economic policy as well as social affairs build on long standing relationships. Way before the creation of the common Jobcenter, collaboration had been practised on the basis of a local cooperation agreement of the employment agencies and the municipal social welfare centres in region G-B. The composition of the leading civil servants of both authorities has been very stable for the last years and the leading civil servants and their assistants know each other for years. They meet regularly in different contexts, for instance on the Jobcenter but also on the distribution of the European Social Funds. The director of the local employment agency points out that the municipal directorates and the local employment agency reach agreement on matters of the Jobcenter in a consultative manner:

> "The particularity about region G-B is that we do all this in cooperation independent from the formal majority regulations [on the supervisory board]. This is due to the fact that we have been working together for years in a trustful and positive manner. And this has simply continued with the new regulations for the minimum income scheme. We have indeed come even closer. Before, there had once existed a pilot project, MoZArT, on social assistance and unemployment assistance. This was also run in region G-B, and I was already here. Also due to continuity in the persons acting in this region, it exists a good collaboration between the directorate for economic policy, the directorate for social affairs and the employment agency, (…). It is normally not the question who sets the tone, but rather a positive ambition to commonly achieve a good agenda." (G-B-7).

In brief, long standing and continuous bureaucratic relationships exist in region G-B which are additionally strengthened by the practice of the local government to entrust its administration with the municipal part of supervisory authority over the Jobcenter.

7.3.2.2 Local modes of interaction for the delivery of services

In region G-B, the civil servants from the local employment agency and the municipality do not limit themselves onto their supervisory role but tightly and exclusively pull the strings of the operations of the Jobcenter. Strategic decisions on the employment programme, benchmarks and the budget are officially adopted in the sessions of the supervisory board which takes place every two to three months. Both supervising authorities, in addition, have deemed it necessary to institutionalise joint, monthly 'controlling sessions'. On these occasions, civil servants from the municipal directorates and from the local employment agency ask the Jobcenter management to report on current developments. The civil servants discuss current issues and might instruct the Jobcenter management to take concrete actions. The competence-based interactions between civil servants from the municipality and the local employment agency in and around these 'controlling sessions' are thus central to the governance of the Jobcenter in region G-A.

In contrast, third sector organisations, project executing organisations or the social partners are widely excluded from the decision-making process. The umbrella organisations for the welfare associations, business and trade unions in region G-B are each invited to send a representative to the advisory committee of the Jobcenter. The members of the advisory committee describe their influence as very limited. At the occasion of the meeting, the management of the Jobcenter usually presents some performance indicators. Discussions are described as superficial. The issue of the combination of policy fields is thus primarily arranged by the municipal administration and the employment agency, thereby integrating national and local competences but mostly ignoring third sector organisations or the social partners in the decision-making process.

The municipality, the local employment agency and the management of the Jobcenter principally agree on the idea to actively integrate benefit recipients into the labour market and to demand the benefit recipients' active participation in this process. For this purpose, they strive to integrate competences of social welfare with active labour market policy and placement in an approach to activate benefit recipients.

In short, a closed circle between the civil servants of the local administration and the local employment agency defines the principal strategy of how to activate benefit recipients.

Devising and organising the local employment programme and its services

The planning of the local employment programme is a highly centralised process involving the technical expertise of the city administration, the local employment agency and, partly, the Jobcenter. Working groups of specialised civil servants and officers from the municipality, the local employment agency and the Jobcenter are formed to make suggestions. On this basis, the leading civil servants of the local employment agency and the municipality as well as the Jobcenter management negotiate on the composure of the employment programme.

In the planning process, the local employment agency advocates political priorities of the national level. The local employment agency prefers rather short-term and budget conscious training programmes as they can cover many benefit recipients, might rather lead to the achievement of immediate effects of labour market integration and, therefore, serve to deliver on national benchmarking objectives. In contrast, the city administration points out that integration of a benefit recipient into low-paid employment on the regular job market will usually not relieve it from its obligations for payment of housing benefits. In order to respond to the local social and economic situation, the city regards the use of workfare community jobs as important. The city is interested in the application of workfare community jobs for covering communal tasks, for example gardening and landscaping, child care, youth care or other areas. In the planning process, the city also advocates long-term programmes for further education. Both the city and the employment agency also view a need to react to social problems of benefit recipients.

The labour market programme reflects both municipal and the local employment agency's preferences by a high share of workfare community jobs and a large number of training measures. The Jobcenter in region G-B has continuously dedicated up to 50% of its budget for the employment programme to workfare community jobs. Besides the workfare community jobs, short training measures of two to four weeks, for instance on writing an application, are also widely offered. In contrast, the share of long-term, further education programmes offered to long-term unemployed remains small. Social welfare services are offered as well in the framework of the Jobcenter.

Based on the employment programme, training and further education programmes will be ordered via a centralised tendering body organised by the Federal Employment Agency at the regional level. The managing field service personnel of the Jobcenter points out that it is difficult to plan a particular programme with one project executing organisation as central tendering might lead to the delegation of the project to another project executing organisation. Nonetheless, the actors describe that they are able to ask for a wide variety of measures including those that they deem suitable for long-term unemployed and weaker groups of the labour market.

In contrast, procurement of all types of subsidised work is a matter which the local actors decide on. By the supervisory authorities, the Jobcenter was conferred the task to execute this procurement process which includes the widespread workfare community jobs. The Jobcenter and the supervising authorities, however, did not want a discretionary procurement process. Particularly, the conservative city government has taken a more sceptical stance on a traditionally strong municipal alliance with local social enterprises. At the same time, the municipal actors also opposed a completely market-oriented, unrestricted tendering process as they deemed a tighter grip on procurement necessary in order to promote municipal strategic goals. Therefore, the local actors agreed to organise procurement of workfare community jobs as selective tendering. On the basis of the local objectives for workfare community jobs, corresponding project executing organisations are identified through a formal market survey. Those identified are invited to make an offer for the execution of a workfare community job. In this rather hierarchical process, the possibility of field service staff, benefit recipients or welfare organisations to voice their demands is very limited. Thus, instead of using a market-oriented tendering logic or instead of making different local actors participate, award of contract for workfare community jobs is regulated by the local civil servants through a formalised and hierarchical procedure.

In parallel to the remodelling of the organisation of active labour market policy, delivery of social welfare services was also reformed in a crucial manner. The management of the Jobcenter, the director of the local employment agency and the leading civil servants of the city realised that, labour market policy programmes paid by the Federal level needed to be interwoven in a much closer manner with the municipal offers for counselling and rehabilitation. Completely disconnected from the placement activities, in the past, each field for rehabilitation or counselling in region G-B had been subject to the steering requirements of separated departments in the municipal administration for social affairs. Each department had established different arrangements with the service provider organisations. Recognising problems to refer persons from the Jobcenter to a counselling, the management of the Jobcenter but also the director of the local employment agency asked the responsible municipal social administration to make social rehabilitation programmes compatible with the activities of the Jobcenter. Confronted with continuous demands of reorganisation, the municipal directorate for social affairs finally reacted. Its general department put forward a new organisation plan which proposed to inter-organise services with the Jobcenter.

The new organisation plan details requirements and guidelines for counselling, reporting, and benchmarking. According to this plan, it is no longer entirely up to the benefit recipient to contact a social welfare association for help on issues of addiction, debt, and other health or social concerns. Field staff in the

Jobcenter is asked to include social rehabilitation as possible activity requirement in the integration contracts with benefit recipients. A guideline prescribes to staff and the third sector organisations exact procedures of how to interact with a benefit recipient. Indeed, the municipal social directorate has embedded its new organisational approach in a greater reform of its relationships towards social welfare associations. Instead of guaranteed grants to quasi-public welfare providers, the municipality shifts to flat rate payments according to the number of cases treated. As payment for services is made dependent on the application of the new system, the project executing organisations' prior opposition was broken. In the areas of drug counselling, debt counselling, psychosocial counselling and migrant centres, funding for the service provider associations became conditional on the application of this new organisation plan. The director of the umbrella organisation for the welfare associations in region G-B complains that the city did not involve the welfare associations in this reorganisation process.

> "It doesn't exist a process of social planning in this area. (...) At least, it doesn't exist one which would include us, a social planning which would allow us to commonly clarify: 'how many offers do we actually need?' Most of these activities are organised by us, by the welfare associations and their members." (G-B-11).

Furthermore, reacting to current waiting periods of up to six month, the municipality also increased its budget for debt counselling and psychosocial counselling.

In short, the joint organisation of active labour market programmes and rehabilitation programmes in local authority G-B is a matter of very technical and competence-based negotiations between the civil servants of the municipality and the local employment agency. They define key elements and dense regulations of procedures of an employment programme which reacts both to social as well as work-related problems of benefit recipients.

Definition and organisation of placement and counselling

Not only the employment programme comprises both activities for social rehabilitation and active labour market policy measures, but the supervising authorities and the management of the Jobcenter instruct field service staff to actively react to skill, social and health problems of benefit recipients in order to achieve activation into the labour market or programmes.

To place and counsel benefit recipients, both the city and the Federal Employment Agency transferred staff to the Jobcenter. Of the more than 1000 employees, one third was provided by the city and two thirds by the employment agency. Staff was not selected by the management of the Jobcenter itself. In region G-B, the local authority and the local employment agency have kept responsibility for hiring and firing staff. In region G-B the number of persons applying for minimum income benefits had been largely underestimated, when the Jobcenter was found. As a consequence staff had to be quickly increased by almost the double. To respond to this demand, the Federal Employment Agency hired university graduates with very diverse educational backgrounds, or it provided redundant staff from former state companies. The municipal side did not hire additional staff at all as the local government ordered a spending freeze. Instead, the Jobcenter was provided with a 'pool' of municipal staff from areas, as for example nursing, where municipal staff had become redundant. As a result, a third of the employees of the Jobcenter are not trained as social worker or placement officer. Furthermore, as many of the additional employees were only hired for temporary work, the share of temporary employment makes up one third of field service personal.

An obstacle, highlighted by all actors, to achieve activation of benefit recipients are the competences of staff. Training demands are described as high both for unqualified employees but also for trained staff as the latter were either formed for social work or placement but not for both fields. Managing field service personnel of the Jobcenter describes it as difficult to master at a time up skilling and operations. Deficits of staff are pointed out as regards reacting to individual problems of benefit recipients. The civil servants from the supervising authorities and the Jobcenter management explain that those employees not qualified for the job would orient themselves very closely along the legal regulations and other stipulations. This limited ability of many employees to autonomously counsel is explained by a managing field service officer in the Jobcenter:

> "If I am not at ease with the professional requirements of the job, how will I be able to counsel the people? I will restrict myself closely onto actions in accordance with the legal texts and regulations, because I am not able to decide autonomously. This is very problematic, it is indeed awkward." (G-B-1).

As the national legal regulations are considered too broad for staff to handle, directives and instructions prescribed by the Federal Employment Agency as well as by the municipality play an important role in steering the activities of management and staff in the Jobcenter. As stipulated by the Federal Employment Agency, benefit recipients were grouped into five different categories distinguishing between those closer and those more distant from the labour market. In region G-B, the supervising authorities and the management of the Jobcenter use this categorisation for organising targeted counselling and placement of benefit recipients. Field service staff is advised to only offer particular programmes to a benefit recipient. For each category of benefit recipients, the supervising authorities prescribe 'suitable' programmes. For example, benefit recipients in the group considered most distant from the labour market shall be only offered workfare community jobs, counselling or rehabilitation. Furthermore, the categorisation is used to regulate the frequency of contacts between field service personal and a benefit recipient. According to this stipulation, field service staff shall only once a year meet with persons considered most distant from the labour market. Those in the group considered one step closer to the labour market but still not employable are asked to get in touch with a placement officer or a social worker at the Jobcenter once every six months. This categorisation makes the activities of the Jobcenter subject to many bureaucratic requirements as the co-director of the Jobcenter underlines:

> "The social code II is a very short legislative text compared to everything else that had existed before. But short legislative texts in particular pose the risk that many things have to be made applicable for the implementation, through standards, regulations and so on which in turn (…) make the implementation process partly very complex (…)." (G-B-6).

In short, due to field service personnel's deficits, an autonomous counselling and placement approach is described as problematic. The Jobcenter management and the supervising authorities doubt that staff is able to autonomously recognise social and work-related problems of persons difficult to place. Therefore, the supervising authorities dictate detailed terms to case managers how to interact with the benefit recipients.

7.3.2.3 Local techniques of control

Despite the described deficits of field service staff to individually react to the problems of benefit recipients, the Jobcenter management and the supervising authorities aim to guarantee activation of benefit recipients into employment, active labour market programmes as well as rehabilitation programmes by the application of numerous mechanisms of control.

Activities of the Jobcenter and its field service staff are tightly controlled by both national and local benchmarks and indicators. Representing the Federal level, one of the principal interests of the local employment agency is to ensure national benchmarking on the integration of recipients into employment, education and subsidised employment. In general, all actors involved in the governance of the Jobcenter in region G-B have accepted this idea of benchmarking as a very important orientation towards active services for labour market integration.

Not only does the director of the local employment agency continuously advocate the necessity of benchmarking and indicators, but also municipal civil servants discover this technique of the new Jobcenter organisation as a way to guarantee implementation of their proper strategic interests. In contrast to the focus on direct labour market integration, the municipal directorate for social affairs puts up indicators to control the management, field service staff, benefit recipients and project executing organisations with regard to their efforts to progress 'employability'. The municipal directorate has developed a system to control outcomes of the participation in debt counselling and psychosocial counselling. Following a counselling, it is evaluated whether benefit recipients move onto a group considered closer to the labour market, achieve first-time placement on a workfare community job or find a regular job. Control takes place immediately after the conclusion of a rehabilitation programme as well as six months later. Furthermore, the city applies a benchmarking concept to control the Jobcenter with regard to payments of the municipal housing benefits.

Also the manager of the Jobcenter shares the local employment agency's believe that a system of standards, benchmarks and indicators is the only feasible way to ensure activation in a large organisation. In addition to national and municipal controls, the management of the Jobcenter therefore practices internal controls by indicators to reassure the activation of benefit recipients. For this purpose, a comprehensive control table drawn up by the management prescribes down to the teams of four to five staff detailed indicators for benefit payments, counselling and placement on programmes which they have to achieve. The control table reviews those indicators for which the Federal Employment Agency asks to fulfil minimum standards, as for example the frequency of contacts with benefit recipients or the rate of integration contracts signed. Moreover, the control table prescribes in detail the number of unemployed that has to be placed on each labour market policy programme per month. Performance on indicators is published every two weeks. Monthly, the managing field service staff is required to justify their performance in a meeting with the management of the Jobcenter. At a lower level, the managing field service staffs regularly meet with their field staff to discuss their performance. To guarantee reaching the national and municipal objectives, the Jobcenter manager even sets more ambitious internal goals than are formulated by national or municipal objectives. The management of the Jobcenter explains that detailed steering is necessary in order to guarantee that the labour market policy programmes are indeed filled with persons:

> "We have control tables, this is a control table for placement, it includes every goal that we have, (…), split up on each team. And every team manager knows, where he stands

> with regard to the goal. Green means: goal accomplished, yellow means: on course, and red means: not accomplished. And the same we have also for benefit payment, and we also have for example a list, (...) which details placement on programmes. This means, in turn, every Jobcenter has the task to fill programmes, because I need to fill the programmes, which we buy. And this is also controlled by the control table. I can therefore monthly see: where does a Jobcenter stand with regard to placement on each activity?" (G-B-5).

Thus, to secure accomplishment of the national and municipal benchmarks, the general management of the Jobcenter details indicators for controlling field staff and field service management staff with regard to active services, and placement into employment, active labour market programmes and rehabilitation.

The managing field service staff of the Jobcenter experiences the dense system of central, local and internal controlling of benchmarks and indicators as an extremely rigid system, which leaves hardly any discretion in the interactions with the benefit recipients. When it comes to interactions with benefit recipients, managing staff observes that, many of their social workers and placement officers primarily think off the number of persons which needs to be accorded monthly to each labour market programme. The managing field service staff complains about having a too weak influence on planning programmes and setting goals. A field service manager explains how tight the room of manoeuvring is for field staff to interact with the benefit recipient:

> "I have to place a certain number in workfare community jobs monthly. I have to place a certain number onto training programmes, I have to execute all possible things prescribed by numbers which finally leads to the situation that one cannot always find the perfect way for the customer, but, being steered by such benchmarks, one also has to take different ways, and place a customer onto a programme which is not necessarily the best option for him. (...) It is not the range of programmes, defined in the legal texts, which limits us. (...) What I urgently need is some autonomy. I shouldn't be dependent on the fact that I have to fill 30 training programmes in a month. If I fill 30 training programmes by chance, then it is absolutely alright. But it shouldn't be my goal. My goal has to be to find the right activities for the customers, and my goal shouldn't be to fill a number of training programmes." (G-B-2).

Moreover, a reporting system was institutionalised which includes the delivery of social welfare services. According to this reporting system, the welfare associations or rehabilitation centres are principally required to report back to the Jobcenter on the rehabilitation process of a benefit recipient. Despite protests of the welfare associations, the benefit recipients are asked for permission for lifting confidentiality requirements and they are asked to personally transmit data between the Jobcenter and the welfare association. Nonetheless, the third sector organisations finally complied with reporting demands as their funding was made conditional on them (cf. chapter 7.3.2.2).

In brief, not only do the local employment agency, the municipal administration and the management of the Jobcenter agree to control national benchmarks and to put up common standards. Relatively independently, each actor, additionally, applies its own indicators to control implementation of its particular strategic interests. Activities of the third sector organisations and the Jobcenter's general management, managing field service staff and field service staff are closely supervised by directives, reporting, indicators and benchmarking. The goal is to ensure placement by field service staff and the project executing organisations in employment and on programmes for rehabilitation and labour market integration.

7.3.2.4 Towards a bureaucratic activation logic in region G-B

To conclude, civil servants in region G-B achieve activation of benefit recipients through a local co-production of national placement services and municipal social welfare services. Local politicians back activation strategies but widely leave tasks of the Jobcenter organisation to the local civil servants. Thereby, long-standing bureaucratic relationships between the local employment agency and the municipal administration are privileged over a traditional partnership-based local welfare policy approach. While the municipal directorate for labour market policy as well as the one for social affairs tends to lobby for municipal 'social' concerns, the local employment agency puts a greater stress on national provisions for an efficient organisation. The organisation of services to react to social as well as work-related employment obstacles of benefit recipients is thus primarily an outcome of technical and competence-based negotiation processes between the civil servants.

A competence-based, negotiated mode of interaction characterises planning processes of the employment programme, the procurement of social and labour market policy programmes as well as staff policy. The planning of the concrete labour market and rehabilitation programmes offered in region G-B is a highly technical process. Benefit recipients' needs are a matter of categorisations as well as negotiations between leading civil servants and working groups of specialised civil servants from the employment agency, the municipal economic and social department. Procurement of programmes is organised in a hierarchical manner to keep project executing organisations at distant but to be able to enforce local interests.

Given that staff is not deemed capable to autonomously master interactions with benefit recipients in region G-B, the Jobcenter management, the local employment agency and the municipal administration put a focus on dense control mechanisms to achieve activation of benefit recipients in region G-B. Third sector organisations and in particular field service staff is not trusted to autonomously interact with benefit recipients or to be able to autonomously achieve national benchmarks. For targeted counselling and placement, the local actors complement national benchmarks with local standards, indicators and reporting requirements. This adds up to a very rigid local system of control which shall guarantee that project executing organisations and field service staff in the Jobcenter provide active services to benefit recipients in order to surmount obstacles to labour market integration. It is indeed in detail prescribed and supervised by the supervising and managing authorities that field service staff signs integration contracts with benefit recipients and places them into work, training programmes, workfare community jobs, social counselling or rehabilitation.

All in all, activation of persistently unemployed and weaker groups of the labour market receiving minimum income benefits is achieved according to a bureaucratic logic by prescribing a defined set of national placement services and programmes combined with municipal social work services.

7.3.3 Local governance of welfare interventions in local authority G-C

Local governance of assistance to minimum income recipients in city G-C takes place at the backdrop of a strong socio-economic environment. Unemployment is at a level below German average and numbers of minimum income recipients are low. City G-C, situated in a part of former West-Germany, is located in one of the best performing regional economies of the country. The region's strong economy is based on innovation and important sectors of modern medium technology industries. Positive employment effects particularly stem from the large production sector. The regional economy is based on a dense tissue of export-oriented large enterprises, SMEs with extremely competitive international profiles and some of the strongest research hubs in Europe. A positive development of tax incomes contributed to a solid financial situation of the municipality in 2007. Another reason for sound municipal finances was a policy of long-standing budgetary discipline.

The local government is formed by a coalition of the conservative party and the social democrats. The mayor of city G-C is a conservative and the conservatives have a simple majority in the local parliament. Among the priorities of local policy, the conservative mayor stresses the need of a continued budgetary discipline of the local parliament and the municipal administration.

7.3.3.1 Local institutional conditions for the take-up of services and policies

The city counts on a strong tradition of local labour market policy comprising proper local programmes for long-term unemployed and vulnerable persons, particularly for substance abusers. In the local framework of the prior social assistance regime, city G-C had developed approaches at the interface of labour market policy and social services for social assistance seekers. Most prominently figuring among the past municipal approach were public employment schemes which particularly aimed at giving an employment opportunity to persons with drug addictions, psychological and social problems. Past financial efforts of the city's labour market policy resembled those sums now available from national funds for labour market policy activities of the Jobcenter. For the implementation of the local policy approach, long-standing, close partnerships had evolved between the city and local third sector organisations. As a result, a highly established tissue of local social welfare associations and social enterprises exists in region G-C.

When the Jobcenter was created, the municipal department for local finances and economy, which is directed by the city treasurer, was accorded by the local government the municipal supervisory part over the Jobcenter. In addition, the municipality has an official municipal appointee for local labour market policy who is based in the municipal department for local finances. This position of a municipal appointee for local labour market policy is a very established one which has been in existence for many decades. Apart from the municipal appointee for local labour market policy, the treasurer, who simultaneously acts as deputy mayor, also counts on the administrative assistance of a regular civil servant specialised in issues of the Jobcenter only. While the treasurer can thus count on a strong municipal administrative expertise, he himself is described by all interviewees as possessing great detailed knowledge of the processes of the Jobcenter. The treasurer is personally interested in the activities of the Jobcenter. Furthermore, being the head of the municipal department for finances and economy, he has also recognised the financial significance of the Jobcenter for the city.

Apart from the municipal administration, the local parliament plays a particular role in G-C, which contributes to a strong local community. Activities of the Jobcenter are subject to direct demands of accountability by the local parliament. The management of the Jobcenter is regularly asked to appear in front of the parliamentary committees for economic development, housing and health in order to explain activities of the Jobcenter. The strong role of the local parliament is explained by the fact that the city views the Jobcenter as a municipal administration. Based on this interpretation, the city and the local parliament demand the Jobcenter management to involve the local parliament. The deputy manager of the Jobcenter stresses that this is a one-sided perception as the Jobcenter's supervisory authority is formally equally shared with the local employment agency. However, as the deputy manger explains, the city takes its interpretation nonetheless for granted:

> "(...) maybe it is a particularity that in city G-C it exists this municipal view that the Jobcenter is equal to a municipal administration. Maybe this does not exist somewhere else. I always say that this is only how the municipality views it, actually it is not like this. The Jobcenter is not a municipal administration, but from the municipal point of view it is one. They just define it like this." (G-C-3).

However, this municipal interpretation remains unchallenged and increases the lobbying opportunities for the local community. For the third sector organisations and civil society, the prominent role of the local parliament increases their influence. While the official advisory committee of the Jobcenter does not offer much influence, they can instead make their voices heard among the local parliamentarians. The local parliamentarians might then take a decision the Jobcenter has to react to.

The director of the local employment agency, who counts for matters of the Jobcenter on the assistance of one specialised civil servant, accepts that the active role of the local parliament contributes to a strong municipal role:

> "(...) I am firmly convinced that the influence of the municipal authority is strong and (...) that the municipal authority exerts its influence based on the will of the local parliament. In our city this is exceptionally strong (...) that the local parliament strongly takes up this issue and in some cases it decides on a position which the representative in the supervisory board has to stick to. In these cases, the position of the municipal authority is not negotiable (...)." (G-C-1).

The leading civil servants but also the representative from the regional umbrella organisation of the social welfare organisations highlight that the organisation of the Jobcenter provided enough local discretion for the existing local structure of programmes, know-how, organisations and persons to persist. The representative from the local social welfare organisations' regional umbrella observes great continuity of the local partnership-based structures:

> "The reform of the minimum income scheme left (...) a very wide frame to the local structures, no matter if we would talk about the municipality or the employment agency,

(…). This means, it existed room for the local structures. And in city G-C we had (…) 1500 to 2000 hard-to-place persons in public employment programmes. Somehow we had the obligation to deal with them. (…), there was just this particular local problem, (…) which we had reacted to. (…) Also in the form of the organisation we had reacted to this local problem. (…) where these persons with particular social problems were counselled, where they went to, this was all given to a certain extent. (…) and I believe that this tradition impacted on what was then implemented in city G-C." (G-C-7).

In short, a very established and active local partnership coalition of civil servants, third sector organisations, the local government and the local parliament frames the organisation of the Jobcenter in city G-C.

7.3.3.2 Local modes of interaction for the delivery of services

Regular meetings are held between the management of the Jobcenter, the supervising municipal authority, which is represented by the treasurer and the municipal appointee for labour market policy, and the supervising local employment agency, which is represented by its local director. In the framework of six week 'jour fixe' in the town hall as well as four month sessions of the supervisory board, the actors exchange their views. Based on discussions, they reach agreement on the broader guidelines of how to use the budget and how to develop activities of the Jobcenter. Holding the chairmanship of the supervisory board, the city openly points to its decisive voting power. However, the municipal appointee for labour market policy highlights that the decision-making process is usually based on mutuality as both the city and the employment agency would mutually respect their partner's strength and limits:

"The city G-C has never had to take advantage of its decisive voting power. We know as city G-C what we can expect the director of the local employment agency to tolerate. Vice-versa, the employment agency knows that we are not some weak district in the north of the country or I don't know where, but that we are the city G-C and that the acting actors are strong persons! (…) We don't exaggerate this. This means, if we reach a point, where we say, 'okay, by demanding this we would make it impossible for the director of the local employment agency to agree', then we search for a compromise on the supervisory board. The sessions of the supervisory board are very respectful events" (G-C-4).

At the same time, the supervisory authorities do not deem it necessary to intervene in detail into the operations of the Jobcenter as they generally trust in the decision-making capacities of the manager and officers of the Jobcenter as well as the third sector organisations.

All in all, the municipal side was able to convince the local employment agency to share a strategy for the Jobcenter which highlights the importance of work but places a focus on a step-by step reduction of the social problems of the very hard-to-place benefit recipients. To combine programmes and services of social welfare and active labour market policy, they agree on the need to count on the participation of the local community, comprising directing and field service staff both from placement and social welfare services, third sector and other project executing organisations, but also the benefit recipients. In view of a rather low unemployment rate and enterprises that are often ready to qualify employees themselves, the Jobcenter views its primary tasks in developing the employability of long-term unemployed and trying to help them to increase their placement opportunities. Based on this strategy, the manager of the Jobcenter expects field service staff to respect the problems and interests of the benefit recipients and to mutually develop an integration strategy with benefit recipients:

> "(…) what I really want and what I expect is, (…) that our colleagues develop an interest and that they will face everyone who steps into the door with this interest and that they will say, 'where does this person stand?' Where does this person has its visions, what does this person want to reach, what is this person interested in, and that we will then try to collaborate with this person in order to develop a solid integration strategy and the appropriate and existing programmes then have to be used for this integration strategy, (…)." (G-C-2).

In brief, a broad local coalition defines the strategy of Jobcenter G-C. This local strategy is primarily aimed at reacting to non-work related problems of unemployment and to construe attempts of work activation together with the benefit recipients.

Definition and organisation of the employment programme and its attached services

The local employment programme results mainly from discussions between managing staff, field service staff of the Jobcenter, the local welfare associations and social enterprises. Regularly, the general management meets with field service staff and field service directing staff in order to discuss the development of labour market programmes and social service activities. In parallel, the management regularly invites representatives from local social enterprises and social welfare associations to jointly evaluate the development of labour market programmes and social welfare services. In addition, the management and the directing staff of the Jobcenter make regular personal visits to the third sector organisations in order to gain an impression how programmes are run. The management of the Jobcenter explains that it listens to the experiences and arguments of what works best from counselling field service staff and the personnel from the project executing organisations. For the management of the Jobcenter, these discussions form the principal basis of planning activities for the Jobcenter. The deputy manger of the Jobcenter explains how interactions with staff and project executing organisations contribute to shape action:

> "(...) thanks to discussions with counselling staff (...) we get this feedback. In addition, we have regular discussions with personnel from the social enterprises. (...) we ask a lot (...), what proved successful? We also make evaluations. We organised this here in the management, that we said, what were the effects of certain programmes? (...) thanks to the feedback we always get insights on what worked and what didn't work that good, and for us this is our starting point for the consecutive planning." (G-C-3).

Based on this knowledge, the Jobcenter presents a draft of the employment programme to the local parliament and to the supervisory authorities. In front of the parliamentary committees, the management of the Jobcenter regularly explains the activities planned for the Jobcenter. Also in the sessions with the supervisory authorities, the Jobcenter management is required to justify its plans. The local parliamentarians as well as the supervisory authority might demand further adjustments to the employment programme. However, the management of the Jobcenter stresses, that its proper draft is usually not fundamentally changed in this mutual process.

In the planning process, the arguments made by the local community and the local employment agency differ. The Jobcenter and its management, the ruling parties in the local parliament, the municipal administration, and the third sector organisations have a strong preference for publicly subsidised employment. They view it as a way to assist weaker groups of society to partake in society and to increase their employment opportunities. The local employment agency, in contrast, has a stronger preference for qualification than workfare community jobs. It stresses the necessity to also take into account measures which serve directly for the integration into the regular labour market. In light of the many unemployed who do not qualify for training or a job immediately, the director of the local employment agency is however ready to accept the local argument of a last resort option of public employment schemes:

> "If there is no alternative, I prefer a public employment scheme over nothing. Therefore, it is not a great issue to quarrel about for us. It is just an issue, which requires posing the following question: 'is this priority right or shouldn't we also give more weight to qualification and shift the programmes a bit more towards this direction?' This is why we reduced the public employment schemes." (G-C-1).

All actors in region G-C also highlight the importance of providing social welfare services to react to obstacles of the long-term unemployed. The deputy manager of the Jobcenter explains that the use of rehabilitation measures and child care is important to tackle the problems of the unemployed minimum income benefit recipients:

> "We have a good labour market situation and those who are ready for the inclusion into the labour market will find their place, either thanks to our assistance but also through their own job search. What remains are those who are so severely limited. (…) they need these social services, particularly on issues of addiction, alcohol, drugs and problems of debt. In addition, for women, who are single parents, we face the problem of organising places in child care facilities and sometimes psychological assistance is also needed, (…) therefore the use of these social services becomes very important and they are also relied on, (…)." (G-C-3).

Given the widely accepted argument of the local community to focus on those difficult to place, the employment programme reflects a strong preference for social welfare services and publicly subsidised employment. As all actors agree on the necessity of publicly subsidised employment, the Jobcenter makes predominantly use of both workfare community jobs and the more generous publicly subsidised employment schemes. Their share of means spent of total labour market measures is at approximately 50%. Taking into account the varying intensity in support clients need, region G-C has created different varieties of workfare jobs. Usually, the public employment schemes are connected to a counselling which shall help the participant to find out his or her training, qualification or social rehabilitation needs and the opportunities existing to get help. Most of these programmes had been already run in more or less the same way by the municipality before the founding of the Jobcenter. By being 'creative' with the new rules, the municipal actors and the director of the local employment agency explain that it was possible to continue the local programmes in the frame of the new instruments. The most crucial difference arising is that these programmes are now financed out of the federal budget instead of using municipal funds as it was the case before the founding of the Jobcenter. Apart from workfare jobs, the city provided more personal and greater capacities for debt counselling, child care and psychosocial counselling. Waiting periods for debt counselling could be reduced for unemployed minimum income recipients from up to 1 year down to 4 months. The employment programme also comprises further education and short training programmes although they represent only a smaller share of the Jobcenter activities.

The Jobcenter was given the sole responsibility to organise the allocation of active labour market programmes to welfare associations and other project executing organisations. As prescribed by national law, the programmes of further education or training are ordered via the centralised regional tendering authority. For all other programmes, notably the publicly subsidised jobs, the Jobcenter does not make use of public tenders. It directly concludes contracts with local third sector organisation. In this context, the Jobcenter carries on the established local partnerships with the local social enterprises and social welfare associations. The manager of the Jobcenter explains that the existing local partnership-structures facilitated the delivery of programmes in the frame of the Jobcenter:

> "We had a very comfortable situation in city G-C. We could build on a yearlong tradition of local labour market policy. I was very happy to be able to count on a given range of different offers, particularly in the area of the project executing organisations, the social enterprises, but also other municipally co-financed projects or projects from the European Social Funds. As a result, we were able to immediately work together with the project executing organisations, which had already made vast experiences with the different target groups." (G-C-2).

Apart from continuity in the organisation of delivery of labour market programmes, the delivery of social welfare services was being interlinked in a stronger manner with the activities of the Jobcenter. In close cooperation with the counselling centres and the social welfare associations, the management of the Jobcenter undertook steps to facilitate access of unemployed minimum income benefit recipients onto social welfare services via the Jobcenter. Upon initiative of the Jobcenter, cooperation agreements were worked out between the Jobcenter, the social department of the municipality and the local welfare service organisations. As part of these agreements, common guidelines were found on the use of the services. All actors agreed to support labour market integration, by granting minimum income benefit recipients privileged access to social welfare services including debt counselling and child care services in the frame of a quota of designated places. Furthermore, the Jobcenter explicitly nominated one person to manage interactions with social service providers. The Jobcenter management advises field service staff to include the utilisation of social services in integration contracts with benefit recipients. A feedback system also involves regular direct exchanges between the case-manager at the Jobcenter and the social worker at a welfare organisation. While both the Jobcenter and the local welfare organisations agreed on the importance of successful encouragement and assistance, it was also reached consensus that the use of a social service by a benefit recipient remains excluded from sanctions. The management of the Jobcenter was convinced by the social associations' demand to respect an individual's free choice to seek assistance on problems like addiction. The manager of the Jobcenter resumes how the third sector organisations and the Jobcenter commonly developed criteria for offering social welfare services to the unemployed:

> "(…) This means, that in practice, we have an access of roughly 50% of the counselling capacities of debt counselling via our case-management. We just agreed on this with each responsible institution. (…) From the beginning on, we considered interface management as very important. We had one colleague, who put a main focus of his tasks on this interface management. In addition, this means, we have framework agreements with all relevant service organizations and institutions, we have worked out cooperation contracts. (…) Finally, we discussed explicit codes of conduct with the outreach clinics in [G-C], who will meet whom and when, how can the services be implemented." (G-C-2).

In short, the process leading to the definition and organisation of the employment programme is thus a mutual one which is open to arguments from case-managers, the Jobcenter management, the social welfare associations, local parliamentarians and the supervising authorities and to some extent even the benefit recipients. It leads to the mutual definition and partnership-based delivery of a programme comprising both social welfare services and instruments of active labour market policy.

Definition and organisation of placement and counselling

Not only does the programme of the Jobcenter combine offers of social services and active labour market policy but the Jobcenter management also asks counselling field service staff to react to social as well as work-related problems of the unemployed. Together with the benefit recipient, placement officers and social workers shall autonomously determine the intensity of counselling needed as well as the appropriate social or labour market programmes. The Jobcenter manager explains how staff is instructed to autonomously case manage each benefit recipient:

> "We don't distinguish by saying, okay, 'we have customers that might be eligible to a case management and customers who don't need a case management', but the work our colleagues have to do is just to decide how intensive help has to be in a particular case." (…) some cases they will identify as 'there is not much to do at the moment', or 'I can leave the case for some time to a third party', this is for example the case, when the colleagues from a welfare association for housing problems will say, 'we have to treat very different issues during the next three, four months', then, the case-manager can leave it to the social welfare association during the next months, make a note and invite the person again in four months. It means that it is not him who has to move the case on during the four months, but, of course, it can happen, that he has to react to the case, as something happens what is relevant." (G-C-2).

The Jobcenter management trusts in its case-managers' ability to take proper judgements how to individually interact with a benefit recipient, how often to meet with a benefit recipient and what kind of instruments and programmes to select. Therefore, the management of the Jobcenter deems it not as appropriate to make counselling or measures offered to benefit recipients depend on a categorisation of benefit recipients:

> "The present concept of client groupings is not helpful in practice and for the colleagues. (...). Because you have an incredible variety of different people in the Jobcenter and you cannot cope with this variety, this complexity with simply creating four or five categories, that you will, let's put it like this, connect to very shallow integration strategies. That is not our approach and I hope, neither, that one day we will be forced to implement such an approach. (...) our quality has to be assessed with regard to the question, if we will be able to cope with this complexity and variety." (G-C-2)

To master case management, the management of the Jobcenter views it as an opportunity to count on placement officers from the employment agency as well as municipal social workers. Competences are highlighted as being complementary. Personnel from the Federal Employment Agency is accorded expertise in the field of labour market policy while the municipal social workers are praised for mastering issues of counselling and social welfare services. In practice, the Jobcenter counts on 200 municipal social workers and 100 employees of the Federal Employment Agency, of the latter, around 80 are placement officers and around 20 are employees with a different background. Due to the long-standing practices of municipal labour market policy, the municipality was able to provide such a high number of social workers. When the Jobcenter took over the municipal tasks for long-term unemployed, the city was also eager to transfer its counsellors specialised in assisting long-term unemployed to the Jobcenter. Apart from the deputy manager, who originates from the employment agency, all ranks of directing staff are almost entirely compounded of municipal social workers.

Given the high share of trained field service staff, the management of the Jobcenter concentrates on increasing competences of the social workers and placement officers in case management techniques. Apart from case management courses, a very experienced municipal social worker acts as contact person and instructor on case-management issues. In addition, the management asked its counselling field service staff to set-up regular discussion groups for exchanging practices how to counsel best a benefit recipient. Finally, on the occasion of 'event days' in the Jobcenter, social workers from the social welfare associations are invited to meet and discuss with counselling staff the implementation of drug counselling or debt counselling. The director of the local employment agency acknowledges that, thanks to these practices, especially the placement officers sent from the Federal Employment Agency learned about the significance of social welfare measures for long-term unemployed. The manager of the Jobcenter is convinced that placement officers and social workers have learned from each other to master case management:

> "Indeed, [the employees have learned from each other], I am firmly convinced of this. In the beginning, the exchange had proceeded in a hesitant way. Reservations were common. One had to take into account both cultures, but we approached each other in a very positive manner and those voices were raised that said, we are happy, to have a municipal colleague that can help us with the calculation of costs of accommodation, and those from the municipality said, we are relieved to have someone from the Federal Agency, who can help us in dealing with the IT system. These voices are getting continuously numerous and we live that development." (G-C-3).

In short, building on a high share of municipal social workers, the management in Jobcenter G-C supports and entrusts placement officers and social workers to rather autonomously engage in a mutual development process of a case management approach with benefit recipients and third sector organisations.

7.3.3.3 Local techniques of control

Different national and local techniques are applied in region G-C in order to control the delivery of services by the Jobcenter, field service staff and the project executing organisations.

National directives of the employment agency on national management objectives for the integration into employment and education as well as national minimum standards on client contacts are regarded by the local actors as only one aspect of control. The director of the local employment agency explains that the national benchmarks on labour market integration and cost developments serve as a basis for discussions between the Jobcenter and the supervising authorities on how to improve activities. The management of the Jobcenter also highlights the effect of the national minimum standard requirements on local practices. According to his observation, the standard requirement to sign integration contracts helped to institutionalise this practice among field service staff.

Although the idea of benchmarking has been principally accepted by all local actors, the Jobcenter management and the municipal authority are not ready to let national objectives on cost-reduction or placement numbers dominate local activities. The local appointee for labour market policy acknowledges that non-compliance with national benchmarks and minimum standards might put the local director of the employment agency in an uncomfortable situation vis-à-vis its national superiors. If necessary, however, he stresses that the local community would prefer to enter in an argument with the Federal Employment Agency.

Instead of relying too heavily on national benchmarks or standards, the Jobcenter management and the municipality prefer to trust in the field service staff's proper capability of reaching the goal of activation. The local appointee for labour market policy explains why he trusts in the field service staff of the Jobcenter:

> "Us, ourselves we know what we are doing here and how we are doing it, and if it serves some statistical requirements, we do it in order to comply with the minimum standards but we ourselves know very well what we are doing here, because very many of the communal employees work as counselling staff, who have learned as part of their education how to deal with room for manoeuvring, how to comprehensively manage a case. That means, we can have discrepancies of what is controlled and what is happening in the Jobcenter." (G-C-4).

Apart from benchmarks or standards, the manager of the Jobcenter explains that field service staff has to give arguments why it uses certain measures:

> "In a way of quality control, every single colleague will be able to justify his or her actions, or will need to justify his or her actions if asked: 'Why did you deem this reaction as necessary for this person?' And then, the colleague has to explain this decision on the basis of arguments but not on the basis of referring to certain categories." (G-C-2).

The management and the supervising authorities describe this discursive strategy of control as a way to detect problems and to find out ways how to improve approaches. In order to track benefit recipients' development, for example of those taking part in workfare jobs, the case-managers and the management of the Jobcenter regularly exchange with the social enterprises and social welfare associations. The management underlines that he also uses the close direct exchange with the third sector organisations as a way to evaluate the success of programmes:

> "We have an integration quota of the public employment schemes of around 20%. This might sound poor but if we take into account the target group of those measures that is not used to work anymore and confronted with multiple integration obstacles and additionally has psychological problems, then it is a result that is a success. The results in numbers are one aspect, but the feedback, the personal discussions, and the continuous negotiations with the social enterprises repeatedly confirm this." (G-C-3).

To sum up, the federal steering mechanisms on the success of placement activities are only loosely applied – and to some extent even circumvented – by the municipal promotion of a local system that leaves room for proper judgements to field service staff and project executing organisation. This system tends to be based on mutual trust between actors of their capacity to assist citizens with gradual reintegration processes into employment.

7.3.3.4 Towards a participatory logic of activation in region G-C

To conclude, activation in region G-C is achieved by the provision of both services for the rehabilitation and placement into work of unemployed minimum income recipients.

The institutionalisation of an organisational field for the activation of benefit recipients is based on a strongly established local community: an experienced and well staffed municipal administration, an engaged local treasurer, an active local parliament and very established local social enterprises and social welfare associations use their strong relationships and contacts to advocate for the persistence of a local approach. The local community thus actively strives to continue a partnership-based local approach at the intersection of social work and labour market policy focusing on assistance for very vulnerable and hard to place groups of long-term unemployed. Some elements of the national framework as for example the signature of integration contracts, the competences of the Federal Employment Agency's placement officers and the general principle to activate benefit recipients into work are locally adopted. Also the linkages between the Jobcenter and the social welfare services are strengthened due to the initiative of the Jobcenter management. However, overall, the organisation of the Jobcenter is shaped by a long-standing local approach which is based on broad local partnerships.

In this local context, activities are planned on the basis of discussions between counselling staff, Jobcenter management, project executing organisations and the supervisory authorities. These arguing processes on how to best achieve an individual activation of benefit recipients are institutionalised in various ways. Arguing processes on the overall strategy of the Jobcenter take place on the supervisory board and in regular meetings between the local employment agency, the municipality and the Jobcenter management. At the same time, arguing processes are also institutionalised in the form of regular group discussions, phone calls, event days or mutual visits between the Jobcenter management, the counselling field service staff, the social enterprises and the social welfare organisations. As a result, a participatory logic defines how to implement publicly subsidised employment programmes, debt counselling, drug counselling or psychological assistance according to the benefit recipients' needs.

Local actors not only rely on national benchmarks on placement control but reciprocity in defining service delivery produces trust in each other's capacities to find the right solutions. While the national benchmarks and standards guarantee the local acceptance of certain minimum standards such as the signing of integration contracts, local actors explicitly renounce to set detailed indicators or to ask for reports to guarantee the activation of benefit recipients. Instead, the supervising authorities trust in the ability of the well-qualified counselling staff, the well-known project executing organisations and the Jobcenter management to achieve the activation of benefit recipients into work, subsidised employment or social rehabilitation services.

All in all, activation of persistently unemployed and weaker groups of the labour market receiving minimum income benefits is achieved according to a participatory logic by making a strong local community and established providers partake in a discursive strategy of how to use active labour market policy programmes and social rehabilitation services for individualised local approaches.

Taking into account the strong local community, the different arguing processes on service delivery between manifold actors and a trust-based local control process, the co-production of services to activate unemployed comes close to a participatory logic of local governance in city G-C.

7.3.4 Local governance of welfare interventions in local authority G-D

Activities to activate persistently unemployed and weaker groups of society in region G-D face a difficult socio-economic context. Unemployment has been consistently at a very high rate, and the level of minimum income recipients is elevated. Situated in former East Germany, the city is still struggling with the dramatic decline of its heavily industrialised economy. In the aftermath of reunification, up to 90% of industrial employment in the city was lost. In the meanwhile, important investments comprising large state subsidies have been undertaken in order to establish a service and technology oriented economic basis in the city. While some major German enterprises opened production facilities or service hubs in the city, the economic tissue remains incomplete due to a weak basis of SMEs as well as limited research and development activities. Production activities are still underdeveloped and, therefore, remain subject to attempts of local economic policy. The city is governed by an alliance between the social democratic party (SPD) and the conservative party (CDU). The mayor is a social democrat. The difficult financial situation of the city has been aggravated by continuously rising debt rates which the city government has not been able to curb effectively yet.

7.3.4.1 Local institutional conditions for the take-up of services and policies

In reaction to the constant and dramatic decline of employment due to rationalisation, the city had built up a large sector of publicly subsidised, regular paid employment during the 1990s and the beginning of the 2000s. Subsidised both from local, national and European funds, the city financed social enterprises and ran a public company to hire subsidised employees. Recent misuse and lacking accounting of subventions caused a public outcry and high demands of reimbursement by the funding bodies. As a result, not only the local social treatment of unemployment was called into question but, shattered by this financial scandal, the local partnership structures to sustain this approach were discredited.

A particular local approach of working together which would date back before the founding of the Jobcenter does therefore not exist. Due to the recent case of corruption, approaches of local partnership or local bureaucracy are widely discredited. Some of the important persons from the municipality were discharged after misuse of public employment investments had been discovered. Also the current director of the local employment agency took office only after the founding of the Jobcenter. Nobody reports on long standing relationships with another actor. Instead, the civil servants from the supervising authorities mutually question the other partner's competences.

The weakness of local municipal structures persists in the context of the Jobcenter. In the field of labour market policy and social policy, the city lacks proper social strategies, personnel and expertise. The city administration does not count on a department or on experts with an explicit labour market policy profile. Instead, the municipal supervisory authority over the Jobcenter is shared by the directorate for social affairs and the directorate for economic development. Given this situation, municipal civil servants recognise that the city lacks administrative personnel to develop proper concepts for the Jobcenter. In the official context of the Jobcenter, the municipality has chosen a political representation by its leading local government figures. However, the leading local government figures including the mayor are described not being familiar enough with the issues of the Jobcenter in order to be able to intervene in detail.

In contrast to the weakly elaborated municipal structures, the local employment agency as the other supervising authority of the Jobcenter is represented by a very experienced director. Furthermore, three civil servants of the local employment agency, who are specialised on issues of the Jobcenter, assist the director.

In short, a breach of trust has discredited bureaucratic and local partnerships relations in region G-D, leading to a situation of rather weak and fragmented actor relationships.

7.3.4.2 *Local modes of interaction for the delivery of services*

Every three, four months, both supervisory authorities get together to hold a session of the supervisory board. On the supervisory board, the municipality is given the decisive chairmanship as the municipality agreed to accept the Federal Employment Agency's minimum standard requirements, which for instance demand implementation of the benchmarking system. However, initiatives or suggestions with regard to the Jobcenter are rarely undertaken by the local politicians representing the municipality on the supervisory board. The director of the local employment agency remarks that the city forgoes to take advantage of its chairmanship of the supervisory board:

> "The city would have the majority, even with regard to issues of the labour market programme, if the city drafted a proper programme, submitted it to the supervisory board and decided on it, and even if we were all against it, the city could still implement it. However, they don't go that far, but theoretically, they could." (G-D-1).

Discussions on the supervisory board are described as being rather superficial. The sessions merely serve the purpose of taking official decisions on the Jobcenter.

Also apart from the supervisory board, the city rarely seizes actively its authority over the Jobcenter. Renouncing on assuming proper action, civil servants of single municipal directorates usually ascribe responsibilities to other municipal directorates, to the local employment agency or to the management of the Jobcenter. The civil servants from the city administration acknowledge that the city has not yet managed to develop a common strategy with regard to the Jobcenter. A municipal civil servant describes how the city is caught between interests of budget-friendly policies, interests of providing qualified labour for regional economic development and interests of solving the social problems connected to the large number of long-term unemployed:

> "Yes, we just don't have a clear strategic focus. On the one side it is the budget, the regular labour market, but we also have large unemployment, therefore, we also need to offer programmes for publicly subsidised employment." (G-D-5).

In view of a lacking municipal concept what to do with the long-term unemployed, all municipal actors find their common denominator in implicitly or explicitly agreeing that the Jobcenter should at least not cost much. In this situation, municipal budgetary interests regularly prevail over 'social' or 'regional development' interests.

Furthermore, the local administration blocks demands of the local parliament of a more direct parliamentarian influence on the Jobcenter. The municipal administration highlights that the Jobcenter should be governed by its administrative supervisory board and not by parliamentary committees. Instead, representatives of the political parties of the local parliament were granted membership on the advisory board. In region G-D, the advisory board is a large committee made up of 22 local representatives comprising also the social partners, the chamber of commerce and trade, the social welfare associations, representative organisations of unemployed and the municipal appointee for migrants. However, while the advisory board is described as serving as informational basis for the public, it is unanimously regarded as non-influential.

Given the absence of local bureaucratic negotiation processes or larger civic discussion processes, the local employment agency can exert its influence on the Jobcenter in a relatively unchallenged manner. Interpreting its proper supervisory authority in a widely autonomous manner, the director of the employment agency invites the two managers of the Jobcenter every two weeks to instruct them on current issues. The director of the employment agency explains that the management of the Jobcenter, including the deputy manager who was sent by the municipality, has adopted the perspective of the employment agency on many matters.

> "He [the municipal deputy manager of the Jobcenter] is sometimes even rather against his employer when it comes to questions of policy priorities and goal-setting. This is also due to (…) the collaboration we also undertake with him, because he recognises at the occasion of some issues and of some points that our perspective, which we have adopted as employment agency, is rather apt to make things move on." (G-D-1).

Relatively unchallenged, the local employment agency forwards a concept for a transparent, market-oriented approach in region G-D. The strategy of the Jobcenter in region G-D is concentrated on placement into the labour market of those unemployed easier to place. Social problems of persistently unemployed minimum income benefit recipients are not regarded as tasks that the Jobcenter needs to tackle. Resuming the prevailing local strategy, the manager of the Jobcenter points out that cost efficiency concerns prevail over social considerations in the local service delivery:

> "Let's be realistic. A certain group of clients will not have a chance on the first labour market. This is at least consensus among our local supervising authorities. We should not waste money by spending only due to reasons of social policy deliberations (…)." (G-D-2).

In short, exploiting the weakness of the municipal authority, the directing staff of the local employment agency is able to lobby for a cost-efficient strategy concentrating on labour market placement. This strategy is explicitly adopted by the

Jobcenter management while the municipality at least implicitly gives its accord as it is not able to present any alternatives.

Devising and organising the local employment programme and its services

The employment programme is primarily worked out by the management of the Jobcenter and the local employment agency. The regular exchanges with the Jobcenter management give the local employment agency's directing staff the opportunity to lobby for political priorities of the national level. Decisions to shift resources from one activity to another are often taken ad hoc during meetings between the management of the Jobcenter and the directing staff of the local employment agency. If detected by the city, the local employment agency and the management of the Jobcenter together defend such changes on the supervisory board.

The local employment agency has a strong preference for wage subsidies and qualification programmes in order to assist activation into the regular labour market and to accomplish the national benchmarking objectives. Although the city has adopted the position of the local employment agency to some extent, its civil servants still stress the need for subsidised employment. The municipal civil servants consider public employment as a necessary political response to high unemployment: public employment can cover both local social problems and municipal tasks, as for example landscape maintenance. The director of the municipal directorate for economic development also explains that the activation of benefit recipients into regular employment often does not pay off for the city as many benefit recipients would not earn enough to free the city from paying housing benefits:

> "If it is a joint organisation, both should be able to reduce their shares of financing in a parallel manner (…). Only then a real incentive is given for the municipality, so that it really comes up with ideas and also finally tries out new approaches. Otherwise, (…) the share of those who are benefit recipients despite proper incomes continues to increase and we are not relieved from benefit payments." (G-D-5).

Reflecting the preferences of the local employment agency, resources for the local employment programme have been continuously shifted from subsidised employment towards measures for the activation into the regular labour market. Wage subsidies and qualification measures today represent a large share (40%) of the resources used.40% of the resources of the local employment programme are nonetheless still spend on subsidised employment. Thereof half of this share is used for workfare community jobs and the other half for more generous employment schemes. In the programme of the Jobcenter in region G-D, the provision of social welfare services does not play a role.

Based on the employment programme, the Jobcenter orders the programmes for training and further education via the centralised tendering body of the Federal Employment Agency. The director of the local employment agency explains that programmes are not planned before delivery with a particular local project executing organisations. Regarding training and further education programmes, he explains, that commonly worked out projects would not be possible as they could always be allocated to another project executing organisation during the centralised competitive tendering process. In contrast to training and further education, procurement of the different types of subsidised employment is still a local matter organised by the municipal directorate for economic development. At the background of the corruption scandal (cf. chapter7.3.4.1), also the municipality was asked by all actors in the region to increase transparency of the public employment procurement process. Programmes are therefore increasingly contracted out to private project executing organisations that are not any longer involved in the planning of the subsidised jobs. Instead of developing more elaborate programmes with the local social enterprises, cost-efficient strategies are chosen: workfare community jobs are implemented on the basis of a minimum standard financial endowment which is paid to the project executing organisations.

Apart from the delivery of labour market programmes, efforts to coordinate activities between the Jobcenter and the local social welfare services do not exist. The management of the Jobcenter does not consider social problems of minimum income benefit recipients as issues the Jobcenter is responsible to react to. On the other side, a representative of a local umbrella organisation of the welfare organisations highlights that the welfare organisations would often not perceive a needy person's joblessness as their proper problem. Also the responsible municipal directorate for social affairs does not take initiative to link its services of drug counselling, debt counselling, psychosocial counselling or child care to the activities of the Jobcenter. Furthermore, the representative of a large welfare association resumes that it does not make sense for the counselling centres and outreach clinics to cooperate with the Jobcenter as the Jobcenter does not practise a case management on the social problems of the minimum income recipients:

> "I would absolutely not oppose, if a case-manager of the Jobcenter said: okay, now I am approaching this case as a case-manager in a comprehensive manner, and I will see, what is all necessary, I will coordinate and mediate this process and I will overview this process. Maybe, I will invite the concerned actors to a round table on the concrete case, so that we can altogether draw up an integration plan for the benefit recipient. I would not at all oppose such an approach, but this instrument does not exist at the Jobcenter, (…)." (G-D-7).

As a result, staff of the Jobcenter is not aware of the capacities of the social services and they do not know how to make them accessible. If benefit recipients deem it necessary, they can directly contact a social welfare organisation. However, in region G-D, limited municipal capacities and, therefore, long waiting periods from six up to twelve months for counselling sessions are reported.

All in all, the strong role of the local employment agency in the planning process as well as the lacking engagement of the municipal side and its third sector organisations trigger an employment programme which is focused on active labour market policy. The selection of programmes and their delivery process tend to be influenced by efficiency concerns and strategies of cost-minimisation. In consequence, a greater coherence between programmes of active labour market policy and activities for rehabilitation, care and counselling is not achieved.

Definition and organisation of counselling and placement

Not only the focus of the employment programme rests solely on labour market integration but also field service staff is directed by the local employment agency and the management of the Jobcenter to concentrate on an efficient approach of active placement. For this purpose, staff is advised not to spend too much time with single benefit recipients. A more comprehensive approach including social counselling is regarded as not efficient in light of the many benefit recipients. In this context, placement officers, sent from the employment agency to the Jobcenter, are praised to master an efficient approach to placement. In contrast, municipal social workers' ambitions to react to social problems of benefit recipients are regarded as problematic. The management of the Jobcenter views it necessary to explicitly instruct the social workers to focus on placement:

> "We are not responsible for case management on social matters. We need to draw limits for counselling, and larger counselling activities comprising social matters, we have to leave to others. (…). (…)the social welfare services (…) have to take care of these tasks. In these cases, we have to leave it to them. Okay, you have to explain this to people who have done it like this for decades, and this takes time. Those employees who came from the placement agency are more at ease with such an approach as they have never learned it differently." (G-D-3).

To activate benefit recipients, the Jobcenter counts on 800 employees sent by both the city and the Federal Employment Agency. The supervising authorities in region G-D select staff for the Jobcenter as they hold responsibilities for hiring. As national miscalculations on the need of staff also affected Jobcenter G-D, an immediate additional demand of staff arose right after the founding of the Jobcenter. Staff was increased by roughly 300 employees. The federal authority stocked up personnel by providing redundant staff from former state owned companies or by hiring highly qualified university graduates with diverse educational backgrounds– often for temporary employment only. By doing so, the employment agency increased its share of staff up to two thirds. As a result, apart from the deputy manager, the managing positions in the Jobcenter are entirely held by placement officers from the Federal Employment Agency. In contrast, the municipality did engage much less in providing additional staff. As the municipal servants explain, in the whole process of providing staff, the municipality did not actively try to find suitable personnel for the Jobcenter. One reason why the city did not send extra municipal social workers was that its social services were short of social workers themselves. Another reason, pointed out by the municipality, has been the very difficult municipal financial situation which would have made it difficult to hire additional personnel. Instead, similar to the strategy of the employment agency, the city transferred to the Jobcenter staff from different areas of municipal competence where staff had become redundant. A civil servant of the municipal directorate for economic development explains that the creation of the Jobcenter provided the opportunity of 'outsourcing personnel':

> "All in all, this was also an outsourcing process (…). The Jobcenter was a spin-off for both sides, (…). According to this spin-off strategy, one kept the best people rather in its own ranks than actively sending them to the Jobcenter." (G-D-6).

The city and the welfare associations remark that a more individual placement or counselling would not be possible due to lacking numbers of field service staff and problems of qualification. The management of the Jobcenter also points out that staff of its Jobcenter only has a limited ability for mastering social and work-related placement and counselling tasks. According to the managers of the Jobcenter, this also explains why staff requires instructions to renounce on more-time consuming interactions with benefit recipients. The director of the local employment agency judges that the capacities of the Jobcenter's field service staff suffice for a cursory placement approach. Although the civil servants' of the city observe that the intensity of placement and counselling is low, municipal civil servants highlight that the administration of the Jobcenter achieves to function in a very cost-efficient way. A tendency would exist to make use of the measures which can be most easily applied.

All in all, instead of tailor-made or even a participatory approach in dealing with the benefit recipient, the Jobcenter G-D concentrates on a cursory placement approach which is based on efficiency concerns and strategies of cost-reduction.

7.3.4.3 Local techniques of control

In region G-D, control techniques are applied in order to focus management and placement officers of the Jobcenter as well as project executing organisations on achieving placement into employment or subsidised employment.

Control of activities of the management of the Jobcenter, staff and project executing organisations primarily rely on benchmarks for successful placement of the unemployed into employment, education or publicly subsidised jobs. For this purpose, the national benchmarks serve as very important reference. In addition, the local supervising authorities used their discretion to add local benchmarks. The municipality asked for setting local benchmarks for costs of housing as well as for the number of persons that are supposed to be placed on workfare community jobs.

Especially the local employment agency exerts high pressure on the Jobcenter to fulfil the national objectives agreed on. Without any participation from the municipal side, the local employment agency organises a continuous monitoring process. In front of the director of the local employment agency, every two weeks, the managers of the Jobcenter have to justify the performances of the Jobcenter with regard to the national benchmarks on benefit payments and placements into employment, education and publicly subsidised jobs. During these meetings, the importance of achieving high numbers of placement into employment or subsidised employment is stressed by the local employment agency. The managers of the Jobcenter in region G-D acknowledge a strong influence of the employment agency on their measures taken. They identify 'expenses for benefit payments' as crucial indicator. Similar strong attention is paid by the management on achieving the prescribed 'number of integrations of unemployed into labour, education or publicly funded employment'. Not only the management, but all actors in region G-D have accepted the national goals on placement into employment, education or publicly subsidised jobs as a strong guide for action.

To better achieve high numbers of placement and the reduction of benefit payment expenses, placement activities in region G-D are explicitly concentrated on those minimum income recipients who are regarded to have greater chances of employment (re-) integration. Placement services, qualification and employment programmes are concentrated on those unemployed with moderate employment opportunities. Only for these groups of unemployed the use of placement efforts and other resources is considered reasonable by the management of the Jobcenter as well as by the local employment agency. In contrast, reintegration efforts are completely withhold from those benefit recipients who are being internally considered as not able to take-up work. For concentrating resources on groups of unemployed closer to the labour market, local decision makers use a categorisation of the benefit recipients according to their capacities. This categorisation was asked for by the Federal Employment Agency. In region G-D, the categorisation thus serves as a local concept to maximise the outcome of placement activities. The manager of the Jobcenter resumes the local strategy to reach a resource-efficient placement of the unemployed:

> "This is certainly a strategic question, how you deal with a mass clientele and with whom you can reach something or not. (...) One has to pay attention to cost-efficiency arguments. (...) those 20% of our clients most remote are not counselled by us. They only get their monthly benefit payments."(G-D-3).

In contrast, efforts to report on the development of the benefit recipients' employability are not undertaken in region G-D. The managers of the Jobcenter do not consider such a concept as practicable in the framework of the management objectives. The city criticises the lacking focus on employability as a civil servants from the directorate of employment points out:

> "(...) we observe that there exist no activities, which are targeted on developing dynamics in between these categories. This would imply an intensive development of those in the most distant group onto the next category and from the next one towards the following on. We are missing this and we are missing what would be required conceptually to achieve such an innovation." (G-D-6).

In brief, the national benchmarks on the reduction of costs of benefit payments and the placement into employment and education strongly condition local activities of the Jobcenter, its management, its field service staff and the project executing organisations in the regions. This is underlined by a local steering concept which puts a focus onto unemployed with better activation opportunities in order to maximise the Jobcenter's output in terms of cost-reduction and successful placement. During regular monitoring sessions with the Jobcenter management, this market-oriented style of control is strongly promoted by the local employment agency.

7.3.4.4 Towards a market-oriented logic of activation in region G-D

In summary, the organisation of services to activate minimum income recipients in region G-D comes close to a market-oriented logic. Primarily national resources for placement and active labour market programmes are made use of in the local organisation of policies and services. National benchmarking priorities on placement into the labour market and cost-reduction of benefit payments are advocated by the local employment agency, while local social work approaches and services are widely renounced on in the Jobcenter framework. Matching cost-efficiency strategies, placement services concentrate on those unemployed people who are easier to place on the labour market.

Region G-D reveals a shattered local community. Bureaucratic interventions or partnership structure for policies and services are discredited by recent scandals. The structures, local relationships, personnel and experiences of a past local labour market policy, which focused on public employment for the long-term unemployed, are today viewed sceptically by all local actors. Moreover, primarily due to weak structures of coordination and lacking expertise in the local administration, a fragmented local community struggles to develop strong preferences on matters of social welfare policy: the local community does not achieve to put forward concepts how to deal with benefit recipients experiencing different and multiple problems of employment, rehabilitation, counselling or child and family care. Given the lack of a municipal stake in the process, the Jobcenter organisation is dominated by cost-efficiency strategies drawn up by the Federal Employment Agency's local civil servants. In contrast to the local community, a well-staffed local employment agency strongly advocates its preferences on focusing efforts on placement activities in employment or education of the unemployed.

The federal steering and policy instruments for placement activities provide resources which are used at the local level for implementing a market-oriented logic. Local modes of interaction tend to be dominated by cost-efficiency concerns. Expert-negotiations or wider arguing processes on the services to deliver are rare. Instead, crucial relationships of the local organisation tend to be dominated by a logic of competition on scarce resources. Relations between the Jobcenter and the third sector organisations are solely reduced to the procurement process. Project executing organisations are paid a low tariff for their services to recipients. Furthermore, staff is advised to maximise successful placement into employment or education by applying a cursory, quick approach in placement services. At the same time, paying attention to the social problems of the unemployed is regarded as inefficient as it is deemed too time consuming and not leading to immediate results with regard to the integration into the labour market.

The activities of project executing organisations and staff are controlled by placement benchmarking. For this purpose, the national benchmarks on cost-reduction and placement into employment and education are accepted by the local actors as a strong orientation. To ensure the use of the national benchmarks, the local employment agency has institutionalised a regular monitoring process.

Local benchmarks play neither an important role nor do they provide for goals in the area of social welfare services or the employability of benefit recipients.

All in all, the organisation of the minimum income scheme in region G-D comes close to a market-oriented logic of the activation of the unemployed into employment or education. Making use of national resources and competences, the local employment agency can successfully advocate an approach based on a cost-efficient organisation of placement services to capable clients.

7.4 Conclusion: varying local activation approaches in Germany

The chapter illustrated at the hand of four case studies how activation of persistently unemployed and weaker groups of society is achieved in Germany at the local level. The German welfare state has been facing the same challenge as the French welfare state: a rising number of persistently unemployed, weaker groups of society and persons with non-standard employment biographies has become dependent on minimum income benefits.

Reacting to these challenges, the social protection and labour market reforms in Germany are partly calling traditional boundaries between previously fragmented and disparate fields of welfare production into question. Reflecting general developments of the Bismarckian welfare states, as an answer to challenges of long-term unemployment and 'precarious' social situations caused by social and economic changes, the German welfare state centres on the activation of weaker groups into work as a new institutional filter against dependency on assistance benefits. Corresponding to this new institutional filter, the two-tier social protection system was subject to employment friendly reforms. Only for short-term unemployed core workers with a steady contribution record, the principle of status- and job protection remains in place by an unemployment insurance programme. As a crucial step towards a more employment-friendly system, the tax-funded status-oriented unemployment assistance scheme and the tax-funded subsidiary social assistance scheme were merged into a new work-oriented means-tested minimum income scheme against social exclusion. By this step, demands for social protection of persistently unemployed, weaker groups of society and persons with non-standard employment biographies were recalibrated from generous status-based protection onto this work-oriented minimum income scheme which provides benefits at the level of former social assistance. In a parallel step, services and work incentives are stipulated for the work activation of the minimum income scheme recipients. As a further reform parameter, increased labour market flexibility is targeted at creating work opportunities for weaker groups particularly by low-income employment. Taken together, the greater harmonisation of the social protection system, the stipulations for services and work incentives as well as a partly flexibilisation of the labour market add up to a Bismarckian-type of activation in Germany which centres on employment as mode of welfare production for weaker groups.

Discussion of the first hypothesis: activation as a matter of the local organisation

This attempt of employment-centred welfare to decrease pressure from minimum income schemes raises the question how persistently unemployed, weaker groups of society and persons with non-standard employment are assisted to integrate into the labour market. The new work-oriented minimum income scheme stipulates the merging of the previously disparate fields of local social welfare and national unemployment policy: a delivery of both benefit payments and services to minimum income recipients shall be organised by Jobcenters jointly run by the municipalities and the Federal Employment Agency. While constituting a fresh organisation, the division of labour between the two authorities for the tasks of the new minimum income scheme strongly respects the traditional boundaries of the fields of national unemployment policy and local social welfare policy. While the federal government and its Federal Employment Agency account for placement activities and financing unemployment benefits, the municipalities continue to hold responsibility for housing payments and social welfare services. Regulation therefore strongly respects the former boundaries of the two policy fields. The idea is that both authorities achieve to inter-organise the fragmented competences of the two policy fields. As a result, the functioning of the Jobcenter is to a great extent left to the local coordination efforts between the municipalities and the local agencies of the Federal Employment Agency.

As stipulated by our first hypothesis, these attempts to activate the long-term unemployed, vulnerable groups and persons with non-standard employment biographies turn into a matter of local coordination processes of previously fragmented policy fields. The case studies show intense local coordination processes to organise services for the activation of benefit recipients. In the German cases, it depends on the local actors' efforts in as much activation attempts take into account both 'social' and work-related exclusionary factors of benefit recipients: local concepts of case management and the local organisation of staff decide in as much national placement competences and municipal social workers are combined. In the German cases, inter-organised services for the activation of benefit recipients also depend on local agreements and exchanges between the Jobcenter and the local third sector organisations. Finally, the work-oriented national benchmarks require the local level to come up with proper benchmarks and concepts in order to foster activities of the Jobcenter which take into account not only work-related but also 'social' exclusionary factors of benefit recipients. Thus, local coordination attempts are about the attachment of placement services, social counselling, labour market programmes and social services to benefits.

The four German local case studies illustrate that the national reform ambition to activate benefit recipients into work and services is indeed being implemented at the local level. All actors principally agree with the idea to activate benefit recipients and rise up to the challenge to organise services accordingly. Locally developed activation approaches combine services and turn the division of labour between national competences for placement and communal social work competences into inter-organised local fields to co-produce targeted services for the activation of long-term unemployed, weaker groups of society and persons with non-standard biographies. None of the local cases studied contradicts the national reforms. The idea of unconditional benefit payments, which would have matched a traditional social treatment of unemployment in Germany, is neither practised in one of the regions studied nor is it considered an appropriate way to deal with unemployment by the actors in charge of decision-making in the four local cases. As all four German case studies show, the local actors are thus capable to inter-organise local fields for the activation of benefit recipients, but they do so differently.

Discussion of the second hypothesis: variance in the local organisation of activation

As provided for by our second hypothesis, variance in welfare interventions towards benefit recipients can arise due to differences in local structures, modes of interaction and control forms.

In region G-C, an inter-organisation of both placement and counselling activities primarily produces a participatory logic of activation. Actors in this region rely on a long-standing local partnership-based approach for service delivery. Building on each other's competences in social work and active labour market policy, a local concept is organised in practice which individually assists benefit recipients who are very difficult to place. Actors from the field of social welfare policy and labour market policy come together on institutionalised occasions, like for example group discussion fora, mutual visits, information days or 'jour fixe', in order to discuss on how to deliver services. Acting on relatively equal terms, placement officers, social workers, managing staff, representatives from third sector organisations, local politicians, leading civil servants of the municipality and the local employment agency as well as to some extent even benefit recipients are involved in a process of exchanging their experiences and arguments at different occasions and in different constellations forming the basis of a trust-based participatory logic of service delivery. According to the predominant characteristics in structure, interaction and control, the organisation of services in region G-C comes therefore close to a participatory type of activation.

In contrast, inter-organised service reactions to social and work-related beneficiaries' needs in regions G-A and G-B are defined in closed negotiations between civil servants of the local employment agency and the municipality. Decision-making processes predominantly rely on long-standing, entangled bureaucratic institutional structures. The delivery of social and labour market services in the local authorities G-A and G-B is a matter of very technical negotiations and hierarchical instructions. A very dense system of control instructs staff and project executing organisations how to react to both social and labour market problems of benefit recipients. It comprises both national benchmarks, and local benchmarks, exact placement objectives for single programmes and prescriptions for counselling and placement, reporting requirements, and detailed standards of procedures. According to the dominant characteristics in structure, interaction and control, the organisation of services in region G-A and G-B comes close to a bureaucratic type of activation.

In local authority G-D, a local strategy of cost and time efficient placement of those unemployed who are easier to place is given priority. Besides this work orientation, proper local approaches how to deal with 'social' exclusionary factors of long-term unemployed are hardly promoted. In an institutional setting of weakly elaborated relationships, the smallest common nominator, which the local actors are sharing, is a market-oriented approach giving value to transparency and cost-reduction. Cost-minimising strategies dominate in the organisation of placement and active labour market services. In region G-D, a strict local application of the national benchmarks for work integration and cost-reduction shall orient field service staff and project executing organisations towards a market-oriented strategy of placement activities. Overall, according to the dominant characteristics in structure, interaction and control, the organisation of activation in region G-D stipulates a market-oriented approach.

In sum, confirming expectations formulated in our second hypotheses, the cases in Germany reveal local variation in the organisation of activation approaches. In the German case studies, the local co-production of services varies between market-oriented concepts to quickly integrate unemployed clients into the labour market, bureaucratic approaches for enabling the social inclusion of beneficiaries and participatory activation approaches to empower persons to choose among different services.

Local activation approaches: explanatory factors of the national framework

While some local authority and discretion exists for the municipalities and the employment agencies to organise benefits and services to activate weaker groups, the national framework provides crucial legal, financial, and administrative rules and resources for the local organisation. Thereof, the stringent work-oriented minimum income benefit regulation and new organisational instruments strongly influence the local organisation of the German activation regime.

The development of the local cases is influenced by the 'self-help' legacy of the German subsidiary social assistance regulation. While strong work conditionality requirements had been absent in the former German system of unemployment insurance and unemployment assistance, the idea of 'self-help' had already been a guiding principle of former social assistance regulation. Also the new minimum income scheme remains basically subsidiary to self-help in the form of family welfare or income from employment (Jacobi and Mohr 2007: 227). The fresh ideas of 'demanding' and 'promoting' work as well as the important family responsibility for benefit receipt are indeed principles which are very much in line with former conditionality requirements of German social assistance (Lahusen and Stark 2003). By the Hartz-reforms, this conception of 'self-help' has been confirmed as a general principle for the new minimum income scheme.

In addition to the legal conception, it is the work component of the subsidiary principle of German minimum income scheme regulation which is strongly reinforced by new organisational provisions introduced by the national level. In the studied cases, the system of national benchmarks and minimum standards are highly influential on the local organisation. For all local actors, the national benchmarks constitute a crucial point of reference for the local organisation. The national benchmarks serve as important guide for the local approaches' to strive for the activation of benefit recipients into work or education. In addition to the benchmarks, minimum standard requirements of the Federal Employment Agency on the local organisation influence the local approaches. The minimum standard requirements, including stipulations like the signature of integration contracts, locally strengthen the idea to ask minimum income recipients to individually contribute to the success of counselling or placement. In short, as a result of the introduction of national organisational prerequisites like benchmarks and minimum standards, the local implementation of the minimum income scheme is being oriented in a general manner towards activation approaches.

To sum up, the important local room for manoeuvring in the German cases is nationally framed and strongly shaped towards the activation principle by a 'historically' consistent work requirement component of minimum income benefit regulation and by the introduction of new national organisational instruments as benchmarking and minimum standards.

Local activation approaches: explanatory factors at the local level

While the national level thus enhances local activation by stringent national regulation and benchmarks, local dynamics determine the concrete institutionalisation of the German activation regime.

Not only the national framework, but also long-standing local practices make the idea of activation a concept principally shared at the local level in Germany. Already before the founding of the Jobcenter, municipalities had begun to stress the work component of the social assistance regulation. In the framework of the locally run, subsidiary former social assistance scheme, many of the municipalities started to initiate their own 'welfare-to-work' schemes (cf. chapter 6.2). As rising numbers of social assistance seekers had caused increasing local budgetary problems, many municipalities began to give more importance to the conditionality requirements provided by the social assistance regulation and they started to ask benefit recipients in a more rigorous manner to take up work. Benefit recipients were often required to accept workfare community jobs or more generous, public employment subject to social contributions which were run by the municipalities (Gangl 1998). As a result, already before the founding of the Jobcenter, most of the municipalities had accorded increased importance onto the idea to require an individual contribution of benefit recipients and to strive for work-integration of the benefit recipients.

Despite this general acceptance of the activation idea in the German cases, the case studies also show that regional approaches are far from being homogenous. In each local organisational field, we find 'skilled' actors trying to institutionalise different concepts(Fligstein 2001b) how to approach the task of activating minimum income recipients.

In all four case studies, despite being generally committed to activation, municipal actors step up as advocates of social issues which resemble traditional concerns of German local social welfare arrangements. Municipal actors and those from the third sector associations usually stress the need of a more holistic approach comprising the use of social welfare services in order to react to the challenges of minimum income receipt. They view workfare jobs and other schemes of subsidised employment as a good alternative to the benefit recipients' integration into the regular labour market. Their preference for subsidised community work is connected to the ambition to strive for solutions which also help to deal with the social and economic problems of the municipality. Finally, instead of competitive tendering, the municipal actors and the third sector associations prefer local and more direct ways of organising the delivery of services. All in all, the municipal actors carry on many ideas which guided the delivery of social assistance before the founding of the Jobcenter. These local 'social' preferences are usually advocated by the civil servants in the local administration and they are ascribed to the municipal social workers. Interestingly, the municipal mayors usually share these ideas independent from their political affiliation.

In contrast, in all four case studies, the local employment agencies' directing staff steps up as advocates of new organisational principles. They argue in favour of the benefit recipients' integration into the regular labour market and of benchmarks on placement and benefit development. All directors of the local employment agencies have incorporated a strong commitment to a transparent and efficient dealing with resources, benchmarking for cost-control and placement and activities enhancing the activation into the regular labour market. Their goals very much resemble the national targets set by the Federal Employment Agency. The local agencies' directing staff thus steps up as agents at the local level of the strategies set by the national level. Usually, the local agencies' directing staff views the placement officers as an agent of their strategies on the street-level.

While advocates for these different strategies can be found in each local case study, it depends on the institutional positioning of actors in a given local organisational field to determine which organisational strategy will be prevalent in a region (Bourdieu and Wacquant 1992; Fligstein 2001b).

In local authority G-C, a strongly established and active community commonly takes up the charge to organise placement services and welfare services. Resembling the traditional picture of German 'network-based local systems of welfare' (Mignione et al. 2002: 63; cf. also chapter 6.2), a long-standing local partnership for labour market policy exists between an experienced municipality, very established local social welfare organisations and social enterprises, active local parliamentarians, engaged local politicians and other stakeholder of local civil society. In this region, the municipal preferences for an organisation which ensures a stake for many local actors are clearly dominant. The municipality counts on extremely skilled actors lobbying for the interests of the municipality. It counts on a municipal appointee for labour market policy who strongly lobbies for guaranteeing the local interests and the involvement of many stakeholders in matters of the Jobcenter. Furthermore, the local parliament has developed a strong interest in issues of the Jobcenter. In addition, the strong municipal role is manifested at the street-level of the Jobcenter which is mostly made up of municipal social workers. Moreover, local authority G-C, is the only region in the German sample where a local political figure plays an outstanding role: the local treasurer strongly lobbies for guaranteeing a strong municipal stake in the Jobcenter. In region G-C, for the actors, it was therefore a matter of course to continue on the basis of these local structures. Changing the established partnership arrangement would have met fierce opposition of a third sector, engaged local politicians and active local parliamentarians which form an extremely interwoven complex in support of the existing structures. Submitting to this prevalent local partnership structure, the local employment agency can utter its preferences only as one 'new' partner among many established ones. For delivering services to long-term unemployed, the local employment agency was simply incorporated into these partnership structures. As a result, the Jobcenter is dominated by an organisational approach which resembles traits of the former local welfare system: not only do local authorities determine the development of the Jobcenter but also the third sector organisations have a strongly institutionalised role in the decision-making process.

Despite a dense tissue of third sector organisations and reports on past 'partnership' approaches, the new Jobcenter organisation leads to a bureaucratic governance approach in region G-A and G-B. As local politicians and parliamentarians leave matters of the concrete organisation of the new Jobcenter to their local civil servants, long-standing bureaucratic ties are strengthened. Local bureaucrats in region G-A and region G-B eagerly accumulate legal, financial, and administrative resources of the Jobcenter for boosting their proper position. As a result, bureaucratic institutional ties which had evolved between the local employment agency and the municipality for instance in a pilot project to the Jobcenter organisation (MoZArT project, cf. also Fleckenstein 2008 on its relevance for local co-operation), are privileged. In both regions, specialised municipal labour market departments advocate the different local concerns, while the local employment agencies lobby for the goals of the Federal Employment Agency. A constant struggle of both actors to ensure their share in the Jobcenter makes the organisation a matter of bureaucratic interventions and technical negotiations. The ambition of both actors to guarantee their stake in the organisation is evidenced by the relentless interventions of their civil servants in the steering of the organisation. Both the employment agency and the local authority feel a constant need to intervene to indeed ensure that developments proceed according to their preferences. The local organisation therefore results from detailed compromises between the local employment agency and the municipal administration. As a consequence, the chosen organisation of the Jobcenter reflects a 'negotiated' strategy. In both regions, the founding of the Jobcenter has therefore produced a situation which leaves not much room for other actors, such as the social partners or the third sector organisation, in the decision-making process. For example, the social partners and the third sector organisations are 'discarded' onto non-influential advisory boards of the Jobcenter instead of being involved in the formal and particular informal circles of the local administration and the local employment agency. As a result, a rather monopolistic bureaucratic structure is enhanced by the creation of the Jobcenter while elements of a former networked local system of welfare lose relevance, at least in local policies on matters of the minimum income scheme.

Traditional local governance approaches are most radically challenged in region G-D, where the local employment agency can reform the local system in the strongest way. In this municipality, previous local institutional ties between local bureaucracies and the local community were being disrupted. A recent case of corruption has discredited the local bureaucracy as well as its former ties with third sector organisations and local politicians. In local authority G-D, as bureaucratic or participatory approaches are discredited in most of the actors' eyes, the local employment agency's advocates of a more transparent and market-oriented approach step up. The directing staff of the local employment agency successfully lobbies for organising the Jobcenter strongly according to criteria of efficiency. As a result, the local approach to deal with long-term unemployed is changed from a municipal participatory approach into one putting a stronger focus on a market-oriented organisation. Here, the founding of the Jobcenter and the appearance of the local employment agency in the steering of the minimum income scheme thus led to a changing approach towards dealing with minimum income recipients.

To sum up, the new organisation of the Jobcenter has opened a window of opportunity for actors to challenge and in some cases change the previous 'partnership'-based local governance system in Germany. In contrast to the traditional local social welfare system, in region G-D, the local employment agency successfully lobbied for a re-organisation towards a greater market-orientation. In regions G-A and G-B, the entrepreneurial local employment agencies were required to compromise with strongly established local municipal administrations on a 'negotiated' approach. Finally, a highly mobilised third sector but also committed local politicians, local parliamentarians and civil society worked for the continuity of the partnership-based local organisation in region G-C.

To conclude, the successful local institutionalisation of an activation regime for long-term unemployed, weaker groups and persons with non-standard biographies in Germany is a matter of both national as well as local developments. While the national framework leaves much room for the concrete inter-organisation of benefits, placement and social welfare, it shapes the local organisation towards activation. The 'historical' continuity in work-oriented national regulation of the minimum income scheme and the organisational framework enhance a general application of the activation paradigm at the local level. In particular, new national organisational requirements as benchmarking for placement and cost-control as well as minimum standards comprising the nation-wide introduction of integration contracts set important national parameters for the local organisation.

At the same time, given the local room for manoeuvring, the development of local institutions crucially influences the organisational solutions found at the local level. Generally, already before the Hartz reforms, most of the municipalities had tended to turn the focus on activating long-term unemployed or vulnerable assistance recipients by shifting greater attention to the work-requirement component of the former social assistance regulation. At the same time, the new Jobcenter framework brings together actors at the local level who forward different concepts how to activate long-term unemployed. While communal actors continue to lobby for traditional concerns of German local social welfare arrangements, the local employment agency challenges the local organisation by the national 'market-oriented' activation concept. It very much depends on the local institutional positioning of the two actors how the prevalent activation approach evolves in a region. Where local institutions are weakly elaborated, local agents of a market-oriented approach successfully reform the local service delivery system. Where long-standing institutional ties between bureaucracies are locally privileged over local partnerships, a more bureaucratic strategy evolves as a result of closed negotiations between the municipality and the local employment agency. And where a strong institutional partnership of local government, parliamentarians, third sector organisations and local administrations persists, we observe a participatory approach involving manifold local actors in the organisation of activation approaches of long-term unemployed and vulnerable groups.

8. The institutionalisation of employment-centred welfare in France

At the background of increased numbers of recipients of minimum income benefits in France (cf. Fig. 1), in the following chapters, it is analysed how labour market and social policies react to this challenge. We analyse the introduction of activation policies and we investigate into attempts of re-organising the approaches towards unemployed and persons at the risk of social exclusion.

8.1 Labour market- and social policy reforms in France

In reaction to rising unemployment, non-wage labour costs and public deficits, France has introduced labour market and social protection reforms. New government priorities – at least partly – initiate a shift from the social treatment of unemployment towards the activation of unemployed into employment. The French reforms match the typical Bismarckian welfare state reform patterns of activation at the 'margins' (Clegg 2007) and thereby put minimum income schemes into focus.

8.1.1 Changes in the French benefit system

The Bismarckian style French social protection system has been subject to numerous important changes.

A series of changes of the unemployment insurance programme has remodelled the programme into a more employment oriented benefit system (Allocation de Retour à l'Emploi, ARE). Several, albeit smaller reforms have led to an increasingly circumscribed provision of unemployment insurance benefits (Daguerre and Taylor-Gooby 2003: 630). Most significantly, in 2001, given continuous budgetary problems of the unemployment insurance programme, the social partners agreed to restrict entitlement criteria by strengthening the insurance principle. Stricter contributory requirements for accessing unemployment insurance and a reduction of the maximum duration of entitlement from 30 down to 23 months were introduced.

In parallel to the unemployment insurance programme, a specific unemployment assistance programme remains in place for long-term unemployed with a strong contribution record (Allocation spéciale de solidarité, ASS).

Criteria relevant for entitlement to this benefit are significantly stricter than for unemployment insurance and require a long-standing contribution record. Given a further tightening of eligibility criteria, this flat-rate and tax-financed unemployment assistance turns into an exclusive social protection option for older long-term unemployed (Barbier and Knuth 2011a; Clegg and Palier 2012). Simultaneously, marking a further step of a new policy to limit options of exit from the labour market onto social protection, access to early retirement schemes was restricted (Barbier and Kaufmann 2008: 116–118; Daguerre and Taylor-Gooby 2003: 630).

The greater limitations in these more generous, higher-ranking programmes of status-protecting social security benefits have contributed to a constant increase in the number of persons requiring protection against social exclusion (Daguerre and Taylor-Gooby 2003: 630). Particularly younger unemployed, persons with weaker or unsteady contributory records and precarious non-employed increasingly have to rely on the general minimum income scheme against exclusion. Since the introduction of the means-tested 'minimum income for insertion' (Revenu Minimum d'Insertion, RMI) in 1988, the number of assistance recipients has significantly increased. While only 410,000 persons received this assistance at the end of 1989, with 1.3 million recipients in 2005, it has evolved as the most important instrument of basic security in France (Anguis 2007).

Eligibility to the general minimum income scheme against social exclusion still remains independent from the ability to work. However in 2010, the general minimum income scheme was reformed into a new, work-oriented general minimum income programme (Revenu de Solidarité Active, RSA). While the prior minimum income for insertion (RMI) connected benefits to an unspecified activity requirement, the right to claim the new 'active solidarity allowance' is now privileging work conditionality over social insertion (Barbier and Knuth 2011a: 14; Clegg and Palier 2012). Social insertion shall remain an option only for those seriously limited in their work ability (Lafore 2009). Very similar though to the benefit regulation of the prior RMI, benefits for the precarious non-employed remain at a moderate level and do not include housing benefits.

As a result of the introduction of the RSA, coverage of the general minimum income scheme was extended. By merging the flat-rate, means-tested minimum income benefit for single parents (API) into the new general minimum income programme, coverage was extended to single parents. In contrast to the previous regime (RMI), which excluded young people without children, coverage of the new benefit was also extended to all persons under twenty-five years of age who have worked at least two years of the previous three. Apart from the benefits granted to precarious non-employed (RSA *socle*), the generalised minimum income extents coverage in a permanent manner also to employed persons with low-incomes (RSA *socle et activité* or RSA *activité seul*) (Clegg and Palier 2012). Despite this trend towards an increasing broadening of the general minimum income scheme against social exclusion, category-specific flat-rate and income-tested programmes remain in place for older unemployed with a strong contribution record (Allocation equivalent retraite, AER), long-term unemployed with a strong contribution record (ASS, see above), disabled persons, or for asylum seekers and other persons with specific backgrounds (Allocation temporaire d'attente, ATA) (Barbier and Kaufmann 2008: 92–94; Barbier and Knuth 2011a). The extension of coverage nonetheless generalises a 'basic' social protection character of the once marginal minimum income benefit scheme in France (Clegg 2010): with two million benefit recipients in 2011, the tax-financed and work-oriented general minimum income scheme against social exclusion takes a crucial function in a reformed French benefit system whose specialised and higher-ranking programmes of social security have become less encompassing.

Given the increased focus of the higher-ranking status-protecting social security programmes on those unemployed with stronger contribution records, a work-oriented minimum income programme increasingly presents the basic social protection scheme against social exclusion for precarious groups of the labour market, long-term unemployed, and otherwise disadvantaged groups of society in France.

8.1.2 A reformed regulation of services, incentives and work requirements

In parallel to the reforms of the benefit system, over the last decade, a stress on placement, incentives and work requirements has been introduced in policies towards unemployed.

For the insured unemployed, in 2001 'a back to work plan' (plan d'aide au retour à l'emploi, PARE) was adopted by the social partners who are responsible for the governance of the social insurance programme. It aims at work placement of the insured unemployed. As a result of the PARE system, the insured unemployed are now required to search for work and to accept training offers (Barbier and Kaufmann 2008: 85–89). In 2010, furthering the linkage between social insurance and work placement, the local agencies for benefit delivery (ASSEDIC) of the French social insurance (UNEDIC) were integrated with the placement service agencies (ANPE), into one single organisation (Pôle Emploi).

Compared to the fresh employment orientation of the insurance system, however, much more stringent work requirements, incentives and services have been introduced for the general minimum income programme. A series of reforms has reinforced the idea of the minimum income scheme to function as a welfare-to-work scheme: "(…) in the French case the importance given recently to the 'trap' problem as well as the new welfare-to-work approach, represents a major change in the employment and labour market policy regime."(Erhel and Zajdela 2004: 139). While the original minimum income benefit regulation was already based on the requirement for benefit recipients to sign an agreement on participation in 'integration measures' (Clasen and Clegg 2003: 376), social forms of integration were privileged over work obligations. However, consecutive reforms have increased the significance of the linkage between work and income. In 2003, the general minimum income benefit (RMI) was supplemented by a work-based benefit supplement (Revenu minimum d'activité, RMA) which was conditional upon the acceptance of employment. In 2010, the introduction of the active solidarity allowance (RSA), which reformed the former general minimum income programme (RMI), set a clear preference of the linkage between benefits and work over social activities (Clegg and Palier 2012). The new regulation stipulates the requirement for benefit recipients to look for a job by registering at the public employment agency (Pôle Emploi) or the responsible local authority (Département) (Barbier and Knuth 2011a: 14). Social integration activities shall be prescribed from now on to those benefit recipients only who have serious social problems and these activities shall become part of a work-integration process.

To enhance work integration, case-managers (référents) shall sign and coordinate the work integration plan (contrat d'insertion) with each minimum income recipient. The integration contract shall propose an activity responding to the benefit recipient's economic situation, employment, health or social problems or his or her need of education (Avenel 2007). Not least because of the recent minimum income benefit reform, benefit recipients are now principally being treated in the same way as other unemployed 'job-seekers': they should have access to the range of employment policy instruments operated by the public employment services and all other providers (Clegg and Palier 2012). This range of active labour market policy instruments comprises training schemes for the unemployed, temporary subsidised employment in the public and non-profit sectors and subsidised contracts in the market sector for persons who are difficult to place (Barbier 2007: 159).

The regulation for the active solidarity allowance furthermore increases the minimum income benefit recipients' responsibilities (*devoirs*) to comply with the work integration activities proposed by a case-manager. While the former philosophy of the minimum income scheme was based on a mutual commitment approach, the right (*droit*) to the minimum income scheme is now being paralleled by a greater stress on individual duties (Clegg and Palier 2012). In line with the greater stress on individual obligations, the existing sanction regime in the case of non-compliance has been made easier to apply. Partial and temporary withdrawal of the benefit payments is now possible under the new active solidarity allowance regime (Clegg and Palier 2012). The former sanction regime for minimum income benefit recipients only provided for a complete withdrawal of benefit payments which was often considered as being a too harsh option. The greater enforceability of work requirements finally corresponds to a new definition of 'reasonable' employment which was introduced in 2008. It limits the range of reasons for which an unemployed might refuse a job opportunity (Barbier and Knuth 2011a: 13).

In short, in parallel to the increased reliance of persons with unsteady employment biographies, precarious workers and long-term unemployed on the general minimum income benefit, remodelled stipulations for services, incentives and conditionality requirements focus on the take-up of work of minimum income benefit recipients.

8.1.3 An increased flexibilisation of the French labour market

At the background of limited employment opportunities particularly for persons with non-standard employment biographies or otherwise disadvantaged groups, the introduction of several labour market policy elements has been aimed at achieving a new 'full employment objective' in France (Daguerre and Taylor-Gooby 2003).

Flexibilisation of the labour market was not introduced in a comprehensive manner, but geared towards low-income segments. In France, opportunities for atypical employment (contrats aidés, stages, prime pour l'emploi) were stepped up by consecutive labour market reforms (Clasen and Clegg 2003: 370). As part of this approach, the consistently high share of subsidised employment remains a "fundamental feature of French-style activation" (Barbier 2007: 159). Recent subsidised work initiatives were particularly targeted at the long-term unemployed minimum income recipients (Barbier and Kaufmann 2008: 82). For example, in the frame of the RMA, subsidies were paid to employers who hired long-term minimum income benefit recipients. Although the subsidised employment contracts offer a regular employment status, they often do not prevent against low-income receipt or risks of poverty (Barbier 2007: 159).

This principle of low-income employment instead of minimum income benefit receipt is most explicitly put forward by the new regulatory framework for the active solidarity allowance (RSA). In the new regulation of the minimum income scheme, a permanent tax credit was introduced in order to incite take-up of low-income employment. To increase work incentives, a so far marginal and unspecified tax credit (prime pour l'emploi) is now being explicitly targeted at low earners. For this purpose it was attached to the minimum income regulation and the payment mode was shifted from an annual to a monthly subsidy. Employment of long-term unemployed or otherwise disadvantaged groups is thus incited by a top-up for low earners.

Finally, labour market flexibilisation was strengthened through the increased possibilities of atypical employment contracts (Barbier and Kaufmann 2007).

These changes in labour market regulation add up to an attempt to promote employment for weaker groups of the labour market and long-term unemployed by work opportunities in low income employment segments: "(...) despite the existence of a minimum wage, work cannot protect against poverty. (...) in both France and the UK, the principal objective is to avoid social assistance, even if this results in a 'working poor' group who will then require specific transfers." (Erhel and Zajdela 2004: 138).

In brief, changes in the social protection system and a greater stress on services and work requirements go in hand with a partial flexibilisation of the labour market which attempts to increase employment opportunities among low income sectors as an alternative to minimum income benefit receipt for long-term unemployed and otherwise disadvantaged groups of society.

8.1.4 The selective focus of a Bismarckian activation regime in France

The institutionalisation of employment priorities for social and labour market policies in France focuses in a rather selective manner on the activation of weaker and more vulnerable groups. Matching a typical Bismarckian reform trajectory, labour market and social policy reforms in France are in an important manner influenced by the legacy of a status-oriented field of social and labour market policy and the disparate existence of a field of social welfare.

Despite important changes, a system sharing important traits of occupation-related, generous Bismarckian social protection remains in place for short- and long-term unemployed with strong contribution records. On the other hand, a residual and strongly work-oriented means-tested benefit system is institutionalised for recipients of the generalised minimum income scheme (RSA), while other weaker groups (e.g. long-term unemployed with strong contribution records, disabled persons, categories of young) are partly spared out by the new activation attempts.

Reform attempts initiated by national legislation thus remained mainly confined to the boundaries of the single policy fields, notably social welfare and occupation-related social protection institutions. The strong inertia of an insurance based, corporatist institution at the core (UNEDIC) has led to an ever growing fragmentation of programmes and initiatives around this relatively stable core. In labour market and social policy, social partners remain powerful advocates of the insurance system and its institutions as they see a strong interest in preserving corporatism in the formation and management of these schemes (Clasen and Clegg 2003). As a result, reforms did neither reach a comprehensive homogenisation of services and benefits for all unemployed nor a comprehensive flexibilisation of the labour market for all employees (Clasen and Clegg 2003; Daguerre and Taylor-Gooby 2003: 632). Portraying the consequences of French labour market and social policy dualism, fragmentation persists between benefit regulation, administrative structures and services. Given the lack of a comprehensive re-organisation, strong demands of coordination arise (Daguerre and Taylor-Gooby 2003: 632; Clasen and Clegg 2003).

In short, while regulation of labour markets, social benefits and services has been reformed by employment-friendly policies, the policy changes did not achieve coordination or integration of the system of benefits and services for unemployed in a more comprehensive way. This kind of policy reaction typical for a Bismarckian welfare state is explained by the role of social partners conserving the core of an industrial risk community.

8.1.5 Conclusion: activation as new filter against minimum income receipt in France

Summing up, labour market and social policy reforms in France fit into typical Bismarckian attempts to institutionalise an employment-centred welfare production for weaker and more vulnerable groups as a new institutional filter against minimum income benefit receipt (cf. chapter 3.5).

Matching a typical Bismarckian reform trajectory, activation reforms do not principally call into question the fragmented benefit system in France, but lead to an important remodelling of benefits, services and labour markets aimed at the take-up of employment of weaker and more vulnerable groups who had been usually excluded from the labour market in the past. Bismarckian institutions of social insurance or occupation related social protection programmes principally persist but access is increasingly closed off for weaker and more vulnerable groups. Generous unemployment insurance remains in place for short-term and long-term unemployed with a strong contributory record. However, steps were introduced in order to deter insured unemployed from long-term benefit receipt which might possibly lead to minimum income benefit receipt. Reduced duration of entitlement and active labour market policy for work placement require insured unemployed to remain active in order to return to work.

Separate from joint insurance and employment services, social assistance persists as residual benefit programme. In order to react to increased minimum income benefit claims of weaker and more vulnerable groups, several new social and labour market policy measures provide for their activation into work. Particularly for recipients of the generalised minimum income scheme against social exclusion (RSA, formerly RMI), work-conditionality requirements have been introduced. Furthermore, new regulation proposes case management and the use of active labour market policy and social services to enable work integration of minimum income benefit recipients. Also the flexibilisation of labour markets has focussed on the creation of atypical jobs and low-income work opportunities for weaker groups of the labour market, long-term unemployed or low-skilled who are now often in receipt the main minimum income benefit in France.

Employment-friendly labour market and social policy change in France is thus 'selective' as it tends to uphold job-protection and access to occupation-related social protection institutions for persons with standard employment biographies while long-term unemployed, persons with non-standard employment biographies or otherwise disadvantaged groups are activated from assistance receipt into low-paid or atypical employment. To put it into a nutshell, activation reforms in France attempt to introduce activation into employment as a new institutional filter for weaker and more vulnerable groups against the receipt of minimum income benefits.

8.2 The re-organisation of service delivery for minimum income recipients in France

In France, the challenges to activate minimum income recipients are paralleled by a steady trend of decentralisation of minimum income benefit provision and service responsibility. Following decentralisation reforms (2003–2004), a local authority (*Département*) received important competences for social assistance (RMI/RSA). The traditional 'centrally-regulated local system of welfare' is thus subject to change through the decentralising of competences for the minimum income benefit recipients onto the local authority of the departments.

This decentralisation of social assistance inscribes in a broader trend to decentralise tasks of welfare state policy and to increase room for manoeuvring of actors at the regional and local level. The first decentralisation reforms in 'centralised' France in the 1980s initiated a trend to strengthen sub-national levels of authority, namely the regions, the departments and the communes. In the area of employment, local one-stop-shops for all unemployed (Maison d'Emploi), which could be run by sub-national authorities, were strongly promoted by the state from 2004 on in many regions. In parallel, broader attempts were also undertaken to revive the third sector at the local level (Bahle 2003: 13). But also the typically centralised public employment services became subject to attempts of regionalisation and its regional and local agencies were strengthened (Berthet 2002; Borras 2006, 2008; Greffe 2005). As a result of the strengthening of sub-national authorities, third sector organisations and the local public employment agencies, considerable local leeway has developed possible approaches to activate weaker groups of the labour market, long-term unemployed or low-skilled, since those tasks are less monopolised by national actors.

This increased local room for manoeuvring is connected to the expectation that an opening of the separated policy fields and isolated actor relations can be achieved in France at the local level (Berthet 2002, Borras 2008). As *chef d'orchestre* (Lafore 2004), the departments are charged by national regulation with the coordination and integration of work-oriented policies, benefits and services to activate recipients of the general minimum income scheme (RMI/RSA). As a traditionally important actor in the field of social welfare policy, in the course of decentralisation, the department has accumulated not only responsibility for the benefit provision of the minimum income scheme but also competences for several social welfare services. At the same time, the departmental level lacks experiences and competences in active labour market policy (Lafore 2004: 30). At the local level, besides social welfare services provided by a department, recipients of minimum income schemes can access services run by the public employment service (Pôle Emploi), the local agencies of the national ministries, other sub-national actors, action plans for long-term unemployed (Plans Locaux pour l'Insertion et l'Emploi, PLIE), and local one-stop shops for employment (Maison d'Emploi). Concerning this situation, for the departments, the challenge arises to combine its tasks for benefit provision, its competences in social welfare and the 'external' services of active labour market policy: "Since the creation of the RMI, the issue is posed of the articulation between the social and work-related dimension of insertion." (Le Bihan et al. 2006: 8).

Consequently, the institutionalisation of an organisational field for the activation of recipients of the minimum income scheme depends to a great deal on the extent to which the departments are capable to locally coordinate policies and services with the fragmented national and local, public and private, social welfare and active labour market policy service providers and agencies. The decentralisation of competences for the minimum income scheme has raised important issues of the implementation of service delivery. The administration of benefit payments and the coordination with services pose new challenges for the departments (Borgetto and Lafore 2007). The local authorities are confronted with tasks to secure resources for the assistance scheme, to ensure activity requirements in the administration of benefits, to install a case management system and to enable access to suitable services for their recipients.

8.2.1 A local framework for the delivery of diverse benefits and services

The criteria of access and the level of assistance benefits remain regulated nationally. At the same time, the department is now in charge of the former state task of leadership (*chef de file*) in devising (*planification*) services of the minimum income scheme (RMI/RSA) (Borgetto and Lafore 2007; Lafore 2004). Legal provisions oblige the departments to install case-managers and to sign integration contracts with recipients (Borgetto and Lafore 2007). Furthermore, the RSA reform, which was being implemented at the time of research, requires the departments to categorise benefit recipients into a group of persons being able to take up work and a group of persons requiring social counselling first. Local policy activities and services for the assistance recipients shall be put forward in regular departmental plans for integration (*plan départemental d'insertion*; PDI). The local authority's integration plan can be made up of a range of instruments.

8.2.1.1 Financing responsibilities

For financing benefit payments of the minimum income scheme, the departments receive fixed grants from the state. Their volume was fixed at the time of decentralisation of the minimum income scheme. In addition, the departments receive payments from the *Taxe intérieure de consommation sur les produits pétroliers* (TIPP), whose development is not, if not even negatively connected to the development of the number of welfare recipients. For the departments, responsibility for the minimum income benefit can thus pose a financial risk (Aubree et al. 2006 et al.; Borgetto and Lafore 2007; Foucault et al. 2008).

8.2.1.2 *The organisation of services reacting to work-related and social exclusionary factors*

The departments hold responsibility for a set of social welfare services described below (cf. chapter 8.2.1.3). In addition, the departments are free to create proper instruments, for instance for labour market integration. To initiate such additional social welfare or labour market activities for beneficiaries of the minimum income scheme, the departments can develop so called 'facultative' instruments. These activities might comprise health care and rehabilitation services, education or training offers.

For the delivery of social services, the departments more and more tend to rely on third sector organisations. To make use of services of welfare associations, public tenders serve as a new instrument increasingly applied since decentralisation:

> "The decentralisation has in effect in an important manner affected relationships between the departments and the third sector organisations. A new dominant logic of service delivery was introduced which relies on public tenders, the creation of competition and the use of evaluation procedures in order to assess the quality and efficiency of these interventions." (Le Bihan et al. 2006: 8f).

As an alternative to social welfare services and to the creation of proper active labour market policy programmes, the departments have the opportunity to finance complementary capacities for minimum income benefit recipients in the 'normal' active labour market policy instruments described below (cf. chapter 8.2.1.4). For this purpose, the local authority can conclude contractual agreements for example with the sub-national agencies of the state, the public employment services, other sub-national authorities or welfare organisations (Aubree et al. 2006; Le Bihan et al. 2006).

The variety of actors intervening in the services delivered to minimum income recipients can even further increase, if a department makes use of its option to delegate powers to other sub-national authorities. If other sub-national authorities agree, the department can confer onto them elements of the delivery of services and benefits (Lafore 2004: 30). Tasks can be delegated to the municipalities, working groups of several municipalities and municipal organisations. Le Bihan et al. (2006: 6f) observe that such decentralised structures can cause further problems with regard to the consistency of departmental policies towards minimum income recipients.

8.2.1.3 *Social welfare services for minimum income recipients*

In addition to the decentralisation of the social assistance scheme, the second act of decentralisation conferred important social services (care for the elderly, help for people in great difficulty, housing) and 'social assistance for the young' (Fonds d'aide aux jeunes en difficulté, FAJ); social assistance for 18–25 year olds) onto the responsibility of the local authority. The departments are now responsible for measures and the oversight of institutions for the inactive (protection of disadvantaged children, dependents, the disabled, elderly) and for the integration of persons at risk of marginalization, notably persistently unemployed, weaker groups of the labour market and low-skilled.

For activities to accompany and orient benefit recipients, the departments have doubled their staff in the immediate aftermath of decentralisation. Decentralisation of the minimum income scheme 'automatically' led to an increase of the local authority's personnel: social workers, that prior to decentralisation had served the assistance seekers in the state run social field services (Direction départementale des affaires santaires et socials, DDASS), now resumed tasks for the department. As a result, one third of overall departmental staff implicated in the delivery of the minimum income scheme consists of former employees of the state. One fifth of employees to serve benefit recipients, were internally recruited by the local authority from other parts of the departmental administration. Consequently, the departments basically and usually exclusively employ social workers for delivering services to minimum income recipients (Le Bihan et al. 2006).

Staffed with social workers, the departments run proper social welfare centres which offer social counselling to recipients of the minimum income scheme. Apart from social counselling, the social welfare centres are generally a place to go for filing minimum income benefit claims and housing payment demands. The centres also offer the many social services, which the departments have accumulated in the course of the decentralisation process.

Consequently, with the delivery of a variety of social services, but also the leadership for devising various fields of social welfare, the departments fulfil a global role in coordinating and designing social welfare services that had formerly been exercised by the state (Borgetto and Lafore 2007; Lafore 2004).

8.2.1.4 *Active labour market policy services for minimum income recipients*

Apart from social welfare services, the local authority does not hold any responsibility for the regular active labour market policy instruments. Definition, governance, parts of financing and provision of the main labour market policy instruments are principally in the hands of other bodies. The implementation of the key active labour market instruments normally provokes the intervention of a multitude of actors. These instruments, which are enumerated in the following, are normally provided to beneficiaries by the public employment agency, Pôle Emploi. On the basis of written agreements (conventions), other actors as the department might also intervene in the direct provision of some of these instruments to unemployed.

Partly publicly financed work contracts are an important instrument of French labour market policy (Barbier 2007). Among the partly publicly financed work contracts, the CAV (Contrat d'avenir) for the public sector and the CI-RMA (Contrats d'insertion-RMA) for the private sector are exclusively designed for the beneficiaries of the main minimum income benefit[5]. For instance, a private employer who hires a welfare recipient can receive a wage subsidy up to a maximum of 18 months (minimum of 12 months). In addition to work, the subsidised contracts demand activities of social counselling and training (and a sustainable employment for the beneficiary in the aftermath). The department, but other territorial authorities or organisations as well, can ask the departmental agency of the national labour ministry, (Direction Départementale du Travail de L'Emploi et de la Formation Professionnelle, DDTEFP), to supply it with a certain number of CAV or CI-RMA which the department can then offer to its benefit recipients (Aubree et al. 2006; Avenel 2007). In this case, the department will co-finance a certain percentage of a work contract for a beneficiary of the minimum income scheme employed in the private or public sector. If the department wishes, it can also step up itself as public employer of a person subject to a publicly financed work contract. In mid 2008, 179 000 beneficiaries of the minimum income scheme received a wage subsidy (Cazain et al. 2008). Globally seen, this instrument is the most important single measure for assistance seekers (Avenel 2007; Pla 2007).

The *plan local d'insertion par l'économie* (PLIE) presents a multiyear, local integration plan combining social counselling and job placement on the long-term (a maximum of 18 months) for the long-term unemployed. It can spring from the initiative of a sub-national authority. Simultaneously, the plans are under supervision of the regional agency of the national labour ministry (Direction Régionale du Travail, de l'Emploi et de la Formation Professionnelle, DRTEFP[6])

---

5 In 2010, after empirical research for this work, both contracts were merged with two similar instruments into a single contract (contrat unique d'insertion, CUI) for all jobseekers. The principal mechanisms of implementation however remain unchanged.

6 At the time of empirical research for this work, the sub national state agencies were subject to a reorganisation process (2009-2011). As a result of this process, the departmental as well as the regional agency of the national labour ministry were merged

as well as the prefect. Financing of this instrument is accounted for by the European Social Funds (ESF), the state and sub-national authorities who wish to intervene. The number and coverage of local integration plans in a local authority depends crucially on the initiative of the actors intervening in this region.

The *secteur de l'Insertion par l'Activité Economique* (SIAE) supports to different degrees publicly financed employment in enterprises that offer combined work opportunities and social counselling with varying intensity according to the difficulties of long-term unemployed. The sector is under authority and supervision of the departmental agency of the national labour ministry. It is financed by the state, the ESF and sub-national authorities if they wish to engage.

Among the range of 'normal' labour market instruments (droit commun) every unemployed job-seeker should in general have access to placement and other measures supplied by the Public Employment Agency (Pôle Emploi), which are most notably (short) training schemes.

In addition, the regional authorities account for an important part of further and advanced training.

In brief, the departments face the task to guarantee access to the different active labour market policy instruments which are governed and financed by a range of different public and private providers.

8.2.1.5 The department as social welfare provider in need of external competences

To summarise, the department thus evolves as key actor in the field of social welfare (Lafore 2004). Taking into account previous responsibilities of the department, the decentralisation reforms have reinforced the department as most important local authority. However, apart from its narrower competences for social policy and social welfare services, experiences of the departmental level in employment policy are depicted as extremely weak (Lafore 2004: 30). In order to increase capacities in active labour market programmes for minimum income benefit recipients, the department can create its proper programmes or strive for detailed agreements with the different state providers.

---

together with related agencies into one regional agency for economic issues (Direction régionale des entreprises, de la concurrence, de la consommation, du travail, de l'emploi, DIRECCTE)

8.2.2 Coordination and activation through local case management

For the orientation and control of the minimum income benefit recipients, the decentralisation laws prescribe to appoint a case-manager (*référent*) for each beneficiary. On the basis of an integration contract, minimum income benefit recipients are required to search for work, to receive training, to work in a publicly subsidised employment scheme or to contact a social counselling.

8.2.2.1 Coordination and control of access to the different services and programmes

In theory, access and orientation to the manifold services and programmes enumerated above shall proceed via a case-manager who is named by the department for each assistance recipient. However, a minimum income recipient is also free to directly solicit Pôle Emploi or another organisation for placement or social counselling.

For the recipients of the minimum income scheme, access to the different social welfare and labour market policy programmes is possible via a multitude of access points. Principally, most of the labour market policy programmes can be accessed via Pôle Emploi. Usually, the local integration plans combining social counselling and job placement for the long-term unemployed (PLIE), the publicly financed employment schemes in enterprises that offer combined work opportunities and social counselling (SIAE) or the departmental social counselling programmes can be accessed through departmental service centres, too. But also other public social service institutions, like the 'local communal centres for social action' (Centres communaux d'action sociale; CCAS), or even some of the welfare associations can refer minimum income recipients onto the general labour market programmes.

This complex situation raises the question of the linkages between the department, the multiple organisations for placement and social counselling as well as those organisations delivering programmes. Without any exchange it will be de facto impossible for the local authority to account for the outcome of what was agreed on in an integration contract between an assistance recipient and the department. Up to now, the informational devices and data files of the main organisations – Pôle Emploi, the PLIE and the local authority – are not compatible. Moreover, they differ extremely in their sophistication and reactivity.

8.2.2.2 Orientation through case management

The activation of recipients thus depends in an important manner on the organisation of local staff, notably case management by the local authority. The department has the legal obligation to appoint case-managers for minimum income recipients. In practice, the matching of competences of the *référents* with the individual requirements of assistance recipients is a crucial question (Le Bihan et al. 2006: 10) which influences the orientation of the benefit recipients either toward work or social treatment.

The departments can fulfil the legal obligation of case management by nominating the social workers employed by the departmental welfare centres as case-managers. Most of these departmental social workers are charged with tasks of social counselling in local social welfare centres run by the department. Thus, if the departments nominate social workers of their social welfare centres to act as case-manager, it is not evident at all that a placement orientation is offered to the beneficiaries of the minimum income scheme.

As an alternative to nominating social workers as case-managers, the departments can also delegate tasks of case managing to professionals of other service agencies, for example to the public employment service or social welfare associations. In these cases, placement officers of the public employment services or social workers from welfare associations would be appointed as case-manager. For this purpose, contracts between the department and the other provider agencies need to be concluded.

8.2.2.3 The crucial role of case management in the French system

To summarise, in the French system case management plays a crucial role in order to activate long-term unemployed and weaker groups of the labour market. It is connected to the question if recipients are 'counselled' on social issues by social workers or rather 'placed' on the labour market by placement officers. The department itself usually exclusively employs social workers who execute multiple tasks of social counselling and services in the local authority's welfare centres. Furthermore, case management is connected to the issue how rights and obligations of a benefit recipient might be enforced and how benefit recipients are oriented towards the different providers for training, counselling or publicly subsidised work programmes.

8.2.3 Local coordination bodies

Local policy activities and services for the assistance recipients shall be put forward in regular departmental plans for integration (Plan départemental d'insertion, PDI). The departments have the right of initiative for this plan. The parliament of the department has to adopt the plan.

The law provides for the participation of other actors in devising policy activities. Local coordination of policies and services is by law proposed to proceed in the framework of roundtables uniting relevant actors in a territory. The idea of these roundtables is to coordinate activities and to agree on common strategies for the repartition of activities and resources in a territory. Different local roundtables exist. Among these, it exists one for 'insertion' and a separate one for 'employment'. The department holds responsibility to chair the committee for 'insertion' (Conseil départemental d'insertion; CDI) and to animate several subordinate local committees for 'insertion' (Commissions locales d'insertion; CLI) in its local authority.

Avenel (2007) observes that the public employment services and the directorate for integration through economic activities (Le secteur de l'insertion par l'activité économique, IAE), which is a representative body of the welfare associations, usually take part in the meetings of the committee for 'insertion'. Under the level of the department, the *commissions locales d'insertion* (CLI) are supposed to unit local actors to prepare specific, subdivided local integration programmes (Programs locaux d'insertion, PLI). In contrast, the roundtables for employment policy are led by the state. The roundtable of the 'public employment service at the departmental level' (service publique de l'emploi départemental, SPED) shall exercise a crucial role for strategic coordination on labour market policies in a department. The department is not a core member of these regular meetings to coordinate labour market policy. Moreover, at the time of research in 2009, the SPED had virtually reached a dead end. Meetings often did not take place anymore as all actors waited for the implementation of a proposed reform on the organisation of the state agencies at the sub-national level.

Thus, for devising service offers for recipients of the minimum income scheme, the department chairs a mandatory coordination and action planning body for 'reinsertion' and service activities for the assistance seekers are projected in a local authority's integration plan.

8.2.4 The organisation of benefit payment

While applications for benefit payment can be usually filed at the departmental social welfare centres or the municipal communal centres for social action

(Centres communaux d'action sociale; CCAS), the calculation and delivery of benefits is normally administered by the 'pay office for family assistance' (Caisses d'Allocations Familiales, CAF). Prior to decentralisation, the CAF had already been responsible for delivery of benefit payment. Based on contracts with the departments, the CAF have usually continued this task also after decentralisation (Le Bihan et al. et al. 2006: 7). Due to their extensive legal and regulatory expertise, the CAF can act as 'guarantor' that national regulation for benefit payments are respected (Avenel 2006). Responsible for processing and providing benefit payment, the CAF are thus another actor implicated in the service delivery of the minimum income scheme

8.2.5 Conclusion: a fragmented framework for the local activation of benefit recipients

Summing up, the departments can make use of several instruments for the institutionalisation of a local organisational field to activate recipients of minimum income schemes. The local authority chairs an 'insertion' committee to device and to coordinate with other actors a common integration strategy for minimum income recipients. Services and instruments for labour market integration or social counselling can be provided by the department itself, on the basis of contractual agreements or public tenders, by cooperation with other agencies and project executing organisations or by a delegation of tasks to other sub-national authorities. For counselling and placement, the law prescribes the institutionalisation of case-managers. Case management shall implement integration contracts, effectively provide access for recipients to the offers of different services and programmes and apply a sanction regime in the case of non-compliance of recipients.

Despite this strategic role of the local authority for the activation of minimum income benefit recipients, the legacy of the French minimum income scheme of belonging to the 'social welfare system' was though not broadly challenged by decentralisation. Important organisational elements of the social welfare system were transferred onto the local level. The departments 'inherited' social workers from the state run social field services (DDASS) who staffed social welfare centres run by the departments. Moreover, the department does not hold responsibility for any of the main labour market instruments. In addition, participation of the departments in the roundtables for labour market policy in a territory is not guaranteed. Furthermore, scope for manoeuvring for a department could be limited due to risks of financing the minimum income scheme.

The renewal of social welfare into an instrument of activating policy thus requires the local level to master tremendous processes of reorganising tasks of labour market and social policy in order to co-produce targeted and individualised activation of long-term unemployed and weaker groups of the labour market. Having put priority on the organisation of benefit payments in the immediate phase of decentralisation, the departments have in the meantime intensified efforts for the integration of minimum income benefit recipients (Avenel 2007). Nevertheless Borras (2008) observed that the dimension of activating measures had remained weak so far. At the example of four local case studies, these reorganisation processes shall be reconstructed in France.

8.3 The local implementation of activation approaches in France

Taking the examples of four local case studies (local authorities F-A, F-B, F-C, F-D), we investigate into the question of a local co-production of policies and services between the field of social welfare and active labour market policy, between tasks of the national and the local level and between different providers. It is being analysed how processes of re-organisation might result into the institutionalisation of local organisational fields for a targeted and individualised activation of long-term unemployed and otherwise disadvantaged benefit recipients of the general minimum income scheme in France.

8.3.1 Local governance of welfare interventions in local authority F-A

Welfare interventions in local authority F-A proceed at the background of a strong socio-economic situation. Unemployment rates in the local authority have been constantly below the French average. The rate of minimum income recipients is under average compared to other urban departments. The moderate numbers of unemployed and minimum income recipients mirror the positive local economic development. Many of the largest French enterprises as well as some international companies have production or administration sites in the region. Overall, the economy of the department is based on an important production and research sector for the development and production of medium and high-tech technology products, it counts an important service sector including a strong tourism sector and it is still marked by a small but important segment of agricultural production in its surrounding areas.

At the time of research in 2009, the local authority was governed by a socialist president. In the local parliament, the socialist party had an absolute majority.

8.3.1.1 Local institutional conditions for the take-up of services and policies

Since decentralisation, the local authority has increasingly tried to build up services for the activation of assistance claimants. For this policy change, decision-makers of the department highlight as decisive a strong will in political leadership but also bureaucratic expertise.

Since decentralisation, politicians in the government of the department have been engaged in shaping an agenda for the minimum income scheme. The director of the 'insertion policy' directorate of the local administration explains that the latest two vice-presidents of the department which were responsible for insertion policy have been advancing efforts for a greater focus on labour market integration.

> "And then we had a series of vice-presidents in the local government, I arrived at this moment, and I was lucky to have consecutive vice-presidents, (...) which were elected people who had a will to say, 'we need to tackle the issue of labour market integration, we need to provide more means for placement activities, we need to do better in terms of placement activities', in the following, they asked me to put a greater stress on labour market integration in the insertion approaches in the department." (F-A-5).

The politicians favouring a stress on labour market integration delegated implementation of the necessary programmatic and organisational reforms to their administration. The directorate of insertion policy and its director were entrusted with the task to increase the relevance of placement efforts in approaches which had been so far dominated by a social workers' philosophy of a social treatment of benefit recipients. As the director of insertion policy explains, since decentralisation, his directorate has been viewing itself as a 'guarantor' of establishing a new 'culture' of labour market integration:

> "It was also one of the reasons why they [the government] repositioned my directorate in 2004. They positioned it really like a directorate which serves to support the field service staff of the RMI and particularly to help them how to change towards taking into account placement in the most adequate way. That's why I don't have proper field service staff, I know the instruments to spread and I have a culture which I shall try to promote, this means to support the personnel of the local agencies and the directorate for efforts against exclusion and to direct the local social workers to practice placement and labour market integration efforts and to apply those instruments to the clients who are not necessarily those who will themselves orient towards the take-up of work." (F-A-5).

However, not only in the field but also in the central administration of the local authority, adherents of a social work respective social treatment approach remain strong. This is expressed by a division of tasks for the minimum income benefit recipients between an 'insertion' policy directorate oriented towards labour market integration efforts and a directorate for 'efforts against exclusion' oriented towards a social approach. This constellation makes a stringent approach of the local authority difficult as a high-ranking civil servant of the regional employment agency observes. A division thus exists between civil servants who are in favour of an activation approach and another group in the administration consisting mostly of social workers who remain attached to a traditional social treatment approach. The director of the insertion policy directorate explains the development of these two groups:

> "Back in 1998 I found a situation which had not changed a lot. The social workers were still very much attached to this idea, 'we have to work on their social *insertion* first, and we later on, once we will have repaired the people, we can place them onto the labour market. (...) Particularly here [in the administration], we witnessed a differentiation to appear between a certain number of people who were really in favour of this turn: we will take care of a person in a comprehensive manner and we will find solutions for his or her work integration and in parallel we take care of its social problems. They began opposing the culture of the social workers who still remained attached to their traditional position, 'we will first need to take care of the social issues before we think about placement." (F-A-5).

Apart from the political figures and the administrative competences, several welfare associations exist in the region. Often, they run their initiative in partnership with other welfare associations for which they receive funding from the state or the local authorities. A representative from an important welfare organisation in the department explains that the third sector in the local authority interprets its role and its approaches as being independent from any state or sub-national policy:

> "It's one of our political priorities to try and hold on to a certain equality in the relationships between us constituting the civil society which works in the sector of the general interest, (...) and the public authorities, that we rather remain in a partnership relationship instead of receiving instructions as a supplier, (...) we try to resist and to find ways for having more equal relationships. I think the efficiency of the system of insertion is also related to a certain equilibrium, a mutual recognition of the initiatives that emerge from the civil society, the public authorities, and the economic sector." (F-A-6).

In brief, institutional relationships resembling a local partnership structure exist which are though influenced by an ideological separation between politicians and civil servants in favour of 'activation' and civil servants, social workers and welfare associations in favour of a 'social treatment' of long-term unemployed and vulnerable groups.

8.3.1.2 Local modes of interaction for the delivery of services

Since decentralisation, the local authority and its civil servants have the opportunity to shape interactions for the delivery of services and policies. The local interactions are influenced by conflicts on how to deal with benefit recipients.

All civil servants interviewed underline the necessity to invest in efforts for labour market integration in order to make benefit recipients find work and to reduce costs for benefit payments. However, several high-ranking civil servants in the local authority report that many of the civil servants working at the department but also the staff in the social welfare associations would primarily stress the necessity of a social work approach. A civil servant of the local authority points out that the regulation of the RMI can be interpreted as a social treatment approach:

> "We are referring to a law which primarily remains a social right. (…) this means that the RMI privileges the social issues over the economic question." (F-A-5).

A representative from a social welfare association makes a statement which exemplifies the still dominating position of many social workers and civil servants in the local authority:

> "We first need to solve the social problems in order to later support labour market integration efforts." (F-A-6).

The director of the insertion policy directorate opposes this philosophy and highlights the importance of work for the inclusion of the individual:

> "No, often it goes the other way around, and the feeling of utility is more important for inclusion (…) when they people work, when they earn money, they feel useful, and they fell useful for their families and they do not feel guilty (…)." (F-A-5).

In brief, the local authority struggles to formulate a common activation strategy for minimum income recipients.

Devising and organising the local employment programme and its services

Although the department is not part of the state-led local committee for employment policy, its local government tries to shape an active labour market policy dimension. The director of the local administration's insertion policy directorate points out the development of a local agenda since decentralisation which shifts efforts on the assistance claimants' labour market integration. Acknowledging the advantages of the established labour market policy programmes, the local authority attempts to financially support existing local partnerships, like the local action plans for long-term unemployed (PLIE) or the publicly subsidised sector of enterprises (SIAE). The local service delivery system for the activation of recipients of the minimum income scheme is thus based on these existing local partnerships which consist of the state, the sub-national authorities and third sector organisations. The local authority only creates additional measures if its decision-makers deem that certain services lack completely.

On the basis of the local authority's co-financing activities, the civil servants of the local administration's insertion policy directorate try to take actively part in the governance of the numerous established partnerships for labour market programmes. As agreements on the organisation of service provisions of these partnerships usually rely on mutual steering and co-financing of different 'partners', the local authority's civil servants attempt to put forward their arguments on the necessity of placing long-term unemployed and disadvantaged groups. The local authority tries to influence ongoing discussions on the governance bodies of the local partnerships in such a manner that its recipients will particularly benefit from the general labour market policy programmes.

In the frame of the local support for active labour market policy, the local authority has signed a convention on the co-financing of the local action plans (PLIE) existing in the region. The local authority also agreed to a convention to co-finance publicly subsidised enterprises that offer work opportunities for long-term unemployed or weaker groups of the labour market (SIAE) which combine work opportunities with social counselling efforts. To set an extra incentive for these enterprises to employ minimum income benefit recipients, the department grants additional funding on top of the general subvention for each beneficiary hired. Based on a convention, the local authority and the regional public employment service agreed on the creation of common training measures reserved for minimum income recipients only. The convention comprises the following agreement: as the regular labour market instruments (droit commun) of initial three months training offered by the public employment agency were judged by both actors as too short for many assistance recipients, the department will finance an additional three month of training. Furthermore, on the basis of public tenders, the department has created significant numbers of places in social counselling offered by welfare associations. Despite its active role in most of the main labour market instruments for the long-term unemployed or weaker groups of the labour market, the local authority only orders a restrained number of publicly financed work contracts to offer them directly to their beneficiaries. In addition, the local authority also organises public tenders to incite third sector organisation to create a few new programmes combining social counselling and active labour market component. The department thus offers social counselling and co-finances the main labour market instruments existing for the long-term unemployed.

Summing up, the local authority co-finances the main active labour market instruments in its territory in order to increase active labour market policy support for the minimum income recipients. By active interventions of its civil servants in the existing local partnerships, the local authority tries to launch its arguments on the necessity for better access conditions of minimum income benefit recipient to training, subsidies work or counselling programmes.

Definition and organisation of placement and counselling

To realise the activation of recipients of the minimum income benefit into work or into the training, social counselling and employment programmes, a case management system is crucial. Regulation of the minimum income scheme stipulates the signature of integration contracts between the benefit claimant and the case-manager ('referent') in order to determine suitable activity requirements.

When competences were decentralised to the local authority, the department decided to carry on the traditional 'social work' organisation according to which social workers are charged with the counselling of minimum income recipients. This means that case management, the signature of integration contracts, and implementation of work-oriented activity requirements is under the sole responsibility of the social workers of the local authority's social welfare centres.

After decentralisation, leading civil servants of the local administration's directorate for insertion policy though recognised that active placement efforts and the signing of integration contracts were not common among the social workers, who also exert other social counselling tasks besides those for the minimum income benefit recipients. To improve the implementation of an activation approach, the social workers were offered special training courses. In parallel to these training offers, separate local agencies for the minimum income scheme were created by the local authority in order to support the social workers and the social welfare centres. In contrast to the social welfare centres, these local agencies employ not only social workers but also medics, psychologists and contracted placement officers from the public employment service Pôle Emploi. The latter are salaried by the local authority for their deployment in the local authority's agencies. These mixed teams of professionals are supposed to give information and advice on 'how to activate' to the social workers of the social welfare centres. Furthermore, staff of the local agencies for the minimum income scheme shall receive recipients if they have specific problems (social, psychological, health, employment).

Although the social workers in the welfare centres occasionally take into account advice from the departments' local minimum income agencies, leading civil servants of the department recognize that an active case management approach is not widespread. Job placement as part of case management remains a problem. Furthermore, the social welfare centres and the social workers in F-A de facto deny the signature of integration contracts. While they might work out integration contracts, the central administration of the department has to sign these documents. As the director for the insertion policy directorate points out, a very heavy administrative charge arises for the central administration which it is hardly able to handle. This de facto blocks the implementation of case management and activity requirements.

In practice, case management shall proceed as follows: after having filled an application for benefit payment, benefit claimants are, later on, invited to a 'roundtable' which reunites the benefit recipient with social workers of the local authority and placement officers of Pôle Emploi deployed in the local authority's agencies. This roundtable takes a decision whether a benefit recipient requires a social counselling or is ready for job placement. After this 'categorisation', the benefit recipient is invited to see a social worker at a social welfare centre in order to work out an integration contract. These roundtables were only recently installed in order to meet new stipulations of the RSA legislation which require a categorisation of benefit recipients (cf. chapter8.2.1). The question of how to organise such a 'categorisation' had provoked fierce debates between the 'pro-activation' policy oriented directorate for insertion policy and another fraction consisting mainly of the social workers in the local and central administrative services of the local authority which was rather opposed to the idea of a 'categorisation'. After long discussions, the 'social workers' arguments were accepted that such a categorisation, if at all practised, required a very careful decision process. Thus the categorisation makes the local system even more complex and raises questions on the effectiveness of the activation process of the benefit seekers.

In short, the activation strategy of the local authority lacks a proficient case management system to place recipients on the basis of integration contracts into work or the existing social and labour market programmes. Those civil servants in the local administration lobbying for a more stringent case-management approach repeatedly fail to advance their arguments in debates with a strong fraction of 'social workers'. Instead, efforts to accompany and orient benefit claimants remain confined to the field of social work and the traditional social treatment by social workers.

8.3.1.3 *Local techniques of control*

The problems to institutionalise an activation logic in placement and counselling generally raise the issue how the department attempts to control the implementation of its policies.

The local authority does hardly develop any mechanisms to control the implementation of case management and the service delivery of the project executing organisations. Theoretically, the agencies, associations and companies which train, counsel or employ the benefit recipient, are supposed to report back to the responsible case-managers. Apart from this very general stipulation, the local authority, however, renounces on any further efforts to control the activation process of a benefit recipient. The department does not make use of any significant technique of control. It does not prescribe the tasks of the social workers and counsellors in a bureaucratic manner by very detailed regulation and standards. For instance, the department does not prescribe how many recipients a social worker or counsellor shall accompany. Also, mutual control by frequent exchanges between social workers, the responsible administration of the department or the local minimum income agencies remains weak. Furthermore, the local authority does not set any management objectives to be reached by social workers, placement officers and other staff in the social welfare centres, the local agencies of the minimum income scheme or the project executing organisations. For example, it does neither set any detailed or periodic objectives of the numbers of persons to be placed on specific active labour market policy programmes nor does it set any steering provisions with regard to the frequency and nature of contacts a counsellor is required have with clients.

In short, field service personnel of the department and the project executing organisations both have wide discretion how to interpret the department's concept of case-management and activation. As a result, the content of integration contracts, the information exchange between the different organisations and the support offered to a benefit recipient remain completely discretionary decisions of the social workers in charge. Despite an employment programme stressing active labour market policy, the lack of control of case management by the local authority favours the persistence of a traditional culture of social work in the implementation of the minimum income scheme.

8.3.1.4 *Programmatic renewal but organisational continuity: social treatment in local authority F-A*

Department F-A tries to build up a local organisational field for the activation of recipients of the minimum income scheme. Since decentralisation, the local authority has committed important resources to the active labour market programmes for benefit recipients but nonetheless does not achieve to organise an activation approach.

The local authority's civil servants of the directorate for insertion policy are charged by reform oriented local politicians to actively try to influence and convince the actors of existing local partnerships to focus efforts on minimum income recipients. To increase support for long-term unemployed and vulnerable groups, the local authority co-finances the extension of active labour market programmes. It thereby supports the important local partnerships for active labour market policy, which exist between local, national, public or private service providers in the department.

In contrast to a service offer comprising both programmes to increase social and labour market competences of benefit recipients, the challenge of case management reveals the difficulties to combine competences and actors from the different fields of social work and active labour market policy. Due to their strong arguing power, a highly established fraction of social workers in both administration and social welfare associations is able to dilute ideas of reform-oriented actors of the insertion policy directorate. New concepts for a more stringent activation approach are repeatedly subject to controversial and long local debates. The final agreements found have a tendency of being overly complex for implementation and they do not change principal organisational mechanisms. Furthermore, coordination of a more active approach of counselling is not ensured by explicit control techniques. As a result, activation of benefit recipients remains confined to the field of social welfare and social work: it persists being a matter of highly discretionary decisions of social workers. The failure to implement the signature of integration contracts is an example which illustrates that the traditional culture of social work and social treatment thereby persists. Consequently, the implementation of services for an activation of long-term unemployed and disadvantaged groups remains contested in this region.

To conclude, the local authority aims to activate recipients of the minimum income scheme but does not achieve to fully institutionalise an organisational field for the activation of benefit recipients. This is notably due to the continuous dominance of a local social treatment culture and its adherents in the process of implementing the benefit scheme. While programmes offered to the benefit recipients enlarge the range of services through local partnerships with national and local actors delivering active labour market policy, case management is not effectively intertwined between the field of social work and labour market policy and different national, sub-national, private or public providers. Instead it remains confined to the field of local social work. Case management continues to be solely enacted by the department's social welfare centres, their managers and social workers who tend to support a social treatment of unemployment.

8.3.2 Local governance of welfare interventions in local authority F-B

Welfare interventions in region F-B face a very difficult socio-economic situation. Being situated at the outskirts of a strong French economic urban region, a couple of larger French industrial and service sector companies are located in the department which attract employees from the whole region. At the same time, the share of low-skilled and non-skilled persons, comprising a significant low-skilled migrant population, is very high in the department. Given a strong employment decline of the formerly important local industrial basis (for example: the local automobile production branch lost roughly 25% of employment between 2003 and 2008), employment prospects of the low-skilled population in the traditional local industrial branches have been limited. The socio-economic situation of the local authority is thus divided into an economic structure which is able to attract well-educated employees from the whole region and a social structure which is characterised by a local polarisation of the social problems of the overarching region. As a result of this situation, since the introduction of the general minimum income scheme against social exclusion, the rate of benefit recipients in this local authority has been constantly on the rise (but one year) reaching a level which is among the highest of the French departments. Also unemployment rates are much higher than the French average.

The steady rise in the number of benefit recipients has aggravated financial problems of the local authority. Constantly increasing local expenditures for the minimum income benefit, which are not being fully reimbursed by the state, have contributed to a difficult budgetary situation of the local authority. Compared to other department, the financial situation of the local authority F-B in 2008 was characterised by a very high debt. In 2008, expenditures for the minimum income benefit made up one fourth of the local budget and thus represented the biggest share of the budget.

Traditionally, the local authority has been governed by parties situated on the left or radical left of the political spectrum. While the communist party had repeatedly held the local presidency in the past, at the time of research, in 2009, a socialist president governs the local authority.

8.3.2.1 *Local institutional conditions for the take-up of services and policies*

In region F-B, institutional relationships between the local authority and other sub-national authorities, agencies or private providers are weakly elaborated. Instead, the relationships particularly between the local authority and the local or regional state agencies are prone to conflict. Devolved authority is primarily used to politically oppose the decentralisation of responsibilities for social policy. Local decision-makers repeatedly point to the difficult financial situation of the department for which they blame the central state. Decision-makers of the local authority blame the central state and the general conditions of decentralisation to provide insufficient support to local policies. The local authority's policy is to demand the central state and the Employment Agency to increase its efforts for minimum income benefit recipients.

In short, particular institutional relationships relevant for activities towards minimum income recipients are weakly developed in region F-B and are not promoted by local policy which opposes central government policies.

8.3.2.2 *Local modes of interaction for the delivery of services*

Local authority F-B invests limited resources into programmes and services for the activation of minimum income recipients. Instead it primarily fulfils its core obligations for social policy, comprising payments to minimum income benefit recipients. In addition, the local authority also voluntary runs supplementary, passive benefit programmes, for example for older persons. These additional programmes make up more than 5% of the local budget. This stress on a passive local social policy approach matches a social treatment of unemployment which is still a guiding concept in the local administration. The statement of a manager of a local authority's minimum income agency illustrates in practice the local approach to the minimum income scheme. The idea is to endow people with a minimum income but to refrain from implementing active inclusion policy:

> "Us, we are here for advise, information and reception. (…) In any case, we, our role is to inform them [the recipients] with regard to the law and legal regulations, (…). But then, they act on their own risk and fate, but, me, I am not here for judging them. If you need, I can assist you, I can help you, (…). But then, the rest, this is up to them to decide, these are adult persons." (F-B-9).

Devising and organising the local employment programme and its services
In line with its stress on passive policies, the local authority is not significantly involved in the governance of the important active labour market policy programmes.

The local authority generally states its reluctance with regard to the state defined active labour market instruments. In the talks with the decision-makers of the administration, the civil servants raised several doubts on the success of the instrument. In contrast, interviewed civil servants of the state-run agencies suspect the department to renounce on a promotion of the regular active labour market instruments due to political reasons. The civil servants of the state-run agencies accuse the department of generally opposing central government's policies due to the department's disapproval of the financial conditions of decentralisation.

Following recent political leadership change of the government of the department, some limited attempts were initiated to improve an active support for recipients of the minimum income scheme. As a result, the local authority co-finances the state-run, publicly financed work contracts albeit only very restricted numbers. Moreover, the department declines to step up as public employer for these subsidised employment opportunities. The department also engages in the governance and financing of the local action plans (PLIE) for the counselling and placement of long-term unemployed. Nonetheless, the department has not yet created broader activities for its beneficiaries. Instead, decision-makers of the local authority continuously campaign for the state and the Employment Agency to take greater responsibility for a specific service offer to minimum income recipients.

In short, apart from its social policy spending activities, the department does only to a very limited extent engage in the local implementation of active labour market policy instruments for long-term unemployed or persons difficult to place.

Definition and organisation of placement and counselling

Even though the local authority does not develop much of a proper offer of active labour market policy and social welfare programmes for the benefit claimants, an option remains to refer recipients to the general services and service offers of other agencies, notably the public employment services. To do so, an efficient case management would however be necessary.

The appointment of a case-manager for a benefit recipient and the implementation of integration contracts on work and activity requirements were viewed by the local authority as a more formal demand it had to comply with. The local authority dealt with these national legal stipulations by simply adding case management as an additional task to the departmental social welfare centres. Thereby, the social workers of the social welfare centres take up case management as further task of the already numerous missions of social counselling which they have.

Despite decentralisation, the organisation of staff thus reveals much continuity of a social work approach. Many of the social workers, who are now working at the local authority's social welfare centres, had originally come from the state-run social field services. Before decentralisation, they had been responsible for the numerous social tasks of the state-run social field services, amongst these the minimum income scheme. After decentralisation, they principally continue executing similar tasks in the departmental services. Local authority F-B thus continues to leave case management and counselling of benefit claimants exclusively in the field of social welfare but renounces on establishing a connection with placement. Crucial assignments such as proposing activities to benefit claimants, signing integration contracts, and enforcing activity requirements remain entirely in the hands of the social workers in the social welfare services.

Practically, the signature of integration contracts and activation into work, social counselling or active labour market programmes shall proceed as follows: after having requested benefit payments, several weeks later, claimants are invited by postal mail to present themselves at one of the social welfare centres. At the occasion of such a meeting, benefit claimants shall discuss their situation with a social worker. Both shall work out an integration contract comprising activity requirements for the benefit claimant.

However, decision makers of the department recognize that an active role of counselling that would involve job placement or the working-out of integration contracts is barely exercised by the social workers and the social welfare centres. In contrast, acceptance of the idea to work out integration contracts is low among the social workers who formally shall act as case-managers. A statement of a social worker responsible for a social welfare centre exemplifies the 'social workers' stance on integration contracts:

> "A case management process is not efficient if I try to force someone by putting a knife on his throat; it needs to be a voluntary process instead. (…) The possibility of sanctions exists in the legal regulation but this is not an option for us." (F-B-4).

This inertia of a social work approach is furthered by another agency of the local authority which exists in parallel to the local social welfare centres. After decentralisation, the local authority created additional local agencies for the minimum income scheme. Although branded as 'new', however, like the local social welfare centres, these agencies were also staffed with social workers (and few psychologists). The tasks put forward by the department for these local agencies have been twofold: on the one hand, they are supposed to support the social welfare centres' counselling and case-management of benefit recipients through information, supervision and evaluation. On the other hand, the local minimum income scheme agencies might invite beneficiaries to take part in counselling sessions or workshops on social, psychological, health or employment related issues. In practice, however, the local agencies did not introduce any organisational change. Civil servants of the department and the local agencies' officers describe exchanges between the local social welfare centres and the local minimum income scheme missions as extremely rare. Also exchanges between the local authority's agencies and other actors in the region, as for example the public employment services, are very rare. Instead, the statements of the directing social workers of a local agency show that the local agencies for the minimum income scheme indeed share the traditional social work philosophy.

Stipulated by the new legislation of the RSA, the local authority F-B is obliged to categorise benefit recipients into the being able to take-up work and those requiring a social counselling first. Although regulation of the RSA was already in force at the time of research, the department had not yet made up any concrete on how it would organise this categorisation.

In brief, the organisation of case-management chosen by the department after decentralisation thus leaves social workers in crucial positions of which they make actively use in order to work against the implementation of an activation approach of benefit recipients.

8.3.2.3 Local techniques of control

The implementation of case management as a social work approach raises further questions on the department's efforts to control and supervise not only the behaviour of benefit claimants but also the activities of staff and organisations who deliver policy action.

The department does not build up any important techniques of control of its staff, be it by quantifiable objectives, detailed role descriptions or processes of mutuality and trust-building. For instance, the local authority renounces on setting steering provisions with regard to the frequency and nature of contacts, detailed or periodic objectives for specific programmes persons have to be placed on.

Since recently, the local administration's directorate for 'insertion policy' has developed plans to introduce contract-based goals and obligations for the organisations and associations that deliver policy action. The idea of the civil servants of this unit in the local administration is that contracted quantitative objectives might serve as an indicator for evaluating the development of programmes. As one statement of a social worker of the local administration exemplifies, the social workers managing the social welfare agencies and the local agencies for the minimum income scheme, which deliver policy action, are strongly opposed to these suggestions made by the insertion policy unit of the local administration:

> "There are things that you can't quantify, so, I am against this. Social aspects are not quantifiable. (...) it's nice to have quotas that shall be stimulating for our work. But unfortunately, it's difficult to practice such things because we work with human beings. We are not a factory, we don't produce persons in terms of monthly numbers. I am sorry, but this is much more complex what we are doing. I don't view this positively to try to quantify. It bothers me." (F-B-2).

So far, the civil servants of the insertion policy unit have not succeeded to reach the implementation of management objectives in a broader way. As a statement of a director of a local social welfare centre shows, the social workers have shifted to a strategy to prepare contracts but only for statistical purposes.

> "Sometimes you have persons that don't need a contract. But we give them a contract for 3 months instead of for six or longer. Then, we can redo the contract after three months. Like this, we can renew the contract and the person has four contracts a year and we easily achieve the numbers given. This has nothing to do with what the persons need or have to do, it is just in view of the objectives we shall achieve." (F-B-4).

In brief, efforts for control or supervision of the delivery of local authority's services and policies remain generally weak. No particular control mechanism has been set in motion in a significant way to ensure national premises for the activation of benefit recipients.

8.3.2.4 Continuity of a social treatment approach in local authority F-B

Opposed to the decentralisation of social policy and the national activation reforms, the local authority widely refrains from initiating local programmes or supporting approaches for the activation of benefit recipients. The local government uses its decentralised authority to politically oppose the central state and to demand engagement of the Employment Agency for minimum income recipients. Simultaneously, social workers occupying key positions in the local administration are left scope to continue implementing a social treatment of unemployment. Despite the national prescriptions for case management and integration contracts, the local authority F-B thus implements the minimum income benefit as an administration of unconditional benefit payment.

The local authority favours a passive social policy approach and refrains from initiating a particular service organisation for the recipients of the minimum income scheme. Despite its difficult financial situation, resources are still voluntarily used for additional benefit programmes instead of investments in active labour market policy. At the same time, the local authority also forgoes the opportunity to coordinate a better access of the minimum income benefit recipients on the programmes and services run by other actors in the region, as for example the public employment agency. This denial to locally coordinate services for the activation of recipients of the minimum income scheme is exemplified by a complete lack of an effective local case management system. Development of counselling, placement and case management therefore illustrates how the service structure in the department misses the integration of national and local levels' competences, social and labour market policy fields and public and private actors. In local authority F-B, the crucial task of activation of a benefit claimant still remains a highly discretionary decision of social workers. A mutual obligations' approach of active case management and placement efforts is an idea though not broadly accepted by the service agencies and its social workers.

Similar to case management, also recent initiatives for new steering mechanisms as management objectives or a categorisation of beneficiaries are only adopted in a 'superficial' way. The local administrations' directorate for insertion policy, which is responsible for the local implementation of such approaches, neither achieves a broader application of the new instruments nor are they accepted by social workers, associations and organisations servicing the recipients of the minimum income scheme. This lack of control constitutes a further obstacle for institutionalising a local framework for the activation of benefit recipients.

Overall, the local governance confirms the strong institutional cleavage between 'normal' unemployment policy and its related services on the one side and social welfare on the other side. Overall, weak or conflict-loaded local relationships between the national and department levels, social welfare and labour market policy fields as well as public and private actors have so far blocked the institutionalisation of a local organisational field for the activation of minimum income recipients. Instead of developing a local dimension for the activation of beneficiaries, the minimum income scheme in region F-B remains focussed on the administration of an unconditional assistance payment.

8.3.3 Local governance of welfare interventions in local authority F-C

Welfare interventions in region F-C take place at the background of a very positive socio-economic environment. The rate of unemployment has been consistently below the French average and, compared to other urban departments, numbers of minimum income recipients are under average. These positive developments result from the fact that the department is situated in one of the strongest economic regions in France and Europe. The region belongs to one of the most competitive regions in Europe due to its solid industrial basis, comprehensive knowledge resources as well as a successful development of highly innovative technologies, research intensive products, and services.

At the time of research, the government of the department has been led for more than twenty years by the same president. The president is affiliated to the French conservative party and has been leading a centre-right coalition majority in the departmental parliament for the last two decades. The conservative government and its president but also the socialist opposition are principally in favour of initiating proper local efforts in labour market and social policy for the minimum income recipients.

8.3.3.1 Local institutional conditions for the take-up of services and policies

Since decentralisation, the local government and its president have actively strived for a local policy to activate recipients of the minimum income benefit into work. The extremely committed local president is described as key figure for the turn towards an activation strategy. The director of the local administration's directorate for 'insertion policy' highlights the importance of political initiative:

> "A political will. (…) This is decisive. If you can't count on a president of the department who (…)… our president is very active on this issue, he intervened a lot, he was very interested in things, (…), he took initiative for passing a [national] law on these questions, so, I think one really needs a political will." (F-C-3).

Simultaneously, the responsible local administration's directorate for insertion policy is eager to apply to practice its strong expertise on how to organise services and policies. Comprising twenty civil servants, the local directorate for insertion policy is a strong division of the local administration which shapes strategic, budgetary and cooperation questions of the local minimum income scheme policy. The very experienced director of the local administration's directorate for insertion policy is not only highly committed to assist long-term unemployed and disadvantaged groups with their integration into the labour market but also has a vision how to do so. In addition, the director counts on excellent contacts with other actors in the region due to her long-standing professional experiences she has gained in the region.

Furthermore, the local president and the director of the local administration count on a strong relationship with the regional employment agency. The local president and the local administration are open to the opinion and ideas of the directing staff of the regional employment agency. Particularly the vice director of the regional employment agency has accumulated important experiences and contacts in the field of local work integration approaches for persons difficult to place due to a series of different professional positions he has been holding in the local territory. The vice director of the regional employment agency explains that he has a strong vision how to organise services for persons more difficult to place which he is eager to share with the decision-makers of the department:

> "It was me who developed the concept from A to Z. This goes back to two events. I had been director of the local public employment agency for a long time and in this function I was always sensible to issues of the insertion of long-term unemployed, it was my personal sensibility, (…) and I found an approach interesting (…). And secondly… the prefect here, he had nominated me as president of two local insertion commissions when the state was responsible for this. (…) Back at this time, I really got to know the services of the local authority and therefore, when the department became responsible for the RMI and its organisation, us, the ANPE and the department, we construed this new organisation together." (F-C-7).

Not only bureaucratic ties are strong but also those with the third sector. The local community of the department F-C is a very active one with a historically developed, dense tissue of welfare associations. Already before decentralisation, the social welfare associations had been involved in approaches to assist minimum income benefit recipients. Although these approaches conferred to a social work treatment of the benefit recipients, to implement its new programme, the local authority F-C could build on existing partnerships and this very active local community. The director of the local directorate for insertion policy points out the importance of this local community for a proper local approach:

> "(…) among the factors which were key, it was also the fact that it exists this associative tradition (…) in the department [F-C] which does not exist in all the departments, there are some departments which would not have been able to do this because they simply didn't have such a network of *insertion* associations which had already existed in [F-C] way before decentralisation, (…)." (F-C-3).

In brief, a developed local partnership structure between the third sector, the political arena and different administrative bodies exists. In addition, key actors of this partnership structure are ready to advance an activation approach.

8.3.3.2 Local modes of interaction for the delivery of services

Advocated by the local president since decentralisation, labour market integration of the minimum income recipients has become a local priority. The local president, the director of insertion policy of the local administration and the vice-director of the regional employment agency all stress that the minimum income benefit is at a time a right and an obligation. Most of the actors in the region share this understanding as the following statement of the local administration's director for territorial development exemplifies:

> "(…) when the department took up competence for the RMI, we did a large operation which was named "out of sight", this means that all the persons that didn't respond to our mails were disentitled from the RMI. Because the RMI, this is a right, but in order to make use of this right certain duties exist, and if a person does not want to respond to its duties, which comprise a regular contact with a case-manager, he or him will be disentitled form the RMI." (F-C-3).

The president of the department and the civil servants view this mutual obligations' approach as a necessity not least due to the financial burden, which the department has been facing since decentralisation. A high-ranking civil servant points to a volume of benefit payments of up to 70 million euro which had not been covered by the state at the moment of decentralisation. Driven by the objective to achieve the benefit recipient's activation into work, the department aims to assist persons' of becoming proper 'actors' of integration efforts. A high civil servant of the local authority explains the prevailing local concept for activation which is based on the idea to actively promote 'self-reliance' of recipients:

> "(…) the recipients not only need to be listened to or given money. But it depends on how we can assist them to become an actor of their proper life (…). (…) for each case, we put in place a gateway towards integration and this track depends on the abilities of the person (…). For example, if the person is very close to taking up an employment activity, we have a contract with Pôle Emploi and Pôle Emploi will be responsible for the case-management of this person. If we have someone who needs training or further education, we might have a specific association for this purpose and we will ask this association to take up the case management for this person, and finally, we, as Département, we will rather counsel those recipients of the minimum income scheme that need social counselling before they can really tackle the route for integration." (F-C-3).

The local authority is not only ready to invest in social counselling but also in active labour market policy in order to make beneficiaries find work. As the director of the local administration's directorate for *insertion* policy explains, the department needs to apply proper efforts for work integration to reduce costs for benefit payments:

> "(…) I think we have widely demonstrated that what you don't invest in instruments for insertion or placement, you will repay in entitlements. And it is really like this, only if you have an organisation which identifies the people, assists them and also controls them in a certain manner, you can hope for mastering the development of benefit payments. Otherwise, it turns out as a disaster." (F-C-2).

In short, in combination with its core competences in social welfare services and counselling, the department also aims to organise a proper active labour market policy for the recipients of the minimum income benefit.

Devising and organising the local employment programme and its services

The department becomes an influential 'player' in the field of labour market policy itself. As the regular active labour market programmes are run by other authorities and providers, the local authority and its civil servants try to shape these programmes towards a better access for the minimum income benefit recipients. Representatives of the state, other sub-national authorities, and social welfare associations, which are involved in the different active labour market policy programmes implemented in the territory, all stress a close co-operation with the local authority. Usually, the local authority makes financial contributions to the different programmes and thereby gets access to their governing bodies. The local authority then actively intervenes in the local partnerships by engaging in collective processes to reach agreement on the organisation of service provision and by taking part in mutual steering processes. On the governing bodies, the local authority attempts to convince the different actors governing a programme to reserve high access capacities for the minimum income benefit recipients. The director of the local directorate for insertion policy explains how the civil servants of the directorate have been striving for building up relationships and partnerships with the active labour market policy providers in the region:

> "We developed institutional relations with Pôle Emploi… in the beginning, it's true, it was not simple as we were part of completely different system and we needed to get to know each other, to sketch out the modalities of collaboration, etc., well, this took some time, but now it is functioning smoothly. The same applies for the PLIE, finally, everything was a matter of partnership working which needs time to establish and which requires permanent discussions, (…)." (F-C-3).

As part of its employment programme, local authority F-C finances an important number of publicly subsidised work contracts, and steps up itself as an employer of 400 minimum income recipients who are on a publicly subsidised work scheme (CAV). The local authority F-C is also involved in the governance and financing of the four local action plans for long-term unemployed (PLIE) in its territory. In addition, the local authority engages in the governance and financing of a number of publicly subsidised enterprises (SIAE), which combine employment with activities of social counselling. The local authority also concluded an agreement with the regional authority about specific training programmes for recipients of the minimum income benefit.

This combined strategy of financial efforts and arguing is well illustrated in the field of training: participation of recipients of the minimum income scheme in training programmes offered by the regional authority had so far been very low. The civil servants of the local directorate for insertion policy identified this as a problem. In reaction to this problem, the director of the local directorate for insertion policy but also the local president lobbied for guaranteed numbers of places for recipients of the minimum income scheme in certain regional schemes of advanced training. The region was susceptible to the arguments of the local authority as its regional parliamentarians and government figures were principally interested in boosting a regional profile in employment policy. From the perspective of the region, long-term unemployed were generally considered as group for whom such a regional initiative would make sense for. The local authority took advantage of this situation by explaining to the regional authority that it would consequently be a good idea to particularly support minimum income recipients. As the director of the local integration policy directorate explains, after long debates and a financial offer of the department, the region finally agreed to dedicate special capacities to benefit recipients of the minimum income benefit:

> "Our discussion with the region, they have been very long and very complex and we concluded them by signing a convention with the region. I think, we are one of the few local authorities which did so. The problem of the region is that they are responsible for training since decentralisation but the funds transferred by the state normally don't permit, I mean, they make it difficult for the region to pay attention to persons who do not belong to their traditional clientele. (…) the region said 'we want to do something in the area of employment, but we don't have the means to do so' (…). So, we had a very long discussion process with them and finally we decided to share the costs." (F-C-3).

In addition, the local authority has created a number of new service offers in collaboration with the local social welfare associations. The essence of these collaborations with welfare associations is to offer activities that include both social and employment measures particularly apt for benefit recipients difficult to place. For the delivery of these services, the public authority will usually rely on public tenders.

In short, by a mixture of financial participation and strong lobbying, the directorate for insertion policy and the local president have built up a diverse employment programme for the recipients of the minimum income scheme. As a result of partnership working on the basis of mutual memoranda of understanding and public tenders, the local authority achieves to facilitate minimum benefit recipients' access to services and programmes which cover a wide range of both social counselling and active labour market policy.

Definition and organisation of placement and counselling

At the background of the various programmes and services delivered by different organisations in the region, case-management becomes a key issue to assist and activate recipients of the minimum income benefit. It relates to questions how benefit recipients are referred to suitable service offers and how they are made to fulfil activity obligations.

Since decentralisation, as explained by two high-ranking civil servants of the local administration, the local president has been advancing the idea to accompany each benefit recipient and to set up a new system for case-management.

> "Today it's the department, before it was their [the 'pay office for family assistance', CAF] charge to assure that each benefit recipient of the RMI had a case-manager. Since 2004 it's us who are responsible. And the local president took this question very seriously and it was therefore one of his objectives that every benefit recipient of the RMI would have a case-manager. Because when it was the CAF, which took care of it, due to a lack of resources, there were people who had received the RMI for two years and they had never been in touch with someone." (F-C-3).
>
> "When we took charge of the RMI in 2004, we had to do an enormous work in order to re-establish a case-manager for each benefit recipient. It took us until April 2006 to re-appoint case-managers for all RMI recipients. On the basis of an activity we called 'operation out of sight', we re-established contact with more than 6.000 persons, who had not been seen for a long time, in order to assess their situation and to appoint a case-manager for them." (F-C-2).

The local president's primary objective was to reduce the so far dominating influence of a social work approach on the benefit recipients. As the director of the local authorities directorate for insertion policy explains, the social workers from the local authority and those transferred from the state's social field services to the local authority were not considered being capable of practicing an activation of benefit recipients.

> "As they had been principally in the hand of social workers, interactions with the benefit recipients for a long time rather consisted of a social counselling." (F-C-2).

After consultations with the regional employment agency, the local president and the local civil servants took up propositions of the regional employment agency's vice president to delegating the task of case-management to professionals in external organisations. Step by step, the local authority concluded agreements on external case management with different organisations. These agreements principally described the obligation for external case-managers to work out integration contracts with prescribed numbers of benefit recipients and to engage in information exchanges with the local authority. Under the condition that the external organisation fulfils its obligations, the local authority compensates the organisation it cooperates with for the salary of the external case-manager. The director of the local authority's directorate for insertion policy explains the local authority's strategy to conclude such agreements with the regional public employment agency and a range of other organisations:

> "In contrast to other departments, we made a different choice, it is a political choice. (…) what other departments did was to create internally case-managers for placement. They usually appointed social workers for this task who then received a couple of training courses and that was it. We didn't opt for this choice. Because traditionally, historically, the departments have much more a competence in social issues than in placement matters. So, the choice we opted for, it was to rely on those people who had competences in placement matters, which means Pôle Emploi and the other associations, and also the PLIE (…)" (F-C-2).

As a result of agreements with various organisations, the local authority can draw on a wide variety of external case-managers in terms of profession and specific competences. First, for case-management with a strong focus on job placement, the local authority draws on roughly 100 contracted placement officers who work at Pôle Emploi. Second, in order to react to benefit recipients with a more complex bundle of problems, the department has created case-management tasks in between placement and social work. For this 'socio-professional' counselling, the local authority relies on case-managers in up to 80 organisations comprising larger but also numerous smaller associations with very specific competences, like for example counselling for young unemployed artists, etc. Finally, as a third, and traditional area attached to social assistance in France, social workers of the social welfare centres of the local authority as well as social workers from other social welfare organisations continue to offer social counselling as case-managers.

The civil servants of the local authority and other involved actors report that this reorganisation of case management was only possible through strong political leadership and intense arguing processes. In the beginning, the many social welfare associations in the territory were opposed to submerge on a contractual basis onto an activation approach. When the local authority made its reform plans public, the placement agencies, welfare associations and all other important organisations operating in the department were invited to public discussions. As the director of the local insertion policy directorate recalls, at these occasions, the local authority's president put clearly forward the local reform ambitions:

> "It wasn't very easy because the things we wanted to do, they had not existed before. (…) in 2004, with the decentralisation, it took place a radical change, (…), and it was

indeed a tricky issue in the beginning to make them understand that there was a turn and that it was now the department which would implement a proper policy. There was a reunion, I remember, it was in December 2003 where the president, reunited them. So, a large gathering took place and it was sent out a very strong political message and they all got it." (F-C-3).

Furthermore, strong bureaucratic expertise was important to indeed implement the new case management system. As their director explains, the civil servants of the directorate for insertion policy have been constantly engaged in discussing and advocating the activation concept of the local authority with organisations delivering the services:

"I have five specialised civil servants who do all this work and if things get more complicated, of course, I might also intervene. We have really close relationships with all those organisations. (...) What we try to do is to always deal with the problems when they arise and to have constant contact with them, we don't want to sit and wait for the big reunions. (...) That's the daily work of the five specialised civil servants. They not only intervene for solving problems, but they also intervene for discussing, for observing, for knowing how things work and also for answering to questions. In the course of their activities, they are directly in touch with the associations, with the important persons in the territory, in order to solve things which do not work well but also to make things progress and for this it is necessary to get involved in the political debates, the strategies, and the technical aspects." (F-C-3).

When the various organisations in the region recognised that they were given a role in the implementation process, they were increasingly convinced by the local authority's plans. According to the account of the director of the local insertion policy directorate, it required these continuous efforts for establishing acceptance of the local authority's activation approach among the organisations employing the case-managers.

"Later on [after the political announcement], rather on an administrative level, we had to deal with the objections of one or another person, with some it went well, with others it was more difficult. (...) But it's true it was a very crucial thing that we engaged in discussions, in exchanges, etc. and now, five years later, things have indeed become stable. We are now working with them [the welfare associations] hand in hand for the implementation of the RSA and we will continue to rely on them. But it's true, for them it was pretty new to respond to such a clear political strategy, because they felt a bit deprived of their capacity to imagine, and to do what they wanted to do, as it had been the case prior to our reform." (F-C-3).

To put case-management into practice, the local authority F-C pioneered on a fast registration and categorisation procedure of benefit claimants. On the day a person claims benefit payment, he or she simultaneously has to answer to a formal questionnaire on his or her social situation, professional experience and level of education. Based on this survey, the benefit recipient will be immediately put in contact with a case-manager either with placement, mixed background or social work background. Together with the benefit recipient, the case-manager then works out an integration contract spelling out each person's activity requirements.

While interactions with the benefit recipients are then primarily in the hands of the external case managers, the local authority coordinates the counselling and placement process. Several small subordinate agencies coordinate and control in subdivided territories of the local authority the placement, counselling and case-management activities between the external case-managers, recipients and project executing organisations. The local agencies organise very regular case conferences with all the case-managing placement officers, social workers and counsellors in the local territory which they are responsible for. Moderated by civil servants of the local authority, these case conferences are described by participants to allow for intensive discussions and arguing processes on the management of cases.

First of all, these roundtables enable the department to keep up its authority on the content of integration contracts. The roundtables give the local authority the opportunity to inform the case-managers on the social and active labour market instruments it aims to offer to the minimum income benefit recipients. The director of the local administrations' territorial policy directorate describes that trust in the case-managers' proper decision-making competences, e.g. to place a recipient onto a certain programme, has strongly evolved thanks to the regular roundtables.

> "(…) we inform them on the regulation of the RMI, on the policy priorities, on our whole service delivery organisation, and then, regularly, in line with current developments, we invite them, and we, for example, organise a half-day workshop (…) on issues how to get into touch with counselling centres because this is often a problem. Step by step, we present them the different instruments, each time there is something important, we invite them to a reunion and we do a presentation for them. We are indeed always in touch with them. During the last five years, our relationships have really become… we have really reached a very close and common understanding with them." (F-C-3).

Second, as a result of these case conferences, it can be decided to change the case-manager for a particular recipient. As the vice-director of the regional public employment service explains, the principle idea is to recognise when a benefit recipients might shift from a social counselling to a placement service:

> "A (…) committee exists where we talk about the situation of the persons who are being activated. So that those persons who are in a social counselling with a case-managing social worker will not be stuck forever in a situation of social counselling because nonetheless, at some point a person needs to find himself back on the labour market." (F-C-7).

Third, the round-tables also serve the purpose to increase exchange between the different providers, case-managers and project executing organisations in order to guarantee coherence of the local approaches, which is not evident due to the incompatible informational devices and databanks of Pôle Emploi, the PLIE or the local authority. For example, due to the participation of the case-managing placement officers of Pôle Emploi in the roundtables, the case-managing counsellors of the welfare associations are learning what the placement agency offers to benefit recipients. The director of the local administration's directorate for territorial development explains the ambition to facilitate a coherent approach through organising the roundtables:

> "We really undertake important efforts to achieve a personalised counselling process of each benefit recipient of the RMI, either with the associations that we finance, with the municipal social centres, or with Pôle Emploi (…). The idea is also to practice a coherent approach in view of the situation of the benefit recipients and an approach which is coordinated with the other partners. This means, that in [the area x] the municipal social centres won't chose one approach with Monsieur Dupond and we will chose other activities with him and in the end no one knows what is really done. You know what I mean. We want to reunite our efforts and try to achieve as much coherence as possible." (F-C-3).

In brief, implementation of the minimum income scheme in local authority F-C proceeds by discussion and arguing processes in local roundtables between the actors involved in case management and service provision. Civil servants from the local authority and other observers point out that the organisational changes (initial questionnaire for a benefit claimant, delegation of case-management, local agencies of the department, regular local roundtables and local case-conferences), which have been put in place by political initiative and constant coordination efforts, were decisive to introduce access to job placement for benefit recipients based on a mutual obligations' approach.

8.3.3.3 *Local techniques of control*

As highlighted, the local authority is in general confronted with the coordination of a multitude of agencies – either of internal or external case management staff or of organisations delivering labour market and social welfare programmes in the framework of the integration strategy put forward by the local authority for its benefit recipients. To ensure implementation of the local activation approach, the local authority has developed sophisticated mechanisms for the control of staff, organisations and associations delivering policy action.

Contracted quantitative objectives are one aspect of controlling the organisations and associations delivering policy action in the framework of the activation strategy of the local authority. Decision-makers of the local authority explain the use of contracted objectives by pointing to their duty to control the spending of public money and to justify action before departmental deputes. Objectives set for policy action are regularly agreed on in a mutual process between the local authority and the organisation that will realise policy action. Measures that aim to integrate beneficiaries into work on the short- or long run will be evaluated with regard to numbers of 'positive outcome' meaning integration into employment or further education. Successful integration into employment is normally considered as permanent employment or fixed-term employment for at least six months. Part-time is hereby considered as a successful integration by the local authority and it is de facto often aimed at by the local authority and its organisations delivering policy action. Directing staff of the department explain this local objective by pointing out that part-time employment normally allows a beneficiary to drop out of the local authority's responsibility for benefit payment (formerly RMI, now RSA *socle*). This logic principally remains the same for the local authority in the RSA. According to regulations of the RSA, the state overtakes financial responsibility and Pôle Emploi shall offer services for those who work (part-time) but still remain eligible for RSA payments (RSA *chapeau*).

However, the local authority points out that contracted quantitative objectives are only one indicator for evaluating the development of programmes and services. Through the frequent exchanges of the local authority's experts with associations and organisations, the implementation of service measures is controlled. Regular attendance of the local authority's experts in steering committees on labour market programmes or the local roundtables between the local authority's civil servants, external case-mangers and project executing organisations create a sense of mutuality between the different actors.

While some welfare associations had warned of 'creaming effects' as a consequence of the introduction of quantitative steering objectives, they, too, acknowledge today, that control strategies of the local authority value different aspects. Representatives of the welfare associations do not feel that their case-managers are pressured by the local authority to take action only towards quick labour market integration or to assist only those unemployed easier to place. Representatives of the social welfare associations and other observers repeatedly highlight fruitful and mutual relations with the local authority that have evolved since decentralisation. Based on regular discussions and arguing processes, trust-based relationships evolve that serve to oversee and guarantee implementation.

In short, while local benchmarks mirror incentives for the local authority to activate benefit recipients into part-time employment, direct communication between the local actors creates trust-based relations which ensure the transformation towards a system of individualised services for placing and counselling benefit recipients.

8.3.3.4 Towards a participatory activation logic in local authority F-C

Decentralised budgetary responsibility and the few legal provisions are interpreted by entrepreneurial local actors as both an opportunity and incentive to reorganise existing local partnerships into a joint organisational approach for the activation of assistance recipients.

In local authority F-C, an elaborated local partnership structure of close relationships between the third sector, the political arena and the different local administrations exists. Re-organisation of this partnership structure towards an activation approach is driven by reform-oriented local political leadership, skilful local civil servants and conceptual advice from the regional employment agency.

In addition to its core social counselling competences, the local authority develops a proper local focus on active labour market policy and placement. Based on conceptual advice of the vice-president of the regional employment agency, the local president and the local administration's insertion policy directorate have advocated important changes. Local financial incentives, a series of agreements as well as 'good arguments' were key to make an initially opposed third sector act according to the local activation strategy. By doing so, the local authority is able to exploit a rich local tissue of third sector organisations and other providers. In the frame of this approach, the important active labour market programmes reserve explicit capacities for minimum income recipients. Furthermore, counselling and placement tasks are delegated to a large number of contracted case-managers in external organisation, notably, the public employment services, the communes, but also to up to 80 very different local associations which opens up multiple opportunities as well as obligations for benefit recipients to frequent case-managers either for job placement, for socio-professional or social counselling.

In order to control implementation of the local activation approach by external case-managers' and organisations delivering labour market as well as social welfare policy programmes, the local administration's directorate for insertion policy has developed different mechanisms. Attempts to control by benchmarks for the integration into employment and particularly part-time employment are explained by budgetary motivations set by the national framework. Moreover, the local authority supervises implementation of case management as well as social and labour market programmes by very close exchanges and trust-building measures with welfare associations, placement agencies as well as placement officers and social workers.

Taken together, local resource-sharing, intensive local arguing processes of various actors on the right service offer, and mixed control techniques come close to a participatory concept for active inclusion. As a result, a local organisational field is institutionalised which opens up various options of counselling, training, subsidised work or job-placement (in part-time employment) for long-term unemployed and disadvantage groups receiving assistance payments.

8.3.4 Local governance of the minimum income scheme in local authority F-D

Welfare interventions in local authority F-D face a difficult socio-economic situation. Given a traditional focus on the industrial production of low technologies, the urban core of the department has been struggling with its transformation towards a stronger service economy. Despite a difficult transformation process, strong potential for a service-based local economy can be found in the tourism and trade sector. However, the transformation process has not yet triggered a significant improvement of the employment situation. Unemployment in the department is therefore above the French average. Since the introduction of the RMI, the local authority's level of minimum income benefit recipients has been constantly among the highest of the French departments.

The local authority has been a stronghold of the political left for the last decades. At the same of research, a socialist president is at the head of the local government. The local president governs the department on the basis of an absolute majority of the socialist party in parliament.

8.3.4.1 Local institutional conditions for the take-up of services and policies

Leading civil servants of the local authority explain that the local authority and its president regarded the decentralisation of the minimum income scheme as a matter that required developing activation strategies to deal with and reduce the high number of benefit claimants. As key to implement the changes, the strong political leadership of the departmental president is repeatedly highlighted. The local president gave out the strategy that the minimum income scheme shall be at a time a right and an obligation.

On the basis of this political announcement, the local president widely delegated the task of devising a service delivery system to the local authority's 'insertion policy' directorate. Given the political importance that the local president accorded to a strategy to reduce the high numbers of benefit recipients, the local president was principally ready to back all the moves of the insertion unit of the local administration as the director of the RMI directorate explains:

> "(…) me, now, I have the possibility to do everything, the president of the local authority, he follows me, I can thus develop an offer for the insertion of the benefit recipients (…)." (F-D-6).

The local authority's insertion policy directorate is a well-staffed branch of the local administration with a president who is described by other local actors as a very entrepreneurial figure. By making reference to the local president's slogan on the minimum income benefit being 'a right and an obligation', the civil servants of this directorate were able to justify all their reform activities as the following statement by one civil servant shows:

> "It's a policy that merits being rigid, (…) we control who has the right, who doesn't have the right will be expelled from benefit payments, (…), we ask for signing contracts, we ask the people to obey their contracts and we put a strong priority on employment that the people exit benefit payment, and we try to facilitate their access to employment." (F-D-1).

Apart from the elaborated bureaucratic structures, numerous welfare associations, economic associations or community organisations have been for a long time involved in social and employment policy. The community-based, social or economic associations form a dense tissue in the local authority. Well developed local partnership structures thus exist between these non-profit and profit organisations as well as the public providers. The local authority's directorate for insertion policy views this existing local partnership structure as an advantage it aims to exploit for its policy.

In short, at the background of an institutionalised local partnership structure, the insertion policy directorate of the local administration is entrusted by the local president to reform the local service delivery system towards a mutual obligations' activation approach.

8.3.4.2 *Local modes of interaction for the delivery of services*

As the following statement of a civil servant of the RMI directorate illustrates, decision-makers of the local authority explain their efforts and the local investments in labour market policy programmes by the necessity to make the assistance recipients find work and reduce costs for benefit payments:

> "(…) the RMI has become a burden for the local budgets and employment makes people exit from benefit payment, so it allows us economise on benefit payments." (F-D-8)

For this purpose, the local president asked his administration to put a stress on labour market integration activities. In line with this demand, the leading civil servants of the insertion policy directorate attempt to put a focus of the service delivery system on labour market policy programmes and placement activities.

Devising and organising the local employment programme and its services

The local authority invests proper resources in active labour market policy programmes and aims to actively shape a local employment programme. Apart from its core competences for social counselling, the principal strategy of the local authority is to intervene secondary to the main active labour market policy programmes which are run in the region. The idea is thus not to build up proper local active labour market policy programmes from scratch but to collaborate with the established providers in order to make their activities better respond to the beneficiaries' specific problems.

Coordination takes primarily place between civil servants in the governance of concrete active labour market policy programmes. The leading civil servants of the local administration's directorate for insertion policy usually try to influence the governance of the relevant active labour market policy instruments. Through negotiations with the actors involved in the governance of a programme, the civil servants of the local administration's directorate for insertion policy attempt to achieve better access conditions for the minimum income benefit recipients. Usually, the local authority offers to co-finance capacities of existing programmes. In turn, the civil servants of the local authority ask for detailed quota which exclusively reserve places for minimum income benefit recipients in the relevant active labour market policy programmes. The negotiations of the civil servants of the local administration's directorate for insertion policy with their counterparts from the state or the regional authority normally lead to the conclusion of detailed conventions on each actor's obligations.

The civil servants of the local administration's directorate for insertion policy are very successful in their negotiations on quotas for minimum income benefit recipients. In practice, the local authority participates in the co-financing of all the main labour market programmes which the leading civil servants of the department consider apt for activating benefit claimants. Explicitly demanded for by the local authority, the relevant providers have accepted quotas to guarantee a certain number of places for recipients of the minimum income scheme. In the sector of publicly financed enterprises (SIAE), the local authority co-finances those enterprises that offer social counselling in parallel to work. Another local programme for labour market integration supported by the local authority are the local action plans for long-term unemployed (PLIE). In negotiations with the regional authority, the civil servants of the local administration's directorate for insertion policy also reached agreement on the reservation of places for minimum income benefit claimants in certain regional schemes of advanced training. The department also co-finances a high number of publicly financed work contracts. Finally, the local authority also counts on the delivery of social counselling by welfare associations on the basis of competitive public tenders.

Despite the local civil servants successful negotiating approach, this strategy also raises criticism. The director of the regional administration for training, for example, is of the opinion that the regional training offers which are not specified by law to a particular target group should generally be accessible to everyone. He explicitly argues against the local authority's strategy that aims to lobby for privileging minimum income recipients' access to active labour market services:

> "Only signing a convention with the local authority that exclusively aims at the minimum income recipients, this poses a problem. It is not the role of the regions to finance the training programmes for the minimum income recipients." (F-D-3).

In short, in addition to its core offers of social counselling, the department also improves minimum income benefit recipients' opportunities to take part inactive labour market policy programmes. In interactions with the important active labour market policy providers, local co-financing offers and the local authority's civil servants' negotiating ability are key for the promotion of quotas in training programmes or subsidised employment schemes for minimum income benefit recipients.

Definition and organisation of placement and counselling

The different programmes offered by organisations to assist social and labour market integration raise the question of how access to these programmes by benefit recipients is organised. To achieve activation in such a complex service delivery system, the department has taken significant steps for a reorganisation of case-management.

After the decentralisation of the minimum income scheme, leading civil servants of the local administration's directorate for insertion policy identified the need to completely reorganise case-management. They reached the conclusion that the previous system of social counselling had been inefficient and not appropriate to activate benefit claimants. Decision-makers of the local authority identified the predominant role of actors from the social welfare system as problem of the previous system. The civil servants of the local authority were therefore of the opinion that continuity of a system based on the local social welfare centres and social workers would inhibit a mutual obligations' activation approach. Directing staff of the local administration's directorate for insertion policy therefore deemed it absolutely necessary to ban the influence of the local welfare services and the social workers on the benefit recipients' integration efforts. Instead, the local authority aimed to introduce greater placement activities apt for long-term unemployed or weaker groups of the labour market. The department aimed at a case management system which would comprise job placement, too.

According to the ideas of the local authority's high civil servants, reorganisation was primarily supposed to give job placement a more central role in case management activities. However, the public servants of the department analysed a lack of proper staff for implementing job placement. Decentralisation had only led to a transfer of additional social workers onto departmental services, notably from the state. Nonetheless, the local authority's public servants were explicitly against simply according case management to social workers. At the same time, the local authority did not want to hire additional permanent staff. The local authority's decision-makers recognised that, all competences needed for a case management system could be found in the different services in the region which had so far been operating in an uncoordinated manner. Based on this recognition of a lack of proper staff in the field of job placement, the department chose to delegate the task of case management almost entirely to external professionals working in different organisations in the region.

For the delegation of case management, the local authority usually concludes an agreement with those organisations in the region that employ field service personnel with relevant competences for placement or social counselling activities. The contracted field service personnel of these external organisations are then appointed as official case-managers for benefit claimants of the minimum income scheme. The agreement on which this decentralised case management is based usually describes in detail the charge of a case-manager. The main duties of the contracted case-managers are to work out integration contracts with benefit recipients and to respond to the control requirements of the local authority.

In return, the local authority compensates for the salary of the external case-manager.

For case management with a strong focus on job placement, the local authority refers recipients to contracted personnel at the local chambers of commerce. Besides placement, a great number of case-managers contracted by the local authority fall into a category that is described as 'socio-professional' counselling. Case-managers falling within this category are depicted to combine competences both in job placement and social work. This case management approach is carried out by external counsellors from numerous and very different organisations operating in the region. The third case management approach provides for benefit claimants the option to contact a counsellor with strong competences for social counselling. This social counselling finally remains a matter of the social workers of the social welfare centres and other social welfare associations.

The reform plans put forward by the local authority initially met harsh criticism of other local organisations. Especially the third sector organisations were opposed the local plans as they did not want to submerge under a policy solely defined by the department. Many of the third sector organisations did not wish to lose their rather autonomous role in assisting persons in need. Key to bring about organisational change was the strong political ambition of the local authority and the empowerment of the insertion policy unit to order the changes. In the course of this strategy, the local authority made further funding to the third sector conditional on compliance. Furthermore, the local authority was able to circumvent opposition in some way by giving important tasks of service delivery to the local chamber of commerce which was an actor supporting the activation approach.

In practice, the local authority implements a case management system for which it has pioneered in the run-up to the RSA reform: on the day a person files an application for the minimum income scheme, he or she will simultaneously have to answer to a survey on his social, professional and educational situation. On the basis of this categorisation, the beneficiary will be directly proposed a case-manager. At the occasion of the first meeting with a case-manager, a benefit recipient signs an integration contract detailing activity requirements. Overall, as the following statement of a civil servant of the RMI directorate illustrates, departmental civil servants describe the introduction of a questionnaire for the orientation of benefit claimants and the delegation of case management as key to ease benefit claimants' access in particular to job placement:

> "We get hold of the persons in the moment when they ask for benefit payments, because otherwise, if we would contact them only six months or one year later, and if we would

not have done anything in between, we would certainly increase the social problems that might arise." (F-D-1).

To guarantee that interactions between external case-managers and benefit recipients proceed according to the premises of the local authority, the insertion policy directorate aimed at a tight regulation process. Civil servants of the local authority in practice regulate placement and counselling activities by authorising the content of each integration contract that is worked out between the external case-managers and the benefit claimants. Case-managers have to send every integration contract, after signature by a benefit recipient, to the local minimum income agencies. Then, the personnel of the local agencies will scrutinise each integration contract with regard to content and activities proposed by a case-manager.

The integration contracts are a practical tool to regulate implementation of the local authority's policy: they put down the exact activities proposed to benefit recipients. Moreover, these contracts reflect the rights and obligations agreed on between the benefit claimant and the department. If local staff of the local authority disagrees with the activities agreed on between a case-manager and a benefit claimant, the local authority amends in a unilateral manner the activities written down. The staff in the local agencies of the minimum income scheme might also give order of reassignment of a case-manager to a benefit recipient if the current case-manager is not deemed suitable any longer.

The decision-makers of the local authority recognize the significant administrative charge which is caused by this way of controlling the case management process. However, they deem this as absolutely necessary in order to guarantee the local authority's control over the activation process, namely case management, signature of integration contracts and placement onto social or labour market programmes. For this purpose of regulating the placement and counselling process, several local agencies have been created by the local authority. As exemplified by the following statement of a civil servant of the RMI directorate, the local authority's public servants believe that it would be otherwise very difficult to guarantee the activation the benefit recipients into work, social or labour market programmes: such an approach might not be evident for every case-manager and therefore interactions have to be regulated tightly:

"This organisation allows us to delegate to the case managers the placement activities without at the same time losing control on the whole process, we follow them regularly although it is a bit complicated to organise this. (…) This control is important because it depends on the processes on the ground if they case managers will follow the strategy of the RMI directorate (…)." (F-D-7).

In short, the department tightly regulates the activation process of a case management system which heavily relies on external organisations and their case-managers. A considerable bureaucratic process is put in place by local field service staff of the local authority. The staff of the local authority will scrutinize each integration contract worked out between the external case-managers and the benefit recipients. Thereby, the local authority can unilaterally intervene in the activation process, for instance by determining the activities proposed to a benefit claimant.

8.3.4.3 Local techniques of control

The local authority has developed explicit control mechanism to ensure an activation of benefit recipients by external case-managers and the project executing organisations.

Organisations delivering services financed by the local authority are asked to reach contracted objectives. Civil servants of the department commonly explain the use of benchmarks by pointing to their duty to supervise the spending of public money and to justify action before departmental deputes. Delivered services are measured with regard to numbers of 'positive outcome' meaning integration into employment or further education. Successful integration into employment is normally considered as permanent employment or fixed-term employment for at least six months. From the perspective of the local authority, part-time work is considered as a successful activation. Part-time work is indeed often aimed at by the department and the project executing organisations. This particular aim arises out of the situation that activation into a part-time job will relieve the department from any further obligations even though a recipient might remain eligible to benefit assistance. This mechanism was valid for the RMI and it principally will remain in force for the RSA. In the RSA, the local authority finances benefits for those not working (*RSA socle)* while the state has to account for those persons who are working part-time and still remain eligible for minimum income payments (*RSA chapeau*). In these cases, the state is required to finance the supplements. Furthermore, the legal texts propose that Pôle Emploi provides the necessary active labour market services for these 'working-poor'. A higher-ranking civil servant of the local authority explains this focus on part-time employment as a goal:

> "(…) from the RMI, there is one door to exit it, this means, I need to have a proper income, if I don't have any other income, its only work that helps, it is an obligation to work at least more than the RMI gives to me, as a result, the goal needs to be at least part-time

> work integration." (F-D-2). "(...) And according to the new logic it means that we in fact need to try to reduce our number of people in the RSA socle in order to make them access to the RSA chapeau. By doing so, we are transferring the responsibilities." (F-D-2).

Local authority F-D equally tries to measure services rather dedicated to social integration. Decision-makers acknowledge that this is a difficult task.

However, leading civil servants of the local authority point out that contracted quantitative objectives are only one indicator for evaluating the development of measures. In addition, organisations and associations will be regularly demanded to deliver written reports on their service activities. These reports serve as further instrument of evaluation and control of the service delivery system for the department. One of the main tasks of some of the experts working in the departmental administration consists of supervising a written reporting system which requires organisations and associations to constantly inform the local civil servants on their implementation of service measures. A leading civil servant of the RMI directorate of the local authority explains this control strategy based on requirements for reporting:

> "We achieve to evaluate all our activities that we are financing. (...) And we base our further financing on these evaluation reports." (F-D-1).

In brief, the local authority controls delivery of placement, counselling and training by mechanisms of benchmarks and a broader reporting system. A goal put forward by the benchmarks is the activation into part-time employment as this relieves the local authority from its benefit payment obligations.

8.3.4.4 *Towards a bureaucratic activation logic in local authority F-D*

Since decentralisation, local authority F-D has achieved to coordinate services at the local level for the activation of minimum income recipients. Financial pressure due to high numbers of minimum income recipients and the opportunity to shape a proper local policy are viewed by both political and administrative actors of the local authority as an incentive to activate assistance recipients. For this purpose, primarily the insertion policy directorate of the local authority devises a local service delivery system which combines the competences for subsidised employment of the national labour ministry's departmental agency, training offers of the regional authority, social counselling of third sector organisations as well as placement by the local chamber of commerce.

The department can exploit for its service delivery system an established tissue of third sector organisations, for-profit providers and the local state agencies. The department invests important resources in order to incite providers of the existing local partnerships structure to turn the focus of activities onto assisting the recipients of the minimum income scheme. For expanding local services beyond social counselling, civil servants of the local directorate for insertion policy negotiate with the relevant providers on co-financed quotas in active labour market policy programmes. In some instances, the local authority also counts on the delivery of new service offers by the welfare associations or the local chambers of commerce on the basis of competitive public tenders. To make this service delivery system for the activation of minimum income benefit recipients work in practice, the department puts a strong focus on organising an efficient case management system. For this purpose, the local insertion policy directorate closely regulates case management of counsellors or placement officers in external organisations as the local chambers of commerce or different welfare associations. Empowered by the local president, the local insertion policy directorate thus arises as the central body organising the local service delivery system: the civil servants of the directorate for insertion policy negotiate with other civil servants of the public authorities on a service offer and they closely regulate case-managers and project executing organisations' activities.

To ensure the coordination of contract-based case-management or organisations and associations delivering social counselling or active labour market policy services, the department has developed different mechanisms of control. The diverse programmes for training or subsidised work schemes are usually controlled by quantitative objectives on their success of placing benefit recipients into (part-time) work or further education. This sets a framework for undertaking active placement and counselling. However, the department is reluctant to give away too much decision-making power to case-managers or project executing organisations: civil servants of the department therefore scrutinise and control implementation by reporting and tight regulation of activities. This huge administrative work is necessary as other forms of control as trust or more detailed management objectives are not applied.

To conclude, the department organises services for the activation of recipients of the minimum income scheme which tend to follow a bureaucratic logic of activation.

8.4 Conclusion: varying local welfare interventions in France

This chapter showed at the example of four case studies how activation of long-term unemployed and disadvantaged groups of society is realised in France at the local level. The French welfare state has been confronted with the same challenge like other Bismarckian countries including the German welfare state:

increased numbers of long-term unemployed, disadvantaged groups of society and persons with non-standard employment biographies have been claiming minimum income benefits.

The labour market and social policy reforms in France are partly questioning the persistence of the classical 'Bismarckian' fragmentation which divided welfare state institutions between a labour market policy for workers on the one side, and family income respectively social policy for weaker and more vulnerable groups on the other side. In the face of new risks of long-term unemployment and vulnerable situations, which are caused by social and economic transformations, French labour market and social protection reforms follow Bismarckian patterns of change: given the increasing social and economic fragility of family support and the status-oriented nature of social insurance, activation is institutionalised as a new institutional filter for weaker and more vulnerable groups against the increased risk of dependency on minimum income benefits.

In line with this new employment filter, social protection options have been circumscribed. Given financing problems of corporatist social insurance, entitlement is increasingly reserved for persons with strong contributory records and social insurance benefits are linked to 'return-to-work' placement activities. Furthermore, options for category specific long-term assistance or early retirement were limited, too. While the employment-friendly character of 'higher-ranking' institutions has been thus partly increased, the reforms have simultaneously caused a recalibration of social protection claims of long-term unemployed and disadvantaged groups onto the 'last-resort' safety net. In order to take pressure from this residual welfare option, the French minimum income benefit regulation has been step by step re-regulated from social *insertion* in to a work-oriented character. Much more pronounced than for the corporatist unemployment insurance system and thus 'selective' in its effect, social policy reform introduces work requirements and work incentives for recipients of the general minimum income benefit. As a complementary component of this new institutional filter, work opportunities, particularly in the area of low-income employment, have been opened up for long-term unemployed and disadvantaged groups by a partial and thus 'selective' flexibilisation of the French labour market. Furthermore, minimum income benefit recipients are now being treated as 'regular' job-seekers who shall have access to placement and counselling services.

All in all, employment-friendly reforms of the social protection system, the focus on services and the flexibilisation of the labour market in France match a Bismarckian strategy of activation, which concentrates on employment as a new mode of welfare production for groups formerly excluded from the labour market.

Discussion of the first hypothesis: activation as a matter of the local organisation

The labour market and social policy reforms raise the issue of how long-term unemployed and weaker groups of the labour market might be assisted with their activation into the labour market. Since the implementation of a decentralisation reform in 2004, the political authority to direct attempts of the activation of benefit recipients was transferred to the departments. For this task, however, the departments were only provided with the principal elements of the traditional 'social work' organisation of the minimum income scheme. According to this organisational frame, the local authority commands a set of obligatory social welfare services, it is accorded chairmanship of an 'insertion' committee to draw up an 'insertion strategy', and it was transferred staff comprising exclusively social workers. The latter had already been a central pillar of the 'social treatment' approach in the local social field services of the state before the decentralisation of the minimum income system. Thus, to serve the minimum income recipients, the department has inherited from the state the structures of the social welfare system, notably the social workers and the chairmanship of the roundtable for insertion. However, the department did not gain resources and competences from the field of active labour market policy. Instead, the services and programmes for training, placement, further education or subsidised employment are held by a number of different actors, notably the state and its regional agencies, the public employment services, other sub-national actors or even private actors. Despite recent reforms to activate benefit recipients, the organisational framework for services and policies did not call into question the demarked fields of social welfare and active labour market policy. Re-organisation processes, like the unification of services (Pôle emploi) of insurance benefit payment and placement services for the status-based unemployed, remained principally confined to the boundaries of each policy field. As a result, the activation of the minimum income benefit recipients is to a great extent left to the coordination efforts between the departments, the employment agencies, the state, the regional authorities and the third sector.

As suggested by our first hypothesis, the attempts to activate disadvantaged persons, persistently unemployed, or persons with non-standard employment biographies turn into an issue of the local coordination of formerly disparate and fragmented policy fields. The case studies give evidence of the requirement of intense local coordination processes in order to organise services and policies for the activation of benefit recipients. In the French cases, it is widely up to the local level, in as much benefits, work requirements, active labour market policy and social counselling are interlinked with each other. Apart from benefit payment and social counselling, increased access opportunities to the manifold active labour market policy programmes depend on the local authorities' engagement to find co-financing arrangements and quota agreements for minimum income benefit recipients with the relevant providers. Furthermore, it completely depends on the local authority to organise an efficient case management which is needed to ensure benefit recipients' access to the different providers for social counselling or active labour market policy programmes. Moreover, given the variety of providers of services, the ability of the local authority to organise an efficient case management determines whether activity requirements are in practice linked to benefits. In the French local studies, coordination efforts and an efficient case management system thus turned out as extremely important in order to realise a co-production between benefit recipients, the local authority and the many providers of services and programmes work.

As the four French case studies show, this fragmentation of providers and policies is only partly challenged by the French local authorities. The local authorities deal not in a consistent manner with the national reform objective of an activation of benefit recipients into work. Generally, two reactions by the local authorities can be observed. Either, the local authorities deem the tasks conferred to them as completely unacceptable. In this case, they use their local discretion to politically oppose the central state and they will deliver the minimum income scheme rather as unconditional benefit according to a social citizenship logic. Alternatively, the local authorities view their new budgetary responsibilities and the few legal regulations imposed as an incentive to attempt to actively reduce the number of benefit recipients and the charge of benefit payment. In these cases, the local authorities try to actively institutionalise proper local service delivery systems for the activation of benefit recipients into work. In these regions, the idea is to grant rights and assisting services to benefit recipients while simultaneously demanding their active participation in integration efforts. However, as the case studies have shown, the ability and the way the local authorities are able and willing to organise a local co-production of the fragmented services differs strongly.

To conclude, the first hypothesis of the institutionalisation of local organisational fields, which achieve to reduce the fragmentation of policies and providers, can only partly be partly confirmed in the French cases. The case studies show that an activation approach of combined services and work incentives is not consistently applied at the local level. This raises questions on the exact variety existing and the causes of theses inconsistencies (cf. discussion below).

Discussion of the second hypothesis: variance in the local organisation of activation

As stipulated in our second hypothesis, variety in the organisation of welfare interventions in the realm of the minimum income scheme can arise due to differences in local institutional structures, modes of interaction and control forms.

In local authority F-C, placement and counselling services are primarily organised according to a participatory model. A local political ambition put forward is to make the region's rich tissue of local third sector organisations and other providers contribute to an activation approach. At the occasion of roundtables, public discussions, steering committees or mutual visits, the civil servants of the insertion policy directorate and the local politicians argue that it is necessary to sign integration contracts and to activate benefit recipients. During these occasions, the civil servants or even politicians of the local authority regularly discuss ideas how to activate benefit recipients with the case managers, project executing organisations, welfare associations, the public employment services or the representatives from the other sub-national authorities. On the basis of this discursive strategy, which is furthered by monetary incentives and the signature of mutual agreements, the local authority achieves to integrate diverse service offers of a very rich local tissue of various providers and approaches into their proper local concept for the activation of minimum income benefit recipients. Control of the numerous external case managers and project executing organisations is not only assured by quantitative indicators on the number of persons activated into (part-time) work or further education but also by the round tables and regular discussion fora, which provide a common and trust-based understanding of the necessity to sign integration contracts with benefit recipients and to activate benefit recipients into work or work-related activities.

While local authority F-D builds on a similarly active and diversified local partnership structure, it attempts to coordinate the various local training, employment and training activities rather in a bureaucratic manner. Empowered by the local president, who wishes a reduction of benefit recipients, civil servants of the insertion policy directorate put a focus on negotiating technical details, lay down detailed regulations and make financing conditional on compliance. By doing so, they tightly regulate service delivery by project executing organisations and contracted case-managers. In order to control the implementation of an activation approach, the local insertion policy directorate requires case-managers and other actors to respect standards and to report back in detailed ways on activities. Given the numerous actors and very manifold situation for which local authority F-D has to find regulations for, this bureaucratic approach of activation causes considerable regulatory activity for the civil servants of the insertion policy directorate and its subordinate field services.

While local authority F-A is situated in a similarly active and institutionalised local partnership structure of various actors, it fails to forge a coherent organisation of services for the activation of minimum income benefit recipients. Although local politicians announce their preferences for activation policies and the local authority co-finances activities for placement, the implementation of a coherent service delivery system widely fails. Charged with this task, the local directorate for insertion policy is neither given enough political support nor does it succeed to broadly convince reform opposed local actors of the necessity to activate benefit recipients. Furthermore, the local authority does not apply reliable mechanisms to control the implementation of policies and services. As a result, a social treatment approach remains in practice, which is not compatible with activity requirements and work integration.

Finally, local authority F-B, does neither count on any established institutional relationships with third sector organisations or the state-run agencies, nor does it attempt to initiate those in the area of counselling and placement. Instead, local politicians demand the state and the employment agency to step up activities for disadvantaged groups and long-term unemployed. As a coherent service delivery organisation is not in the focus of local initiatives, a social treatment of minimum income benefit recipients remains in place in the local administration.

In the French cases, the local co-production of services thus alters between participatory activation approaches for empowering autonomous citizens' capabilities, bureaucratic approaches for enabling the activation of beneficiaries and a social treatment of standardised benefits for social citizens.

Between social treatment and activation approaches: explanatory factors of the national framework

The contested character of activation at the local level in France provokes analysing the national framework for possible explanatory factors. Despite the turn towards activation in social and labour market policy regulation, the case studies disclosed that the national framework for the local organisation does not necessarily provide coherent enough financial, regulatory, technical and administrative rules and resources to implement activation approaches. In the local case studies, we explored that the national financing mechanism of the local budget, the historical development of the national regulation of the minimum income scheme and national organisational resources constituted most influential 'national' factors on local action.

A shift towards a local activation approach is most directly enhanced by the national financing conditions. The decentralisation of the minimum income scheme has transferred a considerable budgetary responsibility onto the departments. As the departments receive fixed state grants for benefit payments, whose volume was defined at the time of decentralisation, national financing does not exactly account for the actual evolution of expenses. This means that the local authority itself might need to account to a certain extent for the financing of the minimum income benefit payment. An increase in numbers of benefit recipients in a local authority, can thus force the local authority to limit its expenses in other local policy areas or to borrow extra monetary resources. In the local cases studied, issues of local financing of the minimum income benefit were therefore generally a major concern for the local authority's politicians and civil servants. As a result, activation into employment was discovered by local politicians and civil servants as one possible way to respond to the budgetary risks. As the state takes over financing responsibilities from the local authority for the 'working poor' minimum income benefit recipients (since 2010: RSA *châpeau*), a particular incentive arises for the local authorities to focus strategies on the activation into part-time or low-income employment. At the same time, the national financial mechanism does not consistently provoke local activation policy as a response. As illustrated in the case study F-A, in face of a difficult financial situation, the local politicians fully resorted to a policy of lobbying for additional national resources instead of choosing local activation. The national financing mechanism thus incites activation as one possible local strategy while also leaving room for other local strategies.

Apart from the national financing mechanism, the local developments in the cases studied were influenced by the legacy of the French minimum income benefit regulation. As became evident at the example of the contested local priorities, the history of the French regulation of the minimum income scheme does not constitute a coherent reference for a work orientation. Originally, the French 'politique d'insertion' had been based on a very broad concept of social exclusion. Although activity requirements have been stipulated from the beginning, regulation of the French minimum income scheme initially favoured a broader concept of social integration instead of focussing on the take up of work. Step by step, the minimum income scheme has been re-regulated towards a stronger work-orientation (cf. chapter 8.1). However, even though the recent RSA reform is described as the most explicit turn of the minimum income benefit towards a workfare scheme (Barbier and Knuth 2011b; Clegg and Palier 2012), it still leaves for local actors ample room for interpretation whom to categorise as a benefit recipient exclusively being in need of a 'social counselling'. In the cases studied, this incoherence in the development of the regulatory framework allowed for different interpretations of the national regulation. For some actors, *social insertion* still constituted the prevailing frame of reference. For other actors, a mutual obligations' approach of work integration has become the principle point of reference. This contested legacy of the national minimum income benefit regulation thus opened up a wider room for local interpretation forming at a time a reference for those local actors attached to *social insertion* and those attached to *activation*.

Besides the evolution of national regulation, local developments were strongly influenced by the local organisational resources provided by the national level. The staff resources, local committee chairmanship authorities and service competences handed over to the department, indeed increased its organisational resources in the field of social welfare but not in the area of active labour market policy and placement competences. This 'decentralisation' of the prior national social welfare organisation (Lafore 2004) particularly raised issues of placement competences in the area of staff resources. The social workers who had constituted a central pillar of the 'social treatment' approach in the social field services of the state (cf. chapter 6.2) now staffed a local administration which was already dominated by professionals having a distinct social work background. Thus, as the local authority was equipped with key organisational elements of the prior social welfare system, activation was a much contested issue at the local level.

Although the national financing mechanisms of the local budget can incite local activation strategies, which confer to national regulation suggesting part-time or low-income employment take-up for minimum income benefit recipients, this is a much contested event. The national regulation's legacy of the minimum income regulation and the organisational instruments set a framework for local action in France which allows for strong variance to arise between local authorities implementing activation and other cases of continuous practices of social treatment.

Between social treatment and different activation approaches: explanatory factors at the local level

Given the discordant national framework for local activation, local dynamics strongly determine the institutionalisation of the French activation regime.

While the activities of the local authorities are embedded in existing local institutional structures and relationships, the case studies illustrate that actors advancing very different concepts appear in the local organisational fields (Fligstein 2001). These actors advocate different strategies of how to deal with the minimum income recipients. In all four case studies opponents and proponents of an activation reform could be identified.

Opponents of the new activation approach adhered to the traditional idea of a social treatment of benefit recipients. Social workers, local administrations' directorates for *social exclusion issues*, welfare associations and other partners of the local authority could constitute these adherents of the social treatment approach. Some of these actors had strongly incorporated a social work approach in the realm of their profession (social work). This group of actors therefore remained strongly committed to approaches of the typical French social welfare system. Their preference was clearly in favour of continuity of the established social welfare system of rather standardised benefit payment. These actors thus constituted firm proponents of upholding a *social insertion* approach.

In contrast, in all four case studies, adherents of a new activation approach stepped up which were ready to challenge the established local organisation. These actors were susceptible to the new activation approach in national social and labour market policy regulation. The reform-oriented actors oriented their activities along concepts like 'the minimum income scheme is at a time a right and an obligation'. These actors had a clear preference in favour of re-organisation of the local service delivery system. They were normally ready to pioneer and step up as entrepreneurs of a new approach. Usually, they were familiar with organisational concepts how to achieve an activation of benefit recipients. They viewed the necessity to make benefit recipients sign integration contracts, to introduce efficient case-management and to control, for example, by benchmarks. While their organisational strategies how to achieve activation could differ, the reform-oriented actors agreed that the approach of the 'social workers' posed an obstacle to implement an activation strategy.

Rather independent from their political partisanship, local government heads and vice-presidents could constitute a crucial fraction of this reform-oriented group of actors. Ready to make use of decentralised political authority, they viewed activation as an appropriate strategy to take pressure from the local budget and as a concept for shaping a proper local policy profile. Given the French *cumul de mandates* (accumulation of mandates) a local mandate can also give a national politician, as for example in local authority F-C, the opportunity to directly apply national reform premises. Among the local civil servants, proponents of an activation reform were often found in the *insertion* policy directorate of a local authority's administration. Decentralisations had given these civil servants of the local administration the new and somewhat undefined task of *insertion* policy, which now served as an opportunity to boost the importance of their proper directorate. In some cases, a local activation approach was also supported by directing staff of the employment agency or the state agencies. Given their closely defined position in the hierarchy of the national-run organisations, engagement in the local approaches offered a new and discretionary area of activity.

While lobbyists of these two contrasting strategies (activation or social treatment) could be found in each local case study, the local institutions and the institutional positioning of the rivalling actors determined which organisational strategy could finally emerge as dominant in a region.

In region F-A and F-B, despite decentralisation, adherents of the traditional social work system remain in key institutional positions to determine the organisation of the minimum income scheme. In region F-B, the reform willing directorate of insertion policy not only lacks support by local politicians but also suffers from weakly institutionalised relationships with other reform-oriented actors like the state-run regional agencies. As local politicians mobilise their political authority to ask the central state and the public employment services to assist benefit recipients, the dominant role of the social workers in the central administration, the local field services and case-management is not being called into question. In this situation, strong obstacles arise to implement new organisational issues as for example a benchmarking system. In region F-A, the difficulties to surmount the legacy of a broadly institutionalised social welfare system are even more striking. While politicians are generally in favour of investing in an activation strategy, the case management system, the field service agencies and the third sector remain attached to a social treatment approach in the tradition of the social welfare system. In the discussion in the central administration on how to organise a service delivery system for the benefit recipients, the 'social workers' are continuously able to defend the current practices against changes suggested by the 'reformers' of the directorate for insertion policy. As a result, in both local authorities national prescriptions for 'case management' or 'signature of integration contracts' are just shallow categories applied in a system which is still dominated by actors in favour of implementing the minimum income benefit as a social treatment.

By contrast, in local authority F-C and F-D actors advocating the activation of benefit recipients occupy key positions in institutionalised local partnerships between the local political arena, local administrations and third sector organisations. In both local authorities, the local presidents are strongly committed to an activation strategy. They form strong reform alliances with the civil servants' of the directorate for insertion policy and, in the case of local authority F-C, they also collaborate with the employment agency. In order to reform the system, the 'reformers' introduce key changes in case management and find reliable ways of control. Concerning case management, tasks are delegated to external placement officers. As a result, the directorate for social exclusions issues, the social welfare centres and the social workers do not play any longer a crucial role in the implementation of the activation approach. In addition, the reform-oriented local politicians and civil servants in the two local authorities strive for efficient control mechanisms of the implementation of the local activation approaches. In local authority F-D, the local president gives strong authority to the *insertion* policy directorate which establishes tight controls for external case managers and project executing organisations through standards and a detailed reporting system. In local authority F-C, the president and the local directorate of insertion policy rather rely on their positive 'reputation' among the local community as a basis serving to convince other local partners to commit to an activation approach. In both local authorities F-C and F-D, national prescriptions for case management, signature of integration contracts or greater budgetary responsibility are thus locally used by actors eager to reform the system towards an activation of benefit recipients.

To conclude, the local institutionalisation of an activation regime for long-term unemployed, weaker groups and persons with non-standard biographies in France is a matter of both national as well as local developments. Despite the social and labour market policy's priority on activation, the national framework leaves much room for interpretation of the concrete inter-organisation of benefits, placement and social welfare services. The discordant history of the national regulation of the minimum income scheme and the decentralised social work organisation make activation at the local level a highly contested issue. Only the national financial mechanism of the local budget gives a certain incentive to activate benefit recipients into part-time and low-income employment as stipulated by the reformed social and labour market policy objectives in France.

While the national framework thus offers resources for local actors to practice in a surprisingly autonomous way the delivery of services to minimum income recipients, the interplay of established structures and the institutional positioning of advocates of competing ideas are crucial to understand why in some regions the minimum income scheme is still practised as a social treatment and why it is reorganised towards an activation of benefit recipients in other regions. As proponents of a 'social workers' remained in crucial local positions in local authority F-A and F-B, the structure and legacy of the minimum income scheme as an approach of social treatment was not challenged. In contrast, in local authority F-C and F-D, local politicians and civil servants of the *insertion* policy directorate formed entrepreneurial reform coalitions in order to break with the legacy of social treatment. In these regions, explicit service delivery systems, which combine placement, counselling and activity requirements, are built up for the activation of minimum income recipients. As reliance on civil servants' authority is greater in region F-D, the service delivery system is more structured according to a bureaucratic logic. As reform willing actors in local authority F-D, can resort to strong reputation and long-standing credibility, the service delivery system is reformed by arguing processes according to a participatory activation approach. Developments in France thus show that the organisation of an activation approach is highly contingent on local circumstances.

9. Conclusion: local coordination of fragmented Bismarckian welfare states

Responding to rising numbers of minimum income recipients, activation into employment evolves in France and Germany as a fresh approach to deal with new challenges of inclusion arising. Thereby displaying a more general trend of Bismarckian-type continental welfare states, employment centred welfare presents a new attempt of the inclusion of long-term unemployed, weaker groups of society or unemployed persons with non-standard employment biographies. As this book has shown, the typically fragmented Bismarckian welfare state architecture makes the activation of persistently unemployed and vulnerable groups evolve as a process which is highly contingent on the local inter-organisation of once disparate minimum income benefit arrangements with services for placement, training, rehabilitation or care.

In general, the rising number of benefit recipients of minimum income schemes in continental European countries was conceptualised as a problem of typical Bismarckian institutions of welfare and work requesting new filter functions against the risk of minimum income receipt. The 'division of labour' of Bismarckian institutions between labour market policy for 'workers' and family welfare or passive social policy for weaker and more vulnerable groups has decreasingly proved as robust option. With regard to family welfare, fragilities have arisen due to increasing rates of family breakdown, female employment careers and the partly erosion of socially secured male breadwinner careers. In parallel, changes in production, deindustrialisation and rising atypical employment have undermined options of socially secured employment and stable male-breadwinner careers. Finally, faced with increasing demands, access to more generous category specific and work-status related, higher-ranking social protection programmes has been limited stepwise in attempts to reinstate basic insurance principles. Taken together, new economic and social risks have increased claims on means-tested minimum income schemes, which had been originally installed as a disparate, residual benefit programme for those 'extreme outsiders' which were not 'filtered' by the Bismarckian welfare state institutions of family welfare, socially secured employment or generous higher-ranking social protection programmes.

This rise in the numbers of minimum income beneficiaries, however, turned the fragmented and passive character of the Bismarckian welfare state increasingly into a problem requiring new solutions especially for the inclusion of weaker and vulnerable groups. Diffused by the EU and other international organisations (Armingeon 2007; Visser 2009), new concepts have been put forward for safeguarding inclusion opportunities of weaker and more vulnerable groups in face of new social and economic risks arising. Replacing a focus on social protection, at the core of these concepts is the idea of activation into employment as a new and general premise against social exclusion and for a sustainable welfare state (van Berkel and Valkenburg 2007: 8). The flexicurity concept added a qualitative dimension to the debate on an employment-centred welfare state, by proposing ideas on enabling both labour market inclusion as well as protection (Clasen and Viebrock 2009). Taking up this challenge to offer broader and more universal access conditions to work, qualification, income replacement, rehabilitation or care also for the weaker groups of society, a reformulated agenda for social and labour market policy has arisen (Schmid 2002; Barbier 2004; Clasen and Clegg 2006): a reform agenda has evolved which comprises the institutionalisation of flexible labour markets, work incentives, integrated and employment-friendly social protection systems as well as active labour market policies and social welfare services facilitating work take-up. Especially the Open Method of Coordination proved able to 'irritate' so far passive Bismarckian welfare states (Heidenreich 2009), which has triggered questions how social and labour market policy reforms have responded to increased numbers of minimum income recipients in continental European.

Reforms in continental European countries, however, did not lead to a radical overhaul of the Bismarckian system but to a very specific institutional remodelling. This remodelling aims at the institutionalisation of employment-centred welfare as a new institutional filter against dependency on minimum income receipt.

First, more far-reaching reforms of the integration of social security systems enabling more egalitarian protection are inhibited in continental Europe by the inertia of contribution-based social security programmes. As these higher-ranking protection programmes though couple entitlements in an increasingly strict manner to 'workers' with steady contribution records (Clasen and Clegg 2006; Palier and Martin 2007; Hemerijck and Marx 2010), means-tested minimum income programmes are being established as an increasingly generalised protection mechanism which covers weaker and more vulnerable groups, long-term unemployed and persons with unsteady or low employment records (Palier 2010) as well as 'precarious' workers. At the same time, benefits of tax-financed general minimum income programmes tend to remain at a residual level and subsidiary in nature. In continental Europe, realignments of social security thus strengthen the two-tier character between an ever more exclusive contribution-based 'higher-ranking' Bismarckian system for 'workers' and general 'last-resort' minimum income programmes for needy workless groups, long-term unemployed, unemployed persons with unstable employment biographies or precariously employed.

As claims on social protection are increasingly channelled onto still residual minimum income programmes, a more flexible labour market evolves as an alternative to assistance benefit receipt. In continental Europe, changes in labour market regulation weaken the exclusive character of Bismarckian employment relations and create employment opportunities particularly in low-paid or 'atypical' work. In line with continental European policy trends, changes in France and Germany exemplified the introduction of more flexible employment contracts or in-work benefit schemes (Clegg 2007) as new alternatives to minimum income benefit receipt. Among the continental European countries, France stands out with the introduction of the RSA stipulating a broad in-work benefit programme for low-paid employees (Clegg and Palier 2012). Also Germany focuses on exemptions from social contributions for low-income work (Mini- and Midi Jobs) and pays top-ups for low earners (Barbier and Knuth 2011a: 6; Eichhorst et al. 2008b). Labour market reforms have thus removed access barriers for low-skilled, weaker groups of the labour market or long-term unemployed which were previously excluded by the rigid Bismarckian employment model. Apart from a flexibilised segment of part-time, non-permanent or low-paid jobs, however, a rigid segment of permanent and well-protected jobs persists giving rise to a significant dualism in continental European labour markets (Palier 2010; Palier and Thelen 2010). This partial flexibilisation of so far rigid Bismarckian labour markets nonetheless constitutes a crucial element of a new institutional filter of minimum income schemes: in order to take pressure from minimum income programmes, it attempts to move benefit recipients from a position of 'extreme outsiders' into the labour market.

Besides greater labour market opportunities, social services are increasingly used in continental Europe to focus on easing the employment barriers of persistently unemployed, disadvantaged groups of society and persons with non-standard biographies. Social expenditures' share for services has reached moderate levels. Perhaps even more important, although typically passive Bismarckian welfare states still reserve a high share of public social expenditures for passive benefits, the rationale of service provision in continental Europe changes from a concept based on upholding the status of workers into a tool for activating weaker and more vulnerable groups into work (Bonoli 2010). Social welfare services like child care and active labour market policies are in an increasingly explicit manner applied in connection with attempts to facilitate the take-up of work (Kröger and Sipilä 2005; Rostgaard 2002). Exemplifying such trends in continental Europe, the German Hartz reforms have stipulated a comprehensive set of placement services, training programmes and social welfare services for minimum income benefit recipients (Dingeldey 2007; Eichhorst et al. 2008b). Also the French RSA reform has suggested to treat minimum income recipients as 'normal' jobseekers who require not only social work services but also services of active labour market policy (Barbier and Knuth 2011a: 14). The rationale of using services as alternative to assistance receipt (Nelson 2011) thus constitutes a general trend in continental Europe and therefore compounds a further pillar of a new institutional filter against minimum income receipt.

Apart from increased employment opportunities and social services, activation from social benefits into work is enhanced by the application of work requirements, incentives and other workfare elements. In continental Europe, the application of work requirements and work incentives in the social protection system is most strongly concentrated on recipients of minimum income benefits (Clegg 2007, Martin and Palier 2007). In line with these 'selective' tendencies, the introduction of new regulation or the reinterpretation of traditional Bismarckian subsidiarity requirements has served the purpose of remodelling minimum income schemes towards the take-up of work (Clegg and Palier 2012; Knuth and Barbier 2011a, 2011b). At the same, also the higher-ranking social security programmes have become more employment-friendly albeit in a more implicit manner. Although typical Bismarckian non-conditional benefit support remains in force for the insured unemployed (Clegg 2007), the shortening of unemployment insurance in both France and Germany (Daguerre and Taylor-Gooby 2003: 630) as well as the suppression of status-oriented long-term unemployment benefits in Germany (Eichhorst et al. 2008b) display continental European examples of increased work take-up incentives which are also set for the insured unemployed. Taken together, these changes in the social protection programmes add up to a comprehensive employment-friendly remodelling of the continental European social protection systems: the cuts in the higher-ranking systems as well as the strong application of work requirements and work incentives in minimum income schemes function as a tool for the activation of minimum income benefit recipients but also as a general deterrent of long-term benefit receipt. The introduction of various workfare elements in the social security system thus constitutes a further pillar of a new institutional filter against minimum income receipt of disadvantaged groups, persons with non-standard employment biographies and persistently unemployed.

Summarising the nature of these important and selective social and labour market policy changes in continental Europe, Bismarckian institutions change to the extent that they can function as employment-centred filter against minimum income receipt: employment, social services and workfare elements are replacing family welfare, male-breadwinner family salaries or generous social protection as a new and specifically Bismarckian institutional filter against risks of minimum income receipt of weaker and more vulnerable groups. While processes of European diffusion and national regulation have thus paved the way for this new priority on employment incentives, work requirements, social welfare services and active labour market policy in continental Europe, a crucial local dimension is opened up by the strong focus of the Bismarckian activation regime on persons difficult to place, who are dependent on minimum income benefit provision.

The activation of long-term unemployed and vulnerable groups from minimum income provision into work 'automatically' opens up a local dimension as local authorities play an important role in the provision of minimum income benefits and social welfare services (rehabilitation, care, social work) in continental Europe. Traditionally, continental European welfare states have reserved a prominent role for the local level in the provision of disparate and subsidiary minimum income benefits and social welfare services (Mingione et al. 2002; Saraceno 2002) for the 'extreme outsiders'. Furthermore, tendencies of decentralisation have often (re-)invigorated a local basis of minimum income benefit programmes and social service competences in continental Europe (Bahle 2003; Finn 2000). Exemplifying the first case, Germany's social assistance and social welfare service systems have always been strongly based on the local level. Displaying the latter case, in France, local authority for social welfare services and the general minimum income programme was recently strengthened by the decentralisation of competences for benefit and service delivery. Local authorities are thus conferred an important role in the Bismarckian activation regime.

In addition to the outstanding role of local authorities in social welfare services and minimum income benefits, the increased focus of Bismarckian welfare state policy on supporting services, incentive setting and work requirement enforcement makes the realisation of policies depend on the local level. This policy mix, which is aimed at surmounting the different obstacles to labour market activation of long-term unemployed and otherwise disadvantaged groups, is principally about improving a person's individual capacities, correcting individual behaviour and increasing an unemployed person's activity motivation (van Berkel and Borghi 2007; Eichhorst et al. 2008a). In order to react to these individual requirements, targeted and often multiple service reactions are required which involve tailor-made incentives, placement, training, or counselling services (van Berkel and Valkenburg 2007). As such processes of assisting and guiding unemployed towards the take-up of employment strongly rely on the service delivery part of the policy process, its outcomes are highly contingent on the local context (Kaufmann 2009: 88–106). Partially challenging the national uniformity of benefits and regulation in continental Europe, the new activation policy approach raises questions of situated, local processes of service delivery (Salais and Villeneuve 2004).

The important role of local authorities and the necessity of the local level to organise a targeted delivery of different services, however has raised questions how so far disparate minimum income programmes might be combined with work incentives, social welfare services and active labour market policy. Mirroring the fragmented Bismarckian welfare state's character, an unemployment policy for 'workers' was typically divided from a poverty policy for minimum income recipients in continental Europe. This division concerned three areas: first, different from a coherent activation approach, policy fields' logics could vary between 'status-based' unemployment policy for workers and a separate 'social work treatment' of minimum income recipients. Second, in the Bismarckian multi-level system, local tasks of minimum income benefits and social work competences were often separated from a national provision of placement, qualification or benefit delivery for 'workers'. Third, in continental Europe, public providers typically granted an important say to the social partners in issues of labour market policy and active labour market policy whereas the third sector organisations were often involved in the local provision of social welfare services and minimum income benefits. In sum, this fragmentation between isolated policy fields, different competences in the multi-level system and separated public and private providers has raised the question how the activation of long-term unemployed and vulnerable groups might be organised at the local level in continental Europe.

In order to overcome this fragmentation and to provide tailor-made work incentives, social welfare services and active labour market policy, the local level offers opportunities of co-produced welfare interventions. Co-produced welfare interventions describe possibilities to offer tailor-made interventions by locally combining different actors, multi-level competences and various policy fields which are relevant for these approaches. Such co-produced welfare interventions are about the institutionalisation of distinct local organisational fields (Scott 2001) for the activation of minimum income recipients. The institutionalisation of such local organisational fields refers to coordinated interventions of different providers, competences and policy levels along the objective of activating long-term unemployed and otherwise disadvantaged groups. Locally co-produced interventions therefore present an approach to cope with the fragmented character of Bismarckian welfare states, which relied on organising access to employment, qualification, income protection or care according to narrow and confined categories and different providers. This observation led to the first hypothesis: *The decentralised structuring of local organisational fields for the activation of persistently unemployed and vulnerable groups of society challenges the fragmented Bismarckian welfare state architecture by local coordination processes between the local and central level, between fields of labour market and social welfare policy and between public authorities, third sector organisations, private providers and social partners.*

Taking into account both the traditionally discretionary character of social assistance in continental European welfare states as well as the renewed decentralisation tendencies, the local co-production of services and policies to activate benefit recipients might however proceed in different ways at the local level. Varying organisational solutions might arise at the local level how to deal with the problem of fragmentation and how to organise coordination. Activation is thus not only a matter of different programmatic priorities differing between a market-oriented focus on work incentives for welfare clients (Eichhorst et al. 2008a: 5; Lødemel and Trickey 2001), bureaucratic strategies of defining beneficiaries' needs for labour market integration (Serrano Pascual 2007), or participatory approaches promoting autonomous citizens' capabilities (Salais 2003; Sen 1999). It is also a matter of the organisation of local service delivery system. The local conditions for taking up services and policies, modes of regulating interaction between the manifold actors at the local level, as well as the local techniques for controlling coordinated action, influence the direction of activation strategies. First, existing local institutional structures might vary in their disposition for the take-up of decentralised policies and services. Existing local institutions might alter between a market-oriented configuration of weak and isolated actors, a bureaucratic entanglement of decentralised public agencies or locally bound partnerships. Second, local interactions between actors for the co-produced delivery of policies and services can alternate. The delivery of services can be a matter of forms of competition between rational actors, a bureaucratic issue of regulation by experts or a participatory process of local arguing between numerous stakeholders. Third, the local co-production is also conditioned by the way control techniques for goal-attainment of coordinated policies and services are locally implemented. Local control strategies can vary between outcome-oriented benchmarking approaches, bureaucratic attempts of detailed standard setting or participatory approaches based on trust and reciprocity. To analyse the varying local structures, interactions and control types in a systematic manner, three different ideal-types of the local organisation of service delivery organisation were related to the competing strategies of activation. In a second hypothesis, the assumption was formulated that *the existing local institutional structures, the modes of local interaction and the techniques to control service delivery can pattern activation according to a market-oriented, a bureaucratic and a participatory organisation of co-produced services.*

In an empirical inquiry, the two hypotheses on the local dimension of activation were tested against local developments in eight regions in France and Germany. As France and Germany remodel their social and labour market policy from a social treatment of unemployment towards the activation of persistently unemployed and otherwise disadvantaged groups, the question arises on how placement, counselling and stronger work requirements are organised for minimum income benefit recipients. Reforms in both countries display the arising challenges for the local level to deal with features of a typically fragmented Bismarckian welfare state organisation.

In France, national organisational provisions still define the general minimum income scheme as a field apart from 'normal' institutions for unemployed: while benefit pay offices and placement services were integrated into one single national agency for the insured unemployed, responsibility for the minimum income benefit recipients was largely decentralised. Although decentralised competences replace a former centralised system of welfare, the principal local competences and organisational capacities have remained confined to typical areas of the French social welfare system which has been marked by the interventions of social welfare services, welfare associations and social workers (Fraisse 2009; Mingione et al. 2002). This has raised the question how actors at the local level might organise a local co-production, which can merge the local authority's tasks for assistance benefit delivery and social welfare services with placement or training services run by other providers. Given the French minimum income scheme's strong tradition of a social work approach (Morel 2004), such combined services for the activation of minimum income recipients were not at all evident (Lafore 2004). In France, local developments have therefore evolved around issues of how to improve benefit recipients' access to placement or training services.

In Germany, national organisational reforms went further than in France by the merging of social assistance and long-term unemployment assistance into one minimum income benefit scheme. A former networked local system of welfare was replaced by a framework organisation for 'Jobcenters' integrating delivery of minimum income benefit payments, placement services of the national employment agency and municipal social welfare services. The principal division of competences in these newly found Jobcenters, however, has been based on the traditional division between a mostly nationally organised unemployment policy and a municipal social welfare system. Despite the founding of a common Jobcenter, the close inter-organisation of national placement competences and capacities with municipal social welfare arrangements, comprising the interventions of social workers and social associations, has therefore not been evident at all. In Germany, similar to the case studies in France, local challenges therefore evolved around issues to inter-organise both placement and social welfare services.

The organisational difficulties to merge the fields of social welfare and labour market policy into a co-produced activation approach illustrated the great challenges projected by the Bismarckian reform path onto the local level in both France and Germany. Given the particular Bismarckian reform path, the local case studies thus evidenced that it was essential to establish local organisational fields of co-produced services in order to institutionalise attempts of employment-centred welfare in both France and Germany.

As explored by the case studies, the local handling of the challenge of fragmented policies and services differed significantly not only between France and Germany but also in the single welfare states. In the single local cases, however, it was possible to observe certain coherence with regard to the local institutional setting, the interaction patterns for delivering services and the local techniques applied for controlling services. It was thus possible to identify distinctly different local organisations of service delivery. As a result, in the two Bismarckian welfare states analysed, welfare interventions coexisted for market-oriented concepts to quickly integrate unemployed clients into the labour market, bureaucratic approaches for enabling the social inclusion of beneficiaries, participatory concepts of activation to empower persons to choose among different inclusion options and even unconditional minimum income benefits for social citizens.

A participatory logic of welfare interventions to activate minimum income recipients could be observed in regions F-C and G-C. In both cases, local institutional conditions revealed the existence of long-standing local partnerships. Close ties existed between local authorities, national placement services at the local level, social associations and other project executing organisations. In meetings such as case-management conferences, local round-tables, mutual visits, common workshops or public planning conferences the different actors exchanged experiences and defined services. Decisions of the right services to offer were often found on the basis of arguing processes between the many actors. Despite the existence of benchmarks to control for service outcomes, in both cases actors primarily trusted in each other's ability to bring in crucial service competences for the targeted activation of benefit recipients. As a result, the co-production of both social and placement services resembled a participatory mode in regions F-C and G-C.

Different from this participatory approach, regions F-D, G-A and G-B leaned towards a bureaucratic organisation of service delivery to activate minimum income recipients. Long-standing bureaucratic ties in G-A and G-B helped in establishing combined placement and social counselling services. While such a bureaucratic entanglement between agencies could not be observed in region F-D, interactions to define service delivery in F-D proceeded nonetheless in a bureaucratic manner similar to practices in G-A and G-B. In all three regions, decision-making was a privilege of civil servants considered as having the right competences. Highly technical bargaining on the organisation in regions G-A and G-B as well as detailed instructions by central administration going down to the street-level in all three regions resembled a bureaucratic mode of interaction. In line with this bureaucratic approach, benchmarks on the outcome of services were complemented by detailed guides of action, reporting or standards in order to ensure a tightly defined activation process of benefit recipients. As a result, the co-production of both social and placement services came close to a bureaucratic logic in regions G-A, G-B and F-D.

Different from this bureaucratic organisation, welfare interventions in region G-D resembled a market-oriented type of activation. Here, institutions producing approaches in social matters were weakly elaborated. This local fragmentation of institutions did not allow developing a broader local strategy besides cost-containment. Staff or project executing organisations were advised to interact with benefit recipients in the most time-efficient manner. Instead of local planning processes, decisions were left to the selection criteria of quasi-markets. In region G-D, techniques to control activation processes relied on benchmarks on cost reduction and numbers of activated unemployed. As a result, the organisation of service delivery came close to a market-oriented logic of activation.

While the sample gave evidence of cases of the institutionalisation of activating services in both France and Germany, in two cases of the sample, crucial organisational elements for the implementation of an activation approach were lacking. In the French sample, regions F-A and F-B continued to practise an approach of endowing social citizens with money but mostly refrained both from promoting as well as demanding the activation of benefit recipients. Local institutions here illustrated a broad and active local opposition against activation reforms. Decision-making to define possible services to activate minimum income schemes was mostly avoided. Techniques to control services of field service staff or welfare centres local management were largely absent. As a result, in both regions F-A and F-D, in practice, benefit recipients continued being subject rather to a classical Bismarckian approach of 'social treatment' than an activation into unemployment.

All in all, the case studies principally confirmed both our hypotheses on a) the local capacities to challenge Bismarckian features of fragmentation between providers, policy levels and policy fields by the creation of distinct organisational fields for the local co-production of activation, and b) the possibility of variance of decentralised and co-produced service delivery models between local organisations of market-oriented, bureaucratic or participatory models in one and the same welfare state (cf. Tab. 4). While the labour market and social policy reforms have clearly opened up a local dimension of a Bismarckian activation regime in both France and Germany, the varieties and inconsistencies arising in such local reactions to the fragmented Bismarckian welfare institutions require further explanation.

Tab. 4: Local organisations of welfare interventions in France and Germany

Local Authority	**F-A**	**F-B**	**F-C**	**F-D**	**G-A**	**G-B**	**G-C**	**G-D**
Socio-economic Situation	Strong	Weak	Strong	Weak	Weak	Strong	Strong	Weak
Government Partisanship	Left	Left	Conservative	Left	Left	Conservative	Conservative	Left
Concept of the Individual	Social Citizen	Social Citizen	Autonomous Citizen	Beneficiary	Beneficiary	Beneficiary	Autonomous Citizen	Client
Mode of Interaction	Arguing	Avoidance	Arguing	Competence-Based	Competence-Based	Competence-Based	Arguing	Competition-Based
Local Conditions	Local Partnerships	Local Opposition	Local Partnerships	Local Partnerships	Integrated Public Agencies	Integrated Public Agencies	Local Partnerships	Local Fragmentation
Techniques of Control	Absent	Absent	Trust and Reciprocity, Bench-marking	Standards and Reporting, Benchmarking,	Bench-marking, Standards and Reporting	Bench-marking, Standards and Reporting	Bench-marking, Trust and Reciprocity	Bench-marking

Source: own representation.

Activation reforms as selective local appropriation in a dynamic local-national system of welfare

The differences explored in the local organisation of welfare interventions give rise to asking for explanatory factors of the specific local developments. It raises the question why some local authorities organise services for the activation of benefit recipients, why they do so in different ways and why other regions turn their back on the institutionalisation of employment-centred welfare.

Taking into account the empirical inquiry, we can now embed our structural argument on the influence of different local institutional settings in a wider explanatory model on the local implementation of activation policy reforms: as exemplified by the case studies in France and Germany, the local organisation of services and policies to activate minimum income recipients is a process of actors' selective local appropriation in a local-national system of welfare. This local process of selective appropriation (Zeitlin 2005: 480–481; 2009: 231–233) is a matter of dynamic interrelations between (1) structures of the local organisational field, (2) external influences on the local structures primarily exerted by national developments and (3) the production and reproduction of the local structures by actors at the local level.

First, the structures of a local organisation field for appropriating activation reforms are predetermined by 'path-dependent' process of established rules and routines of practice. Mechanisms of 'policy feedback' (Pierson 1993) constitute coordination effects and a selection of institutions (Pierson 1993: 624-628; Thelen 1999: 392-395) between paths of local partnerships, bureaucratic entanglement and local fragmentation. Pre-existing institutionalised local relationships and governance arrangements of how actors from the field of labour market and social welfare, from the national and local level, from the private and public sector would deal with each other, enormously influenced local responses to issues of activating long-term unemployed and vulnerable groups of society. Relying on a record of trustful and reciprocal local collaboration approaches, as exemplified by regions F-A, F-C, and G-C, a broad set of actors tackled in a participatory manner the challenge of organising activating labour market and social welfare services. Illustrating the same phenomenon, in the regions G-A and G-B, established working relationships between a small circle of civil servants from different administrations did not only facilitate solving the task of organising an activation approach but also resulted in an organisation based on standards, detailed premises and rules. In turn, as exemplified in case F-B, weakly established relationships between local authorities and other crucial providers can also negatively affect the institutional capacities to organise an activation approach.

Local institutionalised paths are therefore crucial to understand how actors at the local level selectively appropriate the task to active benefit recipients.

While local organisational fields show a certain stability of practices, established local patterns of the reproduction of concept, rules and resources can be challenged by external influences leading to the application of activation reforms. External influences can cause local moments of 'crisis' for the organisation of local approaches triggering a 'window of opportunity' for radical changes of local service delivery systems. Given the remarkable stability of local institutions, external influences will however rather incite local instances which give rise to opportunities of the incremental reinterpretation and stepwise remodelling of existing local institutions and practices (Crouch and Farrell 2004; Streeck and Thelen 2005). Those external factors producing influences on the local governance can be narrowed down by a discussion of a summary of the local case study series in France and Germany. As a summary of the results shows, the categories of local socio-economic situation and government partisanship are too shallow variables to explain external mechanisms of influence (cf. Tab. 4). Notwithstanding increasingly European processes' effects on the local level (Graziano 2010), the present study particularly confirmed the national governments' role as crucial supplier for the local organisational field in terms of concepts, resources and rules. Instead of a mechanism of centralised implementation of activation reforms, developments in France and Germany showed how the national level rather spans a framework of rules and resources effecting local possibilities to organise the implementation of activation reforms. The national framework, which thus enables local processes of selective appropriation of activation reforms, can notably vary in the area of legal conception, financial regulation, and organisational instruments.

A mechanism of influence relevant for the local appropriation of activation reforms is the national conception of minimum income schemes, which construes a reference for the actors at the local level on how to deal with benefit recipients of the minimum income schemes. In Germany, the legal principle of social assistance has evolved in a very coherent manner in the past. Since the creation of the social assistance scheme, it conveys the idea of 'self-help' meaning that benefits are subsidiary to family help or income from work. In face of rising numbers of benefit recipients, German local authorities and other actors of the former social assistance regime had increasingly shifted their focus on the work component. As a work-oriented approach had already been established as municipal practice, it was a matter of 'common sense' for these actors to implement the activation premises put forward by the Hartz reforms. In contrast,

French legal regulation of social assistance has a history of an unconditional approach of social treatment. Only recently, successive reforms have put a stress on work requirements in the regulation of the main minimum income scheme. This change in regulation opened up room for interpretations at the local level between those actors still adhering to the social work approach and those ready to apply activation into work as a new solution for dealing with rising numbers of benefit recipients. As a result, a social treatment practice was still dominating in local authorities F-A and F-B, while the service delivery systems in local authorities F-C and F-D had shifted towards a mutual obligations' approach. In short, the room for interpretation, which legal texts offer in terms of different solutions but also in terms of changes over time, influences the variance of local approaches towards benefit recipients. A narrower scope of interpretation of German minimum income legislation has furthered a strong institutionalisation of the activation principle in local practices while the more ambivalent evolution of the French legal conception allows a local social treatment to persist besides local activation approaches.

A further mechanism of influence relevant for the local appropriation of activation reforms is the national financial regulation of minimum income schemes and services. Both in France and Germany, financial incentives tend to gear local practices towards the activation of benefit recipients. In Germany, the local actors can decide on the mix of expenditures for services in the realm of a national fund clearly earmarked for active labour market policy programmes. At the same time, the financing mechanism of benefit payments does not establish a clear-cut incentive to integrate benefit recipients into any job: low-income jobs on the regular labour market might free the Federal Employment Agency from its unemployment benefit payment obligations but do not necessarily relieve the municipal partner from its housing benefit payment obligations. Some municipalities therefore view nationally subsidised employment programmes as a better option than other activation efforts. Other municipalities try to facilitate the transition into full-time jobs, for example by increasing local child care offers for needy part-timers. In contrast, national financial support to the local authorities in France tends to reward local action towards activating benefit recipients into part-time or low-paid jobs. As national reimbursement for benefit payments does not fully cover the actual development of benefit payments, a local incentive exists to reduce the number of benefit recipients by activating them into the labour market. However, this financial mechanism is not strong enough in order to provoke activation in a linear manner in all the cases studied. Furthermore, making activation more difficult, the national framework does not provide to the local authorities an extra budget earmarked for active labour market policy. In short, the tightness of the linkage between national financial regulation and local labour market activation can vary. Despite certain incentives for local activation, which are set by national financing regulations of the local budget in both France and Germany, particularly the national financing frame in France is not coherent enough to necessarily promote local activation.

Another mechanism of influence relevant for the local appropriation of activation reforms are organisational prerequisites set by the national framework. In both Germany and France, national organisational elements and resources crucially influence the organisation of local service delivery systems. In Germany, the new organisational prerequisites as national benchmarking, standards for the introduction of integration contracts, requirements for public tendering and the provision of placement officers are very crucial factors in explaining how the national framework contributes to local activating services. Particularly the very stringent national framework for benchmarking supports implementation of services oriented towards the activation of benefit recipients in all four regions studied. While the benchmarks and the other organisational instruments generally promote local actors' adoption of the activation approach, this does, however, not necessarily mean that they implement a market-oriented service delivery model, which is favoured by the national framework of benchmarks and competitive tendering. Instead, the national organisational framework still leaves enough discretion for the local actors to decide on crucial organisational areas as the programming of active labour market policy, the case management organisation, local control techniques and the tendering of both subsidised employment and social welfare services. Compared to this stringent organisational framework in Germany, the French national framework for local service organisation is much less comprehensive. The most striking differences are that the French organisational framework completely renounces on establishing a national system of benchmarks and abstains from providing placement officers for the local organisation. Instead, the national framework for the decentralised social assistance scheme introduced only three relevant organisational prerequisites for the local level: the local authorities overtaking responsibility for the service delivery system were asked to install case managers, integration contracts and a categorisation between benefit recipients capable to work and those not. Although these national stipulations were implemented in all the regions studied, the local rationale of application differed strongly. Case-management, integration contracts and the categorisation of benefit recipients serve in some regions as elements for institutionalising a service delivery system oriented towards the activation into work while their implementation in other regions fails to develop a connection to an activation approach. In short, depending on the coherence of national organisational prescriptions and provisions, the scope for local interpretation varies. While in Germany, local discretion exists *how* to apply case management, integration contracts or benchmarks for the activation of benefit recipients, in France, discretion exists *whether* to use the national organisational provisions for a targeted activation approach.

To summarise, national legal conception, financing mechanisms and organisational prerequisites set crucial parameters for processes of the local selective appropriation of activation reforms. In France, the national framework has developed remarkable discretion for local action of a system which had been formerly depicted as a centralised local system of welfare. In France, the ambivalent legacy of 'social insertion' regulation, a lacking local budget for active labour market policies, and a lose organisational framework renouncing on benchmarks and the provision of placement officers sets a national framework that only moderately advances local service delivery system for the activation of benefit recipients into employment. Compared to France, in Germany a more coherent national framework has developed for a formerly 'networked local system' of minimum income delivery. A national benchmarking system, traditional work requirement components in the minimum income scheme regulation, the provision of placement officers from the Federal Employment Agency and a national budget earmarked for local active labour market policy form a national organisational framework clearly advancing local service delivery systems for the activation of benefit recipients into employment. While local processes of selective appropriation are pre-structured in Germany for organising one of the three activation strategies, the lose national framework in France makes it possible for a local authority to implement the minimum income scheme still as a guaranteed benefit or to initiate proper services for the activation of beneficiaries. Given these intentional and also unintentional effects of the particular configuration of a national framework on the local level finally raise the question of the role of local actors in the production and re-production of the local institutional structures.

Beyond the importance of local institutional structures, which we highlighted above, the empirical inquiry revealed important dynamics of the production and reproduction of these structures by social actors (Giddens 1984): "(…) embedding structures do not simply generate constraints on agency but, instead, provide a platform for the unfolding of entrepreneurial activities." (Garud et al. 2007: 961). 'Skilled' actors (Fligstein 2001b) appeared in each local case study who were ready to advocate distinct concepts how to organise a local service delivery system. Matching the observation that organisational fields like local service delivery systems distribute different power positions to actors (Bourdieu 1977; Bourdieu and Wacquant 1992), the positioning of those institutional entrepreneurs (Garud et al. 2007) differed between the regions studied. In each local organisational field, 'incumbents' and 'challengers' gathered behind opposing concepts how to organise local service delivery (Fligstein 2001b). Incumbents are those actors attempting to preserve the current situation as it guarantees them a dominant position in a local field. Challengers, in contrast, prefer change as the current situation only allows them to survive at a lower level of resources. Actors' success of advocating distinct ideas then crucially hinges on their 'relative' power of making others cooperate (Hacker 2005). The actors' relative power to make others cooperate depends on their abilities to exploit current institutions for different cooperation strategies comprising direct command, agenda setting, brokerage, or the creation of a common identity. By applying these strategies, the goal of skilled actors is to stabilise those agreements between actors which can manifest their proper positions:

> "(…) the process of institution building takes place in the context of powerful actors attempting to produce rules of interaction to stabilize their situation vis-à-vis other powerful and less powerful actors. Fields operate to help reproduce the power and privilege of incumbent groups and define the positions of challengers." (Fligstein 2001b: 108).

In short, the theory on skilled actors adds a further explanatory component of the process of selective local appropriation of activation reforms.

Embedded in distinct local institutional structures, 'skilled' actors selectively appropriated the national concepts, rules and resources provided for local welfare interventions. Although activation had become 'common sense' at the local level in Germany, strategies between actors at the local level differed in respect to how to organise service delivery. While actors of the 'local community' aimed to preserve elements of a former networked local system of welfare, newly empowered local agents of the Federal Employment Agency stepped up as advocates of a market-oriented concept of service delivery. However, despite the important national concepts, resources and rules available for the local employment agencies for advancing a market-oriented organisational strategy, its wider implementation only succeeded in region G-D where institutions of local partnership and local bureaucracy were associated with failure. In the other cases, the newly empowered local employment agency faced strong 'incumbents' represented by actors of the local community. In regions G-A and G-B, where established municipal labour market policy units were charged by local government to rather exclusively assume the role as 'preserver' of local communal interests, the local organisation was permeated by detailed bureaucratic regulations and steering requirements resulting from continuous negotiations between the local employment agency and the municipal administration. As illustrated in case G-C, it required a 'politically' mobilised local community of local government figures and local parliament to preserve a typical German networked local system of welfare and to make the local employment agency join as only one actor in a set of different local actors contributing to this participatory concept of service delivery. Thus, in Germany, the local appropriation of a reformed national framework evolves either as negotiation process on a 'bureaucratic' organisation between the local employment agency's civil servants and an established local administration, as a matter of consensus on a 'participatory' organisation if the local community's political mobilisation is strong, or as a 'market-oriented' application of national premises by the local employment agency if municipal institutions are weak.

In contrast to Germany, given the more open national framework described above, local actors in France diverged more radically on the strategies they locally appropriated. While leaders of decentralised government and RMI/RSA directorates of the local administration could be eager to seize the national frame for shaping a proper local activation approach, a social treatment of benefit recipients was still adhered by many social workers, social welfare associations and sometimes local politicians as well. Presenting a major force of inertia, as practices in regions F-A and F-B illustrated, reform-opposing actors could occupy key positions in the local political arena or the local administration. Furthermore, they actively defended a social treatment approach by 'sabotaging' or arguing against reform. In these regions, national requirements of case management or integration contracts were locally appropriated in a way which did not enable the organisation of an activation approach in practice. In order to however make actors in established local institutional structures co-produce an activation approach, it required successful reform-oriented local entrepreneurs. The successful challenging of local social treatment practices though did not only depend on the appearance of reform-willing local government leaders but also necessitated a strong empowerment of the RMI/RSA directorates in the local administrations. If such 'reform-alliances' were formed, they either used direct command strategies to forge a 'bureaucratic' service delivery system as in the local case F-C or they relied on their strong reputation in order to convince other local 'partners' to contribute to a participatory service system for the activation of benefit recipients. A key to the successful implementation of both strategies was to keep the most reform-opposed 'incumbents' in the social welfare directorates, centres and associations out of the service delivery system and to cooperate with the moderate ones. In short, only where reform-oriented civil servants could build alliances with reform-oriented governance leaders, it was possible to instruct or convince other local actors to commit to the organisation of an activation approach and to break the opposition of social workers otherwise still adhering and practising a social treatment of benefit recipients.

The processes of selective local appropriation in a local-national system of welfare thus detail the mechanisms behind the evolution of local service delivery systems for the activation of benefit recipients. By renouncing on broadly centralised processes of implementation, national frameworks like in France or Germany provide local room for manoeuvring for organising targeted and individualised services for activation. While actors in charge of organising such local service delivery systems refer in their actions to the rules, resources and concepts provided by a distinct national legal, financial and organisational frame, they locally interpret the appropriate way how to implement the national framework. As a result, the institutionalisation of service delivery systems becomes a process highly contingent on the local level: this process of selective local appropriation is locally determined by institutional path dependencies of local co-operation and the dynamic positioning of actors' adhering to different strategies of how to deal with minimum income benefit recipients.

To conclude, by shifting modes of inclusion for weaker groups from social policy and family welfare towards labour market activation, Bismarckian countries have opened up an important local dimension of the welfare state: activation into the labour market becomes contingent on the local abilities to overcome features of Bismarckian fragmentation in the organisation of access to individually required services, be it placement, training, help for rehabilitation or child care. As the local handling of minimum income schemes in France and Germany has illustrated, the organisation of welfare interventions proceeds as a local process of the selective appropriation of a distinct national framework for the activation of persistently unemployed and vulnerable groups. This process of local selective appropriation of activation reforms principally increases welfare interventions dependency on distinct local circumstances. The existence of particular local institutions can turn into a prerequisite to enable services in different ways. On the other hand, the lack of some localities of such prerequisites can make the application of new welfare state policies difficult. Also policies become more dependent on individual policy entrepreneurs. The process of local selective appropriation was to an important extent contingent on the readiness of few or single local institutional entrepreneurs to advance the application of activation reforms. Mechanisms of local selective appropriation can thus lead to pilot models or exemplary regions. Other regions where such policy entrepreneurs are less brilliant, visionary or assertive can struggle to provide broad access to placement, training, or help for rehabilitation to long-term unemployed and disadvantaged groups. Those contingencies of local process can only be reduced if the national framework itself attenuates the fragmentation of policies and services and thus facilitates the coordination of the necessary services for the activation of long-term unemployed and vulnerable groups. While a more integrated framework for a local organisation of placement, social welfare and work incentives has enabled the local implementation of activation approaches in Germany, the still very fragmented framework for a local organisation of placement, social welfare and work incentives makes the local handling of minimum income schemes in France extremely prone to the volatilities of local institutions and the success of local institutional entrepreneurs.

Literature

Abrahamson, P. (2005): Coping with urban poverty: changing citizenship in Europe? In: International Journal of Urban and Regional Research, Vol. 29, No. 3: 608–621.

Alber, Jens (1995): A framework for the comparative study of social services. In: Journal of European Social Policy, Vol. 5 No. 2: 131–149.

Alber, Jens; Standing, Guy (2000): Social dumping, catch-up, or convergence? Europe in a comparative global context. In: Journal of European Social Policy, Vol. 10, No. 2: 99–119.

Agnuis, Marie (2007): La population des allocataires du RMI: tendances d'évolution et disparités départementales. In: Études et Résultats, No. 568.

Armingeon, Klaus (2007): Active labour market policy, international organizations and domestic politics. In: Journal of European Public Policy, Vol. 14, No. 6: 905–932.

Armingeon, Klaus; Bonoli, Giuliano (2006): The politics of post-industrial welfare states. Adapting post-war social policies to new social risks. London: Routledge.

Atzmüller, Roland (2009): Institution building and active labour market policies in Vienna since the 1990s. In: International Journal of Sociology and Social Policy, Vol. 29, No. 11/12: 599–611.

Atkinson, Anthony B. (1989): Social Insurance and Income Maintenance. In: Anthony B. Atkinson (ed.): Poverty and Social Security. Hemel Hempstead: Harvester Wheatsheaf: 204–124.

Aubree, Loic; Barry, Heveré; Baillion, Jean N.; Mauguin, Jocelyne (2006): L'action sociale extralégale et facultative des départements. In: Etudes et Resultats, No. 537: 25–37.

Avenel, Cyprien (2006): Les conséquences de la décentralisation sur la gestion du RMI. In: cahier européen, No. 04: 1–20.

Bahle, Thomas (2003): The changing institutionalization of social services in England and Wales, France and Germany: is the welfare state on the retreat? In: Journal of European Social Policy, Vol. 13, No. 5: 5–20.

Barbier, Jean-Claude (2007): The French activation strategy in a comparative perspective. In: Serrano Pascual, Amparo; Magnusson, Lars (eds.): Reshaping welfare states and activation regimes in Europe. Bruxelles: P.I.E. Lang (Saltsa – joint programme for working life research in Europe, No. 54): 145–172.

Barbier, Jean-Claude; Kaufmann, Otto (2008): The French strategy against unemployment: innovative but inconsistent. In: Eichhorst, Werner; Kaufmann, Otto; Konle-Seidl, Regina (eds.): Bringing the Jobless into Work? Experiences with Activation Schemes in Europe and the US. Berlin, Heidelberg: Springer-Verlag Berlin Heidelberg: 71–119.

Barbier, Jean-Claude; Knuth, Matthias (2011a): Comparing social protection in France and Germany. Books & Ideas. Online available at: http://www.booksandideas.net/Comparing-Social-Protection-in.html, (accessed on 12/11/2011).

Barbier, Jean-Claude; Knuth, Matthias (2011b): Protection against unemployment. In: Sozialer Fortschritt, No. 1–2: 15–24.

Barbier, Jean-Claude (2004): Systems of social protection in Europe. Two Contrasted Paths to Activation, and Maybe a Third. In: Lind, Jens; Knudsen, Herman; Jørgensen, Henning (Eds.): Labour and employment regulation in Europe. Bruxelles: PIE Lang: 233–253.

Barbier, Jean-Claude; Fargion, Valeria (2004): Continental inconsistencies on the path to activation – Consequences for social citizenship in Italy and France. In: European Societies, Vol. 6, No. 4: 437–460.

Barbier, Jean-Claude; Ludwig-Mayerhofer, Wolfgang (2004): Introduction: The many worlds of activation. In: European Societies, Vol. 6, No. 4: 423–436.

Baumol, William J. (1967): Macroeconomics of Unbalanced Growth: The Anatomy of Urban Crisis. In: American Economic Review, Vol. 57, No. 3: 416–426.

Beck, Ulrich (1983): Jenseits von Stand und Klasse? Soziale Ungleichheiten, gesellschaftliche Individualisierungsprozesse und die Entstehung neuer sozialer Formationen und Identitäten. In: Kreckel, Reinhard (ed.): Soziale Ungleichheiten. Göttingen (Soziale Welt, Sonderband 2): 35–74.

Behrendt, Christina (2002): At the margins of the welfare state. Social assistance and the alleviation of poverty in Germany, Sweden and the United Kingdom. Aldershot: Ashgate.

Bekker, Sonja; Wilthagen, Ton (2008): Europe's pathways to flexicurity: Lessons presented from and to the Netherlands. In: Intereconomics: Review of European Economic Policy, Vol. 43, No. 2: 68–73.

Berkel, Rik van; Borghi, Vando (2008): Introduction: The governance of activation. In: Social Policy & Society, Vol. 7, No. 3: 331–340.

Berkel, Rik van; Møller, Iver Hornemann (2002): The concept of activation. In: Berkel, Rik van; Møller, Iver Hornemann (eds.): Active social policies in the EU. Inclusion through participation? Bristol: Policy Press: 45–72.

Berkel, Rik van; Valkenburg, Ben (2007): The individualisation of activation services in context. In: Berkel, Rik van; Valkenburg, Ben (eds.): Making it personal. Individualising activation services in the EU. Bristol: The Policy Press: 3–24.

Berthet, Thierry; Cuntigh, Philippe (2002): Employment policy and territories. In: Céreq Training & Employment, No. 46: 1–4.

Beyer, Jürgen; Höpner, Martin (2003): The disintegration of organized capitalism. German corporate governance in the 1990's. In: West European Politics, Vol. 26, No. 4: 179–198.
Billari, Francesco C.; Kohler, Hans-Peter (2004): Patterns of low and lowest-low fertility in Europe. In: Population Studies, Vol. 58, No. 2: 161–176.
Blanchard, Olivier (2006): European unemployment: the evolution of facts and ideas. In: Economic Policy, Vol. 21, No. 45: 5–59.
Blanchard, Olivier; Wolfers, Justin (2000): The role of shocks and institutions in the rise of European unemployment. The aggregate evidence. In: The Economic Journal, Vol. 110, No. 1: C1-C33.
BMAS (2007): Grundsicherung für Arbeitssuchende Sozialgesetzbuch. Fragen & Antworten SGB II. Published by Publikation Redaktion Bundesministerium für Arbeit und Soziales Referat Information. Bonn.
Bode, Ingo (2006): Disorganized welfare mixes: voluntary agencies and new governance regimes in Western Europe. In: Journal of European Social Policy, Vol. 16, No. 4: 346–359.
Bonoli, Giuliano (2010): The political economy of active labour market policy. Dissemination and Dialogue Centre (Edinburgh). Edinburgh. (Working Papers on the Reconciliation of Work and Welfare in Europe).
Bonvin, Jean-Michel; Farvaque, Nicolas (2007): A capability approach to individualised and tailor-made activation. In: Berkel, Rik van; Valkenburg, Ben (eds.): Making it personal. Individualising activation services in the EU. Bristol: The Policy Press: 45–65.
Bonvin, Jean-Michel; Orton, Michael (2009): Activation policies and organisational innovation. The added value of the capability approach. In: International Journal of Sociology and Social Policy, Vol. 29, No. 11/12: 565–574.
Borgetto, Michel; Lafore, Robert (2007): Le droit de l'aide et de l'action sociales à l'épreuve de 'l'acte II de la' décentralisation. In: Recherches et Prévisions, Vol. 24, No. 87.
Borghi, Vando; Berkel, Rik van (2007): New modes of governance in Italy and the Netherlands: The case of activation policies. In: Public Administration, Vol. 85, No. 1: 83–101.
Borghi, Vando; Berkel, Rik van (2008): Review Article: The Governance of Activation. In: Social Policy & Society, Vol. 7, No. 3: 393–402.
Borras, Isabelle (2006): Les maison de l'emploi, guichet unique et outil de coordination das les territoires. In: Actualité de la formation permanente, No. 199: 23–30.
Borras, Isabelle (2008): Les responsabilités des collectivés locales dans la politique de l'emploi: innovation ou expérimentation. In: Cahier de Recherche, No. 12: 1–32.
Börzel, Tanja A.; Risse, Thomas (2000): When Europe Hits Home: Europeanization and Domestic Change. In: European Integration Online Papers.

Bosch, Gerhard (2004): Towards a New Standard Employment Relationship in Western Europe. In: British Journal of Industrial Relations, Vol. 42, No. 4: 617–636.
Bourdieu, Pierre (1977): Outline of a theory of practice. Cambridge, England: Cambridge University Press.
Bourdieu, Pierre; Wacquant, Loïc (1992): Invitation to a reflexive sociology. Chicago, Illinois: University of Chicago Press.
Bredgaard, Thomas; Larsen, Flemming (2007): Implementing public employment policy: what happens when non-public agencies take over? In: International Journal of Sociology and Social Policy, Vol. 27, No. 7/8: 287–300.
Buhr, Petra (1999): Vorbild Schweden? – Armut und Sozialhilfe in unterschiedlichen Wohlfahrtsstaaten. In: Leviathan Zeitschrift für Sozialwissenschaft, Vol. 27, No. 1: 218–237.
Casas, Ramón P. (2005): Setting minimum social standards across Europe. Observatoire social européen.
Cazain, Sophie; Mirouse, Isabelle; Hennion, Marie; Nauze-Fichet, Emmanuelle (2008): Le nombre d'allocataires du RMI au 30 juin 2008. In: Études et Résultats, No. 657.
Champion, Cyrielle; Bonoli, Giuliano (2011): Institutional fragmentation and coordination initiatives in western European welfare states. In: Journal of European Social Policy, Vol. 21, No. 4: 323–334.
Clarke, John (2008): Reconstructing nation, state and welfare: The transformation of welfare states. In: Seeleib-Kaiser, Martin (ed.): Welfare state transformations. Comparative perspectives. Basingstoke: Palgrave Macmillan: 197–209.
Clarke, John; Gerwirtz, Sharon; Hughes, Gordon; Humphrey, Jill (2000): Guarding the public interest? Auditing public services. In: Clarke, John; Gerwirtz, Sharon; McLaughlin, Eugene (eds.): New managerialism, new welfare? London: SAGE Publ: 250–266.
Clarke, John; Gerwirtz, Sharon; McLaughlin, Eugene (2000): Reinventing the welfare state. In: Clarke, John; Gerwirtz, Sharon; McLaughlin, Eugene (eds.): New managerialism, new welfare? London: SAGE Publ: 1–26.
Clasen, Jochen (1999): Beyond social security: The economic value of giving money to unemployed people. In: European Journal of Social Security: 151–179.
Clasen, Jochen (2005): Reforming European welfare states. Germany and the United Kingdom compared. Oxford: Oxford University Press.
Clasen, Jochen; Clegg, Daniel (2003): Unemployment protection and labour market reform in France and Great Britain in the 1990s: Solidarity Versus Activation? In: Journal of Social Policy, Vol. 32, No. 3: 361–381.

Clasen, Jochen; Clegg, Daniel (2006): Beyond activation: Reforming European unemployment protection Systems in post-industrial labour markets. In: European Societies, Vol. 8, No. 4: 527–553.

Clasen, Jochen; Viebrock, Elke (2006): Das Genter System der Arbeitslosenversicherung – immer noch gewerkschaftliches Rekrutierungsinstrument oder sozialpolitisches Auslaufmodell? Dänemark und Schweden im Vergleich. In: Zeitschrift für Sozialreform, Vol. 52, No. 3: 351–371.

Clasen, Jochen; Viebrock, Elke (2009): Flexicurity – a state-of-the art review. RECWOWE Publication, Dissemination and Dialogue Centre. Edinburgh. (Working Papers on the Reconciliation of Work and Welfare in Europe, REC-WP 01/2009).

Clegg, Daniel (2007): Continental drift: On unemployment policy change in Bismarckian welfare states. In: Social Policy & Administration, Vol. 41, No. 6: 97–617.

Clegg, Daniel (2010): From insurance or insertion to rights and responsibilities: the shifting logics of unemployment protection in France. In: Nevile, Ann (ed.): Human rights and social policy. A comparatative analysis of values and citizenship in OECD countries. Cheltenham: Elgar: 83–100.

Clegg, Daniel; Palier, Bruno (2012): Implementing a myth: work conditionality in French minimum income policy. In: Lødemel, Ivar; Moreira, Amilcar (eds.): Workfare revisited. Oxford University Press.

Crouch, Collin; Farrel, Henry (2004): Breaking the Path of Institutional Development: Alternatives to the New Determinism in Political Economy. In: Rationality and Society, No. 16: 5–43.

Czommer, Lars; Knuth, Matthias; Schweer, Oliver (2005): ARGE – moderne Dienstleistungen am Arbeitsmarkt: eine Baustelle der Bundesrepublik Deutschland. In: Hans-Böckler Stiftung. 104 (Arbeitspapier).

Daguerre, A.; Taylor-Gooby, P. (2003): Adaptation to labour market change in France and the UK: Convergent or parallel tracks? In: Social Policy & Administration, Vol. 37, No. 6: 625–638.

Derlien, Hans U. (2000): Co-ordinating German EU policy. Failing successfully? In: Hussein, Kassim; Peters, Guy; Wright, Vincent (eds.): The national co-ordination of EU Policy: The Domestic Level. Oxford: Oxford University Press: 54–78.

Di Maggio, Paul J.; Powell, Walter W. (1983): The iron cage revisited: Institutional isomorphism and collective rationality in organizational fields. In: American Sociological Review, No. 2: 147–160.

Dingeldey, Irene (2007): Between workfare and enablement – The different paths to transformation of the welfare state: A comparative analysis of activating labour market policies. In: European Journal of Political Research, No. 46: 823–851.

Du Gay, Paul (2000): Entrepreneurial governance and public management: The anti-bureaucrats. In: Clarke, John; Gerwirtz, Sharon; McLaughlin, Eugene (eds.): New managerialism, new welfare? London: SAGE Publ: 62–81.

Ebbinghaus, Bernhard (2001): When labour and capital collude. The political economy of early retirement in Europe, Japan and the USA. In: Ebbinhaus, Bernhard; Manow, Philip: Comparing Welfare Capitalism. Social Policy and Political Economy in Europe, Japan and the USA. London: Routledge: 77–101.

Ebbinghaus, Bernhard; Hassel, Anke (2000): Striking deals: concertation in the reform of continental European welfare states. In: Journal of European Public Policy, Vol. 7, No. 1: 44–62.

Ebbinghaus, Bernhard; Visser, Jelle (1997): Der Wandel der Arbeitsbeziehungen im westeuropäischen Vergleich. In: Hradil, Stefan; Immerfall, Stefan (eds.): Die westeuropäischen Gesellschaften im Vergleich. Opladen: Leske + Budrich: 333–376.

Eichhorst, Werner; Kaufmann, Otto; Konle-Seidl, Regina; Reinhard, Hans-Jürgen (2008a): Bringing the jobless into work? An introduction to activation policies. In: Eichhorst, Werner; Kaufmann, Otto; Konle-Seidl, Regina (eds.): Bringing the jobless into work? Experiences with activation schemes in Europe and the US. Berlin: Springer: 1–17.

Eichhorst, Werner; Grienberger-Zingerle, Maria; Konle-Seidl, Regina (2008b): Activation policies in Germany: From status protection to basic income support. In: Eichhorst, Werner; Kaufmann, Otto; Konle-Seidl, Regina (eds.): Bringing the jobless into work? Experiences with activation schemes in Europe and the US. Berlin: Springer: 17–67.

Elster, Jon (1991): Arguing and bargaining in two constituents assemblies. The Storrs Lectures. New Haven: Yale Law School.

Elster, Jon (1998): Deliberative democracy. Cambridge: Cambridge University Press (Cambridge studies in the theory of democracy).

Enjolras, Bernard; Laville, Jean Louis; Fraisse, Laurent; Trickey, Heather (2001): Between subsidiarity and social assistance – the French republican route to activation. In: Lødemel, Ivar; Trickey, Heather (eds.): An offer you can't refuse. Workfare in international perspective. Bristol: Policy Press: 41–70.

Erhel, C.; Zajdela, H. (2004): The dynamics of social and labour market policies in France and the United Kingdom: between path dependence and convergence. In: Journal of European Social Policy, Vol. 14, No. 2:125–142.

Esping-Andersen, Gøsta (1996): Welfare states in transition. National adaptations in global economies. London: Sage Publ.

Esping-Andersen, Gøsta (1999): Social Foundations of Postindustrial Economies. Oxford: Oxford University Press.

Esping-Andersen, Gøsta (2002): Why we need a new welfare state. Oxford: Oxford University Press.

Esping-Andersen, Gøsta (2006): Warum brauchen wir eine Reform des Sozialstaats? In: Leviathan Zeitschrift für Sozialwissenschaft, No. 1: 61–81.
European Commission (2007): Towards Common Principles of Flexicurity: More and better jobs through flexibility and security. Online available at http://ec.europa.eu/social/BlobServlet?docId=2756&langId=en, (accessed on 8/10/2009).
EU COM 412 final (2008a): Renewed social agenda: Opportunities, access and solidarity in 21st century Europe. Communicationfromthecommission to the European Parliament, the Councily, the European Economic and Social Committee and the committee of the Regions. Published by Commission of the European Communities. Brussels.
EU COM 418 final (2008b): A renewed commitment to social Europe: Reinforcing the Open Method of Coordination for Social Protection and Social Inclusion. Communication from the commission to the European Parliament, the Council, the European Economic and Social Committee and the committee of the Regions. Published by Commission of the European Communities. Brussels
EU COM (2009): Commission Working Document. Consultation on the future 'EU 2020' Strategy. Published by Commission of the European Communities. Brussels.
European Commission (2010): Proposal for a council decision on guidelines for the employment policies of the Member States. Part II of the Europe 2020 Integrated Guidelines. Published by European Commission.(193/3).
European Council (2000): Lisbon European Council 23 and 24 march 2000. Presidency Conclusions. Online available at http://www.europarl.europa.eu/summits/lis1_en.htm, (accessed on 07/06/2010).
European Expert Group on Flexicurity (2007): Flexicurity Pathways. Turning hurdles into stepping stones. Online available at http://ec.europa.eu/social/BlobServlet?docId= 1519&langId=en, (accessed on 8/10/2009).
European Union (1997): Treaty of Amsterdam. European Union. Brussels.
Eurostat (2011a): Employment Statistics. Online available at http://epp.eurostat.ec.europa.eu/tgm/table.do?tab=table&language=de&pcode=tsiem010&tableSelection=1&footnotes=yes&labeling=labels&plugin=1, (accessed on 18/11/2011).
Eurostat (2011b): Employment Statistics. Online available at http://epp.eurostat.ec.europa.eu/tgm/table.do?tab=table&init=1&language=de&pcode=tps00073&plugin=0, (accessed on 18/11/2011).
Eurostat (2011c): Labour Market Policy Expenditure. Online available at http://epp.eurostat.ec.europa.eu/tgm/information.do?tab=table&plugin=0&language=en&pcode=tps00077, (accessed on 18/11/2011).
Ferrera, Maurizio (2005): The boundaries of welfare. European integration and the new spatial politics of social protection. Oxford: Oxford University Press.

Ferrera, Maurizio; Hemerijck, Anton (2003): Recalibrating Europe's Welfare Regimes. In: Zeitlin, Jonathan; Trubek, David M (eds.): Governing work and welfare in a new economy. European and American experiments. 1.publ. Oxford: Oxford University Press: 88–128.
Ferrera, Maurizio; Hemerijck, Anton; Rhodes, Martin (2000): The future of social Europe: recasting work and welfare in the new economy. Report for the Portuguese presidency of the European Union.
Finn, Dan (2000): Welfare to Work: the local dimension. In: Journal of European Social Policy, Vol. 10, No. 1: 43–57.
Fischer, Georg; Tholoniat, Luc (2006): The European Employment Strategy in an enlarged EU. In: Zeitschrift für Arbeitsmarktforschung, Vol. 1: 123–142.
Fleckenstein, Timo (2008): Restructuring Welfare for the Unemployed: The Hartz Legislation in Germany. In: Journal of European Social Policy, Vol. 18, No. 2: 177–188.
Fligstein, Neil (2001a): The architecture of markets. Princeton N.J.: Princeton University Press.
Fligstein, Neil (2001b): Social skill and the theory of fields. In: Sociological Theory, Vol. 19, No. 2: 105–125.
Flynn, Norman (2000): Managerialism and public services: Some international trends. In: Clarke, John; Gerwirtz, Sharon; McLaughlin, Eugene (eds.): New managerialism, new welfare? London: SAGE Publ: 27–44.
Foucault, Martial; Madies, Thierry; Paty, Sonia (2008): Public spending interactions and local politics. Empirical evidence from French municipalities. In: public choice, Vol. 137, No. 1–2: 57–80.
Fraisse, Laurent (2009): The third sector and the policy process in France: The centralised horizontal third sector community faced with the reconfiguration of the state-centred Republican model. In: Kendall, Jeremy (ed.): Handbook on third sector policy in Europe. Northampton: Edward Elgar.
Francis, Richard M. (1998): Predictions, Patterns, and Policymaking: A Regional Study of Devolution. In: Publius, Vol. 28, No. 3: 143–160.
Gallie, Duncan (2007): Employment regimes and the quality of work. Oxford: Oxford University Press.
Gallie, Duncan; Paugam, Serge; Jacobs, Sheila (2003): Unemployment, poverty and social isolation: Is there a vicious circle of social exclusion? In: European Societies, Vol. 5, No. 1: 1–32.
Gangl, Markus (1998): Sozialhilfebezug und Arbeitsmarktverhalten. Eine Längsschnittanalyse der Übergänge aus der Sozialhilfe in den Arbeitsmarkt. In: Zeitschrift für Soziologie, Vol. 27, No. 3: 212–232.
Garrow, Eve; Hasenfeld, Yeheskel (2010): Theoretical approaches to human service organizations. In: Hasenfeld, Yeheskel (ed.): Human services as complex organizations. 2nd ed. Thousand Oaks Calif.: Sage Publ.: 33–57.

Garud, Raghu; Hardy, Cynthia; Maguire, Steve (2007): Institutional entrepreneurship as embedded agency: An introduction to the special issue. In: Organization Studies, Vol. 28, No. 7: 957–969.
Genova, Angela (2008): Integrated services in activation policies in Finland and Italy: A critical appraisal. In: Social Policy & Society, Vol. 7, No. 3: 379–392.
Gerring, John (2004): What Is a Case Study and What Is It Good for? In: American Political Science Review, Vol. 98, No. 2: 341–354.
Giddens, Anthony (1984): Die Konstitution der Gesellschaft. Grundzüge einer Theorie der Strukturierung. Frankfurt am Main: Campus Verl.
Giddens, Anthony (1991): Modernity and self-identity. Self and society in the late modern age. Reprint. Cambridge: Polity Press.
Gläser, Jochen; Laudel, Grit (2006): Experteninterviews und qualitative Inhaltsanalyseals Instrumente rekonstruierender Untersuchungen. Wiesbaden: VS Verl. für Sozialwiss.
Gornick, Janet C.; Meyers, Marcia K. (1997): Supporting the employment of mothers: Policy variation across fourteen welfare states. In: Journal of European Social Policy, Vol. 7, No. 1: 45–70.
Gornick, Janet C.; Meyers, Marcia K. (2003): Families that work. Policies for reconciling parenthood and employment. New York, NY: Russell Sage Foundation.
Gough, Ian (1994): Means-testing in the Western World. In: Social Security, No. 43: 24–44.
Gough, Ian (2001): Social Assistance Regimes: A Cluster Analysis. In: Journal of European Social Policy, Vol. 11, No. 2: 165–170.
Gough, Ian; Bradshaw, Jonathan; Ditch, John; Eardley, Tony; Whiteford, Peter (1997): Social Assistance in OECD Countries. In: Journal of European Social Policy, Vol. 7, No. 1: 17–43.
Graziano, Paolo; Vink, Maarten P. (eds.) (2008): Europeanization. New research agendas. Basingstoke: Palgrave Macmillan.
Graziano, Paolo (2010): From local partnerships to regional spaces for politics? Europeanisation and EU cohesion policy in southern Italy. In: Regional and Federal Studies, Vol. 20, No. 3: 315–333
Green, Anne; Orton, Micheal (2009): The integration of employment services at sub-national level: a case study of the 'City Stragety' initative in an English sub region. In: International Journal of Sociology and Social Policy, Vol. 29, No. 11/12: 612–623
Greffe, Xavier (2005): Local employment developement: The French model. In: Scott; Considine, Mark; Eberts, Randall W.; Giguere, Sylvain; Greffe, Xavier; Murphy, Fergus; Parkinson, Michael; Arzeni, Sergio Abrams (eds.): Local governance and the drivers of growth. OECD. Paris.
Hacker, Jacob S. (2005): Policy Drift: The hidden politics of US welfare state retrenchment. In: Streeck, Wolfgang; Thelen, Kathleen Ann (eds.): Beyond

continuity. Institutional change in advanced political economies. Oxford: Oxford University Press: 40–82.
Guibentif, Pierre; Bouget, Dennis (1997): minimum income policies in the European Union. Lisbon: União des Mutualidades Portuguesas.
Hammarström, Anne; Janlert, Urban (2002): Early unemployment can contribute to adult health problems: results from a longitudinal study of school leavers. In: Journal of Epidemiology and Community Health, Vol. 56: 624–630.
Hanesch, Walter (2001): From Welfare to Work. Neue Reformkonzepte in der Sozialhilfe in Europa. In: Stelzer-Orthofer, Christine (ed.): Zwischen welfare und workfare. Soziale Leistungen in der Diskussion. Linz: Sozialwiss. Vereinigung: 167–192.
Hasenfeld, Yeheskel (1992a): The nature of human service organizations. In: Hasenfeld, Yeheskel (ed.): Human services as complex organizations. Newbury Park, California: Sage Publ.: 3–23.
Hasenfeld, Yeheskel (1992b): Theoretical approaches to human service organizations. In: Hasenfeld, Yeheskel (ed.): Human services as complex organizations. Newbury Park, California: Sage Publ: 24–44.
Hasenfeld, Yeheskel (ed.) (2010): Human services as complex organizations 2nd ed. Thousand Oaks Calif.: Sage Publ.
Häußermann, Hartmut; Läpple, Dieter; Siebel, Walter (2008): Stadtpolitik. Suhrkamp Verlag: Frankfurt am Main.
Heidenreich, Martin (2004): Beschäftigungsordnungen zwischen Exklusion und Inklusion. Arbeitsmarktregulierende Institutionen im internationalen Vergleich. In: Zeitschrift für Soziologie, Vol. 33, No. 3: 206–227.
Heidenreich, Martin (2009): The Open Method of Coordination: a pathway to the gradual transformation of national employment and welfare regimes? In: Heidenreich, Martin; Zeitlin, Jonathan (eds): Changing European employment and welfare regimes. The influence of the open method of coordination on national reforms. London: Routledge: 24–48.
Heidenreich, Martin; Bischoff, Gabriele (2008): The Open Method of Co-ordination: A way to the Europeanization of social and employment policies? In: Journal of Common Market Studies, Vol. 46, No. 3: 497–532.
Heidenreich, Martin; Künzel, Sebastian (2010): Integrated employment policies and the challenges of interorganisational co-operation. In: Katia Vladimirova (ed.): Transformations in Labour: Social Security and Social Dialogue. Sofia: CIELA: 27–63.
Heidenreich, Martin; Zeitlin, Jonathan (eds.) (2009): Changing European employment and welfare regimes. The influence of the open method of coordination on national reforms. London: Routledge.
Hemerijck, Anton; Marx, Ive (2010): Continental welfare at a crossroads: The choice between activation and minimum income protection in Belgium and the Netherlands. In: Palier, Bruno (ed.): A long goodbye to Bismarck? The

politics of welfare reforms in continental Europe. Amsterdam: Amsterdam University Press: 129–152.
Hinrichs, Karl (2010): A social insurance state withers away. Welfare state reforms in Germany – Or: Attempts to turn around in a Cul-de-Sac. In: Palier, Bruno (ed.): A long goodbye to Bismarck? The politics of welfare reforms in continental Europe. Amsterdam: Amsterdam University Press: 45–70.
Hood, Christopher; Scott, Colin; James, Oliver; Jones, George; Travers, Tony (2002): Regulation inside government. Waste-watchers, quality police, and sleaze-busters Reprinted. New York: Oxford University Press.
Hooghe, Liesbet; Marks, Gary (2001) Multilevel governance and European Integration, London: Rowman and Littlefield.
Huo, Jingjing; Nelson, Moira; Stephens, John D. (2008): Decommodification and activation in social democratic policy: resolving the paradox. In: Journal of European Social Policy, Vol. 18, No. 5.
Hvinden, Bjorn (1999): Activation: a Nordic Perspective. In: Heikkilä, Matti (ed.): Linking welfare and work. Dublin: European Foundation for the Improvement of Living and Working Conditions: 27–42.
Hughes, George (ed.) (1998): Imagining Welfare Futures. London: Routledge.
Isett, Kimberley R.; Mergel, Ines A.; Le Roux, Kelly; Mischen, Pamela A.; Rethemeyer, R. K. (2011): Networks in public administration scholarship: Understanding where we are and where we need to go. In: Journal of Public Administration Research and Theory, Vol. 21: 157–173.
ISSA 2011: International Social Security Association: http://www.issa.int/Topics/About-social-security (accessed on 16/07/2011).
Iversen, Torben; Wren, Anne (1998): Equality, employment and budgetary restraint: The trilemma of the service economy. In: World Politics, Vol. 50, No. 4: 507–546.
Jacobi, Dirk; Mohr, Katrin (2007): Rushing towards employability-centred activation: the ‚Hartz reforms' in Germany. In: van Berkel, Rik; Valkenburg, Ben (eds.): Making it Personal: Individualised activation services in the EU. Bristol: The Policy Press: 217–244.
Jahoda, Marie (1982): Employment and unemployment: A social psychological analysis. New York: Cambridge University Press.
Jewell, Christopher J. (2007). How caseworkers respond to need in the United States, Germany, and Sweden. New York: Palgrave Macmillan.
Johansson, Hakan; Hvinden, Bjørn (2007): Re-activating the Nordic welfare states: do we find a distinct universalistic model? In: International Journal of Sociology and Social Policy, Vol. 27, No. 7/8: 334–346.
Jørgensen, Henning (2004): Labour market and employment policies activated? In: Lind, Jens; Knudsen, Herman; Jørgensen, Henning (eds.): Labour and employment regulation in Europe. Bruxelles: PIE Lang.

Kalleberg, Arne L. (2000): Nonstandard employment relations: Part-time, temporary and contract work. In: Annual Review of Sociology, Vol. 26: 341–365.

Kantel, H. D. (2008): Grundsicherungsarbeit. Armuts- und Arbeitsmarktpolitik nach Hartz IV. Wiesbaden: VS Verlag für Sozialwissenschaften.

Karamessini, Maria (2008): Continuity and change in the southern European social model. In: International Labour Review, Vol. 147, No. 1: 43–70.

Kaufmann, Franz-Xaver (1994): Staat und Wohlfahrtsproduktion. In: Derlien, Hans-Ulrich; Mayntz, Renate (eds.): Systemrationalität und Partialinteresse. Festschrift für Renate Mayntz. 1. Aufl. Baden-Baden: Nomos-Verl.-Ges.: 357–380.

Kaufmann, Franz-Xaver. (2001): Social security, in N. J. Smelser and P. B. Baltes (eds) International encyclopaedia of the social and behavioural sciences, vol. 21: 14435–9. Amsterdam: Elsevier.

Kaufmann, Franz-Xaver (1997): Schwindet die integrative Funktion des Sozialstaates? In: Berliner Journal für Soziologie, Vol. 7: 5–19.

Kaufmann, Franz-Xaver (1998): Wohlfahrt, Arbeit und Staat unter den Bedingungen von Individualisierung und Globalisierung. In: Geiser, Thomas (ed.): Arbeit in der Schweiz des 20. Jahrhunderts. Wirtschaftliche, rechtliche und soziale Perspektiven. Bern: Haupt: 1–26.

Kaufmann, Franz-Xaver (2009): Sozialpolitik und Sozialstaat. Soziologische Analysen. Wiesbaden: Verl. für Sozialwiss.

Kazepov, Yuri (2008): The subsidiarisation of social policies: Actors, processes and impacts. Some reflections on the Italian case from a European perspective. In: European Societies, Vol. 10, No. 2: 247–273.

Kazepov, Yuri (2010): Rescaling social policies: towards multilevel governance in Europe. Farnham: Ashgate

Kemmerling, Achim; Bruttel, Oliver (22005): New politics in German labour market policy? The implications of the recent Hartz reforms for the German welfare state. Wissenschaftszentrum Berlin. WZB Discussion Paper.

Kenworthy, Lane (2004): Egalitarian capitalism. Jobs, incomes, and growth in affluent countries. New York, NY: Russell Sage Foundation.

Kinder, Tony (2003): Mrs Miller Moves House. The Interoperability of Local Public Services in Europe. In: Journal of European Social Policy, Vol. 13, No. 141: 141–157.

Knuth, Matthias (2009): Grundsicherung 'für Arbeitssuchende': Ein hybrides Regime sozialer Sicherung auf der Suche nach seiner Governance. In: Bothfeld, Silke; Sesselmeier, Werner; Bogedan, Claudia (eds.): Arbeitsmarktpolitik in der sozialen Marktwirtschaft. Vom Arbeitsförderungsgesetz zum Sozialgesetzbuch II und III. Wiesbaden: VS Verl. für Sozialwiss.: 61–78.

Korpi, Walter (2003): Welfare-State regress in Western Europe. Politics, institutions, globalization and Europeanization. In: Annual Review of Sociology, Vol. 29: 589–609.

Kröger, Teppo; Sipilä, Jorma (eds.) (2005): Overstretched: European families up against the demands of work and care. Malden: Blackwell. Malden: Blackwell Publ. Ltd.

Künzel, Sebastian (2012): The local dimension of active inclusion policy. In: Journal of European Social Policy.

Lafore, Robert (2004): La décentralisation de l'action sociale. L'irrésistible ascension du 'département providence'. In: Revue française des affaires sociales, No. 4: 19–34.

Lafore, Robert (2009): Le RSA: la dilution de l'emploi dans l'assistance. In: Revue de Droit Sanitaire et Social, No. 2: 223–235.

Langan, Mary (2000): Social services: Managing the third way. In: Clarke, John; Gerwirtz, Sharon; McLaughlin, Eugene (eds.): New managerialism, new welfare? London: SAGE Publ: 152–167.

Lahusen, Christian; Stark, Carsten (2003): Vom fördernden und fordernden Wohlfahrtsstaat. In: Lessenich, Stephan (ed.): Wohlfahrtsstaatliche Grundbegriffe. Historische und aktuelle Diskurse. Frankfurt: Campus Verl.: 353–372.

Le Bihan, Blanche; Martin, Claude; Rivard, Thierry (2006): L'organisation du RMI et son volet insertion dans neuf departments depuis la décentralation. In: Études et Résultats, No. 535.

Leibfried, Stephan; Obinger, Herbert; Castles, Francis G. (2005): 'Old' and 'new politics' in federal welfare states. In: Leibfried, Stephan; Obinger, Herbert; Castles, Francis G. (eds.): Federalism and the welfare state. New world and European experiences. Cambridge: Cambridge University Press: 307–355.

Leibfried, Stephan; Tennstedt, Florian (1985): Armenpolitik und Arbeiterpolitik. Zur Entwicklung und Krise der traditionellen Sozialpolitik der Verteilungsformen. In: Leibfried, Stephan; Tennstedt, Florian (eds.): Politik der Armut und die Spaltung des Sozialstaats. Frankfurt am Main: Suhrkamp Verlag: 64–93.

Leisering, Lutz (2003): Nation state and welfare state: an intellectual and political history. In: Journal for European Social Policy, Vol 13 No. 2: 175–185.

Leisering, Lutz; Voges, Wolfgang (1992): Erzeugt der Sozialstaat seine eigene Klientel? Eine theoretische und empirische Analyse von Armutsprozessen. In: Leibfried, Stephan (ed.): Armut im modernen Wohlfahrtsstaat. Opladen: Westdt. Verl. (Kölner Zeitschrift für Soziologie und Sozialpsychologie Sonderheft, 32): 446–472.

Leitner, Sigrid; Lessenich, Stephan (2003): Assessing welfare state change. The German social insurance state between reciprocity and solidarity. In: Journal of Public Policy, Vol. 23, No. 3: 325–347.

Levy, Jonah D. (1999): Tocqueville's revenge. State, society, and economy in contemporary France. Cambridge Mass.: Harvard University Press.

Lindbeck, Assar; Snower, Dennis J. (1989): The insider-outsider theory of employment and unemployment. Cambridge, Mass.: MIT-Press.

Lindsay, Colin; McQuaid, Ronald W. (2008): Inter-Agency co-operation in activation: comparing experiences in three vanguard 'active' welfare states. In: Social Policy & Society, Vol. 7, No. 3: 353–365.

Lindsay, Colin; McQuaid, Ronald W.; Dutton, Matthew (2008): Inter-agency co-operation and new approaches to employability. In: Social Policy& Administration, Vol. 42, No. 7: 715–732.

Lødemel, Ivar; Trickey, Heather (2001): A new contract for social assistance. In: Lødemel, Ivar; Trickey, Heather (ed.): An offer you can't refuse. Workfare in international perspective. Bristol: Policy Press: 1–39.

Lødemel, Ivar; Schulte, Bernd (1992): Social assistance: a part of social Security or the poor law in new disguise? In: European Institute of Social Research (ed.): Reforms in Eastern and Central Europe: Beveridge 50 years after. Leuven: Acco.

Ludwig-Mayerhofer, Wolfgang (2005): Activating Germany. In: Bredgaard, Thomas; Larsen, Flemming (eds.): Employment policy from different angles. 1. ed. Copenhagen: DJØF Publ.: 95–114.

Luhman, Niklas (1981): Politische Theorie im Wohlfahrtsstaat. München: Olzog.

Luhman, Niklas (1982):The differentiation of society. New York: Columbia University Press.

Lumann, Niklas (1984): Soziale Systeme: Grundriss einer allgemeinen Theorie. Frankfurt: Suhrkamp.

Luhman, Niklas (1987): Soziologische Aufklärung 4: Beiträge zur funktionalen Differenzierung der Gesellschaft. Opladen: Westdeutscher Verlag.

Marshall, Thomas H. (1965): Class, Citizenship, and Social Development. New York: Achor Books.

Madsen, Per Kongshøj (2002): The Danish model of 'Flexicurity' – A paradise with some snakes. European Foundation for the Improvement of Living and Working Conditions Interactions between Labour Market and Social Protection. Brussels. Online available at http://www.eurofound.europa.eu/ewco/employment/documents/madsen.pdf, (accessed on 2/10/2010).

Madsen, Per Kongshøj; Plougmann, Peter (2002): Flexibility, employment development and active labour market policy in Denmark and Sweden in the 1990s. Edited by Center for Economic Policy Analysis. New School University. New York. CEPA Working Paper 2002–04. Online available at http://www.newschool.edu/cepa/papers/archive/cepa200204.pdf, (accessed on 08/10/2009).

Mahony, James; Thelen, Kathleen (2010): Explaining Institutional Change. Ambiguity, Agency, and Power. Cambridge Mass.: Cambrigde University Press.

Mayring, Philipp (2005): Qualitative Inhaltsanalyse. Grundlagen und Techniken. Weinheim: Deutscher Studien Verlag.

McKee-Ryan, Frances; Song, Zhaoli; Wanberg, Connie R.; Kinicki, Angelo J. (2005): Psychological and physical well-being during unemployment: a meta-analytic study. In: Journal of Applied Psychology, Vol. 90, No. 1: 53–76.

Mingione, Enzo; Oberti, Marco; Pereirinha, José (2002): Cities as local systems. In: Saraceno, Chiara (eds.): Social assistance dynamics in Europe. National and local poverty regimes. Bristol: Policy Press: 35–79.
Monge, Peter R.; Contractor, Noshir S. (2003): Theories of communication networks. Oxford: Oxford University Press.
Monteleone, Raffaele; Mozzana, Carlotta (2009): Integrated employment policies for disabled people: Organisational innovation between obstacles and opportunities. In: International Journal of Sociology and Social Policy, Vol. 29: 649–661.
Morel, Sylvie (2004): Workfare and insertion: How the U.S. and French models of social assistance have been transformed. In: Gilbert, Neil; Parent, Antoine (eds.): Welfare reform. A comparative assessment of the French and U.S. Experiences.10 Vol. New Brunswick, New Jersey: Transaction Publishers (International Social Security Series): 93–142.
Møller, Iver H.; Hespanha, Pedro (2002): Patterns of exlusion/inclusion and people's strategies. In: Berkel, Rik van; Møller, Iver Hornemann (eds.): Active social policies in the EU. Inclusion through participation? Bristol: Policy Press: 137–156.
Mückenberger, Ulrich (1985): Die Krise des Normalarbeitsverhältnisses – hat das Arbeitsrecht noch Zukunft. In: Zeitschrift für Sozialreform, Vol. 31: 415–475.
Nelson, Kenneth (2011): Social assistance and EU poverty thresholds 1990–2008. Are European welfare systems providing just and fair protection against low income? In: European Sociological Review.
Niklasson, Lars (2007): Joining-up for regional development. How governments deal with a wicked problem, overlapping policies and fragmented responsibilities. Statskontoret. Report No. 2.
Newman, Janet (2000): Beyond the new public management? Modernizing public services. In: Clarke, John; Gerwirtz, Sharon; McLaughlin, Eugene (eds.): New managerialism, new welfare? London: SAGE Publ.: 45–61.
Nolan, Brian; Whelan, Christopher T. (2010): Using non-monetary deprivation indicators to analyze poverty and social Exclusion: Lessons from Europe? In: Journal of Policy Analysis and Management, Vol. 29, No. 2: 305–325.
Obinger, Herbert; Rieger, Elmar; Leibfried, Stephan (eds.) (2009): Wohlfahrtsstaatlichkeit in entwickelten Demokratien. Herausforderungen, Reformen und Perspektiven; Festschrift für Stephan Leibfried. Frankfurt am Main: Campus Verl.
OECD (1994): The OECD Jobs Study.OECD. Edited by Organisation for Economic Co-operation and Development. Paris.
OECD (2007a): OECD Economic Surveys France. Edited by Organisation for Economic Co-operation and Development.

OECD (2007b): Activating the unemployed: What countries do. OECD Employment Outlook. Edited by Organisation for Economic Co-operation and Development. Paris.

OECD (2009): Tackling the jobs crisis. OECD Employment Outlook. Edited by Organisation for Economic Co-operation and Development. Paris.

OECD (2011a): Employment Statistics. Online available athttp://stats.oecd.org/Index.aspx?DataSetCode=FTPTC_I, (accessed on 18/11/2011).

OECD (2011b): Employment Statistics. Online available athttp://stats.oecd.org/Index.aspx?DatasetCode=EPL_OV, (accessed on 18/11/2011).

Osborne, David; Gaebler, Ted (1997): Reinventing government. How the entrepreneurial spirit is transforming the public sector. Reading, Mass.: Addison-Wesley.

Osborne, Stephe; McLaughlin, Kate (2004): The cross-cutting review of the voluntary sector: Where next for local government voluntary sector relationships? In: Regional Studies, Vol. 38, No. 5: 573–582.

Ostner, Ilona (1998): Quadraturen im Wohlfahrtsdreieck. Die USA, Schweden und die Bundesrepublik im Vergleich. In: Lessenich, Stephan; Ostner, Iona (eds.): Welten des Wohlfahrtskapitalismus. Frankfurt: Campus: 225–252.

Pal, Leslie A.; Weaver, R. K. (2003): The government takes away. The politics of pain in the United States and Canada. Washington, DC: Georgetown University Press (American governance and public policy series).

Palier, Bruno (2010): The long conservative corporatist road to welfare reforms. In: Palier, Bruno (ed.): A long goodbye to Bismarck? The politics of welfare reforms in continental Europe. Amsterdam: Amsterdam University Press: 333–385.

Palier, Bruno; Martin, Claude (2007): From 'a Frozen Landscape' to structural Reforms: The sequential transformation of Bismarckian welfare systems. In: Social Policy& Administration, Vol. 41: 535–554.

Palier, Bruno; Thelen, Kathleen (2010): Institutionalizing Dualism: Complementarities and Change in France and Germany. In: Politics and Society, Vol. 38, No. 1: 119–148.

Peterson, Paul E.; Rom, Mark C. (1990): Welfare magnets. A new case for a national standard. Washington, DC: Brookings Institution.

Pestoff, Victor (2009): Towards a Paradigm of Democratic Participation: Citizen Participation and Co-production of Personal Social Services in Sweden. In: Annals of Public and Cooperative Economics, Vol. 80: 197–224.

Pestoff, Victor; Brandsen, Taco (2009): Public governance and the third sector: opportunities for coproduction and innovation? Paper presented at the conference of the European Group of Public Administration. St. Julians.

Pestoff, Victor; Osborne, Stephen; Brandsen, Taco (2006): Patterns of co-production in public services. In: Public Management Review, Vol. 8: 591–595.

Pfeffer, Jeffrey; Salancik, Gerald R. (1978): The external control of organizations. A resource dependence perspective. New York, NY: Harper and Row.
Pierson, Paul (1993): When effect becomes cause. Policy feedback and political change. In: World Politics: 595–628.
Pierson, Paul (1995): Dismantling the welfare state? Reagan, Thatcher, and the politics of retrenchment. Cambridge: Cambridge University Press (Cambridge studies in comparative politics).
Pierson, Paul (2001): Coping with permanent austerity. Welfare state restructuring in affluent democracies. In: Pierson, Paul (eds.): The new politics of the welfare state. 1. publ. Oxford: Oxford University Press: 410–456.
Pla, Anne (2007): Sortie des minima sociaux et accès a l'emploi. Premiers résultats de l'enquète de 2006. In: Études et Résultats: 2–8
Pochet, Philippe; Zeitlin, Jonathan (eds.) (2005): The Open Method of Coordination in Action: The European Employment and Social Inclusion Strategies. Brussels: PIE-Peter Lang.
Powell, Walter W. (1990): Neither market nor hierarchy: Network forms of organization. In: Staw, Barry M.; Cummings, Larry L. (eds.): Research in organizational behavior. Greenwich, Connecticut: 295–336.
Preunkert, Jenny (2009): Chancen für ein soziales Europa? Die Offene Methode der Koordinierung als neue Regulierungsform. Wiesbaden: Verlag für Sozialwissenschaften.
Provan, Keith G.; Milward, H. B. (1995): A preliminary theory of interorganizational effectiveness. A comparative study of four community mental health systems. In: Administrative Science Quaterly, Vol. 40, No. 1: 1–33.
Przeworski, Adam; Teune, Henry (1970): The logic of comparative social inquiry. New York: Wiley-Interscience (Comparative studies in behavioral science).
Rauch, Dietmar (2008): Central versus local service regulation: Accounting for diverging old-age care developments in Sweden and Denmark, 1980–2000. In: Social Policy & Administration, Vol. 42, No. 3: 267–287.
Rieger, Elmar; Obinger, Herbert (2009): Wohlfahrtsstaaten in entwickelten Demokratien. Eine Einleitung. In: Obinger, Herbert; Rieger, Elmar; Leibfried, Stephan (eds.): Wohlfahrtsstaatlichkeit in entwickelten Demokratien. Herausforderungen, Reformen und Perspektiven; Festschrift für Stephan Leibfried. Frankfurt am Main: Campus Verl.: 11–22.
Rindfuss, Ronald R.; Guzzo, Karen B.; Morgan, Philip (2003): The changing institutional context of low fertility. In: Population Research and Policy Review, Vol. 22: 411–438.
Rose, Nikolas (1999): Powers of freedom. Reframing political thought. Cambridge: Cambridge University Press.
Rostgaard; Tine (2002): Caring for children and older people in Europe: a comparison of European policies and practice. In: Policy Studies, Vol. 23, No. 1: 51–68.

Ruggie, John (1982): International regimes, transactions, and change: Embedded liberalism in the postwar economic order. In: International Organisation, Vol. 36.

Salais, Robert (2003): Work and welfare: Toward a capability approach. In: Zeitlin, Jonathan; Trubek, David M (eds): Governing work and welfare in a new economy. European and American experiments. 1.publ. Oxford: Oxford University Press: 315–344.

Salais, Robert (2008): Capacités, base informationnelle et démocratie délibérative. Le (contre) exemple de l'action publique européenne. In: Munck, Jean de; Zimmermann, Bénédicte (eds.): La liberté au prisme des capacités. Armatya Sen au-delà du libéralisme. Paris (Raisons pratiques, 18).

Salais, Robert; Villeneuve, Robert (2004): Europe and the politics of capabilities. Cambridge: Cambridge University Press.

Saraceno, Chiara (2002): Introduction: exploring social assistance dynamics. In: Saraceno, Chiara (ed): Social assistance dynamics in Europe. National and local poverty regimes. Bristol: Policy Press:1–34.

Scharpf, Fritz (2000): The viability of advanced welfare states in the international economy. vulnerabilities and options. In: Journal of European Public Policy: 190–228.

Scharpf, Fritz W. (2002): The European social model: Coping with the challenges of diversity. In: Journal of Common Market Studies, Vol. 40, No. 4: 645–670.

Schmid, Günther (1997): Arbeitslosigkeit und Beschäftigung in Europa: Ansätze zu einer Theorie der Beschäftigungsregimes: Statistische Informationen zum Arbeitsmarkt. Reutlingen: Metzler-Poeschel: 15–39.

Schmid, Günther (2002): Wege in eine neue Vollbeschäftigung. Übergangsarbeitsmärkte und aktivierende Arbeitsmarktpolitik. Frankfurt/Main: Campus-Verl.

Schmid, Günther (2006): Sharing Risks. On social risk management and the governance of labour market transitions. In: Wissenschaftszentrum Berlin. WZB discussion paper.

Schmid, Günther; Gazier, Bernard (2002): The dynamics of full employment. Social integration through transitional labour markets. Cheltenham: Elgar (Labour markets and employment policy).

Schmid, Josef; Hörrmann Ute; Maier Dirk; Steffen Christian (2004): Wer macht was in der Arbeitsmarktpolitik? Maßnahmen und Mitteleinsatz in den westdeutschen Bundesländern. Münster: LIT Verlag.

Scott, William R. (2001): Institutions and organizations 2. ed. Thousand Oaks, Calif.: Sage (Foundations for organizational science).

Seeleib-Kaiser, Martin (2008): Welfare state transformations in comparative perspective: shifting boundaries of 'public' and 'private' social policy? In: Seeleib-Kaiser, Martin (ed.): Welfare state transformations. Comparative perspectives. Basingstoke: Palgrave Macmillan: 1–13.

Sen, Amartya Kumar (1985): Commodities and capabilities. Amsterdam: North-Holland

Sen, Amartya (1993): Capability and well-being. In: Nussbaum, Martha C.; Sen, Amartya (eds.): The quality of Life. Oxford: 30–53.

Sen, Amartya (1999): Developement as freedom. Oxfort: Oxfort University Press.

Serrano Pascual, Amparo (2007a): Reshaping welfare states: activation regimes in Europe. Introduction. In: Serrano Pascual, Amparo; Magnusson, Lars (eds.): Reshaping welfare states and activation regimes in Europe. Bruxelles: P.I.E. Lang (Saltsa – joint programme for working life research in Europe, No. 54): 11–34.

Serrano Pascual, Amparo (2007b): Activation regimes in Europe: A clustering exercise. In: Serrona Pascual, Amparo; Magnusson, Lars (eds.): Reshaping welfare states and actives regimes in Europe. Bruxelles: P.I:E. Lang (Saltsa – joint programme for working life research in Europe, No. 54): 275–316.

Statistische Ämter des Bundes und der Länder (2008): Soziale Mindestsicherung in Deutschland 2006. Published by Statistische Ämter des Bundes und der Länder. Wiesbaden.

Streeck, Wolfgang; Hassel, Anke (2003): The crumbling pillars of social partnership. In: Kitschelt, Herbert; Streeck, Wolfgang (eds.): Germany: Beyond the Stable State. London: Frank Cass: 101–124.

Streeck, Wolfgang; Thelen, Kathleen A. (2005): Introduction: Institutional change in Advanced Political Economies. In: Streeck, Wolfgang; Thelen, Kathleen Ann (eds.): Beyond Continuity. Institutional change in advanced political economies. Oxford: Oxford University Press: 1–39.

Sztandar-Sztanderska, Karolina (2009): Activation of the unemployed in Poland: from policy design to policy implementation. In: International Journal of Sociology and Social Policy, Vol. 29, No. 11/12: 624–636.

The Commission of the European Communities (2008): Commission Recommendations of 3 October 2008 on the active inclusion of people excluded from the labour market. Edited by European Commission. Official Journal of the European Union, No. 867.

Taylor-Gooby, Peter (2004): New Risks, New Welfare: The Transformation of the European Welfare State. Oxford: Oxford University Press.

Thelen, Kathleen (1999): Historical Institutionalism in Comparative Politics. In: Annual Review of Political Science, Vol. 2: 369–401.

Visser, Jelle (2009): Neither convergence nor frozen paths. Bounded learning, international diffusion of reforms, and the Open Method of Coordination. In: Heidenreich, Martin; Zeitlin, Jonathan (eds.): Changing European employment and welfare regimes. The influence of the open method of coordination on national reforms. London: Routledge: 37–59.

Vogel, Joachim (1999): Der europäische 'Welfare-Mix'. Institutionelle Konfiguration und Verteilungsergebnis in der Europäischen Union und in Schweden. Eine Längsschnitt- und vergleichende Perspektive. In Peter Flora und Heinz-Herbert Noll (eds.): Sozialberichterstattung und Sozialstaatsbeobachtung im Spiegel empirischer Analysen. Frankfurt a. M./New York: Campus: 73–110.
Voges, Wolfgang; Jacobs, Herbert; Trickey, Heather (2001): Uneven development – local authorities and workfare in Germany. In: Lødemel, Ivar; Trickey, Heather (eds.): An offer you can't refuse. Workfare in international perspective. Bristol: Policy Press: 71–103.
Weber, Max (1921/1972): Wirtschaft und Gesellschaft. Grundriss der verstehenden Soziologie. Tübingen: Mohr.
Whiteside, Noel (2007): Unemployment revisited in comparative perspective: Labour market policy in Strasbourg and Liverpool, 1890–1914. In: International Review of Social History, Vol. 52: 35–56.
Williamson, Oliver E. (1979): Transaction cost economics: The governance of contractual relations. In: Journal of Law and Economics, Vol. 22, 1979: 233–261.
Williamson, Oliver E. (1981): The economics of organization: The transaction cost approach. In: American Journal of Sociology, Vol. 87: 548–577.
Wilthagen, Ton (1998): Flexicurity: A new paradigm for labour market policy reform. Wissenschaftszentrum Berlin. Berlin. Wissenschaftszentrum Berlin. WZB discussion paper.
Wilthagen, Ton; Tros, Frank (2004): The concept of 'flexicurity': a new approach to regulating employment and labour markets. In: Transfer, Vol. 10: 166–186.
Wilthagen, Tom (2007): Flexicurity pathways. turning hurdles into stepping stones. Report by the European Expert Group on Flexicurity. Brussels.
Witzel, Andreas (2000): Das problemzentrierte Interview. In: FQS – Forum Qualitative Sozialforschung, Vol. 1, No. 22.
Yin, Robert K. (2007): Case study research. Design and methods 3. ed., [Nachdr.]. Thousand Oaks, Calif.: Sage (Applied social research methods series, 5).
Zeitlin, Jonathan (2003): Conclusion: The Open Method of Co-ordination in Action: Theoretical promise, empirical realities, reform strategy. In: Zeitlin, Jonathan; Trubek, David M (eds.): Governing work and welfare in a new economy. European and American experiments. Oxford: Oxford University Press: 447–503.
Zeitlin, Jonathan (2009): The Open Method of Coordination and reform of national social and employment policies: influences, mechanisms, effects. In: Heidenreich, Martin; Zeitlin, Jonathan (eds.): Changing European employment and welfare regimes: the influence of the open method of coordination on national reforms. London: Routledge: 214–246.
Zimmer, Annette; Appel, Anja; Ditrich, Claudia; Lange, Chris; Sittermann, Birgitt; Stallmann, Freja; Kendall, Jeremy (2009): Germany: on the social policy

centrality of the Free Welfare Associations. In: Kendall, Jeremy (ed.): Handbook on third sector policy in Europe. Multi-level processes and organized civil society. Cheltenham: Elgar: 21–42.

Zirra, Sascha (2010a): Die Europäisierung nationaler Beschäftigungspolitik. Europäische Koordinierung und institutionelle Reformen. Wiesbaden: Verlag für Sozialwissenschaften / Springer Fachmedien Wiesbaden GmbH Wiesbaden.

Zirra, Sascha (2010b): Domestic Europeanization. Institutional Entrepreneurs and Welfare State Change. Edited by RECWOWE Publication, Dissemination and Dialogue Centre. Edinburgh. Working Papers on the Reconciliation of Work and Welfare in Europe, No. 9.

www.ingramcontent.com/pod-product-compliance
Ingram Content Group UK Ltd.
Pitfield, Milton Keynes, MK11 3LW, UK
UKHW021420091026
15624UKWH00010B/273

9 783631 651070